Asia Bible Commentary Series

JOB

GLOBAL LIBRARY

The gravitas of suffering finds its clear sense in the book of Job. The simple yet forceful elucidation of Dr. Mona P. Bias, rendered in this tender commentary, provides the reader with a necessary comforting balm in embracing the ironic blessing of pain. Having been a spectator of her own journey through the incessant locus of Job's concern, I find Dr. Bias's work a serious necessity for deep thinking amidst our present darkness.

Russell Diwa
Senior Pastor,
Biblical Community Church, Texas, USA

Commentaries on books of the Bible differ in their emphasis – theological, pastoral, expository, devotional, or literary. In my assessment, this one is refreshingly helpful, with a good balance between something too heavy and technical and that of being overly devotional. Topics raised – attributes of God, pastoral comments relating to counseling, suicide, among others – speak to the reader on practical issues of the faith. Asian flavor effuses through insights and stories reflected everywhere. Most of all, Dr. Bias surfaces her high view of God amidst pain and suffering. Of such was also Job's stance.

Richard Lai
Missionary,
Creative Access Nation

One of the aims of the Asia Bible Commentary Series is to have an exposition of the books of the Bible with the Asian psyche and cultural context in mind. This work on the book of Job fulfilled that aim. Job is a difficult book to understand but with this commentary it is now easier to read. Difficult texts and concepts are explained in ways that a layperson can grasp. I therefore highly commend this book to anyone who is interested in knowing God's purpose and explanation for pain and suffering in and through the life of his faithful servant Job.

Andrew Liuson
Chairman, Cofounder, and Former President,
Cityland Group, Philippines

I believe Dr. Mona P. Bias has given us a key that unlocks the book of Job, especially for those who say the book is too hard to understand. This commentary is a brilliant work that integrates extensive literature review, personal studies, and Asian cultural insights. It not only gives us a glimpse into how God fulfills his eternal purposes in our life but also into how he enables us to have integrity in pain, endurance in suffering, confidence in his actions, and hope in his ultimate victory over all evil. This book is an important tool to disciple the church in Asia and elsewhere.

Bekele Shanko
Vice President,
Campus Crusade for Christ International

Written for the Asia Bible Commentary Series, Dr. Mona Bias's commentary on the ancient book of Job is destined to take its place as one of the leading evangelical commentaries available today to the church. Building on her earlier translation work in Job, this commentary draws on the best of contemporary scholarship to give us a superbly balanced resource of rich commentary blended with practical insights for life, particularly regarding the human struggle with pain and suffering. Dr. Mona's scholarship is a goldmine of rich insight for those of us wanting to benefit from the fascinating account of Job. As a leading Asian scholar, Dr. Mona writes in a way that will be of particular blessing for other Asian believers but also for those of us in all parts of God's wide domain. I enthusiastically commend her work to all seeking better to understand this intriguing part of God's word.

J. Paul Tanner, PhD
Vice President and Academic Dean,
The Arab Center for Biblical Studies

Asia Bible Commentary Series

JOB

Mona P. Bias

General Editor
Andrew B. Spurgeon

Old Testament Consulting Editors
**Yohanna Katanacho, Joseph Shao,
Havilah Dharamraj, Koowon Kim**

New Testament Consulting Editors
Steve Chang, Finny Philip, and Samson Uytanlet

© 2024 Mona P. Bias

Published 2024 by Langham Global Library
An imprint of Langham Publishing
www.langhampublishing.org

Langham Publishing and its imprints are a ministry of Langham Partnership

Langham Partnership
PO Box 296, Carlisle, Cumbria, CA3 9WZ, UK
www.langham.org

Published in partnership with Asia Theological Association

ATA
QCC PO Box 1454–1154, Manila, Philippines
www.ataasia.com

ISBNs:
978-1-83973-959-0 Print
978-1-83973-960-6 ePub
978-1-83973-961-3 PDF

Mona P. Bias has asserted her right under the Copyright, Designs and Patents Act, 1988 to be identified as the Author of this work.

All rights reserved. No part of this publication may be reproduced, stored in a retrieval system or transmitted, in any form or by any means, electronic, mechanical, photocopying, recording or otherwise, without the prior written permission of the publisher or the Copyright Licensing Agency.

Requests to reuse content from Langham Publishing are processed through PLSclear. Please visit www.plsclear.com to complete your request.

Unless otherwise stated, Scripture quotations are from the New International Version, copyright © 2011. Used by permission. All rights reserved.

British Library Cataloguing-in-Publication Data
A catalogue record for this book is available from the British Library

ISBN: 978-1-83973-959-0

Cover & Book Design: projectluz.com

Langham Partnership actively supports theological dialogue and an author's right to publish but does not necessarily endorse the views and opinions set forth here or in works referenced within this publication, nor can we guarantee technical and grammatical correctness. Langham Partnership does not accept any responsibility or liability to persons or property as a consequence of the reading, use or interpretation of its published content.

This work is dedicated to:
My ministry partners,
mentors,
and students

CONTENTS

Commentary

Series Preface xi
Author's Preface xiii
Acknowledgments xv
List of Abbreviations xvii
Introduction 1
Commentary on Job 17
Selected Bibliography 285

Topics

Undeserved Suffering 14
Presumptive Theology 15
Job's Wealth 19
The Names of God in the Book of Job 22
Ha Satan: Function or Proper Name? 28
Suicide and How to Seek Help 36
The Retribution Concept: When it Becomes Flawed 48
Sheol and the Afterlife 63
Traditional Beliefs and Experiences 69
Job's Monotheistic View of God 76
Criticism: Subjective and Objective 83
The Contrasting Activities of God 87
Job's Emotional State 89
Mediation in the Asian Context 114
A Typical *Tongtong* Process 115
God's Discipline and Punishment 134
Polygamy in the Old Testament and in Asia 161

Asian Perspective on Imprecatory Prayer 165
The Relevance of Job 32 to Elihu's View of Suffering 200
The Relevance of Job 33 to Elihu's View of Suffering 209
The Relevance of Job 34 to Elihu's View of Suffering 220
The Relevance of Job 35 to Elihu's View of Suffering 225
The Relevance of Job 36 to Elihu's View of Suffering 232
The Relevance of Job 37 to Elihu's View of Suffering 239
The Origin of Life and the Purpose of Our Existence 257

SERIES PREFACE

What's unique about the Asia Bible Commentary Series? It is a commentary series written especially for Asian Christians, which incorporates and addresses Asian concerns, cultures, and practices. As Asian scholars – either by nationality, passion, or calling – the authors identify with the biblical text, understand it culturally, and apply its principles in Asian contexts to strengthen the churches in Asia. Missiologists tell us that Christianity has shifted from being a Western majority religion to a South, Southeastern, and Eastern majority religion and that the church is growing at an unprecedented rate in these regions. This series meets the need for evangelical commentaries written specifically for an Asian audience.

This is not to say that Asian churches and Asian Christians do not want to partner with Western Christians and churches or that they spurn Western influences. A house divided cannot stand. The books in this series complement the existing Western commentaries by taking into consideration the cultural nuances familiar to the Eastern world so that the Eastern readership is not inundated with Western clichés and illustrations that they are unable to relate to and which may not be applicable to them.

The mission of this series is "to produce resources that are biblical, pastoral, contextual, missional, and prophetic for pastors, Christian leaders, cross-cultural workers, and students in Asia." While using approved exegetical principles, the writers strive to be culturally relevant, offer practical applications, and provide clear explanations of the texts so that readers can grow in understanding and maturity in Christ, and so that Christian leaders can guide their congregations into maturity. May we be found faithful to this endeavor and may God be glorified!

Andrew B. Spurgeon
General Editor

AUTHOR'S PREFACE

It all began as I was preparing for my comprehensive doctoral exams. One day, I received a letter, stating that the late Dr. Larry Waters and I had been given the task of producing a commentary on the book of Job. My initial thought was that if I did graduate, I did not even know if I would pass the comprehensive examination that followed.

The day I submitted my dissertation, I boarded the plane and came back home to the Philippines. Around that time, Dr. William P. Welty, Director for the International Standard Version (ISV) Foundation, asked me to translate the book of Job from Hebrew into English. After I had completed this task, Dr. Bruce Nicholls happened to visit me at the school to remind me that Dr. Waters and I had been assigned to work on the commentary which had been put on hold for some time. What encouraged me to agree to write was his remark, during our conversation, that India needed an explanation for pain. Yet, in my mind, I was asking myself how and where I could begin, until I remembered that I had just completed the translation of Job. That gave me hope to take up the challenge and so, Dr. Waters and I began writing a commentary on Job, of which the first edition was completed and published in 2011. I can now say that whenever the living God asks us to do something, either he has already prepared us for it, or he will prepare us as we go along.

As to this second revised edition, I started working on this in 2019 with my colleagues in Rootword Writer's Fellowship, but we were prevented from meeting to write by the onslaught of COVID-19 in 2020. On account of the restrictions due to the pandemic and other commitments, I was not able to resume work on this book until 2022. This pandemic brought unprecedented pain and staggering losses into our lives. Again, the question of suffering raised its head. People have been forced to ask questions they never asked before: Where is God? If he is alive, why did he allow this pandemic to come to our shores? If he loves us, why does he not help us? And if he cares at all, why is he silent despite all our prayers? When will all this suffering come to an end?

The book of Job is indeed a masterpiece par excellence, in both its content and presentation. Apart from human suffering, it addresses almost every other branch of study, including theology, missions, psychology and logotherapy, biology, geology, astronomy, geography, law and justice, faith and life experiences in general.

Job

Suffering is universal. No one is exempt from it. What happened to Job, however, is not necessarily the plan that God has ordained for you. If you are going through some pain, it is alright to cry and fully entrust the disappointment or painful experience to God. Choose to believe that the living God will sovereignly see you through any circumstance. He cares for you more than you could ever imagine.

It is my prayer that as you read through each chapter of the book, you will have a unique and refreshing encounter with our Lord Jesus Christ. May he pleasantly surprise you and bless you tremendously. May you experience his presence and *shalom*.

For the greater glory of our Lord and King!

ACKNOWLEDGMENTS

The writing of this book, and its subsequent revision, would not have been possible without the team that helped publish the first edition. I am forever grateful to the following:

Dr. Bruce Nicholls: he was the one who invited me and the late Dr. Larry Waters to work on the book of Job. He convinced me that people need an explanation for pain and suffering, a question which Job can address, at least to some degree.

Dr. Larry Waters: he was my colleague in writing the first edition of the book of Job with the Asia Bible Commentary Series (ABCS). It is impossible to extricate my work from him or his work from mine. Therefore, I maintain that this revised edition is to be treated as our joint work. Although he had already gone ahead to be in the presence of the Lord, his words and counsel will live on with this work.

The ATA editorial board: Dr. Andrew B. Spurgeon was the first to read our manuscripts when we started working on the first edition of the book. He continued to guide me and kindly responded to my questions as I worked on the current revision. His attention to detail and invaluable input greatly improved this work. Dr. Joseph Shao encouraged me to continue writing as "an Asian and for Asians." His questions allowed me to think through significant issues.

The reviewers: Dr. Andrew Liuson, whose all-out support in the publication and marketing of the book reminded me that there is a real dearth for Asian contextualized writing. Dr. Eugene H. Merrill, in his kind affirmation of my writing, was the first person who initiated me into academic writing when he asked me to do a book review for *Bibliotheca Sacra*.

Rootword Writer's Fellowship: Comprised of Dr. Federico Villanueva, Dr. Rod Santos, and myself, this group was formed after a workshop for writers with Langham. Dr. Bruce Nicholls coordinated the workshops, which were conducted by Ms. Isobel Stevenson and Ms. Julie Belding.

ATA-Langham gave me this chance to revisit the book of Job. I learned much and have grown in the process.

For this revised edition, I am immensely grateful to the following: Ms. Barbara Black, who invested her time, patiently "crossed the t's and dotted the i's," and gave valuable and meaningful feedback for this work.

Dr. B. J. Barron and Sylvia Barron, who located, purchased, and mailed me the recent work of Stephen Vicchio on Job, which I have referred to so many times in this work. They provided video clips of music to encourage me to keep writing until I finished.

Ms. Neri Mamburam, who, while I was writing, pleasantly surprised me time and time again with a packed lunch.

My ministry partners, who are committed to Jesus Christ, to the fulfillment of the Great Commission, and to his workers: Biblical Community Church, TGIF Bible Study Group, Oak Harbor Fellowship, Andy and Linda, Agnes and Raken, Bob and Shirley, BJ and Sylvia, Henry and Tess, Jurgen and Michaela, Kiko and Amie, Lou and Ruby, Malou and Ely, Michelle and Mike, Trix and Ian, Ursula and Rolf, Grace, Gretel, Hanzel, Irene, Juliet, Laiza, Mariz, Mirzi, and Neri. Because of them, I am still in the ministry and fulfilling God's calling for me.

My cheering team through the years: Dr. Christine Liu Perkins, Dr. Chong Hiok and Margaret Chan, Drs. Teody and Evelyn Pajaron, Dr. Somdee Poosawtsee, Dr. Ananda Perera, Dr. J. Paul Tanner, Dr. Layne Turner, Dr. Henry Tan, Dr. Tom and Cynthia Roxas, Prof. Don Glenn, Dr. Ron Watters, Drs. Keith and Jeannette Shubert. They are a part of my spiritual formation and professional development.

Above all, I give praise to the living God for who he is and how he revealed himself to me while working on this revision. He is *Yahweh Yir'eh*, who provided what I needed – especially wisdom and strength. He is *Yahweh Rophe*, who brought healing and refreshing to my soul. He is *Yahweh Ro'eh*, who has continually encouraged and guided me.

LIST OF ABBREVIATIONS

BOOKS OF THE BIBLE

Old Testament
Gen, Exod, Lev, Num, Deut, Josh, Judg, Ruth, 1–2 Sam, 1–2 Kgs, 1–2 Chr, Ezra, Neh, Esth, Job, Ps/Pss, Prov, Eccl, Song, Isa, Jer, Lam, Ezek, Dan, Hos, Joel, Amos, Obad, Jonah, Mic, Nah, Hab, Zeph, Hag, Zech, Mal

New Testament
Matt, Mark, Luke, John, Acts, Rom, 1–2 Cor, Gal, Eph, Phil, Col, 1–2 Thess, 1–2 Tim, Titus, Phlm, Heb, Jas, 1–2 Pet, 1–2–3 John, Jude, Rev

BIBLE TEXTS AND VERSIONS

Divisions of the canon

NT	New Testament
OT	Old Testament

Ancient texts and versions

LXX	Septuagint
MT	Masoretic Text

Modern versions

KJV	King James Version
NASB	New American Standard Bible
NIV	New International Version
NKJV	New King James Version
NLT	New Living Translation

Journals, reference works, and series

ABC	*Africa Bible Commentary*
ABCS	Asia Bible Commentary Series
ABD	*Anchor Bible Dictionary*
ANET	*Ancient Near Eastern Texts*
BDB	Brown F., S. R. Driver, and C. A. Briggs. *A Hebrew and English Lexicon of the Old Testament*

BCOTWS	Baker Commentary of the Old Testament Wisdom and Psalms
BKC	Bible Knowledge Commentary: Old Testament
CBQ	*Catholic Bible Quarterly*
COS	*The Context of Scripture*
EBC	Expositor's Bible Commentary
HALOT	*The Hebrew Aramaic Lexicon of the Old Testament*
HAT	*Handbuch zum Alten Testament*
HUCA	*Hebrew Union College Annual*
ICC	International Critical Commentary
ISBE	*International Standard Bible Encyclopedia*
ITQ	*Irish Theological Quarterly*
JBL	*Journal of Biblical Literature*
JSOT	*Journal for the Study of the Old Testament*
JSOTSup	Journal for the Study of the Old Testament Supplement Series
NAC	New American Commentary
NCBC	New Century Bible Commentaries
NET Bible	New English Translation Bible
NIB	New Interpreter's Bible Commentary
NIBC	New International Biblical Commentary
NICOT	New International Commentary on the Old Testament
NIDOTTE	*New International Dictionary of Old Testament Theology & Exegesis*
NIVAC	NIV Application Commentary
NSBT	New Studies in Biblical Theology
SABC	*South Asia Bible Commentary*
Them	*Themelios*
TOTC	Tyndale Old Testament Commentary
TTC	Teach the Text Commentary
TWOT	*Theological Wordbook of the Old Testament*
WBC	Word Biblical Commentary
ZAW	*Zeitschrift für die Alttestamentliche Wissenschaft*
ZPEB	Zondervan Pictorial Encyclopedia of the Bible
VTSup	Vetus Testamentum Supplements
WBC	Word Biblical Commentary
YJS	Yale Judaica Series
ZAW	*Zeitschrift für die alttestamentliche Wissenschaft*

INTRODUCTION

The book of Job pictures the main character in constant battle with intense suffering, in long debates with his three friends, and, finally, in a personal encounter with God himself. Pain and suffering, which was Job's most pressing problem, is the main theme of the book. Pain is universal, and it levels the playing field for everyone. Pain can take many forms and its intensity and length vary from person to person. It can be transient or permanent in the way it affects a person's well-being. Pain is no respecter of persons, affecting both rich and poor, young and old, people living in ancient times and those living in the present. At the time of writing, countries, families, and individuals continue to reel under the havoc that COVID-19 has brought into the lives of people all over the world. Many have died, with some of them not even knowing what hit them. War broke out in Ukraine in 2022, forcing people to seek refuge in nearby countries as their cities were destroyed.

In such a time as this, there is so much that we can gain from studying the book of Job. For instance, the book helps us gain a deeper understanding of both human nature in its many facets and God and his influence in the world. It will also, hopefully, help us to find new answers to some vital questions: Why suffering? Why injustice? Why does God allow calamities? The author hopes that this book will answer some of readers' questions about pain and suffering, justice and injustice, good and evil in the world, and help to deepen their understanding and strengthen their faith in a loving God.

THE PURPOSE OF JOB

The main purpose of the book of Job is to show that the proper relationship between God and human beings is based solely on the sovereign grace of God and our submissive faith response. A secondary purpose is to show how God uses both adversity and prosperity to lead his people to maturity. A related purpose is to show God's great sovereignty over Satan and to demonstrate how God can use the devil's worst attacks for his own purposes and for his people's good. Some additional purposes are to show the dynamics of God's person as he deals with his people – not with mechanical, legalistic rules but with infinite variety and love – and to demonstrate to all the universe God's great ability to reproduce his love in his people so that they are able to respond in worship even when they do not understand.

JOB

RATIONALE FOR STUDYING THE BOOK OF JOB

Below are some common reasons people study this magnificent book:

- It deals with the issue of suffering, especially undeserved suffering, which helps us:

  to discover whether there is any meaning to suffering,

  to learn about the proper and improper responses to undeserved suffering,

  to learn appropriate and sensitive ways to counsel people who are in pain.

- It informs us about God and his sovereignty, his grace, and his mission.
- It introduces us to the age-old conflict between God and Satan.
- It considers God's justice in the light of questions about why good people frequently suffer and why bad people often prosper.

These and other reasons help us to see why the book of Job is such a valuable part of the canon of Scripture. Many scholars, theologians, authors, and critics have commented on both the book's uniqueness and its greatness. The book has a rightful place among outstanding works in world literature. It is theologically rich and honest,[1] sometimes considered the work of a genius.[2] As poetry, it is ranked high among the poetry of the world, resembling no other text in the canon.[3] Many who read the book – whether philosophers, rationalists, mystics, skeptics, or existentialists – are fascinated with Job. They find in Job an expression of their own temperament or an illumination of their own problems.[4] In Job, "poetry and philosophy, passion and truth, are united in one of the supreme achievement of the human spirit."[5] Indeed, it remains "unmatched in the writings of the Old Testament for its artistic character, its grandeur of language, depth of feeling, and the sensitivity with which the meaning of human suffering is explored."[6] Moreover, the book "comes very

---

1. C. L. Seow, *Job 1–21: Interpretation and Commentary* (Grand Rapids: Eerdmans, 2013), 2.
2. Edgar Jones, *The Triumph of Job* (Nashville: Abingdon, 1968), 11.
3. Robert Alter, *The Writings*, vol. 3 of The Hebrew Bible: A Translation with Commentary (New York: Norton, 2019), 457.
4. Robert Gordis, *The Book of God and Man: A Study of Job* (Chicago: University of Chicago Press, 1965), vi.
5. Gordis, *Book of God*, 8.
6. R. K. Harrison, *Introduction to the Old Testament* (Grand Rapids: Eerdmans, 1969), 1022.

Introduction

close to our psyche and finds a permanent home in our minds and hearts."[7] It is very relevant, for it has a contemporary feel to it – existential realities, suffering, injustice, and persecution.[8] It is "one of the supreme offerings of the human mind to the living God and one of the best gifts of God to men."[9]

The message of the book of Job is relevant to our times, especially given the issues that we are presently facing – individually, locally, and worldwide – with the pandemic, wars and the prospect of wars, and calamities of various kinds.

TITLE

Similar to Esther, Job is also named after its hero rather than its author, even though the man Job might have recorded many of the details. The etymology of the name Job (*'iyyov*) is quite uncertain. It could be derived from the Hebrew word *'oyeb*, which means an "enemy," "assailant,"[10] or "an object of enmity."[11] The name is also connected to an Arabic root word *'yb*,[12] meaning to "repent" or "return."[13] An Arabian provenance for the story of Job makes its Arabic meaning of "restoration" or "repentance" more likely, particularly because "Job was a native of North Arabia, and the whole setting of the story is Arabic rather than Hebrew."[14]

AUTHOR

Numerous suggestions have been made about the authorship of Job. These include Job himself (Barnes, Fausset, Lowth), Elihu (Lightfoot), Moses (Talmud, Kennicott, Rawlinson, Archer), Solomon (Luther, Delitszch, Grotius), an unknown writer at the time of Solomon (Rosenmueller), Hezekiah (Zoeckler), Ezra (Warburton), and an Israelite (Seow).

---

7. Naveen Rao, "Job," in *SABC*, ed. Brian Wintle (Grand Rapids: Zondervan, 2015), 580.
8. Katharine J. Dell, "Introduction" in *Eerdmans Commentary on the Bible: Job* (Grand Rapids: Eerdmans, 2019), http://www.perlego.com/book/2985430/eerdmans-commentary-on-the-bible-job-pdf.
9. Francis I. Andersen, *Job: An Introduction and Commentary*, TOTC 14 (Downers Grove: InterVarsity Press), 15.
10. *HALOT*, s.v. "*'iyyob*."
11. Tyler F. Williams, "*yb*," *NIDOTTE* 1:370.
12. Root word refers to the lexical form of a word, from which other words are derived.
13. Stephen J. Vicchio, *The Book of Job: A History of Interpretation and Commentary* (Eugene: Wipf & Stock, 2020), 46.
14. Gleason L. Archer Jr., *A Survey of the Old Testament Introduction*, 3rd ed. (Chicago: Moody Press, 1994), 503. The Sultanate of Oman has a tomb dedicated to Job (Nabi Ayoub) in Jabal Al Qar, 25 km from Salalah.

Barnes argues that Job himself was the author on the following grounds: (1) the arguments favoring a patriarchal age, and (2) the foreign cast of the work – Arabic words, nomadic habits, illustrations from sandy plains and deserts, and awareness of nature and the arts.[15] While Barnes adds the suggestion that Moses could have written the concluding sentence in the book about Job's age and death, he also gives several arguments against Moses as the author: (1) the style is not that of Moses; (2) Moses used the name Yahweh in his poetry, whereas Job uses other names; (3) Job includes numerous Arabic words; and (4) Moses may not have been familiar with Arabic customs, opinions, and manners.[16] Although authorship cannot be established with certainty, we know that the author was acquainted with Egypt, familiar with world literature, belonged among the intellectuals of his day,[17] and was a poetic genius. Pope acknowledges that "in the heart of the book, in the Dialogue (chapters iii-xxxi), there is a characteristic literary excellence which suggests the influence of a single personality."[18] Moreover, Sarna points to numerous poetic features (linguistic, literary, and others) of the prose sections of Job (Job 1–2; 42:7–17), which indicate that it "is certain that the prologue and the epilogue belong together and are the work of a single author."[19]

DATE

Views about the date of the composition of the book vary widely, ranging from the time of Abraham to 200 BC. This work presupposes the patriarchal period. It has even been claimed that the book of Job may be the oldest book in the world and should be recognized as the first biblical book to be written down. The events described happened before the rest of the stories of the Bible were written, and the book includes no references to the Mosaic law, the Levitical system, the exodus, the temple, or even the exile.[20] Smick explains that the

---

15. Albert Barnes, *The Book of Job* (Grand Rapids: Baker Books, repr., 1996), 31–32.
16. Barnes, *Book of Job*, 31–32.
17. Marvin H. Pope, *Job*, AB 15 (Garden City: Doubleday, 1973), xli.
18. Pope, *Job*, xli.
19. Nahum H. Sarna, "Epic Substratum in the Prose of Job," *JBL* 76 (Mar 1957), 13.
20. See Archer, *Survey of Old Testament*, 508. There is a greater divergence of opinion here than on almost any other book of the Bible. The many views may be grouped as follows: time of Abraham (Bar Qappara); patriarchal age (Archer); time of Moses (Talmud, *Baba Bathra* 14b: "Moses wrote his own book and Job"); time of Solomon (Keil, Haevernick, Luther, Delitzsch, E. Young, M. Unger, E. Merrill); time of Hezekiah (Hengstenberg, Zoeckler); time of Manasseh (Ewald, Hitzig; reason: Job 9:24, "The earth is given into the hand of the wicked"); just before the Assyrian captivity, ca. 750 BC (F. Andersen); right after the Assyrian captivity, between Isaiah and Jeremiah, in the seventh century (W. T. Davison, O. B. Gray); the time of Jeremiah

Introduction

whole book (or part of it) may have existed outside Israel as an oral tradition until an unknown Israelite, under divine inspiration, gave the book its present literary form. This would explain the non-Israelite flavor of the book. Job may have lived in the second millennium BC and shared a tradition that was similar to the Hebrew patriarchs.[21]

APPROACH

The traditional approach to studying a book in the Old Testament is to begin with its background, author and unity, date of composition and source, canonicity, purpose of the book, and the text. This approach is still followed, with some modifications. For instance, Dell added to these traditional elements the changing landscape.[22]

Recent works tend to veer away from the traditional approach mentioned above. There is a movement from the historical approach to a "more literary approach that takes books as they stand, and as the reader experiences them, without too much concern for their pre-history."[23] Further, there has been a shift from the author to the reader, where the context of the reader is of prime importance.[24]

A recent work of Vicchio starts by examining how the book has been interpreted through the centuries by three major religions: Judaism, Christianity, and Islam. He lists the scholars and the literature written in each time period using these categories, each with their subsections: Premodern (until

---

(Steinmueller, Gunkel, Pfeiffer, Terrien); time of the exile (Albright, Tur-Sinai, Cheyne; reason: Job 12:17–19); and the postexilic period (sixth century: A. B. Davidson, Kittel; fifth century: Driver, Dhorme, Gordis, Talmud *Baba Bathra* 15a; fourth century: Peake, Budde, Jastrow, Eissfeldt; third century: Cornhill; second century: Siegfried).

21. Elmer Smick, "Job", *The Expositors Bible Commentary - Abridged Edition*, ed. Kenneth Barker and John Kohlenberger (Grand Rapids: Zondervan, 2017), 742. There are "many conservatives opting for the time of Solomon or a little later. This has in its favor the fact that wisdom and wisdom literature are closely connected to Solomon and his time." See Charles Dyer and Gene H. Merrill, *The Old Testament Explorer: Discovering the Essence, Background, and Meaning of Every Book in the Old Testament* (Nashville: Word, 2001), 376.

22. In addition to author, date, context, audience, and theological themes, Dell includes the reception of the book through the centuries, the different approaches to its study, and the questions being raised by contemporary scholars (Dell, "Introduction" in *Job*). She also explained that at present, "anyone writing on a biblical book needs to state their method and presuppositions." See her other work, *Job: An Introduction and Study Guide: Where Shall Wisdom Be Found?* (London: T&T Clark, 2017), 2, https://www.perelgo.com/book/395380/job-an-introduction-and-study-guide-where-shall-wisdom-be-found-pdf.

23. Dell, *Job: An Introduction*, 2.

24. This, however, is significant "only in light of postmodern hermeneutical concerns" (Dell, *Job: An Introduction*, 3).

AD 1500), Early Modern (AD 1500–1800), Modern (AD 1800–2000), and Contemporary (AD 2001 to present).[25] After presenting this history of the interpretation of the book, Vicchio deals with the text of Job itself. Likewise, Davy begins his work by presenting reasons for his choice of the book of Job as source material for "biblical reflection on the mission of God" and then deals with select texts that relate to *missio Dei*.[26]

THE RELIGIOUS SETTING

Job's offering for his family (1:5) suggests a time like that of Abraham, when religious rites were a domestic matter, carried out apart from any organized form of corporate religion. This is seen, for instance, when the heads of families served as priests and mediators between God and their families: Noah (Gen 8:20), Abraham (Gen 12:7), Isaac (Gen 26:25), and Jacob (Gen 31:54). Job's piety is demonstrated in that he offered burnt offerings regularly (1:4–5). Then at the end of his ordeal, he prayed for his friends after they had offered the burnt offering that Yahweh asked them to sacrifice. Consequently, Yahweh accepted Job's prayer on behalf of his friends (42:8–10).

The three friends' legalistic view of sin and suffering – a view also shared by Job – was evidently the espoused orthodoxy of the time. God was conceived of as a "cause-and-effect" deity. The friends' wrong view of God resulted in a wrong view of Job and his sufferings. It also produced an incorrect view of how God delivers his people and helps them grow in their faith. Because they failed to understand God's way of extending mercy and grace to the undeserving, the friends interpreted as blasphemy Job's refusal to accept their solutions to his suffering.

ATTRIBUTES OF GOD IN JOB

Given the issues that we are now facing – individually, locally, and worldwide – with a pandemic, the prospect of wars, and calamities of various kinds, the book of Job seems particularly relevant to our times. Through the story of Job, the book presents several attributes of the true and living God.

---

25. Vicchio, *Book of Job*, 1–45. This work is very helpful for our purposes as he traces the history of the views on subject matters presented from the earliest documentation and sources of information.
26. Tim J. Davy, *The Book of Job and the Mission of God* (Eugene: Wipf & Stock, 2020), https://www.perlego.com/book/1990350/the-book-of-job-and-the-mission-of-god-pdf.

Introduction

God's Presence

Humanly speaking, God's presence is manifested in the form of his blessings on people, enabling them to enjoy success in undertakings, good health, material wealth, and good social standing. Before the calamities came, Job enjoyed all these blessings and acknowledged that these were the expression of God's presence, for he claimed that "God's intimate friendship blessed my house, when the Almighty was still with me" (29:4–5). When the calamities came, however, Job experienced silence, and thus a sense of God's absence.

Regardless of Job's perception of God and how he felt when the calamities came, the living God was present with him even in his pain and suffering. Although Job did not know it, it was Yahweh who granted *Satan* permission to "lay a finger" on Job's possessions but prohibited him from harming Job himself (1:12). Later, God allowed *Satan* to harm Job but not to take his life (2:6). Elihu argued that God's perceived silence – "he hides his face" – which can also mean the withdrawal of blessings, did not mean that God was not at work behind the scenes (34:29–30). In his time, and in his own way, Yahweh appeared and revealed himself to Job (38–42). Yahweh, having heard the disputations of the three friends against Job, accused them, "You have not spoken the truth about me" (42:7). Yahweh was there all the time, even when Job did not sense it.

God, the Creator

Natural World

Yahweh, as the Creator of the heavens and the earth and everything in it, sovereignly sustains all things. He laid the foundations of the earth (38:4–7). He knows the origin of the dawn and its effects on the earth (38:12–15). He created the intricate primeval oceans and knows the vast expanse of the earth (38:16–18), the origins of light and darkness (38:19–21), and the source of the hail, lightning, flood, rumbling thunder, and rain (38:22–26). He is aware of the different forms and state of water (38:28–30).

Living Beings

Yahweh heads the heavenly council (1:6; 2:1). Moreover, in "his hand is the life of every creature and the breath of all mankind" (12:10) for it is the breath of the Almighty that gives life (33:4). He provides food for the animals – from the mighty lion and to the humble raven (38:39–41). He knows the birth pangs and birthing season of all his creations, including the goat and the deer (39:1–4). He created eagles with unique visual acuity so they can recognize prey from afar (39:27–30). He is powerful to subdue "Behemoth" (40:15–19) and "Leviathan" (41:1–34) because he created these.

God's Relationship with Humanity

As for his dealings with humanity, Yahweh protects and provides for his people (1:10). The lowly – those who mourn – are lifted to safety (5:11). While he frustrates the plans of the crafty so that they do not succeed in whatever they are planning (5:12), he does not reject a blameless person (8:20). He delivers the poor from the power of the mighty (5:15) and rescues his people from various calamities (5:19–21). He is their "redeemer" (19:25). Although Job accuses God of being deaf to his cries, God does hear the cries of his people and may sometimes respond through dreams and visions (33:15). He does not act wickedly and does not pervert justice (34:12) – even though he is omnipotent (36:22) and has the power to do whatever he wants. He is awesome and "beyond our understanding" (36:26), majestic in strength, and just in all his ways (37:23). He restores and doubly blesses those who trust in him (42:10).

God's Greatness

Several aspects of God's greatness are revealed in the book. Job acknowledged *the greatness of God's person* in the concluding chapter of the book, confessing, "Surely I spoke of things I did not understand, things too wonderful for me to know" (42:3). The greatness of God's person is seen not only in God's sovereignty over all things but also in the dynamism of his ways. The way God dealt with Job demonstrates that he is not a whimsical tyrant or mechanical deity, responding to mere outward conformity as the worldly wise might expect.

The greatness of God's power is seen in his creation and in the preservation of all that he created in the universe (38–41). It is God's laws that command the whole spiritual and physical world, just as the power of his love is able to command the love and devotion of persons without mere material rewards.

The greatness of God's program is universal and eternal, not a mere response to sudden problems. Looking at the case of Job, God's perceived plan went beyond *Satan's* atrocious actions against Job (1:6–7). Yahweh for his part meant for Job to experience and have a meaningful encounter with God. This was he whom Job himself desired to one day meet (19:26–27). Job realized that it is God who directly commands all spiritual and physical intelligences, holding each accountable at a coming day of reckoning.

The greatness of God's purposes (1:8–12; 2:3) for humans is not to pamper them with an easy life in the here and now but to perfect them for eternity.

INTRODUCTION

The process, however, may involve pain and suffering as was the case of Job. This fulfills another purpose of demonstrating to all the sovereignty of God and the greatness of his wisdom and grace as he patiently deals with individuals.

The greatness of God's people is seen in the true children of God, who love and serve him in faith and not just because of what he gives them. As they recognize the greatness of his person, power, plan, and purposes, God's people make themselves available to God, in worship and service, allowing him to refine them through trials so that they may come forth as gold (1:20–22; 23:10).

ASIAN THEOLOGY

Asia is home to many gods. Just like in the Ancient Near East (ANE), people groups in Asia have their own local gods. Just as Israel worshiped Yahweh, and the Philistines and the Canaanites believed in Dagon and Baal respectively, in pre-Hispanic times, people groups in northern Luzon, Philippines, paid homage to a god called *Kabunian*, who was considered their Supreme Being. In time, *Kabunian*[27] was equated with the Judeo-Christian God, whom they call today as *Apo Dios* (Almighty God) – where the word *Dios* is a Spanish term for God. Astral deities such as the sun and the moon were and are still worshiped in secret by some people of the older generation. Baucas acknowledges that the spirits – whether of the living or the dead – as well as inanimate objects such as the forest and rivers were also worshiped. Moreover, these spirits are thought to have the power to travel from place to place to respond to the needs of those who still believe in their power.[28]

The God who is presented in the book of Job is not the product of accretion. Right at the beginning of the story, he is introduced as the Supreme Being, reigning over angels who do his bidding (1:6; 2:1). Unlike the name of the local god *Kabunian*,[29] God's name is not coined by his worshipers. On the contrary, God himself revealed his personal name to Moses and, through Moses, to his people (Exod 3:14–15). This personal name – Yahweh – is one

---

27. *Kabunian* is a local deity. With the coming of Roman Catholicism to the Philippines, *Kabunian* was attributed some of the descriptions of the Christian God until it became natural for the locals to think of *Kabunian* as equal and the same as the Christian God.
28. Blano L. Baucas, *Traditional Beliefs and Cultural Practices in Benguet* (La Trinidad: New Baguio Offset Press, 2003), 7.
29. In the name *Kabunian*, the central idea is of prayer, as "buni" means prayer. By adding the prefix "ka" and the suffix "an," to "buni" a free translation of the term could be "the one to whom we pray." It remains necessary to allow a believer of *Kabunian* to describe him, to check if his descriptions match that of the God presented in the book of Job or the Bible.

of the names for God that is found in Job, along with the names *El*, *Elohim*, *Eloah*, *Shadday*, and *Adonay*.

The book of Job recognizes only one sovereign God, who is the giver of life to every living being (12:10; 33:4). This God performed many awesome and unfathomable deeds (5:9; 9:10). He is omnipotent (36:22), awesome (36:26), majestic, just, and righteous (37:23). He revealed himself to Job out of the storm (38:1), established the laws of heaven and earth (38:4), and none of his purposes can be thwarted (42:2). He is the God who cares for his people – delivering the poor from their oppressors (5:15) and vindicating those who have been wronged (42:10–17). All these qualities combine to describe the one true God, and neither the gods in the ancient world nor those in Asia today, nor indeed *Kabunian*, can lay claim to all these qualities.

The few traditionalists who still believe in *Kabunian* or in "split-level Christianity"[30] often attribute pain and suffering to the spirits of deceased relatives. When someone falls sick with an unexplained ailment, the family invites a native priest to perform some rituals to try to discern the cause of the illness. More often than not, it is believed that the spirit of the deceased relative needs some item, such as a blanket or food, and that the sickness is a way of making known these demands. The sick person would need to offer an animal and give what the spirit demanded, and all this would be communicated through the native priest.

Job's friends were completely convinced that sin could be the only reason for Job's unexplained pain and suffering and that there was no other explanation for it. Job, however, without denying that sin could be the cause of his pain and suffering, insisted that in his case, it was God himself who was afflicting him (6:4). Job did not believe that his suffering was the result of sin but, rather, that God was responsible for his suffering. At no point, however, did Job attribute his pain and suffering to the spirit of the dead and other gods as is the case in many Asian religions.

In Job, the head of the family is shown acting as the priest. This is comparable to the role of the native priest in a local community in many Asian societies.

---

30. In this context, it would be the belief both in *Kabunian* and the ancestral spirits and some components of Christianity.

Introduction

THE UNIQUE CONTRIBUTIONS OF THE BOOK OF JOB

- The book of Job offers some answers to the question of why the righteous suffer.
  This early revelation from God supplies the answer to one of humanity's greatest problems: Why does God, if he is both loving and sovereign, allow the righteous to suffer? Throughout the book, various answers to this question are propounded. *Satan* suggests that suffering is a tool with which he can force anyone to renounce God (1:11; 2:4–5). The three friends suggest that suffering is always a punishment for sin (4:7–9; 8:3–6; 11:13–15). Elihu gives ten categories of suffering and suggests that God uses suffering to teach his adherents (33:13–18, 29–30). Job initially felt that suffering was only for the wicked, and for wrongdoers and not for the righteous (7:20), but later learned that suffering is God's refining process to produce "gold" – that is, the best in people (23:10).

- The book gives the reader a rare look at actions around God's throne (Job 1–2).
  Just as the last book of the Bible emphasizes God's throne during times of trial (Rev 4–5; 21), this earliest book (possibly written even before Genesis) pulls back the heavenly curtain for a brief view of God's throne room (see also 1 Kgs 22:19–23). God's complete sovereignty and his great concern for the plight and affairs of humanity are stressed on each of these rare occasions.

- The book introduces the reader to humanity's great enemy – the devil (1:6).
  Assuming that the book of Job is the most ancient biblical book, it is significant that its first chapter introduces man's great adversary – Satan. Satan is described here in simple, unmistakable terms, not as an evil *force* but as a real person who challenges God, has tremendous power over nature, and harbors great enmity toward those who serve God. Satan's actions, however, are always under close scrutiny by God, controlled or restricted by God, and used to fulfill God's purpose. Believers are not to be ignorant about Satan's scheming ways (2 Cor 2:11).

- Job's attitude and conclusion in the final chapter should lead the reader to reject compensation or assumption theology (42:5–6). The three friends' basic error was to assume that they were righteous because they were rich and that they were holy because they were healthy. While Job himself probably held this view, which was the orthodox position of that time, his experience of suffering shattered that view. Recalling the prosperity of the wicked, Job began to discern that health or wealth in this life do not indicate a person's standing with God. True religion is described as trusting God regardless of rewards in this life, with a view to the final day of resurrection and reckoning (19:25).

- The book introduces the concept of a mediator and a redeemer. In his despair, Job longed for a mediator to plead his case before God and before men (9:32–33). In the debate with his friends, Job expressed both his bewilderment over what was happening to him and his declarations concerning what he believed about God. In Job 19:25, Job acknowledged that he had a "redeemer" (*go'el*), who, he hoped, would finally and ultimately vindicate him.[31] Even though Job was not aware of the identity of this redeemer whom God would send, he searched after him and, by faith, held on to this belief. The concept of a "mediator" is not uncommon in Asia, where a meditator is often necessary to maintain *shalom* at home, in business dealings, and in settling conflicts and maintaining peaceful relationships with others in the community.

LITERARY STYLE

The literary form of the book is that of two short prose narratives (the prologue and the epilogue), with the main section consisting of poetic speeches (disputation speeches) in between. Smick acknowledges the book's A-B-A structure – prose narrative-poetic speeches-prose narrative – a structure that it shares with other ancient compositions such as the Code of Hammurabi. Smick attributes this style and structure to the author's creative composition

---

31. Or the "avenger of blood." See *HALOT*, s.v. "go'el."

and not mere arbitrary compilation.³² The prologue introduces Job, the main character, the problem he faced, and the reason behind it. The poetic sections move the plot forward to the climax, which is Yahweh's speeches, capturing the depths and heights of Job's pain and suffering, which were aggravated by his friends' flawed accusations. The epilogue presents the resolution of the problem: Job was vindicated and his friends, proven wrong, offered the sacrifice that God required (42:7–10).

Zuck further suggests that the book is "probably a composite of a lawsuit (several legal terms are frequently used by Job, his friends, and God), a controversy dialogue or wisdom disputation, and a lament. Job voiced many laments against himself, God, and his enemies."³³ It seems not merely probable but certain that the book actually has the elements of a lawsuit, which will be traced at its major points in this commentary. The disputation type of speech – which will be tackled in the response of Job to the first speech of Eliphaz – has some similarities to the oral-antiphonal communication practices among the *Ibaloy*, a people group in the northern part of the Philippines.³⁴

With regard to content, the basic concept of wisdom has always been connected with skill and "know-how" – that is, showing ability and competence in a given field. Wisdom literature challenges readers to discover the "know-how" presented in the book of Job so that they might achieve competence in dealing with questions related to suffering. The book of Job enables readers to learn how to challenge false concepts about suffering and how to maintain a loving and meaningful relationship with their sovereign God in the midst of suffering.

---

32. Smick, "Introduction," in *Job*.
33. Roy B. Zuck, "Job," in *BKC*, ed. John F. Walvoord and Roy B. Zuck (Wheaton: Victor Books, 1985), 1:716.
34. This antiphonal style of communication is observed when on special occasions and after the leading person has made a statement about the celebrant or deceased, a group would respond by singing back the words or the sentence back to the lead person. This alternates between the lead person and the singing group until the former has finished relating the story or presenting what he wanted to share.

UNDESERVED SUFFERING

The book of Job is a combination of divine and human understanding on how to address the major issues involving a person's relationship with God. The book continually asks, "Do righteous people suffer undeservedly?" The book also labors with the concept of *theodicy*, which is a defense of God's justice and righteousness in light of the evil, injustice, and undeserved suffering in the world. We may define undeserved suffering as *suffering that is not traceable to any specific act of personal sin*.

Job is unquestionably a book dealing with human suffering. Even though the suffering of the innocent[1] is not the author's sole purpose, the theme of undeserved suffering is prominent. The book shows that the believing sufferer can question and doubt, face the hard questions of life with faith, maintain an unbroken relationship with a loving God, and arrive at a satisfactory resolution for the issues of personal and collective injustice and undeserved suffering.

Today, many believers suffer, and so they are able to identify with Job. As Andersen says, "The problem of suffering, human misery, or the larger sum of evil in all its forms is a problem only for the person who believe in one God who is all-powerful and all-loving."[2] Without this belief, a person may simply dismiss suffering as "life" or as something uncontrollable by a limited God or gods.

Suffering, then, is the major issue that forces consideration of the deeper questions related to it, especially that which affect the lives of those who have a loving, intimate relationship with the true and living God. The book of Job serves as a dependable and useful model for believers of any generation to deal with the problem of the relationship of God with his children during times of undeserved suffering.

---

1. Matitiahu Tsevat, "The Meaning of the Book of Job," *HUCA* 37 (1966): 195. Though the word "innocent" disturbs some, it is used here in the sense of innocence of any wrongdoing as the basis for the suffering Job endured, not innocence in the sense of having no sin or culpability as a fallen human being.

2. Andersen, *Job*, 64–65. This is not to say that a nonbeliever does not struggle with the same questions, but if an unbeliever's questions do not lead to a relationship with God, then they are normally used as excuses for not believing in God and as reasons to dismiss divine claims without struggling with the biblical issues. The believer, however, struggles with the seeming inconsistencies and incongruities, attempting to harmonize these difficulties with faith in what is known of God in his word.

Introduction

PRESUMPTIVE THEOLOGY

A *presumptive theology* is a system of faith founded on *assumptions* related to human observations, prejudice, or dogmatic tradition. In other words, God is defined by observations, preconceived ideas and prejudices, beliefs or principles, be it religious or not, that were kept and passed on from one generation to the next. Presumptive theology is, first, a reward-and-punishment lifestyle related to an individual's performance (that is, what I do for God in life). Second, it is a set standard of *assumed* values (that is, what I accept as true about God and life, and how I personally respond or react to life and God). Under this system, the Christian life becomes either *a tit-for-tat* or *quid-pro-quo* repayment for services rendered or a let's-make-a-deal proposition.

These concepts are illustrated by *Satan's* question to God, "Does Job fear God for nothing?" (1:9). This question has two dangerous accusations, demonstrating both the *quid-pro-quo* and the let's-make-a-deal concepts. First, the accusation that Job serves God only because God protects and prospers him, and second, that God buys worshipers like Job by giving prosperity and protection. Although this may seem ludicrous, almost all of us accept one or both these assumptions at some time in our lives.

This false presumptive theology persists in Asia. This view says that because we are sinners, we deserve what we get or even harsher treatment. This belief is supported by dysfunctional relationships that reaffirm our worthlessness. Furthermore, this philosophy slithers down its evil path straight through the doorways of suffering people every day. When a baby dies, when a wife is killed in an automobile accident, when a business fails, when we succumb to incurable illnesses, or when a calamity hits us, we are often told, simplistically, that this is because we are sinners and live in a sinful world.

So, is God to be held to a strict set of regulations based on human interpretations of his relationship with humankind? How does the book of Job handle this question and its connection with undeserved suffering, while still demanding faith in an omnipotent, sovereign, and loving God? The book of Job attempts to do the following: (a) reveal the role that Satan may sometimes take in the life of a believer in God with regard to human suffering; (b) show how the three counselors, while presenting some truth, did not follow true retribution theology but, rather, used assumption theology[1] as a method of explaining suffering that is related to *Satan's* original attack on Job; (c) trace the emotional state and psychological well-being of Job in his journey of pain; (d) present Elihu's answers to the questions about Job's suffering; (e) point to Yahweh's assessment of Job's complaint and suffering and explain his correction of Job and his three counselors; (f) summarize the variety of lessons Job learned from his suffering; and (g) affirm that there is a reason and purpose for pain and suffering.

---

1. The term "assumption theology" suggests the concept of "payment" in kind, a *quid pro quo* arrangement. Job's accusers said God is somehow under obligation to humankind and is confined to giving exact payment to individuals.

We turn now to the text of the book of Job, to consider its meaning and message to us and for us at a time when we are still reaping the ill effects of COVID-19. Job begins with a prologue (1:1–2:13) that is followed by the disputation speeches (3:1–42:6) and concludes with an epilogue (42:7–17). Both the prologue and epilogue are in narrative form, and while the prologue states Job's identity and social standing before various calamities beset him, the epilogue describes his life and successes afterward.

OUTLINE

The Prologue	1:1–2:13
Job's Opening Lamentation	3:1–26
Three Sets of Dialogues	4:1–27:23
First Cycle	4:1–14:22
Second Cycle	15:1–21:34
Third Cycle	22:1–27:23
Interlude on Wisdom	28:1–28
Three Sets of Speeches	29:1–42:6
Job's Speech	29:1–31:40
Elihu's Speech	32:1–37:24
Yahweh's Speech	38:1–41:34
Job's Recantation	42:1–6
The Epilogue	42:7–17

JOB 1:1–2:13
THE PROLOGUE

As a narrative, Job has the basic elements of a story: character, setting, and plot. The characters in the heavenly realm are God, the angels, and *Satan*.[1] On the earth are Job, his children, the raiders, messengers, Job's wife, and the three friends. As to the setting, events happen in heaven and on earth. The plot includes different scenes, starting with the conversation between God and *Satan*, in which God gave *Satan* permission to destroy Job's possessions and to afflict him physically to test and prove Job's sincerity and faithfulness to God.

1:1–5 INTRODUCING JOB

Job 1 will try to answer the following questions: Who was Job? What circumstances led to his pain and suffering? How did he respond to his losses? How is God introduced? What role did *Satan* play in this catastrophe?

The first five verses describe the character, possessions, family, and reputation of Job, who lived in the land of Uz. Although the location of Uz is not known with certainty, three places are consistently suggested and staunchly supported by their proponents: south of Damascus, a place in Edom, and a locale in northern Arabia.[2] Seow points to somewhere in the Transjordan, in the region of southern Edom or northern Arabia.[3] Evidence seems to favor

---

1. The noun *satan* in a military and political context can mean an adversary or opponent (1 Sam 29:4, 1 Kgs 5:18, 11:14, 22–23). In a legal context, it can mean accuser, opposing party, or one who hinders a purpose. See *HALOT*, s.v. "satan." For this work, we retain the translation *Satan*, but italicize this to indicate his function as adversary. See further discussion on the word at the end of the chapter.
2. Those who support an Uz near Haran south of Damascus include F. Andersen, Kraeling, Tur-Sinai, and Leon Wood. Uz was a son of Aram, from whom the Arameans descended (Gen 10:23; 1 Chr 1:17) and also a nephew of Abraham (Gen 22:21); thus, Uz is associated with the Arameans. Josephus says that Uz, a son of Aram (Gen 10:23), founded Trachonitis and Damascus. See Josephus, *Ant.*1.6.4 (Thackeray, LCL). Pope explains that "Byzantine and Arab tradition place Job's homeland in the Hauran near Nawa and Sheikh Meskin. . . . The monastery Deir Ayyub near Damascus is another witness to this tradition." *Job*, 3. Rasmussen suggests though uncertain, a place east of Edom, edge of the Arabian desert. See Carl G. Rasmussen, *Zondervan NIV Atlas of the Bible* (Grand Rapids: Zondervan, 1989), 255. Archer settles on Northern Arabia as the location of Uz, which the Septuagint identifies as the land of Aisitai. (*Survey of the Old Testament*, 505).
3. Seow, *Job 1–21*, 44.

the latter since Job lived near the desert (1:19) in a fertile land that sustained agriculture and livestock (1:3, 14).

1:1 Job's Righteousness

Verse 1 describes Job as "blameless" (*tam*) and "upright" (*yashar*). These terms form a word pair that is used again in 2:3. "Blameless," in this context, means being ethically and morally outstanding and having integrity. Being "upright" suggests that Job's way of life was in accordance with God's will and, therefore, pleasing to God. Job "shunned evil" (1:1, 8; 2:3) because of his reverent fear of God – which is also one of the themes of this book. Reverence translates into worship and obedience, which explains why Job shunned evil. Job took God seriously. This involved obeying and respecting God as supreme. Job also hated anything that was contrary to God's character (1:1). God and the writer clearly agreed that Job was an upright person who enjoyed a close relationship with Yahweh (29:4).

1:2–3 Job's Accomplishments

Not only was Job an upright and devout man of God, but he was also known as the greatest man among all the people of the East.[4] In God's sight, not only is a person's faith and righteousness important but their family and professional life must also reflect that relationship. In the Hebrew mindset, the numbers seven and three indicate completeness. Therefore, Job's "seven sons and three daughters" (1:2) reflect God's favor. The seven sons in particular are significant. Ruth was described as better than seven sons (Ruth 4:15). In the culture of the time, having many children was seen as a blessing – a father with seven sons did not have to worry about his future since he had sons to defend him and further the interest of the family.

Job's professional life was equally successful. He was a rancher who possessed extensive property for grazing sheep, camels, oxen, and donkeys. A "large number of servants" helped him manage and care for his family and properties (1:3). Such possessions allowed Job to enjoy a high social status so that he earned the reputation of being the greatest person among his people. Readers may wonder: Is it possible for one person to possess as much livestock as Job did? Yes!

---

4. The MT has *bene qedem* (literally, "sons of the East"). It is a group of people referred to in Old Testament texts: Genesis 29:1; Judges 6:3, 33; 7:12; 8:10; 1 Kings 4:30; Isaiah 11:14; Jeremiah 49:28; Ezekiel 25:4, 10. Seow identifies them with "people across the Jordan, anywhere from Haran in Aram in the north of Kedar in Arabia in the south" (*Job 1–21*, 268).

JOB'S WEALTH

Job is described as the "greatest man among the peoples of the East" (1:3b) during the patriarchal period and in ancient times. One aspect that contributed to his greatness was his wealth. As was a common in agricultural communities of the time, Job's wealth is expressed in terms of the size of his flocks and herds – that is, the number of all his livestock and servants.

During those times, it was quite possible for one man to amass such great wealth. Beginning with a small number of each of these animals and reckoning their individual maximal reproduction capability over many years, the numbers could well correspond to the numbers given in the text (1:3; 42:12). For instance, if a rancher today has 100 healthy female cows – given that a cow gives birth to one calf every year and female calves (heifers) are ready for gestation by the time they are two years old – and following the pattern of cow birthing of female-male-female-male offspring,[1] these 100 original female cows could birth 300 female cows within five or six years. Of course, this would only be possible provided the cows were healthy and enjoyed the best possible living environment – spacious and good grazing land, a fresh water source, being free from plague, and safe from predators. These conditions seem to have been met in the case of Job's herds.

Original: 100 Healthy Female Cows

First year	100 female cows
Second year	100 male cows
Third year	100 female cows
Fourth year	100 male cows
Fifth year	100 female cows

Cows usually have a life span of 18–20 years. They can still give birth when they are 8–10 years of age, although the quality of the heifer diminishes. The farmer or rancher would usually pair the cow with a high breed bull to improve the quality.

Job had 500 yokes of oxen (or a pair of oxen, hence 1,000 oxen) before the calamities. God blessed him by doubling this number after the calamities. Following the pattern of birthing female-male-female-male offspring, and that the first female offspring can also give birth when they are two years of age, a rancher who starts with 1,000 oxen can easily double this figure in 5 years.

> **Original: 1,000 Healthy Female Sheep**
> The life span of a sheep is 12 years. An ewe is ready for gestation 10–12 months from birth. It can give birth twice a year and produce 2–6 offspring each time.
>
> First year   1,000 original x 2 birthing per year x 2 offspring
>   = 4,000 sheep
>
> Second year   1,000 original x 2 birthing per year x 2 offspring
>   = 4,000 sheep
>
> Job had 7,000 sheep. This figure could readily double within five years. Consider also that the first 4,000 offspring are ready for gestation when they are about to start and be age 2.
>
> Job's wealth is also evident in his extensive property. This can be inferred from the number of his livestock and servants. He needed a vast track of grazing land for his animals and a large house for his servants to live.

---

1. This author observed two to three patterns of birthing by cows, but one that caught her attention is this female-male-female-male pattern that was exhibited by one of their cows. This alternate pattern is advantageous to the rancher, but not so much for the caretaker because of the policy that they maintained – the first, third, and fifth offspring belong to the owner while the second, fourth, and sixth offspring belong to the caretaker. In this author's case, all the female offspring of this particular cow went to her family and the male offspring went to the caretaker.

1:4–5 Job's Family

Job was a responsible family man. They had a family tradition where his seven sons would hold feasts on their birthdays to which their sisters were invited (1:4). After a whole circuit of feasts was completed, Job, as head of the family, and acting as priest, would sacrifice burnt offerings for each of his children. The reason Job made these offerings was because he thought that perhaps his children might have secretly sinned and *cursed* God.[5] He feared that they may have treated God lightly or forgotten him in their time of feasting.

---

5. On the word "curse," the actual and proper term for it is *qalal*. The Hebrew text, however, uses the term *barakh*, meaning to "bless." The Masoretes who read the text amended or substituted the term *qalal* to *barakh*, for they did not want to associate the term "curse" with God. The word *qalal* in its various forms can mean the following: "to be light;" "insignificant;" "be laid under a curse;" "be designated, treated, and made accursed;" "to lighten or treat with contempt." See *HALOT*, s.v. "qalal." The same pattern occurs in Job 1:11; 2:5, 9.

Job seemed to have been an ideal parent and spiritual leader of his household. Wanting to make sure that his children's sins, if any, were atoned for, he offered sacrifices for them so that they might have a better relationship with Yahweh. And he did this on a regular basis (1:5). Job's faith was as real at home as it was in the marketplace.

Unknown to Job, he was about to be tested in areas where all human beings are vulnerable: financial status and security, social standing, family, health, and spiritual life. *Satan* would attack three areas that the author, God, and *Satan* himself recognized as Job's strongest points: his integrity, his reverential fear of God, and his refusal to engage in sin. Unlike the reader, who has inside knowledge about what was taking place both in heaven and on earth, Job remained oblivious to all the maneuverings behind the scenes, including *Satan's* accusations against him.

1:6–2:10 JOB'S TESTS

1:6–22 The First Test

In the heavenly assembly, *Satan* challenged Yahweh, suggesting that Job, if he had to suffer the loss of his properties and his family, would curse God. What happens in heaven has a causal effect on things that happen on earth, and we see this in the story of Job. Nonetheless, God remains in control of everything – both in heaven and on earth.

1:6–12 Satan's Accusation against Job

The scene is set in heaven. Similar to – though not subservient to – the practice depicted in ANE texts, God called for a council meeting.[6] On that particular day, the angels (sons of God)[7] who made up the council of Yahweh[8] presented themselves before God. *Satan* also came along with them.

---

6. ANE texts attest to the concept of a divine council in Akkad, Babylon, Ugarit, Canaan, and Egypt. It is sometimes referred to as the Great Assembly. See "The Ba'lu Myth," trans. Dennis Pardee (COS 1.86:246).
7. This designation relates to a divine council, where the "sons of God" are the divine beings that make up that council. This is reflected in the literature and polytheistic culture of the ANE. The chief gods have divine authority, and each has a jurisdiction. Walton explains that in "Old Testament monotheism this concept is revised but not eliminated. It is true that in biblical theology Yahweh needs no advice or consultants (Isa 40:13–14), but it is his prerogative to discuss his plans with others as he wills and to delegate responsibility as his discretion." See John H. Walton, *Job*, NIVAC (Grand Rapids: Zondervan, 2012), 63.
8. Yahweh (YHWH) is God's personal name. It is translated LORD in English Bibles and is used for the first time in Job 1:6. For this work, we will use Yahweh instead of LORD whenever the Hebrew text uses YHWH.

THE NAMES OF GOD IN THE BOOK OF JOB

Yahweh represented by YHWH. These four consonants are also called the tetragrammaton, which is translated "Lord" in English translations of the Bible. Yahweh is God's personal and special covenant name, by which he was introduced and made known to his people, Israel (Exod 3:13–15). While this calls for reverence, "it also connotes God's nearness and concern for man and the revelation of his redemptive covenant."[1] Yahweh, essentially "'faithful presence' is God's testamentary nature, or name (Exod 6:2–4; Deut 7:9; Isa 26:4)."[2]

Jews do not pronounce YHWH for fear of violating the third commandment: "You shall not misuse the name of the Lord your God, for the Lord will not hold anyone guiltless who misuses his name" (Exod 20:7). When encountering the name YHWH in the Hebrew text, the word is not pronounced. Instead, *Adonay* is substituted, or the Hebrew phrase *Hashem* (the name) is used.

The name Yahweh is used 32 times in the book of Job. It first occurs in Job 1:6. Except for Job 12:9, the other 31 occurrences are in the prologue (Job 1–2) and in Yahweh's speeches (Job 38–42).

Elohim is a general term for gods, whether referring to the true living God or to false gods. One way to know if *elohim* in a given OT text is referring to the true God is checking the verb before it. If the verb is singular and is supported by the immediate context or surrounding verses, *elohim* refers to God. If the verb is plural, then *elohim* refers to gods other than Yahweh. At other times, *elohim* can refer to "rulers, judges either as representatives in sacred places or representing majesty and power."[3] *Elohim* is used ten times in the book of Job, mainly by Job in the prologue (5 times) and twice by Elihu in his speeches. Both Job and Elihu acknowledged the transcendence of God.

El is an ancient Semitic term for deity. It is a title that Yahweh claimed for himself (Isa 40:18; 43:12; 46:9).[4] *El* is used of the God of Israel (Num 23:8)[5] and also of a god foreign to Israel (Deut 32:12). At times, it is "applied to men of might and rank,"[6] as well as to angels. It is used 57 times in Job without the usual epithets attached to it. Job and his friends treated *El* as the "common term for the true God"[7] and recognized him as mighty and all-powerful.

Eloah is the singular form of *elohim*. It is "only used in poetry and later Hebrew."[8] While it can refer to heathen gods (2 Kgs 17:33; 2 Chr 32:15), it is usually used to describe the true God (Deut 32:15; Ps 50:22).[9] The term is used 41 times in the book of Job. "It appears to be an ancient term for God which was later dropped for the most part until the return of the exile and after, where there was a great concern for the return to the more ancient foundations. It is not frequently used outside of Job."[10] Job perceived *Eloah* as the one who put a hedge about him (3:23), the one to whom he cried to (16:20), the one who attacked him (19:21), but also the one whom he longed to see (19:26).

> **Shadday** means almighty or powerful and may refer to a deity, a divine name, a mountain, or a mountain range.[11] It can stand alone or be attached to an epithet like *El*, and thus we have *El Shadday* (God Almighty). *Shadday* is used 31 times in Job, more than the combined occurrence in the whole Tanakh or the Hebrew Bible. Job spoke of *Shadday* as the source of the attacks (6:4; 27:2), while Elihu spoke of him as the giver of life (33:4).

---

1. Barton J. Payne, "hawa," *TWOT* 1:212.
2. Payne, "hawa," 1:212.
3. BDB, s.v. "'Elohim."
4. *HALOT*, s.v. "'El."
5. *HALOT*, s.v. "'El."
6. BDB, s.v. "'El."
7. Jack B. Scott, s.v., "'el" in *TWOT* 2 (1980).
8. See *Gesenius' Hebrew-Chaldee Lexicon to the Old Testament*, s.v. "Eloah."
9. *Gesenius' Hebrew-Chaldee Lexicon to the Old Testament*, s.v. "Eloah."
10. Jack B. Scott, "'eloah," *TWOT* 2:43.
11. *HALOT*, s.v. "Shaddai."

The concept of a divine council is not foreign to Asia. This idea is reflected in the bureaucracy of gods and goddesses in Asia's major religions and also mirrored in human affairs. In Hinduism, for instance, Brahman is the Supreme Being, and there are also other gods, who are entrusted with different responsibilities. As mentioned earlier, in the northern part of the Philippines, some tribal groups continue to worship a local deity called *Kabunian*,[9] while, in their cosmogony, there are also lesser gods around him, who each have their roles to play. The main difference lies in the one who calls the assembly and the members of the assembly. In the OT, it is the living God who calls the meeting, and the members of the assembly are the angels (Ps 82:1–8). In the case of Job, the angels and even *Satan* came into the presence of Yahweh to give their reports.

The ensuing conversation between Yahweh and *Satan* began with God's inquiry about where *Satan* had come from. This question was not referring to a place of origin but to what *Satan* had been doing. *Satan's* reply was that he had come "from roaming throughout the earth, going back and forth on it" (1:7).

---

9. Refer to the *Introduction* of this work and under the heading *Asian Theology*.

This led to God affirming Job's moral integrity. While *Satan* acknowledged that Job did indeed revere God, he implied that Job had no good reason to do so since God had powerfully protected Job on every side – Job himself, his household, and everything he owned. Moreover, God had blessed all of Job's work and made him prosperous, as indicated by the increase in his livestock over the years (1:9–10).

Satan denied God's evaluation of Job, accusing God of misjudging Job's real motives and implying that Job served God only for what he got out of it. This was a subtle accusation, not meant for Job alone but also for God. By suggesting that it only needed God to cause the loss of everything he had for Job to curse God, *Satan* initiated the destruction of all Job's properties (1:11), with the ultimate purpose of getting Job to curse God and thus disprove God's favorable assessment of Job. God knew that Job was sincere in worshiping him and that he himself was not blessing Job as a means to gaining Job's faithfulness, and so he said to *Satan*, "Very well then, everything that he has is in your power, but on the man himself do not lay a finger" (1:12). Since *Satan* is limited by God's sovereignty, he cannot do anything that God does not allow. Though God agreed to *Satan's* proposal, he also uttered a prohibition: *Satan* was free to do anything he wanted with everything Job owned, but he was not allowed to harm Job himself. In this way, God set a boundary: while *Satan* could destroy Job's family and possessions, he could go no further.

After leaving God's presence, *Satan* executed his plan to prove to God that Job was not as upright as God had assessed (1:12c). With the aim of destroying the relationship between Yahweh and Job, *Satan* began his attack on Job's integrity.

1:13–22 Satan's Assault on Job's Family and Property

The scene is set on earth. It presents a cause-and-effect scenario. *Satan*, determined to destroy Job's integrity, attacked him, causing the loss of Job's earthly properties and his children. Four messengers came, one after the other, to report the various calamities, starting with the attack of the Sabeans and ending with the most painful news of all – the death of Job's children.

The Sabeans[10] had attacked and stolen all Job's oxen and donkeys and killed his servants, leaving behind only one survivor, who reported the news to Job (1:13–15).

---

10. These are probably nomads from the oasis of Tema. See Seow, *Job 1–21*, 277.

The "fire of God" that fell from the sky and killed the sheep and the servants, might refer to a thunderbolt (1:16). Only one servant escaped to tell the story. This "fire of God" – which, in Elijah's time, had killed fifty soldiers (2 Kgs 1:12) – must have been an awesome and frightening sight. A servant for the camels related what happened next (1:17). Hess, supported by others, claims that the "Chaldeans" referred to in this verse were the earlier unsettled tribes which – together with Aramean groups – had infiltrated Mesopotamia at the beginning of the first millennium BC. They lived in tribal groups and raided cities and caravans.[11] A powerful wind – commonly called *sirocco*[12] – struck the eldest son's house, causing the house to collapse and killing Job's ten children, leaving only one servant to report it.

A common factor in these four calamities that Job experienced was that only one survivor lived to report what had happened. The timing of the events emphasizes the gravity of the situation, with each crippling piece of news overlapped by the reporting of the next one. There is also a downward curve in the devastation, beginning with the loss of Job's oxen and ending with the death of his children. The latter was the most painful of the four calamities for it not only affected Job the most but also meant the end of his posterity and the loss of his own and his wife's security.

Reacting to *Satan*'s first attack, Job got up and "tore his robe," symbolizing his extreme internal turmoil and then "shaved his head" (1:20) – since shaving the head was prohibited in Israel, this is "a neat way of reminding the audience that Job is not an Israelite."[13] Then Job "fell to the ground in worship" (1:20).

Job's reaction to his painful losses and extreme situation was to abandon himself to God's will and hold fast to his loyalty to God. His words, "Naked I came from my mother's womb, and naked I will depart" (1:21a), not only expressed Job's acceptance of all that he had lost but also his recognition of the fundamental truth that he had come into the world with nothing – with no possessions of any kind – and that it was right, in the order of things, that he should leave this world in the same way. His declaration, "The LORD gave and the LORD has taken away; may the name of the LORD be praised" (1:21b),

---

11. See Richard S. Hess, "Chaldea," *ABD*, 1:886–87; J. A. Brinkman, *A Political History of Post-Kassite Babylonia 1158–722 BC* (Rome: Pontifical Biblical Institute, 1968), 260–67.
12. This *sirocco* or east wind is a scorching wind from the desert. It is hot and humid and carries sand and dust in its wake. See "Wind" in *ISBE Online*, www.http://internationalstandardbible.com. The phrase *powerful wind* is used two other times. In 1 Kings 19:11, the wind dug into a mountain and caused a landslide and in Jonah 1:4, a ship thought it would break due to the effect of the wind.
13. Alter, *Writings*, 14. Seow thinks the anonymous composer is an Israelite (*Job 1–21*,, 44).

shows that he was mindful of the truth that all his losses were linked to the sovereign will of God. Whatever the cost to himself, Job was still willing to praise God. His total abandonment to God as a positive act of worship is a striking contrast to the negative fatalism of many people today.

Such an abandonment to God or to some higher being is seen and experienced by many people as a kind of fatalism, a forced acceptance of tragedy or loss as something that is out of one's hands and, unfortunately, cannot be changed. We see an example of this in the Filipino saying *Bahala na* (which means "come what may") – a syncopation of a phrase that might be loosely translated as "God's will be done"[14] – which is often used by people who find themselves in very difficult situations with no immediate solution or relief in view.

The first chapter of Job ends with the recognition that "in all this" – a reference to the cumulative calamities experienced by Job (1:13–19) – "Job did not sin by charging God with wrongdoing" (1:22). Although *Satan's* plan was to prove to God that Job was pious only because God had protected and provided for him, Job's response revealed the opposite. Even after losing everything – except his health and his life – Job did not curse God, as *Satan* had wanted him to do, but remained blameless and worshiped God.

This chapter reminds us that no one – however rich or righteous – is immune from suffering and pain. Although Job was the greatest and a very wealthy person in his time, he too faced undeserved suffering. Job was also an upright person, fully committed to God. We may think that such a person would not be a candidate for adversity, yet God allowed Job to be tested by adversity. This means that believers – even if they have served God faithfully or received abundant blessings from him – are not exempt from suffering. While suffering of some kind is the effect of all *Satan's* machinations, it is also the stage where the watching world can see how God's followers respond to pain. As we have seen in this chapter, Job neither sinned nor blamed God in any way for all that happened to him. Job, therefore, is a shining example for us all! Suffering is thus one of the greatest opportunities for believers to bear witness to their faith by modeling how to handle pain with humility, while remaining faithful to God in and through it all. The problem is that most people do not realize that they are in a spiritual battle or that pain has potential to bring blessings from God.

---

14. See the work of Ed Lapiz, *Paano Maging Pilipino ang Kristiano: Becoming a Filipino Christian* (Makati City: Kaloob, 1997), 33.

Since the events described in the first chapter of Job determine what unfolds in all 42 chapters of this book, the importance of this opening chapter cannot be overemphasized. This chapter takes us behind the scenes and reveals to us the wider scope of the situation and the specific reason for all that happens afterward. It relates how Job, unknowingly, finds himself caught up in a contest between *Satan* and God to prove whether Job's faithfulness to God was sincere. Following God's clear approval of Job's uprightness, *Satan* questioned the motives behind Job's faithfulness and was given the opportunity to disprove Job's sincerity and tempt him to curse God to his face (1:11). The chapter also explains why Job, through no fault of his own, was forced to endure so much physical and emotional suffering, as well as so many difficult spiritual experiences that are described in this book.

Job lost all his properties and livestock, including his faithful servants – except the four who returned to report on what had happened – and, finally, faced the most tragic and painful loss of his ten children. His response of total abandonment to God in the face of all these adversities is outstanding and highly commendable.

As for God, he is shown to be sovereign over all that happened and would happen, both in heaven and on earth. The book describes scenes that take place in both places. In heaven, God is portrayed as being in control of the conversation; on earth, it was God who allowed things to happen and set specific limits on what could happen. God has control over all people – as demonstrated by his former blessing and protection of Job – over circumstances – as seen in the timing of events – and over all creation – as evident in the servant's reference to the "fire" that came from God.

Adversity can turn our hearts toward the living God or away from him. And our response to adversity often reveals the state of our hearts. In Job's case, would he continue to worship God despite the additional calamities that would disturb his once peaceful life? Chapter 2 presents the additional pain that Job had to suffer. How would he respond? What role did God play in this tragedy?

HA SATAN: FUNCTION OR PROPER NAME?

In a legal context, the word *satan* means accuser, opposing party, or one who hinders a purpose.[1] The most important of these meanings in relation to Job would be a heavenly prosecutor, opponent, or adversary. For the first two chapters of Job, the word *satan* is preceded by a definite article (Hebrew definite article *ha* + *satan* = *ha satan* = *the satan*). This is the case in all its 14 occurrences in Job. Alter takes *ha satan* to indicate function rather than a proper name.[2] The word *satan* may also refer to a personal name, but in such instances, it does not have the Hebrew article attached to *satan*. An example of this is the celestial being who incited David to carry out a census (1 Chr 21:1).[3] Walton renames the entity in Job 1–2 and identifies this as the Challenger, to indicate function, rather than Satan, the proper name.[4]

Belcher acknowledges the hesitancy of some scholars to identify *ha satan* in Job 1–2 with Satan because "not much is said in OT about him. However, many passages talk about beings or spirits working against God's purposes (Gen 3:1; 1 Sam 16:14), a role that fits the heavenly being in Job."[5]

While most scholars agree to take *ha satan* as a function rather than as a proper name, Waltke and O'Connor argue otherwise from a grammatical standpoint. Focusing on the article, they explain that there are situations where "the article not only points out a particular person or thing, but it also elevates it to such a position of uniqueness that the *noun* + *article* combination becomes the equivalent of a *proper name*."[6] Following this pattern (article + noun, reversed when transliterated), they cite, as examples, "the lord," transliterated as *ha ba'al*, refers to Baal and "the adversary," transliterated *ha satan* to Satan.[7] Both examples here refer to proper names and not function.

The LXX itself has *ho diabolos*, which can be translated as "the devil" or "the slanderer."

As mentioned earlier, we retain the proper name, hence the term *Satan* is capitalizedand italicized to indicate his function as an adversary.

---

1. See *HALOT*, s.v. "satan."
2. Alter, *Writings*, 12.
3. Alter, *Writings*, 12.
4. Walton, *Job*, 65.
5. Richard P. Belcher Jr., *Finding Favor in the Sight of God: A Theology of Wisdom Literature*, NSBT (London: Apollos, 2018), 79.
6. Bruce K. Waltke and M. O'Connor, *An Introduction to Biblical Hebrew Syntax* (Winona Lake: Eisenbrauns, 1990), 249.
7. Waltke and O'Connor, *Introduction to Biblical Hebrew Syntax*, 249.

2:1–10 The Second Test
2:1–6 Satan's Further Plan to Force Job to Sin
The opening verses of chapter 2 (2:1–3) closely resemble the descriptions found in the previous chapter (1:6–8). The scene is set in heaven, and the conversation between God and *Satan* begins in the same way, and with the same affirmation of Job. God continued to praise Job's integrity and perseverance in faith despite *Satan's* attempt to ruin him. His comments and suggestions to God revealed his motive and role in Job's life.

"On another day" (2:1) does not tell us how much time had gone by before the second test began. What this chapter does reveal is that *Satan* had not given up after his earlier failure to set Job against God. On this particular day, the angels and *Satan* attended another assembly meeting (2:1). The exchange between God and *Satan* opened in exactly the same way as in chapter 1, with God asking the same questions and *Satan* answering in similar fashion (compare 1:6–8 and 2:1–3).

God affirmed Job's integrity and innocence in the face of the loss of his possessions and his children, for which he laid the blame at *Satan's* feet. God also stated that *Satan* had deliberately tried to incite (*suth*)[15] God against Job with the aim of destroying Job without any reason (2:3). *Satan's* retort, "Skin for skin!" implies that with the loss of his possessions and children Job had merely saved his own skin or that his own skin had hardly been scratched.[16] This was perhaps an ironic and symbolic reference to the attack on Job's skin – of boils and lesions that Job will experience after the attack (2:7). Basically, though, *Satan* was cynical in implying that Job was just glad that it was not he himself who had died. *Satan* went on to point out that if only God would afflict (*nakhah*) Job's body, then Job would openly curse God.[17] *Nakhah* can mean to strike so as to wound or kill, and *Satan* was challenging God to allow him to do just this (2:4–5). God agreed but set a boundary as he had done before: Job's life must be spared (2:6).

---

15. The word *suth* is used four other times in the *Tanakh* but in two different ways. First is to like something as when Caleb asked Acsah what she desires (Josh 15:18; Judg 1:14). Second is to attack someone as when Ahab challenged Jehoshaphat to join him in attacking Ramoth Gilead (2 Chr 18:2) and when the chariot commanders wanted to attack Jehoshaphat (2 Chr 18:31).
16. Alter offers this explanation: "What is most precious to a man is his own physical being; in the end, he is prepared to sacrifice everything, even the 'skin' (or lives) of his own dear ones but hurt him badly in his own flesh and bones and he will abandon all his principles of integrity" *Writings*, 468.
17. Literally, "Curse you to your face" as in the NIV text.

As in chapter one, *Satan* indirectly questioned the motives of both God and Job, implying that God was holding back to spare Job and that Job was still worshiping God for self-gain. Illnesses and diseases often weaken human resistance to temptation from the enemy; as a result, more people have probably rejected God on account of suffering and pain than for any other reason.

2:7–10 Job's Integrity in Personal Suffering

Satan immediately moved to attack Job's health. He inflicted him with inflamed and ulcerous boils that covered his whole body (2:7).[18] These resulted in continuous itching, which Job tried to ease by repeatedly scraping himself with a sharp piece of pottery (2:8). A medical doctor describes Job's condition in this way: "From the soles of his painful feet to the crown of his oozing scalp Job was in trouble."[19]

The next scene found Job at the outskirts of the city. Job, who had once sat at the city gates as a judge (29:7), now sat on a dunghill. The MT has it that Job "sat among the ashes" (*'epher*). The LXX uses the word *koprias*, meaning "dunghill," "heap of dung," or "pile of garbage." The LXX also adds the phrase, "outside the city," which the MT fails to include. Continuously scraping his skin with broken pottery, along with the degenerative changes in the skin on his face, might even have made Job unrecognizable (2:12).[20] These painful sores and other deteriorating symptoms caused Job unmatched physical suffering, which only increased over the next few months (7:3; 30:16–17, 27–30).

Apart from physical pain, Job also suffered emotionally. He was grief-stricken over the loss of his children (1:20).[21] Even his friends acknowledged his pain (2:13). There are also indications that Job suffered spiritually. He could not reconcile "the God he had known and the God he was now experiencing."[22]

---

18. *Shekhin*, from an unused root word, probably means "to burn," or "an inflammation" that is an ulcer, boil, or botch. See BDB, s.v. "shekhin." The word is used to describe the festering boils that the living God set on the Egyptians (Exod 9:9–11, compare Deut 28:27, 33). This same word is used for the malignant skin ulcers that Job experienced.
19. Diane M. Komp, *Why Me? A Doctor Looks at the Book of Job* (Downers Grove: InterVarsity Press, 2001), 31.
20. Job's other medical problems included the following: loss of appetite (3:24), insomnia (7:4), hardened skin, running sores, worms, and boils (7:5). He also had difficulty breathing (9:18), loss of weight (16:8), eye difficulties (16:16), emaciation (17:7; 19:20), bad breath (19:17), trembling of the limbs (21:6), arthritis (30:17), blackened, peeling skin (30:28, 30), and fever (30:30).
21. Job was depressed (3:24–25), lacked a sense of inner tranquility (3:26), experienced troubling thoughts (7:4, 13–14), had no taste for life (chapter 3; 9:2); felt uncertain and insecure (9:20), without joy (9:25; 30:31), and lonely (19:13–19).
22. H. H. Rowley, *The Book of Job*, NCBC (Grand Rapids: Eerdmans, 1992), 129.

Moreover, he was distressed over this conflict between his own former experience of God's blessings and a theology that seemed to present God as a capricious despot who delighted in afflicting his servant.[23]

We do not know how much time passed until the next difficult test came: Job's wife suggested that Job give up his integrity. And she seemed to wish for his death when she said, "Curse[24] God so that you may die"[25] (2:9, my translation). If to treat God lightly offends him, more so for someone to curse him. God may strike that person dead. There is a case in many generations after Job and in the time of Moses when an Israelite-Egyptian man "blasphemed the Name with a curse" (Lev 24:11). As a result, he was stoned to death (Lev 24:14).

What might have provoked such an outburst by Job's wife? She must have been still shocked by what she probably perceived as an unjust loss of all human security: her children, her home, her wealth, and her privileged social standing.[26] Job's disaster had hit her too. She also had to watch, day after day, as her husband struggled with unspeakable pain. Perhaps she was only expressing her own perspective and grief over everything that happened to them and her ultimate wish that her husband would do whatever was necessary to end his suffering. Komp explains that "by the time her children and wealth have vanished, and a dreadful dermatological disease afflicted her husband, his wife has a choice in mind for Job: assisted suicide."[27] Can we blame Job's wife for asking Job to curse the living God? Her reaction may seem extreme, and many are quick to criticize her, but we do well to ask ourselves how we might have reacted if we were in her shoes. More important, what should we do to encourage a loved one who is going through a similar situation?

Pain and suffering can cause marital problems even in an almost perfect marriage, and it can make or break a marriage and family. Before the calamities struck, nothing is said about Job's wife. She is introduced and identified in contemporary times by her statement in verse 9. Job, however, did not call his wife a foolish woman but only reprimanded her for "talking like a foolish

---

23. See Job 6:4; 7:17–19; 19:25. Job was terrified by God's silence (23:8–9, 15), his seeming injustice (33:10–11; 34:5), lack of mercy (9:27–31; 33:10–11), and indifference (34:9; 35:3).
24. Job's wife used the Hebrew term *qalal*, meaning "to curse." The Masoretes edited and replaced it with the term *barakh*, which literally means "to bless." See note in Job 1:5.
25. There are two commands in this verse, where the second command may be the result of the first, hence the translation. The NIV has "Curse God and die!"
26. The LXX in Job 2:9 presents some details of how Job's wife felt over everything that happened to her family.
27. Komp, *Why Me?*, 31.

woman" (2:10a) – which focuses attention on her foolish suggestion. Since Job's wife survives to the end of the book, there is no indication that she was judged or punished for her statement.

Job's response to his appalling situation must be one of the most astounding statements of faith found in Scripture: "Shall we accept good from God, and not trouble?" (2:10b). Job's willingness to accept pain and adversity from God means that his worship and service were not dependent on personal prosperity or excellent health.

The narrator's "in all this" – echoing the words from chapter one (1:22) – again sums up the outcome of the test and is a strong affirmation of Job's steadfast integrity in the face of a multitude of negative experiences. Despite all his trials and pain, "Job did not sin in what he said" (2:10). He received a similar evaluation at the end of the first test (1:22). *Satan* could not celebrate. His accusations against Job were disproved for, despite adverse circumstances, Job remained blameless and upright.

Job found himself alone, with nothing but the clothes on his back. He had lost his children, the source of his joy; he had lost the servants who attended to his needs; and even his own wife, by her very words, seemed to have disowned him. Job had become a social outcast, with no standing in the community. Since Job came from an honor-shame culture, he experienced a "loss of face." This humiliation added to the pain he was already experiencing. Once the greatest person in the East, now he had lost everything except his life and his wife. He had become a nobody. It is sometimes thought that rich people have many friends. Would Job find any loyal friends once he lost his wealth and his health?

2:11–13 JOB'S COUNSELORS

Hearing of Job's serious situation, three of his friends came from their respective countries to visit him. They were Eliphaz the Temanite, Bildad the Shuhite, and Zophar the Naamathite. Except for Teman,[28] the other places are difficult to identify. Alter, while acknowledging that the precise location of these places is debatable, considers it likely that they were spread over a few hundred miles to the east of the River Jordan.[29]

---

28. Rasmussen suggests Tawilan, in South Jordan, three miles East of Petra (*Zondervan NIV Atlas*, 254).
29. Alter, *Writings*, 469.

Job's face must have been so disfigured that his friends, as they saw him from a distance, were hardly able to recognize him; when they eventually did, they wept, tore their robes, and "threw dust into the air to their heads" (2:12, my translation). The tearing of robes may symbolize remorse over someone's tragedy or sin (Josh 7:6; 2 Sam 13:19; Ezra 9:3), while throwing dust into the air symbolizes disease and death.[30] The friends sat down with Job for seven days and nights, which was "the period of mourning at the death of a most notable figure (Gen 50:10; 1 Sam 31:13)."[31] Their silence and their sensitivity to his suffering must have brought some comfort to Job, considering that he was alone and in so much discomfort (2:13).

God is well aware of how much adversity each person can cope with, and he sets limits to what he allows to happen in the lives of each of his creations at any given time. While losses and pain can be the result of sin, this is not always the case; often, circumstances out of our control are the fundamental cause of suffering. In Job's unusual and extraordinary case, he was in no way to blame for the circumstances that led to his losses and pain, yet he maintained his integrity throughout *Satan's* second demanding test. Despite his painful experiences and his wife's urging, he did not yield to the temptation to curse God and, thereby, fall into *Satan's* trap. Just as in the first test, the narrator affirms that Job "did not sin in what he said" (2:10, compare 1:22).

Job's second test resulted in a catastrophic amount of pain and loss of health that led to a loss in social standing. Nevertheless, Job remained steadfast, with his integrity intact, thus thwarting *Satan's* plan to destroy him spiritually. Even when his wife challenged him to curse God so that God may strike him dead and thus end his suffering Job refused to do it.

---

30. John E. Hartley, *The Book of Job*, NICOT (Grand Rapids: Eerdmans, 1988), 86.
31. Hartley, *Book of Job*, 86.

JOB 3:1–26
JOB'S OPENING LAMENTATION

Every language in Asia has a word for lamentation. To lament is to express a sense of deep soulful grief and personal mourning. In the Filipino language, this is called *panaghoy*, which is exactly what Job did – although, in Hebrew, this is called the *qinah*.

In his pain, Job decided to go to the outskirts of the city – a place cut off from civilization – to mourn his losses, attend to his oozing wounds, and, possibly, await his expected death. What Job did may be likened, to some degree, to people who believe they are about to die going to Sago Street in Singapore.[1] Locals call this street Death Street. The whole street is lined with houses, where, in times past, people who knew that death was imminent stayed on the second floor. When they died, their lifeless bodies would be moved to the first floor, where their corpse would be washed before burial or cremation.

Chapter 3 of the book of Job will consider the following questions: How did Job feel about the whole situation? What was his foremost and strongest desire? Would he succumb to his wife's suggestion of assisted suicide? How is a lament different from a complaint? Did Job blame God for what had happened to him?

I deviate from Hartley and take verses 3–10 as the curses proper,[2] where verse 10 supplies the reason for these curses. Verses 11–13 are included in the next section (3:11–26) since verse 11 begins the first of a number of rhetorical questions that are interspersed in this section (3:12, 20).

3:1–10 JOB WISHED HE HAD NOT BEEN BORN
3:1–2 Job Cursed the Day He was Born
Seven days and nights passed before Job broke the silence of the dark night of his soul. He cursed the day he had been born, seeing that day as a mistake and as something contemptible (3:1).[3] Those who have suffered greatly in life may express their longing for relief by saying things like "I wish I had never been

---
1. Sharon Teng, "Sago Lane: 'Street of the Dead,'" *BiblioAsia*, vol. 8 (2013), http://biblioasia.nlb.gov.sg/vol-8/issue-4/jan-mar2013/sago-street-dead/.
2. Hartley, *Book of Job*, 88–100.
3. MT has *qalal*. See note in Job 1:5.

born," "I wish I had died at birth," or "I wish I could die now." Job's words of despair did not mean that he was contemplating suicide. Rather, this was a lament on account of his pain, arising from a heart filled with misery. His words do, however, express some dissatisfaction with God's plan since God's will for Job included conception and birth as well as his life and the pain and suffering associated with his present condition.

SUICIDE AND HOW TO SEEK HELP

Although Japan is known for its long-life span, it is also one of the countries with high rates of suicide in the region. As in other parts of Asia, with the onslaught of COVID-19, there was a notable increase in the number of children giving up on life, and Japan had a staggering number of suicides – almost thirty thousand between January 2020 and May 2021 for both known and unknown reasons, including COVID-19 related issues.[1]

Sadly, such suicides continued even once COVID-19 became endemic. All across Asia, there are heart-wrenching stories of families where one family member has been depressed, believing that he or she cannot cope with life anymore, and, in a moment of weakness, gives in and takes their life. Some of these people may have thought that suicide would set them free, but suicide often creates greater problems and brings additional and lasting pain to their families and friends.

If, for some reason, you find yourself feeling trapped, helpless, and without hope, and if this has gone on for a long time, please talk to a family member, a trusted friend, or a mentor. Also seek to be part of an accountability group. Many Asians consider it shameful to visit a counselor or psychologist, wrongly believing that only people with mental problems need to do so. But in crucial moments such as these, where depression drags you down, consider your well-being and seek the help necessary to make you whole again.

If thoughts of suicide begin to nag you or and you feel pushed to the brink, it is all the more urgent to visit your family doctor or talk to your pastor or make an appointment with a counselor. If you are shy, go with a family member or a trusted friend – someone who can support you and also be a great help afterward in encouraging you not to give up. Avoid being alone. Make every effort to pray and read the Bible. Share your thoughts with our heavenly Father and hold on to the promises of the Lord Jesus Christ.

---

1. See the work of Masahide Kodaet al., "Reasons for Suicide During the COVID-19 Pandemic in Japan," JAMA Net Open, 31 January 2022. *doi: 10.1001/jamanetworkopen.2021.45870.* The exact number of suicides was 29,938.

3:3–10 Job's Litany of Curses

This section (3:3–10) focuses on Job's birth, with verse 3 relating to the day of his birth and the night of his conception. Looking back on his life, Job wished that the day on which he was born had perished. Verses 4–5 expand Job's view of "that day" as being one of darkness, gloom, and blackness. Verses 6–9 then expand on "that night" as being nonexistent, barren, and cursed.[4] Job wished that deepest darkness should have engulfed the day of his birth (v. 5) so that it would never have happened, and he would not exist at all.[5]

Job then turned his attention to the night on which he had been conceived. Job desired three things: First, that "that night" would have been seized by darkness so that it had no opportunity to be part of the days and months of the year (3:6) and, as a result, Job would not have been alive and suffering as he now was; second, switching to the metaphor of a woman who was unable to conceive, Job wished that "that night" had been barren so that no new life would have been formed and as a result, there would have been no birth announcement (3:7); and, third, Job desired that the day of his birth be cursed by "those who curse days" (3:8) – probably referring to magicians and those who claimed to communicate with the dead, who were just as ready to wake up "Leviathan." In the Ugaritic literature of Canaan and Phoenicia, eclipses were said to be caused by Leviathan swallowing up the sun or moon.[6]

Job would have reasoned that if only Leviathan had swallowed up the moon, that "night" would never have existed, and he would not have been conceived. Returning to the reality of his situation, Job acknowledged that his mother had conceived and given birth to him; thus, he was not exempt from the distress he was facing (3:10).

Different Hebrew words are used to describe "darkness," which is a common theme in the book of Job. For example, the Hebrew term *khoshekh* is used three times in this chapter (3:4, 5, 9) and 23 times in the rest of the book. The same word is used to describe the primeval darkness that existed before

---

4. Placing "the day" first shows the readers the author was emphasizing "the day." Job wished that the day of his conception would not have happened. This is the first time that the name of God as *Eloah* (singular of *Elohim*) occurs in the book. It occurs 40 other times in Job (compare "Names of God in the Book of Job" on page 22). The word *neharah* ("light") occurs only here in Job.
5. Coppes identified this light with the first rays of the morning sun. See Leonard J. Coppes, "neharah," TWOT 2:560.
6. Roy B. Zuck, *Job*, Everyman's Bible Commentary (Chicago, Moody Press, 1978), 24.

creation (Gen 1:2),[7] before God created light, which is a necessary ingredient for life. Darkness represents nonexistence, and Job wished that the time and day he was born and conceived had never existed or that he had died at birth. As this was not to be, and since his circumstances – his success and position as a man of stature in society – had now been reversed by sickness and suffering, Job preferred death – which he believed would end all pain and suffering – to life on earth.

Job's wife had incited him to curse God so that Job might die and be relieved of his suffering. Job, however, did not curse God but, instead, cursed the day he was born and the night he was conceived because, as he argued, "It did not shut the doors of the womb on me to hide trouble from my eyes" (3:10). This term "shut" (*sagar*) carries a special nuance here because it refers to non-conception and, therefore, the inability to give birth. A classic example of this is Hannah. Because the Lord had "shut" or "closed" her womb, she had no children (1 Sam 1:5–6) until God allowed her to conceive Samuel. Job was saying that had his mother's womb been shut on the night he was conceived, he could not have been conceived and, consequently, would not be experiencing pain and "trouble" (*amal*).[8]

3:11–19 JOB WISHED HE HAD DIED AT BIRTH

Job wished that he had died immediately after birth or through lack of nourishment soon after (3:11–12). In his pain, Job felt that such a death would have been better than his present suffering (3:13). At certain times in our lives, we all ask "why" questions, expressing the common reaction to undeserved or unexplainable suffering. Even men and women of God, when they experienced great suffering, asked questions such as "why?" and "how long?" (Pss 13:1–2; 22:1).

Beginning at verse 13, Job used synonyms arranged parallel to each other to express the complete rest that he desired. Had he died, he would be resting with kings and rulers (3:14) or wealthy princes (3:15). Job acknowledged that death brings peace and a chance to rest with exalted figures.

---

7. Job used other synonyms for darkness, which include *tsalmaveth* (deep darkness, 3:5, compare 10:21, 22; 12:22; 16:16; 24:17; 28:3; 34:22; 38:17), *'ofel* (gloom, 3:6, compare 10:22; 23:17; 28:3; 30:26), and *kimrir* (blackness).

8. This Hebrew term translated "trouble" is a key word in the book for it is used seven other times (1:16; 4:8; 5:6, 7; 7:3; 15:35; 16:2) and it can also be translated in other contexts as evil (4:8) or misery (7:3).

Verse 16 repeats Job's wish not to have survived but to have been buried as a stillborn fetus without having seen the light of day. Light, used four times in this chapter (3:4, 9, 16, 20),[9] is equated with existence and life, just as darkness is equated with nonexistence and death. Job's three references to "rest" (3:13, 17, 26) all signify the rest offered by death, which, for Job, meant no longer experiencing trouble. "There" (3:17), in its immediate context, refers to the "grave" or the equivalent Hebrew term, *Sheol*, the place to where Job as a stillborn baby would have gone. Although *Sheol* is not mentioned in the book until Job 7:9, OT believers accepted that this was the general place where everybody – both the righteous and the wicked – went after death. Job mentioned four specific groups of people who had found rest in that particular place: the wicked, the weary, prisoners, and slaves (3:17–19). His reference to "the small and the great" (3:19a) suggests that social status in life is in view. Job, formerly a significant person in society, had been brought so low because of his circumstances that he longed for relief from his suffering and to be at rest in death. Death would end his great agony, for he would then be free from all trouble (3:10).

3:20–26 JOB WISHED HE COULD DIE NOW

Job addressed several groups of people who wished for death: those in misery, those who anticipated death but did not yet see it (for example, the aged and very sick), and those who longed for death – perhaps because they were in despair (3:20–21). Yet again, Job asked the question "why" (3:20). Both "light" and its equivalent "life" refer back to Job as a sufferer, among those who are bitter – and the phrase "bitter of soul" is used in 3:20 while "bitterness of my soul" is used twice in the book (7:11; 10:1). Job then described the people who were longing and searching in vain for death because they preferred the rest and solace of death to the misery of their present life. They saw death as a cause for great rejoicing (3:22) because it would end all pain and trouble.

Although Job identified with these three groups of people who wished to die, he was not thinking of committing suicide. He had already acknowledged that life and death were both in God's hands (1:21). Job was only requesting that Yahweh take his life because he longed for release from the present severe suffering.

The change from the plural "those" to the singular "a man" (3:23) may underscore the fact that Job was now speaking personally about himself and his

---

9. MT has *'or* for "light." It is used 30 times outside chapter 3 in the book of Job.

own suffering. He was one whose path was "hidden." The parallel line gives the reason: God had "hedged" him in. Job was indirectly saying that his path was hidden or covered because God had placed a wall about him. Job used these metaphors to convey his frustration about the limitations and restrictions he was experiencing because of the troubles that had befallen him and his inability to understand why God would permit such a situation.

Given that Job had embraced his situation – as evidenced by his declaration that "the LORD gave and the LORD has taken away" (1:21) – Job 3:23 should not be interpreted as a statement of blame but, rather, as an acknowledgment that God was in control even when in situations of pain and suffering. Job was only venting his frustration and his inability to understand why things had happened to him the way they did. As Estes explains, Job could not understand where his painful path of life was leading to and felt trapped and imprisoned.[10]

Lamenting and grumbling are different. The book of Psalms has many laments by God's people, both individual and community. While both lamenting and grumbling include pouring out one's soul or venting frustrations to God or someone else, they differ in their purpose and result. A lament is usually directed at God, may lead to a good resolution of the problem, and often ends in praise. Grumbling, on the other hand, often stems from unbelief and a rebellious heart, is more diffused, may be indirectly aimed at God, and seldom has a satisfying outcome.

There is an interesting relationship between Job 1:10 and Job 3:23. *Satan* used the term *sukh* (meaning "hedge" in 1:10) to argue that Yahweh had put a hedge around Job as a protection, leaving Job free to worship God. Job, however, used *sukh* to argue that God was constraining and hedging him in with pain.[11] This seems to indicate that Job had begun to lose any hope of breaking free from his intense suffering.

Unlike Job and his friends, the reader knows that it was not God but *Satan* who instigated these terrible sufferings that Job endured (2:3). While this took place with God's permission, it was *Satan* who initiated this process. Throughout the narrative, we see that although Job held fast to the belief that God was doing all this to him, surprisingly, he never gave up on God. The "hedge" kept Job powerless in his trials. Instead of being a wall of protection

---

10. Daniel J. Estes, *Job*, TTC (Grand Rapids: Baker Books, 2013), 22.
11. Rowley, *Book of Job*, 49.

provided by God – which was *Satan's* accusation (1:10) – the hedge, from Job's point of view, functioned as a wall of affliction that imprisoned him.

In Job 3:24–26, Job continued to direct attention to himself. Beginning with the particle "for" (*ki*), which indicates reason and certainty – and connects back to verse 23, and perhaps even to verse 20 – Job summarized why he wanted to die. Using both a metaphor and a simile, he claimed, "sighing has become my daily food; my groans pour out like water" (3:24). Job's next statement, "What I feared has come upon me" (3:25), is one of the more puzzling verses in this chapter. As already mentioned, Job's suffering was physical, mental (intellectual), emotional, and spiritual. With each loss, and after each new attack, Job feared the next calamity. Verse 25 gives us a glimpse into Job's theological understanding of blessings and curses, and of God's dealings with humanity. Job's situation, which he had so greatly dreaded, is described in negative terms as "no peace, no quietness . . . no rest" (3:26). Job's psychological state was characterized by turmoil and agitation. "In logotherapy,[12] such a state of emotional turmoil is called *noogenic neurosis*[13] if it is the result of an existential vacuum; that is to say, when it is based on a sense of meaninglessness."[14] Job had hit rock bottom, where any sense of meaning of life had left him. And he was simply being honest about how he felt.

Job's cries were not those of a rebellious servant but simply statements of deep pain and agony. Only the godly who have experienced this kind of depth of pain can understand, at least to some degree, Job's despair and deep depression. The calamities had taken a toll on Job. He needed to vent his emotions in a lament – a lament in which he cursed the day he was born, wished he had never been born, and wished he could die and find relief from all his troubles.

---

12. *Logotherapy* is a therapeutic approach that helps people find personal meaning in life. It is a way of treating psychological disorders with special focus on the future and the ability to endure pain and suffering by identifying a purpose for these. See Arlin Cuncic, "What is Logotherapy?" *Verywell Mind*, 8 July 2022, https://www.verywellmind.com/an-overview-of-victor-frankl-s-logotherapy-4159308.
13. *Noogenic neurosis* is a phrase that was coined by Viktor Frankl. It "arises largely as a response to complete emptiness of purpose in life. The chief dynamic is 'existential frustration' created by vacuum of perceived meaning in personal existence and manifested by the symptom of boredom." See James C. Crumbaugh and Leonard T. Maholick, "An Experimental Study in Existentialism: The Psychometric Approach to Frankl's Concept of Noogenic neurosis," *Journal of Clinical Psychology* 20, no. 2 (1964): 1, https://doi.org/10.1002/1097-4679(196404)20:2<200::AID-JCLP2270200203>3.0.CO;2-U.
14. See Marshall H. Lewis, *Viktor Frankl and the Book of Job: A Search for Meaning* (Eugene: Wipf & Stock, 2019), 64 (emphasis added).

Job

It is useful for us all to reflect on questions like this: What is it that I most fear to lose? What is it that could potentially come into my life that might cause me to doubt God's fairness and justice? How do I usually react to negative things that happen to me? Do I tend to blame God when things go wrong?

The shock of the losses started to wear Job down. He became more in touch with his feelings and began to release the emotions that were weighing so heavily on him.

JOB 4:1–27:23

THREE SETS OF DIALOGUES

The judicial process for filing a case in modern times includes proper identification of the case, filing the complaint, serving the summons, arraignment (for criminal cases), a trial, and then the judge's verdict.[1] Job's case was much simpler, and it was conducted in a communal-type setting and as a disputation discourse. Let us now consider the disputation proper.

Job 4–27 trace what happened after Job expressed his desire for death because of the calamities that came upon his life. On account of their age, experience, and status in their respective communities, Eliphaz, Bildad, and Zophar were well-qualified to hear a case and even serve as judges. These three men enlisted themselves to help Job, the defendant in this case.

The friends' speeches were delivered in three cycles. In the first two cycles, all three men spoke, whereas in the third cycle, only Eliphaz and Bildad did so. What is common in all these speeches was that all three friends tried to refute Job's claim to innocence. Job responded to each of their speeches. The broad outline of this section is shown below:

	The Cycles of Speeches		
	First Cycle	**Second Cycle**	**Third Cycle**
Eliphaz	4–5	15	22
Job's response	6–7	16–17	23–24
Bildad	8	18	25
Job's response	9–10	19	26–27
Zophar	11	20	
Job's response	12–14	21	

---

1. Marco Bias, interview by author via Messenger, February 5, 2022. In civil cases and criminal liability, there is the alternative dispute resolution (ADR). If the parties cannot reach a settlement, the court will try to settle this through the judicial dispute resolution (JDR). Where these two processes fail, the trial will start.

JOB

4:1–14:22 THE FIRST CYCLE OF SPEECHES

The original objective of the three friends was to sympathize with and comfort Job (2:11); but on hearing Job's death wish, they set out to correct him, to strengthen him, to convince him of their wisdom, and to urge him to confess the sins he had not even committed. We now consider Eliphaz's speech.

4:1–5:27 Eliphaz Speaks

As we reflect on Job 4, we will consider these questions: Is the law of retribution, as stated by Eliphaz, valid? Do all dreams and visions come from the living God? How can such dreams and visions be authenticated? In what ways was the retribution concept held by Job's three friends flawed? Job 5 prompts us to address these questions: Is the reason for people's suffering always their own sins or those of their ancestors? What are the signs that a person is living a "cursed life"? What are the signs that a person is living a "blessed life"?

4:1–6 Eliphaz's Rebuke of Job

After seven days and seven nights of mourning, Eliphaz, probably the eldest of Job's friends, was the first to break the silence and attempt to encourage Job. Unable to restrain himself any longer, Eliphaz asked permission to be allowed to speak a few words without Job getting impatient (4:2). As a well-meaning friend, Eliphaz acknowledged and commended Job for what he had done for others: instructing, strengthening, supporting, and encouraging those in distress (4:3–4). "Feeble hands" and "faltering knees" depict overwhelming discouragement and helplessness, and the OT describes situations where godly and compassionate people reach out to help those in this kind of situation.

After commending Job, Eliphaz pointed to the reversal of fortune that Job was experiencing. Job now found himself in the same plight as those he had earlier encouraged. Calamities now "discouraged" (*la'ah*)[2] and "dismayed" him (4:5). From Eliphaz's perspective, the calamities overshadowed and suppressed the "confidence" that Job had once manifested. So, by way of rhetorical questions, Eliphaz reminded Job those qualities such as his "piety," which had been the source of his confidence, and his "blameless ways," which had been

---

2. The Hebrew term *la'ah* can mean "to be impatient" or "weary." This is the same word that is used in verse 2a. In this verse, the more appropriate term is "impatient" while in verse 5 is "weary."

the source of his hope,³ should enable him to overcome the multiple crises that he was experiencing (4:6).

4:7–11 Eliphaz's Reasoning about Suffering

Eliphaz then set out to explain the principle of retribution. He began by contrasting the fate of the godly with that of the wicked. He pointed out that no person had ever "perished" or been totally "destroyed" for being "innocent" and "upright" (4:7), and he supported this claim with an observation from agriculture. The activities of plowing, sowing (and planting), and reaping (4:8) present the complete agricultural process, where plowing and sowing are equated to the planning and execution of evil deeds. Those who do these evil acts became so proficient at these activities so that it became their profession in life.⁴ The living God would completely destroy such people (4:9).⁵

Next, Eliphaz illustrated the effect of God's judgment using the metaphor of lions. By nature, lions roar and growl to instill fear in their prey; but if their teeth, the very instrument they need to survive, are broken, they are unable to kill their prey and will starve to death along with their family (4:10–11). Similarly, the wicked will not be able to exploit their victims forever because God will punish them. On the one hand, Eliphaz argued that if Job were indeed innocent and had not sinned against God, he would not perish. On the other hand, God will certainly punish evildoers.

4:12–21 Eliphaz's Report of a Vision

Eliphaz validated his claim by relating his dream-vision of an encounter with an unidentified spirit-being. People in the ancient world believed that dreams and visions were ways in which divine beings communicated with mortals. In the OT, the living God himself made use of this medium of dreams and visions.⁶

Eliphaz had a night vision – an auditory, visual, sensory encounter – in which he received a message from a spirit-being whom he was unable to

---

3. Verse 6 literally translates "Is not your piety, your confidence and your hope, your blameless ways?"
4. *kharash* and *zara'* are participles which when functioning as nouns can serves as *proficio officium* (a profession).
5. The word pair (Heb. *'avad* [literally, "perish"] + *kalah* [literally, "vanish"]) used express the idea that God in his burning anger will certainly and completely destroy those who do such wicked deeds (v. 9).
6. With the coming of Jesus Christ and the completion of the canon of Scripture, God's revelation of his will and purposes through dreams is no longer the norm although there are exceptions.

recognize (4:12–16). He was so scared that his whole body trembled (4:14)[7] and the "spirit" that brushed his face made the hair on his body stand on end (4:15). The MT can be interpreted "a whisper and a sound I hear,"[8] and this whole phrase can be translated "whispering voice" (4:16).

In the Bible, God is portrayed as both the source and the interpretation of people's dreams and visions. Generally speaking, dream-visions as a method of revelation decreased toward the end of the New Testament era and reduced even further with the completion of the canon of Scripture. All that we need to know concerning how to please God and what to do to maintain fellowship with him has already been revealed to us. In addition, believers now have the Holy Spirit to guide them. We cannot, however, be dogmatic about this because Luke, quoting Joel 2:28, acknowledges that there will be visions, dreams, and prophesying in the latter days (Acts 2:17).

In our contemporary setting, we must bear in mind that although God does sometimes speak to people through dreams, not all dreams come from God. If it is claimed that a dream or vision is of God, what is revealed through such a dream must be consistent with what has already been revealed in Scripture and should be referred to the community of faith. As with all forms of revelation, it is essential to evaluate any claims of angelic encounters. Any message from angelic beings that deviates from what is revealed in Scripture or takes rightful worship away from the living God is unacceptable. Angels from God usually acknowledge that they are merely created beings (Rev 19:10; 22:9). They are not to be worshiped, and they draw attention to God and not themselves (Luke 2:13–14).

The content of the revelation received by Eliphaz is found in verses 17–21. Continuing to instruct Job, Eliphaz used rhetorical questions to summarize the message of the angelic being: No human being can be "more righteous than God," who is our Creator (4:17). In making this claim, Eliphaz reminded Job of God's supremacy and perfection and, thus, his high standards when assessing a person. Eliphaz reasoned that if God does not even trust his angel-servants not to make mistakes, how much less will he trust weak, vulnerable, mortals, whose life can be snuffed out at any moment and "crushed more readily than

---

7. There is a figure of speech here, synecdoche: part of the whole where the bones represent the whole body.
8. There is a hendiadys here – two words are connected by an "and" but one word defines the other.

a moth" (4:19).⁹ "Broken" and "unnoticed," human beings perish, and when "the cords of their tent" are pulled up, they may "die without wisdom" (4:20–21). The phrase "die without wisdom" can mean that people die unexpectedly or without understanding what life is all about, which was considered the ultimate disaster for someone from the East.

The message that Eliphaz supposedly received from the spirit-being is true – that is, no human being is, in the strictest sense of the word, upright before God. It is, however, God's prerogative to declare a person righteous on account of that person's faith. This was the case with Abraham, who was considered righteous by God because of his faith (Gen 15:6), a fact also affirmed by the apostle Paul (Rom 4:9).

The existence of angelic beings cannot be discounted. They were present when God created the heavens and the earth (Job 38:7). Jesus Christ himself acknowledged them in his teaching (Luke 15:10). Angels are created beings (Job 38:7; Ps 148:2; Col 1:16), whose main role is to serve as "ministering spirits," especially for believers (Heb 1:14), to participate in guarding and protecting God's people (Ps 91:11–12), and to be God's messengers (Matt 1:20; Luke 1:11–17). Believers need to be aware that there are good angels (1 Tim 5:21) as well as evil ones (Matt 25:41). Moreover, angels must never be worshiped because worship belongs only to the living God (Deut 6:13; Matt 4:10).

This chapter reveals that God is the one who judges and destroys the wicked (4:8–9). He is the Creator of the human race and supreme in righteousness (4:17). He is omniscient, knowing the sin of angels (4:18) and the frailty of the human race (4:19).

---

9. The Hebrew term *lifne* which is usually translated "before" or "in the sight of," can be translated by the term "like." This is a rare occurrence. See Ronald J. Williams, *Hebrew Syntax: An Outline* (Toronto: University of Toronto Press, 1967), 62.

THE RETRIBUTION CONCEPT:[1]
WHEN IT BECOMES FLAWED

The law of retribution as Eliphaz defined it is a half-truth. It is also flawed in that he examined the supposed effects of sin – that is, pain and suffering – and then, without convincing evidence, proposed a hypothetical premise that he (and his friends) treated as a foregone conclusion. Eliphaz started to build his case against Job by assuming that Job must have sinned to merit the suffering he was experiencing.

While it is true that humankind is sinful and God is totally just and holy, it is equally true that God is gracious and forgiving. There is no room for grace in Eliphaz's interpretation and theology.

The basic concept of retribution is reflected in the following statements: You reap what you sow (see Job 4:8; Prov 11:18; 14:14; Gal 6:7); If you do good, you get rewarded; if you do evil, you get punished; and obedience brings blessing; disobedience brings punishment (see Deut 28:1-2, 58–60; 30:9–10). Each of these statements is connected to the "cause-and-effect" concept and are both biblical teachings and universal principles. Perhaps you can recall a time when you heard one of these principles being explained or even experienced it applied in your own life.

There are four fundamental flaws in the view held by Job's three counselors: a flawed premise, a wrong application, the exclusion of God's grace and mercy, and the assumption that this is the only principle by which God governs human affairs and the universe. These flawed beliefs are considered below:

A flawed premise: If, for example, the protasis or the condition (if) and the apodosis or the result clause of a condition (then) are interchanged, this results in a flawed premise.

> "If you do obey" (protasis), "then you get rewarded" (apodosis).
> "If you disobey" or "sin" (protasis), "then you will be punished" (apodosis).

These two statements are correct as they stand. They become flawed, however, when they are interchanged so that the apodosis statement becomes the premise and the protasis statement becomes the conclusion or the cause. For instance,

> Premise: Since you are having a good life,
> That means you are being rewarded;
> You must have been obedient.

> Premise: Since you are going through "undeserved" suffering;
> That means you are being punished;
> You must have sinned.

In the case of Job, the friends erred in their premise and, therefore, their conclusion that the fact that Job was going through suffering must be because he had sinned was false. For them, there was no other explanation, and throughout their debates they set about proving this conclusion. The friends did not have the whole picture and had no clue about what was happening in the spiritual realm. As a result, their words failed to encourage and only brought added pain to Job.

Wrong applications: When flawed retribution concepts are applied to the wrong person or to the wrong situation, this results in wrong applications. For instance, in the case of COVID-19, which was a world pandemic, it would be wrong for someone to conclude that their neighbor got infected because he or she had committed a sin.

Job's counselors applied their flawed principles to a blameless person and declared judgment on him as if they were God himself. Judgment is God's prerogative, for he alone has the right to declare someone guilty. For those of us who are counselors, it is a scary thought that, if we are not careful, we may find ourselves playing God in the lives of our counselees. There is a tendency for counselees to hang on the words of their counselors. Therefore, counselors are in a position to help them – but also to destroy them – with their words. As believers in the living God, may we never forget that we are simply instruments that God can use to point counselees away from us and to God himself.

The exclusion of God's grace and mercy: The blessings and curses section of Deuteronomy, which is the basis of the maxim about retribution, is part of the covenant that Yahweh made with Israel because he loved them and had chosen them to be his people. If they obeyed, they would be blessed; if they disobeyed, they would experience the curses. Job's three counselors treated this maxim as something that was black and white, without providing space for God's purposes and work in the life of Job.

There is an assumption that this is the only principle by which God governs human affairs. The universe however, cannot be governed only by the retribution principle, which is just a small part of transcendent wisdom – that is, the principle by which God manages the universe and everything in it.

How does all this affect us? When we experience undeserved suffering, it is right that we examine ourselves to see if there is sin involved. If there is, we must confess it immediately and invite the Holy Spirit to take control of our lives once again. If it is clear that there is no sin involved, then we must consider if there are other reasons for the suffering. In relation to others, it would be wrong to immediately conclude that they must have sinned when they experience undeserved suffering. We are limited in our perspective. We do not have the whole picture for them, and even they themselves may not have an idea why they are going through the suffering. The right thing to do would be to minister to them with our presence and, if necessary, our resources, too. We can listen, encourage, and comfort them, pointing them to the Lord Jesus Christ, who, in his unfailing compassion, gave this open invitation: "Come to me, all you who are weary and burdened, and I will give you rest" (Matt 11:28).

---

1. This term will be used in this work when referring to the more general and neutral principle of retribution. The term presumptive or assumption theology will be used when it is leaning to its negative aspect – flawed and devoid of the grace of God.

While chapter 4 covers Eliphaz's objections to Job, chapter 5 presents his recommendations and reminders about God's blessings in Job's life.

5:1–16 Eliphaz's Recommendation to Job

Since Eliphaz continued to speak in the second person, addressing Job directly, his words seemed to imply that Job was a fool and a wicked person. This section has very few positive statements (5:1, 17–19); most of what was said is negative and depressing. Eliphaz seemed to be saying that God was judging and punishing Job, and he concluded by appealing to Job to accept and apply his recommendations.

5:1–7 Eliphaz believed that morally bad people find no favor with God

Although Eliphaz challenged Job to call out in prayer, he was really taunting him by saying that even if he did call, no one would respond to him. In other words, Job could not expect deliverance any time soon. Using parallelism to emphasize his point, Eliphaz warned that "resentment" brings death to the "fool" (*'evil*) or the "simple" (*poteh*) person – which may refer to someone who is morally bad or easily deceived because they are inexperienced (5:2). In the book of Proverbs, too, these two terms (*'evil* and *poteh*) are often used to describe a fool, thus linking together these two books, which are both classified as wisdom literature.

Eliphaz shared that he had seen a fool "taking root"[10] and then finding that "suddenly his house was cursed" (5:3). Eliphaz accused a fool of being sure of his footing ("taking root") while the reality was that his whole life was

---

10. Literally, "established."

unsettled, perhaps even cursed. One source of danger might have been litigation in court,[11] where, without defense, the fool's children would be unjustly crushed (5:4). Fools may also become helpless because of people who steal their harvest and their wealth (5:5). This verse illustrates the intensity and thoroughness with which thieves may divest victims of all their possessions. There is a reversal of fortune: the once prosperous foolish person is unable to maintain his status, leaving his children poor and the object of abuse. Eliphaz was so insensitive to bring up the issue of children when he knew that Job was still grieving the loss of his children.

Eliphaz emphasized that hardships and troubles, unlike plants, do not sprout from the ground (5:6) but originate from within a person. It is human destiny that everyone is "born to trouble as surely as sparks fly upward" (5:7). Alter argues that with "the emphasis here on man as a source of trouble, the concrete image of sparks makes better sense: just as a fire sends burning sparks swirling upward, man creates wretchedness all around him."[12]

Eliphaz, as Job's counselor, began with a misinformed and biased assessment of the situation. In his mind, it was a foregone conclusion that Job had sinned, and so he viewed Job's suffering as the consequence of that sin. This led to his declaration that if Job were to call for a mediator, God would not answer and that there would be no one to help him since there was no one really qualified to mediate in his case, neither human beings nor angels. There is some truth in the statement that the wicked bring a curse not only on themselves but also on their families and children. But Eliphaz was wrong because here, he was indirectly referring to Job, whom God had already pronounced upright.

No one is obligated to accept the flawed retribution principle. Mary (not her real name)[13] gave birth to a child with Down syndrome in a culture where this condition is viewed as unacceptable to the extent that babies born with Down syndrome are often abandoned in the hospital. What happens to these babies thereafter is anyone's guess. Grieving more for the baby than for herself, Mary asked, "What sin have I committed to give birth to this precious child in this condition?" We can agree with Eliphaz that calling on God during a desperate situation can turn things around and bring blessing. So it was in Mary's story. Against all odds, Mary and her husband brought the child home

---

11. Literally, "at the city gate."
12. Alter, *Writings*, 28.
13. Real name withheld for the protection of the person and family.

and loved and raised her like any normal child. Although people questioned their decision, in time their decision opened a whole new ministry for the family. They were able to connect with other families who had Down syndrome children but had never made the fact public. Later, nurses at the hospital began to get in touch with Mary whenever a baby with Down syndrome was born, and more and more of these families received the special help they needed through Mary and her husband. The painful situation that had at first appeared to be a curse, when unwrapped, became a wonderful blessing in the form of a vibrant ministry that helped to create a welcoming environment for both babies and their parents.

5:8–16 Eliphaz counseled Job to trust God

In an attempt to empathize, Eliphaz identified with Job, suggesting that if he were in Job's situation, he would lay his case before God and seek help from him (5:8). Using a series of participles (5:9–14) and verbs,[14] Eliphaz described God's countless awesome deeds (5:9): sending rain to water the ground (5:10), lifting up the lowly and comforting those who mourn (5:11), frustrating the plans of the crafty so that they end up accomplishing nothing (5:12), catching the wise in their own shrewdness so that they are unable to differentiate day from night (5:13–14), and delivering the oppressed from verbal abuse by the mighty (5:15).[15] Verse 15 affirms that it is indeed God who delivers the lowly and the oppressed, giving the poor hope that there would be an end to injustice (5:16).

Paul quotes Job 5:13 in 1 Corinthians 3:19. What connects these two verses is the word "wise." Eliphaz advised Job to lay his case before God because the Lord "catches the wise in their craftiness." Paul, in quoting Eliphaz, reminds the Corinthians that "the wisdom of this world is foolishness in God's sight." Therefore, those who think they are wise should watch out for, in time, God will reveal their foolishness, and they will stand accountable before God.

5:17–27 Eliphaz's Reminder of God's Blessings

Eliphaz continued in this positive tone, adding that the one whom God reproves or corrects is blessed. Therefore, he challenged Job not to "despise the discipline of the Almighty" (5:7) but to accept it willingly. Eliphaz went on to

---

14. The verbs in verses 15–16 are imperfect, indicating continuing actions.
15. Seow acknowledges the difficulty of the text of 5:15a. He makes some emendations and argues that salvation will come on the lowly and devastated. See his other work, "Orthography, Textual Criticism, and the Poetry of Job," *JBL* 130, no. 1 (2011), 63-85.

list the blessings that would follow if Job submitted to God's discipline: God inflicts pain but also comforts,[16] injures but also heals (5:18), delivers from every form of calamity and evil, permitting no harm (5:19) – saving from death in both famine and battle (5:20) and protecting from verbal abuse and destruction (5:21).

As he continued with his preview of what would happen if Job accepted God's discipline, Eliphaz focused on the assurance of security that Job could enjoy even in his difficult and dangerous situation (5:22): safety from wild animals since all these creatures would be "at peace" with him (5:23), the security of home and property (5:24), a long line of descendants "like the grass of the earth" (5:25), and, for Job himself, a long life that would culminate with death at a ripe old age – "like sheaves gathered in season" (5:26). This list of blessings ends with a simile or comparison to indicate longevity and death at the opportune time. In contrast to the immoral person referred to in most of the earlier section (5:2–7), here there is mention of prosperity, children, and a safe home; it is a picture of a successful and satisfying life. Finally, addressing Job directly, Eliphaz affirmed that all he had said was well researched and true, and he challenged Job to listen well and put this advice into practice so that he would experience these promised blessings (5:27).

After citing the case of a foolish person to whom God would not listen (5:1–7), Eliphaz urged Job to appeal to God and pointed out the benefits of doing so (5:8–16). He then affirmed that "the one whom God corrects" is blessed (5:17) and urged Job to accept God's discipline so that he might enjoy God's blessings (5:18–27).

Eliphaz's basic arguments were that human beings are mortal, transient, and have no chance of being pure before God, and that sin is always the sole reason for discipline and judgment. Applying this principle to Job, Eliphaz concluded, somewhat presumptuously, that Job's tragedy was the result of moral failure. He then reasoned that because God is holy and Job was sinful, the only way to restore God's blessings was for Job to confess his sin and submit to God's discipline. This is faulty theology since it implies that all bad situations are the result of sin and insists that even if someone is innocent, it is still necessary to confess sin in order to restore lost blessings. This is wrong! The Bible teaches that some suffering is permitted by God to bring him glory; it also shows that, sometimes, suffering remains inexplicable. In Job's case, God himself had declared him blameless and upright. Eliphaz was not an

---

16. Literally, "binds."

empathetic counselor; instead, he was arrogant and condescending, implying that he was a wise man, while Job was a fool.

6:1–7:21 Job's Response to Eliphaz

After Eliphaz's long discourse (Job 4–5), Job was ready to respond by expressing his view of the situation and his feelings, especially his frustration at his friends' lack of empathy. In reflecting on Job 6–7, we will consider the following questions: What has God to do with human pain and suffering? What was the psychosomatic effect on Job of his losses? What did Job require and request from his friends?

6:1–7 Job's Defense of Complaining
6:1–5 Job declared the gravity of his suffering

Job responded to Eliphaz. There are similarities between this type of discourse and the practice of *bakliw* (an antiphonal-responsorial singing and chant) among the *Ibaloys*.[17] On special occasions such as wakes, weddings, and feasts, the elders of the clan and the community form a small group and do a *bakliw*. The leader leads the *bakliw* by telling a story, line by line, in the form of a chant. The group responds, line by line, by chanting – and this action is called *asbayatan*.[18] The content of the *bakliw* usually relates to the occasion. At a wake, for instance, the topic would be the life story of the deceased. On rare occasions, the *bakliw* may even trace ancestry as far back as possible or pass on treasured information to the next generation. On other occasions, the chant may relate a story that brings out a moral lesson for this captive audience or share visions and aspirations for the clan and community.[19] This is one way of preserving treasured traditions.

In Job's response to Eliphaz, he used hyperbole to express his anguish, declaring that if his anguish could be weighed,[20] it would be much heavier than the sand on the seashore (6:2–3). On account of what he was experiencing, Job admitted to uttering rash words (6:3). The admission that "my spirit drinks in their poison" implies that Job felt that his body had absorbed the poison of the "arrows" that the Almighty had shot at him – that is, the losses and pain, coming one after the other, which seemed like overwhelming "terrors"

---

17. As earlier mentioned in the *Introduction*, this is one of the people groups in the Philippines.
18. A free translation to this word is "to respond accordingly."
19. Marco Bias, interview by author via Messenger, March 10, 2022.
20. The same word is used in Job 31:6 where Job requested that he be weighed in a balance to reveal his integrity.

deliberately aimed at him by God himself (6:4). This is the first time that Job pointed to God as the source of his affliction. Contrary to Eliphaz's insinuation that it was Job's sin that accounted for his misfortunes – which would have meant that Job himself was to blame for his suffering – Job believed that the calamities had come directly from God.

Job justified his complaining by reminding his friends that a donkey would not bray nor an ox low if they had sufficient fodder (6:5). Similarly, Job would not have used such harsh words if he had what he needed. He had lost everything: his livestock, servants, children, good health, and social standing – everything except his life and his wife. What he needed was comforting words from his friends and a chance to vent his frustrations. It is usually healthy, when facing undeserved suffering, to be able to express one's frustration. But Job's friends had denied him this freedom despite his great grief. Ellison claims that Job's complaint was torn from him by anguish so that it is far from being a calm reflection of theological reasoning.[21]

6:6–7 Job lost his appetite for food

If food were set before him, Job would have refused to eat, finding it "tasteless." He asked, "Is there flavor in the sap of the mallow?" (6:6). This might refer to the albumen (white portion) of an egg. This loss of appetite was one of the psychosomatic effects of all the calamities Job endured. Moreover, Job reasoned that not allowing him to express his pain through honest complaints was like eating tasteless food without salt, similar to the way Eliphaz had offered him useless words.

Suffering is a universal experience. It was as real in different cultures in times past as it is now. Here are a few lines from the confession of a sufferer in ancient times:

> Praise, praise, do not be bashful, but praise!
> [He it] is, Marduk I entreat (?) him I entreat (?) him.
> [He it] was who smote me, then was merciful to me.
> (35') He scuttled (?) me, then moored me,
> He dashed me down, then grabbed me as (I fell),
> He scattered me wide then garnered me,
> He thrust me away then gathered me in,

---

21. H. L. Ellison, *From Tragedy to Triumph: Studies in the Book of Job* (Grand Rapids: Zondervan, 1958), 37.

He threw me down then lifted me high.[22]

In these lines, the sufferer attributes the calamities to his god, Marduk, who had acted in contradictory ways – for example, wounding and yet also healing him. Job, likewise, was greatly weighed down by his own calamities and, on top of these, the hurtful words of his so-called friends, who falsely accused him of wrongdoing. Despite all this, Job maintained that he was innocent. Suffering is a common experience, and like Job, it is alright to tell the God whom we serve how we are feeling and what we are thinking when we are in pain.

6:8–13 Job's Despair in Suffering

Job desired death. Weighed down by his many troubles, Job longed for God to grant his request (6:8). This request that God would "crush" him and "cut off" his life – that is, that he would die (6:9) – indicates how deeply Job was suffering. Despite the "unrelenting pain" that often accompanies death, Job claimed that he would still find comfort and rejoice because he had "not denied the words of the Holy One" (6:10) – in other words, Job had obeyed God's ethical injunctions. Brutally honest about his thoughts and feelings, Job gave the reasons for his longing to die: It was useless prolonging his life since he would die anyway (6:11), and he had neither the strength nor the resources to help himself to move on (6:12–13). Job was not planning suicide but simply expressing his desire to die and asking that God would take his life.

6:14–23 Job's Disappointment in His Friends

Job's friends were encouragers without substance. In verse 14, Job equated their failure to show loving-kindness (*khesed*) with a failure to show reverential fear of the Almighty (*Shadday*). While referring to his friends as "my brothers," Job accused them of being "undependable," using an extensive simile to liken them to "intermittent streams" (6:15) – treacherous seasonal streams, which have turned to ice[23] (6:16) or dried up and vaporized (6:17) and so fail to supply water. Caravans carrying thirsty travelers from Tema[24] and merchants from

---

22. "A Sufferer's Salvation," trans. Benjamin R. Foster (COS 1.152:486). Foster also included a record of a sufferer with similar experiences to those of Job and which is labeled as the "Babylonian Theodicy" (COS 1.152:492).
23. Literally, "They are darkened by ice. They are completely covered with snow."
24. Tema (*Tayma*) is a desert oasis by a caravan trade route (Isa 21:14), which Jeremiah locates in Arabia (Jer 25:23). Rasmussen suggests that it is 250 miles southeast of the Aqaba/Elath in Saudi Arabia and 200 miles North-Northeast of Medina *Zondervan NIV Atlas*, 254.

Sheba[25] ended up "distressed" and "disappointed" to find that these streams contained no water (6:18–20).

Job declared that his friends had "proved to be of no help" (6:21a) since they had not been there for him when he needed them. He then paused to address his friends as a group.[26] When the friends saw the dreadful things that had happened to Job, fear came over them. And although the friends were physically present, theirs was not a caring presence and their intentions to comfort did not match their words and actions. Job reminded his friends that he never asked for their help – either to pay money on his behalf (as a gift or a bribe) or to save him from his enemies (6:22–23). They had come, promising comfort, but had failed miserably.

We can almost feel Job's pain. Reflect on the last time you were with a friend in pain and ask yourself: Was my friend encouraged by my words and my presence? We must be especially careful not to act like Job's self-appointed counselors. Before meeting a friend in pain, it is helpful to ask ourselves: If I were in this person's shoes, how would I want my friend to act and speak to encourage me? To put a friend at ease, we could begin by saying, "I am here for you. If you need to talk, I am listening. If you want me to say something to help you process, let me know. If you just want me to listen and not say a word, let me know as well. And if you just want us to be together in silence, that is alright, too."

6:24–30 Job's Desires of His Friends

Job's friends were encouragers devoid of empathy. Job challenged them to teach him and to show where he had gone wrong, promising that he would be silent and listen to them (6:24). He acknowledged that honest words may cause brutal wounds but went on to question what his friends' arguments had really proven (6:25). His rhetorical question can be stated as a declarative statement: "You meant to correct what I say, but treated my desperate words as wind"[27] (6:26, my translation). Job pointed out that his friends had taken the liberty of giving advice about life and suffering without allowing him to express his own thoughts on the matter. He accused them of wounding with

---

25. Rasmussen's claim seems uncertain. It is possibly in the southwestern Arabian Peninsula in the vicinity of modern Yemen, although some suggest the horn of Africa, near modern Djibouti *Zondervan NIV Atlas*, 251.
26. The "you" in the Hebrew text is plural – parsed as masculine plural. So, Job was addressing not only Eliphaz, but Zophar and Bildad, too.
27. The NIV editors understood this statement to be a question.

words because they were devoid of compassion and loyalty so that they were willing to "cast lots for the fatherless and barter their friend" (6:27). Religious bigots, self-righteous judges, and those who cling to legalistic orthodoxy have always had trouble knowing how to help those whom they condemn. It is easier to judge people than to help them resolve their problems. The parable of the good Samaritan (Luke 10:30–37) presents examples of people who would not help a person in need because of self-righteousness or misapplied theology. But the good Samaritan, out of his compassion, was willing to give generous, practical help, over and above what anyone could expect. May the living God give us the grace and the resources to respond to people in need and not miss opportunities to be a blessing.

Thereafter, Job prepared for a showdown, requesting his friends to "be so kind as to look at me" and reminding them of his honesty: "Would I lie to your face?" (6:28). Moreover, he begged them to turn back or "relent" (*shuv*)[28] from being unjust, which, in this context, includes making false accusations. If Job's friends did these two things, then[29] they would restore his integrity (6:29),[30] which had been tarnished by their false statements about him. He continued to maintain his innocence. By way of two rhetorical questions, complemented by parallelism, Job vehemently denied any "wickedness" on his lips and the inability to "discern malice."[31]

This chapter reveals that *Shadday*, the Almighty, can be the source of calamities. Job acknowledged this when he claimed that God's arrows were intentionally directed at him (6:4). God is also introduced as the "Holy One," who has the right and the power to end life (6:9–10).

In his response to Eliphaz, Job admitted to using "impetuous" words because of his great "anguish" (6:2–3). For the first time in the book, Job acknowledged that the Almighty played a part in his problem. Job confessed his desire to die (6:8–9) and vented his frustrations over his own sufferings (6:11–13) as well as his friends' lack of empathy (6:14–20). He invited his friends to point out his wrongs (6:24), while also calling them out on their unfair treatment of him (6:25–27). He concluded by maintaining his innocence (6:30).

---

28. *Shuv* can mean "turn back," "return," or "restore." See BDB, s.v. "*shuv*."
29. The construction of the three imperatives to *face* + *turn back* + *restore* allow for the final imperative (restore) to be the result of the first two imperatives.
30. An alternate translation of verse 29 would be: "Repent! Let there be no injustice, then you'll restore my righteousness."
31. Literally, "Is there injustice in my tongue?"

Job felt an overwhelming grief at everything that had happened to him. He was so drained, physically and emotionally, that he felt he no longer had the strength to continue living. In chapter 7, Job continued to describe his discomfort and give expression to his desires, although this time, his words were not directed at his friends but at God. As we consider Job 7, we will address the following questions: What exactly was Job's skin disorder? What was his emotional state? What were his complaints against God?

7:1–6 Job's Discomfort in His Suffering

To describe his painful existence, Job equated a person's fixed time on earth to "hard service" in the military or to the heavy-duty work of a paid laborer or slave (7:1–2). He maintained that irrespective of a person's profession, there was an expectation of and longing for rest[32] and wages at the end of the day (7:2). The synonymous parallelism of "allotted" and "assigned," as well as "futility" and "misery," emphasizes the depth of Job's suffering (7:3). He did not simply stumble on his afflictions but felt that these were intentionally assigned to him. The nights were long, restless, and filled with unending agony (7:4), indicating insomnia.

This was due, at least in part, to Job's disease, which is vividly described in verse 5. Worms are usually found on decaying matter such as corpses. The scabs which covered Job's whole body would have included a hardening of the skin that developed into lumps, accompanied by a continuous flow of pus.[33] This description points to a diagnosis of either malignant boils (chronic furunculosis) or carbuncles. Such infections are usually caused by the bacteria *staphylococcus aureus*, and neglect of this condition may lead to sepsis. Acknowledging the difficulty in identifying Job's exact ailment – because of the long list of possible diseases that were suggested – Vicchio coined the phrase "Disease of Diseases" as a collective phrase to describe Job's ailment.[34] Continuous itching and pain led Job to conclude that his life had passed by quickly and was about to end without "hope [*tiqvah*]"[35] (7:6). "The brevity

---

32. Literally, "shadow."
33. There is a figure of speech here where the effect (release of lesion) is stated but the cause, skin bursting open, is intended.
34. Vicchio, *Book of Job*, 58. Vicchio traces the suggestions for Job's ailment from 200 BCE to the mid twentieth century. The common suggestions include leprosy, elephantiasis, and smallpox. He highlights the diagnosis of Drexelius – candor, depression, elephantiasis, arthritis, nephritis, insomnia – and thinks that these diagnoses are non-sensical.
35. *Tiqvah* can have the meaning: "cord," "hope," "a thing hoped for." See BDB, s.v. "tiqvah."

of human life and the irreversibility of death are a constant theme in Job's arguments with God."[36] Job declared that his life was "but a breath" (7:7).

7:7–21 Job's Desires of God
7:7–10 Life's brevity

Job directed his attention to God, calling attention to the fact that life was no more than a breath and acknowledging that he would not experience or "see" (*ra'ah*) happiness again (7:7). One advantage of this, from Job's perspective, was that the "eye" of the one who "sees" (*ra'ah*) him would no longer have been able to "see" him even though he would "look" for him (7:8). Job seemed to be playing with words by using the same terminology for the *instrument* (eyes) of seeing and the *action* of seeing. Job had felt that God had been doggedly watching him with hostility. He now affirmed that he would soon be gone, and God would not find him even if he were to search for him (7:8b). Through these ramblings, Job acknowledged that God sees and watches over humankind.

Job used a series of metaphors to illustrate his point about the volatile nature of life. He equated a cloud that vanishes from sight and is seen no more to someone who dies and goes to *Sheol* (often, as in the NIV, translated as "grave"), never to come back to life (7:9). He also explained the impossibility of a dead person returning to his former house since "his place will know him no more" (7:10).

7:11–16 Immediate reprieve

Weighed down by the pain of his malignant skin disorder, his unhappy thoughts about the brevity of life, and his friends' unjust treatment, Job admitted that he could not take it anymore but must "speak out in the anguish of my spirit" and "in the bitterness of my soul" (7:11).

Job listed three complaints. First, he used two metaphors – the sea (*yam*) that is limited by the land surrounding it and the sea monster (*tannin*) that is confined to the sea – to describe his feelings of being cornered and hounded (7:12).[37] The Hebrew word *yam* or *yamm* "is also the name of the personified Sea (Yamm), a chaos creature in Ugaritic mythological texts. Since this word is paralleled by another chaos creature (*tannin*, see Gen 1:21), we should view

---

36. Alter, *Writings*, 482.
37. Alter thinks that with this rhetorical question, Job wanted to know "whether he is to be thought of as an undying monstrous god to be kept imprisoned under eternal guard" (*Writings*, 482).

these as creatures that God keeps under watch as he maintains the orderly system."[38] Second, Job complained that he could not even rest because when he tried to find comfort in sleep (7:13), he was frightened by scary dreams and terrifying visions (7:14). Consequently, he preferred "death by strangulation to physical life"[39] (7:15, my translation). Third, Job had lost his zeal for life. He rejected life, just wanting to be left alone, for he believed that his days lacked meaning (7:16). Job found life transitory, and he wanted a reprieve.

7:17–21 Forgiveness before death

Job resumed addressing the unnamed referent (7:14), who – based on the attributes that Job used to describe him – must be God. For instance, this unnamed person can "see everything we do" (7:20) and is able to "pardon . . . offenses" and "forgive . . . sins" (7:21a) and is also the one who will "search" for Job (7:21b; compare 7:8). Once again, Job used rhetorical questions to argue that humankind is not worth God's "attention" that he should "examine" (*paqadh*) and "test" (*bakhan*) them continuously, without reprieve (7:17–18). In the OT, God examined people to either bless or to punish. For instance, Yahweh "examines" the upright to reward them but punishes the wicked (Ps 11:5–7). Job seemed to have believed that God was examining him to punish him. Therefore, Job wished God would avert his gaze and leave him alone (7:19).

In speaking of death, Job rephrased what he had said in verse 8, replacing the word "look" with "search [*shakhar*]" (7:21). He maintained that although God would diligently search for him, he would not find him since Job would "be no more."

Three different words are used to convey the idea of "watching" to express God's omniscience and his very careful attention to and involvement in the life of human beings. God "examines" people either to bless or to punish (7:18–20). He also is the one who dispenses forgiveness (7:21). While we are familiar with the idea that God blesses the upright but punishes the wicked, have we considered the idea that God may send afflictions upon the upright for purposes known only to him? For instance, even Paul, God's faithful servant, had a thorn in the flesh that did not go away. Three times, Paul had asked the Lord to remove it but his request was denied. The context points to pain not as a miscarriage of justice but as the vehicle and the price of deliverance.

---

38. Walton, *Job*, 163.
39. The MT has "these bones." The NIV editors translated the phrase as "body." Here is a figure of speech, synecdoche: part (bones) is used for the whole person or life itself.

Without suffering, Paul would never experience the full revelation of his need, and until he humbly submitted to God's working in and through his pain, it was unreasonable for him to expect the revelation that he sought. In time, Paul had to embrace the fact that God's grace was sufficient for him (2 Cor 12:7–10). Some scholars believe that this thorn was epilepsy; others think it might have been blindness (Gal 6:11) – in which case, it is possible that Paul had only been partially healed from the blindness that occurred during his encounter with the Lord on his way to Damascus (Acts 9:2–18).

Job continued to complain of his discomfort and the psychosomatic effects of the calamities that came: malignant boils, insomnia, and nightmares, leading to a desire for death. He described the Lord's actions against him and boldly asked what sin he had committed that he should become a target for God's arrows. If indeed he had sinned, Job wanted to know when God would forgive him since he was about to die.

Job acknowledged the pain and psychosomatic effects he was experiencing as a result of the calamities. He was covered with worms, scabs, and festering wounds. Yet, it seemed like no one had any sympathy for him – not even his friends. He was confused and longed for an end to his misery and hopeless despair. What disturbed him most was that there seemed to be no end to his suffering. He felt that even God was hounding him and would not leave him alone, even sending him nightmares that robbed him of much-needed sleep. In his anguish and bitterness of soul, Job planned to lodge an official complaint to God.

Many people question whether there is, in fact, divine involvement in human affairs. Job, however, did not hesitate to acknowledge that God was directly responsible for his afflictions. He pointed to God's dogged observation of every move of his life at every moment. Having acknowledged God's involvement, the question of why he allows such suffering could not be avoided. Job could not understand why God was not acting to bring immediate deliverance. There is nothing wrong in asking God "Why?" – as long as we do not move in the direction of questioning God's character and sovereignty.

SHEOL AND THE AFTERLIFE

Although people in Job's time had some vague ideas about an afterlife, this idea was not as developed as it was in the NT. In the OT, people believed they would go to *Sheol* after their earthly life. For instance, when Jacob heard that his sons would need to take Benjamin to Egypt to buy food, he said, "If harm comes to him on the journey that you are taking, you will bring my gray head in grief to Sheol" (Gen 42:38).[1]

Connected to the term *Sheol* is the phrase *gather to my people*, which is a euphemism for death or *going to Sheol*. When Jacob was dying and giving instructions to his children, he said: "I am about to be *gathered to my people* [italics mine]. Bury me with my fathers in the cave in the field of Ephron the Hittite" (Gen 49:29). After completing his instructions, Jacob "drew his feet up into the bed, breathed his last and *was gathered to his people* [italics mine]" (Gen 49:33).

In the OT, there are many views about the afterlife and *Sheol* is viewed in various ways. Here are some of these views: (a) the OT does not contain any belief in the afterlife until the third and second centuries BC; (b) the OT perceives the afterlife as a shadowy, semiconscious continuation of life; (c) the term *Sheol* is used in at least two different ways and may refer to death (the grave) or to the next life; (d) *Sheol*, meaning the netherworld, is divided into two compartments: the lower compartment is for the miserable existence of the bad and the upper compartment is the place where the good await resurrection; (e) *Sheol* is the *netherworld*, which is inhabited by demons and some or all of the dead; and (f) it is only people's bodies that go to *Sheol*, but the souls of the righteous go to heaven.[2]

However, contrary to what is today becoming a consensus – that is, that the OT does not contain a belief in the afterlife until the third and second century BC – this author maintains that there was some knowledge of the afterlife as early as the times of the prophet Isaiah in the eighth century BC and the prophet Ezekiel in the sixth century BC. Merrill explains,

> The most elaborate OT descriptions of the netherworld appear in Isaiah and Ezekiel. Isaiah, speaking of the king of Babylon in the guise of Helel ben Shacher, prophesies his fall from the heights to the depths, to *Sheol* (Isa 14:15//*bor*). . . . Ezekiel condemns Pharaoh in a similar manner, consigning him to Sheol, the place of the pit (*bor*) and the lowest parts of the earth (*'res tahtit*, Ezek 31:16).[3]

In the NT, *Hades* is the equivalent term for what the OT refers to as *Sheol*. The parable of the rich man and Lazarus (Luke 16:19–31) reveals that there is consciousness after death and that there are only two possible destinations: *Hades* or Abraham's bosom. *Hades* is depicted here as a place of torment for the unrighteous and unbelievers awaiting the final resurrection and final judgment (see also Matt 25:41–46; Rev 20:11–15).

"Abraham's bosom" is a synonym for paradise – which is being in the presence of Jesus Christ – and is perceived to be the place where the righteous go, including those who repent of their sins and believe in Jesus Christ even at the last minute, as was the case of the thief on the cross (Luke 23:43).

"Heaven" (Gk. *Ouranos*; Heb. *Shamayim*) without the article, refers to God's throne (Isa 66:1), the place where God dwells (Ps 15:3), and also the place where Jesus Christ is seated (Mark 16:19; Acts 1:9–11; 1 Pet 3:22).

The "new heaven" is a place where, after the first heaven and the first earth pass away, the living God will dwell with his people (Rev 21:1–4). "Heaven" is the "abode of God and of God's angels, the just, and the holy. It is the real home of Christians."[4] It is the final and eternal destination of all faithful believers in the living God and in Jesus Christ our Savior (John 14:1–2).

"The heavens" (Gk. *To ouranos*; Heb. *Hashamayim*) with the article, refer to the sky (Gen 1:6–8), and the place from which the dragon will be cast out from at the end of time (Rev 12:7–12). It should not be confused with "heaven."

Hell (Gk. *Gehenna*) is taken from the Hebrew word *Ge-Hinnom*, which means the "Valley of Hinnom." This was a place outside Jerusalem.[5] It became a garbage dump that was kept continuously burning, hence the imagery used to describe a place for eternal punishment and fire. This place is aptly called the "lake of fire" and will be the final destination of the "beast" and the "false prophet" (Rev 19:20), as well as the devil and his angels (Matt 25:41; Rev 20:10), and the wicked (Rev 21:8). The "lake of fire" is described as the "second death" (Rev 20:14–15).

The Septuagint – the Greek translation of the OT – uses the term *Tartarus* (Gk. ταρταρώσας) in the Yahweh speeches in Job 38–41. Tartarus is a place for the "quadrupeds"[6] and "part" of the "deep"[7] or deepest abyss. In the NT, *Tartarus* is depicted as the place of the angels who had sinned by rebelling against God (2 Pet 2:4)[8] and are in chains awaiting their final judgment (Jude 6).

A nagging question remains: What exactly happens immediately after death? Is there consciousness after death? A concept known as "soul sleep" (Gk. *psychopannychia*) states that "there is a period between one's death and the final resurrection in which oneself (soul) is in an unconscious state."[9] It would seem, though, as already stated, that the parable of the rich man and Lazarus, which indicates that there is consciousness at and after death, contradicts this view. Similarly, the transfiguration (Matt 17:1–8) portrays Moses and Elijah as being aware of what was happening around them.

---

1. This is a literal rendering of the verse using the term *Sheol* as the MT has it, whereas the NIV translates *Sheol* as "grave."
2. D. K. Stewart, "Sheol" *ISBE* 4:472.
3. Eugene H. Merrill, "Sheol" *NIDOTTE* 4:7.
4. Cheryl Kirk-Duggan, "Heaven" in *Dictionary of the Bible* (Grand Rapids: Eerdmans, 2019), 563-64.
5. Donald K. McKim, *The Westminster Dictionary of Theological Terms*, 2nd ed. (Louisville: Westminster John Knox, 2014), 111-12.
6. In this translation, *tartarus* is noted as *netherworld*. Job 40:20 (*NETS*).
7. In this translation, *tartarus* is noted as *netherworld*. Job 41:24 (*NETS*).
8. *Tartarus* in this verse is translated as *hell* in the NIV, KJV, NLT, NASB.
9. McKim, *Westminster Dictionary of Theological Terms*, 300. See also the work of John Calvin, *Psychopannycia or The Soul's Imaginary Sleep*. It is a refutation on the erroneous teaching regarding *soul sleep*.

8:1–22 Bildad Speaks

Job's complaint about the severity of his suffering and his consequent wish for death did not yield a positive response, either from his friends – in the form of empathy or practical help – or from God – in the form of a reprieve. In this chapter, Bildad, another of the three friends, takes up the attempt to counsel Job. Here, we want to consider the questions: How is God's justice expressed in his dealings with both the upright and the wicked? Does God pervert justice?

8:1–7 The Proposition of Justice

Bildad, who is introduced as the Shuhite (8:1), began his speech with a condescending rhetorical question and likened Job's arguments to "a blustering wind" (8:2) – implying that Job's words were loud and abundant but lacked substance. Continuing in the same style, Bildad reminded Job that God does not "pervert justice" or "pervert what is right" (8:3). Bildad's underlying thoughts on retributive justice are evident: If you sin, you will suffer; since you are suffering, you must have sinned. Bildad's oblique message was that Job's suffering must have been the consequence of his sin. But Bildad then went on to claim that Job's children had sinned, and that God had simply permitted them to suffer the consequences of their sins by allowing them to die (8:4). Vicchio brings up the suggestion that Bildad was proposing that "Job's children may be responsible for his suffering."[40] This did not seem to be the case. Bildad was trying to communicate that Job had sinned. He, like his children will pay for the consequences of his sins; but Job need not wait for that to happen. Bildad then gave counsel to Job.

According to Bildad, if Job would diligently "seek" (*shakhar*)[41] God and implore God's favor (8:5), and if he remained "pure and upright," then God would personally intervene on his behalf, not only to restore what Job had lost but to make him even more "prosperous" than before (8:6–7). Bildad repeatedly used the particle "if." Belcher observes that although Bildad is "more direct with Job than Eliphaz, he couches his speeches with possibilities through the use of the word 'if.'"[42]

These verses present Bildad's perspective of God as one who does not pervert justice. On the contrary, God upholds justice by not rejecting the blameless and not supporting the wicked. God blesses the upright and those who seek him (8:5–7).

8:8–10 *The Proof of History*

Bildad commanded Job to learn from the previous generation "and find out what their ancestors learned" (8:8). Job and his contemporaries were young. Despite their accumulated experience, they did not seem to have acquired as much knowledge and understanding as those who had gone before (8:9). Bildad did not doubt that the wise instructions and understanding of their predecessors were available to help Job and his generation (8:10).

Bildad respected the wisdom of the previous generation, which probably refers to elders. In Asia, where showing respect to elders is an important virtue, respect is demonstrated by seeking counsel from elders, acknowledging their presence, and not doing anything that would cause them to lose face. It is also unacceptable to call elders (older people) by their first name. To do so would communicate nonrecognition of their authority and seniority. Depending on age and culture, there may be specific terms that should be used to address an elderly man or woman. To show any disrespect to elders incurs the contempt of the elders themselves or witnesses to the disrespectful act.

---

40. Vicchio, *Book of Job*, 76.
41. Bildad used the same term for "look" that was used in 7:8. This time, he applied it to Job as he advised him to diligently seek God.
42. Belcher, *Finding Favor*, 93.

8:11–19 The Path of Ungodliness

In this section, Bildad described the fate of those who "forget God" (8:13–14). Using "papyrus" and "reeds" as a visual aid, he stated the obvious – these plants cannot grow without "marsh" and "water" (8:11), and they tend to wither even faster than grass (8:12). A similar destiny awaits those who "forget God," which refers to those who desert (Deut 32:18) or reject (Ps 106:21) him. Such people, who are described in the parallel line as being "godless," have no hope (8:13) and cannot be "sustained without the grace and forgiveness of God."[43] This is because they "trust" or "rely on" something "fragile" and flimsy like an unstable "spider's web" (8:14–15). These people are also likened to a young and healthy plant that has received enough water and sunshine and has taken root among the rocks (8:16–17). But once this plant is uprooted, it is as good as dead. It cannot return to its former habitat for other plants would have grown in its place (8:18–19).

The issue here is loyalty to a fixed "cause-and-effect" doctrine that insists that there is a connection between what people do and what happens to them. It is a merger of legalism, judgmentalism, and presumption, which are very much alive and well today. Many of us have grown up with the following mindset: I will be rewarded or compensated exactly for what I do or do not do. Such mindset, however, does not allow for God's grace and his merciful interventions.

8:20–22 The Possibility of Blessing

Bildad concluded by affirming the concept of retributive justice and applying this to Job: "Surely God does not reject one who is blameless or strengthen the hands of evildoers" (8:20). But he also assured Job that he could yet experience the joy of restoration: "He will yet fill your mouth with laughter and your lips with shouts of joy" (8:21). In contrast, Job's "enemies" would be put to "shame" and the homes of the "wicked" would "be no more" (8:22) – in other words, these people would experience losses and shame, just as Job had.

Bildad's attitude is a particularly bad example of how to counsel someone in need. Bildad was clearly more concerned about defending traditional doctrine than he was about helping and comforting Job. His words were cruel and these added to Job's pain. There is a story told of a mother who had just delivered a stillborn baby. While she was grieving the loss of her child, a woman from her church came to visit her and declared, "The reason your baby died is

---

43. Walter C. Kaiser Jr., *The Majesty of God in the Midst of Innocent Suffering: The Message of Job* (Fearn, UK: Christian Focus Publications, 2019), 67.

because you have some unconfessed sin your life!" What foolhardy arrogance to judge someone who is in pain in this way!

When faced with undeserved, unexplained suffering, perhaps we need to embrace this thought: Sometimes, God ordains or allows pain and suffering for purposes we do not know or understand. He may or may not reveal these purposes to us at some future time. In the end, however, our suffering will be used by God for his glory and our benefit, whether we realize this or not. So, instead of adding to people's pain by uncalled for comments, we should heed Paul's admonition to "rejoice with those who rejoice; mourn with those who mourn" (Rom 12:15). Where appropriate, we are to follow the example of Jesus Christ himself, who entered into the pain of Mary and Martha at the death of their brother Lazarus and "wept" (John 11:35) with them, even though he knew that he would raise Lazarus from the dead shortly afterward (John 11:38–44).

Bildad validated his words from history and the tradition of the sages. He pursued the same argument as Eliphaz but couched it differently – insinuating that Job must have sinned to merit the calamities that came upon him and that there could be no other reason for his suffering. Nevertheless, Bildad also added that Job might yet experience God's blessings if only he would seek God.

Bildad espoused the doctrine of retribution. He was a traditionalist, basing his arguments on the traditions of the wise men and the teaching of their ancestors as well as human theology and philosophy. He acknowledged that God does not pervert justice, which is true; but he failed to acknowledge that God does not manage human affairs by retributive justice alone. Bildad tried to make himself seem important and superior by placing a high value on old ideas, even though these ideas could be proven wrong.

Bildad perceived Job's defense as a threat to their established understanding of God and how he works in the world. Like Eliphaz, Bildad argued that the sufferer – in this case, Job – deserved what he was experiencing because God was paying him back for sins he had committed. Bildad did not even attempt to harmonize Job's innocence with traditional doctrine. Instead of listening to Job's plea and explanation, Bildad implied that Job needed to confess some hidden sin that must be the reason for his suffering. Bildad's position was that "what is true is not new, and what is new is not true; that Job is wrong because he is propounding a monstrous new doctrine and Bildad was right, because he is simply repeating an old doctrine, so old that it must be true."[44]

---

44. Samuel Rolles Driver and George Buchanan Gray, *A Critical and Exegetical Commentary on the Book of Job*, ICC (Edinburgh: T&T Clark, 1921), 78.

TRADITIONAL BELIEFS AND EXPERIENCES

Basically, Bildad's argument was that no one, in their lifetime, can depend on learning the necessary wisdom but must depend on the collective insight of past tradition and people. Only then would a person have enough wisdom for living. Wiersbe wisely counters with these words: "To be sure, we today can learn from the past.... But the past must be a rudder to guide us and not an anchor to hold us back.... The fact that something was said or written years ago is no guarantee it is right.... The past contains as much folly as wisdom."[1]

However, truth that has survived the test of time should not be thrown out, as if to say that human experience is more important than sacred doctrine. In the case of Job's experience, the application of sin as the cause of his suffering was incorrect. Bildad's doctrine was not relevant to Job's situation. While sin does bring suffering, this is not so in every case. Often, the one who suffers has done nothing to merit the trouble, and sometimes, wicked and sinful people do not suffer. This is the very dilemma that Job was facing. Traditional doctrine says that sin brings on suffering; experience says that this belief is not necessarily true in all situations – it certainly was not true in Job's case (Job 1–2). A principle emerges: Truth applied in the wrong way becomes wrong. The truth itself is not wrong, but when the truth is misapplied, it is merely an assumption or, at best, a theory.

The chart below, taken from Dr. Roy B. Zuck's class notes, may help explain this principle.

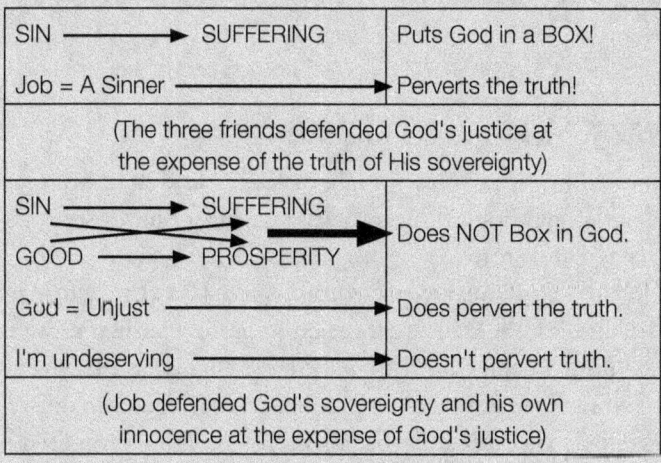

Reading from top to bottom, the top section is the doctrine of tradition, which includes this assumption: A sinner will suffer; thus the sufferer is a sinner.

> This puts God in a box and does not allow for God to use suffering for his purposes and for his glory, as in the case of Christ's suffering, the suffering of the blind man (John 9:1–4), and the suffering of Job. Nor does it allow for situations such as God's decision to raise up and prosper evil nations and kings – such as the Assyrian and Babylonian Empires and rulers – as instruments to carry out his will. But presuming that Job was a sinner because he was suffering, the three counselors *perverted* the truth. They held to that assumption so tightly that they left no room for the possibility that God might be using suffering to accomplish his purpose. In fact, in attempting to defend God's justice, they rejected God's sovereignty and his right to act as God.
>
> The next section of the diagram says that while sin may result in suffering, sometimes, even sinners prosper. Similarly, good people often suffer, but they may also sometimes prosper. This does not put God in a box but agrees that God acts according to his sovereign will and justice for his own glory and purposes. In declaring that God was unjust in allowing his suffering, Job *perverted* the truth. God was not unjust. However, Job's declaration that he was undeserving of the suffering did *not* pervert the truth, and this was the claim that Job held on to even though he did not understand why he was suffering. Job's interpretation of his suffering (i.e., that God is unjust) defends the sovereignty of God but denies the justice of God. The three friends and Job were all struggling to harmonize their theology with experience.
>
> ---
>
> 1. Warren Wiersbe, *Be Patient (Job): Waiting on God in Difficult Times* (Wheaton, IL: Victor Books, 1991), 37.

9:1–10:22 Job's Response to Bildad

Bildad attacked Job even more bitingly than Eliphaz did. In his response, Job only made brief mention of the accusations against him. Instead, he praised God's sovereign and creative power, against which, he confessed, he was helpless. But Job also continued to play with the idea of a chance to stand before God to defend himself. Here are three questions to consider as we reflect on Job 9: Can human beings contend with the Almighty and survive? On what grounds, and in what instances, may people do so? How should we respond when we realize that a calamity that affects us is coming from God himself?

9:1–12 The Greatness of God

Job claimed that he could not contend with his Creator. He responded to Bildad by acknowledging that what Bildad had declared was true – that God does not pervert justice – but he also questioned how "mere mortals" could be vindicated before God (9:2). Job did not think this was possible. "Yet his conviction that God does not pervert justice, prods him to contemplate the impossible, i.e., of pursuing litigation against God."[45] As Job thought further about it, he realized that to "strive" (*rib*) with God is next to impossible (9:3).

This term *rib*, introduced for the first time here,[46] conveys the mood of the whole book. As a verb, it means "to strive," "quarrel," "attack," "lodge a complaint," or "carry a lawsuit,"[47] which is what Job was planning to do. Soulen outlines the typical pattern of a disputation or lawsuit: (a) summons to the offending party; (b) recitation of beneficent acts bestowed in former times upon the offender; (c) accusations against the offender; and (d) calling witnesses to the covenant, both those in heaven and those on earth.[48] Each of these elements are interspersed in the speeches of Job, but could be collected to form a whole package following the outline of Soulen and before Job would make his final appeal and defense in chapter 31. Take, for instance, the summons. Job, as the offended party, repeatedly requested a hearing (13:20–22; 14:15). With regard to beneficent acts, Job listed the blessings that he had earlier received from God (29:2–6). Regarding accusations, Job listed his main accusations against God – that it was God who had caused his suffering and been inattentive to his cries (16:7–14; 19:8–13). As for witnesses, Job called on the earth and "one who is in heaven" (16:18–21).

Job was torn between filing a lawsuit against God and refraining from doing so. He gave several reasons why a person could not or should not file a lawsuit against God. First, since God is all-knowing and all-powerful, no one has ever "resisted" or rebelled (*qashah*) against him and remained "unscathed" (9:4). This term *qashah*, meaning "to rebel" or "to be obstinate," once described the people of Israel, who, on account of their obstinacy, God would have destroyed many times on their way to the promised land had not Moses intervened (Exod 32:9–14; 33:3–5; 34:9). The second reason not to "dispute" with God is because he has dominion over all the earth. In his anger, he uprooted mountains (9:5), and vigorously shook the earth so that its very

---

45. Hartley, *Book of Job*, 166.
46. *Rib* is used in the book seven times as a verb (10:2; 13:19; 23:6; 31:13; 33:13,19; 40:2) and four times as a noun (13:6, 8; 29:16; 31:35) to describe the disputations between Job and his friends and Job with God.
47. See *HALOT*, s.v. "rib."
48. Richard N. Soulen, *Handbook of Biblical Criticism*, 2nd ed. (Atlanta: John Knox, 1981), 170. Examples of this are in Psalm 50, Isaiah 1:2–9, Jeremiah 2:4–13, Hosea 4:1–10, and Micah 6:1–8.

pillars trembled (9:6). And third, God has sovereignty over his creation. He may command the sun not to shine (*zarakh*) or restrict (*khatham*) the light of the stars, demonstrating his power over these luminaries (9:7). God alone created and controls "the heavens," "the sea" (9:8), and the constellations (9:9).

Not only do these verses display the sovereignty of God in creating and maintaining the universe, more important, in this context, they also show that he may sometimes use these created things in his "anger" – mountains (causing landslides, volcanic eruptions, and earthquakes), the sun (eclipses), the sea (storms and tsunamis), the constellations (signs and seasons) – to bring judgment on rebellious people. Job concluded that indeed God performs miracles, awesome deeds which are too many to be numbered (9:10). Under such circumstances, it was clear that no human being, including Job, could contend with God and win.

Job acknowledged that if God should pass by, he would not be able to see him (9:11). This recalls the incident where the Lord, honoring Moses's request, caused his goodness and glory to "pass" by, yet did not permit Moses to see his "face" but only his "back" (Exod 33:18–23). From this incident, we can infer that while God may reveal himself to whomever he chooses, this revelation is only to a limited extent. Job knew that God is invisible to the human eye. He used short rhetorical questions to express the idea that when God "taketh away" (*khathaf*),[49] no one may stop him or ask him to give account of what he is doing (9:12). Yes, God is sovereign. Even King Nebuchadnezzar recognized this when he said of the God of Daniel, "All the peoples of the earth are regarded as nothing. He does as he pleases with the powers of heaven and the peoples of the earth. No one can hold back his hand or say to him: 'What have you done?'" (Dan 4:35).

Job presumed to know not merely what God was doing but even God's attitude in relation to Job's own suffering. In this, Job was being irreverent, if not sinful. We know, however, that Job was struggling with the same issues we ourselves face when we feel that our suffering is undeserved. It also seems likely that Job's response was a reaction toward the three friends' insistence that God always blesses the good but punishes the wicked.

When you feel that God is the one who has caused undeserved pain and suffering in your life, here are some appropriate ways to respond:

---

49. See *HALOT*, s.v. "khathaf."

- Acknowledge that God is just, in control, and knows what is best in every circumstance.
- Ask God for wisdom to know what you should do, and then do it.
- Maintain a humble disposition and a submissive attitude before God.
- Be brutally honest with God about your thoughts and feelings about the whole situation. A perusal of the psalms, especially the lament psalms – both individual (Pss 22; 51) and on a national level (Pss 60; 85; 90) – illustrate how personal you can be with the Lord.

9:13–24 *The Arbitrariness of God*

No one can question what God does. Job continued to explain that God may even choose not to withdraw his anger, as he did when he crushed Rahab's assistants, an oblique reference to the sea and its tributaries (9:13). If Rahab's assistants were crushed by God, how much more might the same be true of human beings like Job? Since God had the power and was in a position to destroy him at will, Job wondered how he could possibly argue his case and defend himself before God in a cross-examination. Job chose to speak less and be cautious with his words (9:14). He added that though he was innocent, he would not argue but, rather, request a favor from his "Judge" (9:15).[50] Job reasoned that even if he did call and God responded, it was doubtful that God would actually listen to him (9:16).

God afflicts without reprieve (9:17–21). Job observed that God had crushed him incessantly with calamities and,[51] without reason, multiplied his wounds (9:17). God had not allowed Job to even catch his breath but, instead, had increased his hardships (9:18). God is stronger than anyone else; he is just, and no one can find fault with him (9:19). In these circumstances, Job felt that he did not stand a chance. Yet, though Job claimed to be innocent, he admitted that his own mouth would condemn him (9:20). This explains, in part, Job's hesitancy to present his case. Job then stated that he had lost interest in life and even admitted that he despised his own life (9:21), echoing many of the thoughts he had already expressed in chapter 7.

---

50. The word *meshofeti* from the root word *shafat* means to "decide," "settle," "pass judgement," "administer justice," "enter into a controversy." See *HALOT*, s.v. "shafat." It is a *poel* participle, functioning as a noun, and an indirect object in 9:15.
51. Literally, "storm."

Job feared that God would not acquit him (9:22–24), claiming that it was "all the same" and that God makes an immediate end to both the blameless and the wicked (9:22).[52] For instance, when calamity suddenly brings death, God scorns the despair of the blameless (9:23); when the land is entrusted into the control of the wicked, God covers the faces of the judges, so that they exercise partiality; hence justice is not served. According to Job, it is no one but God who does these things (9:24). To charge that God's justice is arbitrary is a serious accusation, and the fact that Job had accused God of injustice explains his fear that God would not acquit him. If there is already perceived injustice on the part of a judge, how could a person like Job present his case and expect an impartial hearing?

9:25–35 *The Unfairness of God*

Mortals do not stand a chance before God. Again, Job described the volatility of life, comparing the passing of his days to the swiftness of a royal messenger (9:25), the speed of a papyrus boat, or the rapidity with which an eagle swoops down on its prey (9:26). Even if Job were to forget his complaint and replace his sad expression with a smile (9:27), he would still dread all his sufferings for he feared that God would not acquit him (9:28). This was the same kind of fear that Job described earlier when he admitted that the calamities that he had earlier feared had happened to him (see 3:25). Job's life and future had become uncertain.

Continuing in this vein, Job argued that since he had already been "found guilty," there was little purpose in continuing to "struggle in vain" (9:29). Why should he seek to prove his innocence if God was going to declare him guilty anyway? Job believed that even if he washed himself with soap (9:30), even then God would probably throw him back into "a slime pit" (9:31) – a rather drastic way of expressing the idea that no amount of cleansing could make Job innocent before God. Job also acknowledged that God and Job could not come together for litigation (9:32) since there was no qualified mediator or arbiter (*mokhiakh*)[53] to hear their case and ensure a fair trial (9:33).

Weighed down by his sufferings and frustrated by knowing that the sovereign God is beyond the reach of a mere human being, Job wished desperately

---

52. Verbal participles in Biblical Hebrew may denote continuing or immediacy of action.
53. *Mokhiakh* is a participle from the root word, *yakhakh*, which means to "dispute," "reason together," "judge," "or "rebuke." As a participle, it refers to "one who skillfully renders just decisions," an "arbiter," or "an advocate." Refer to John E. Hartley, "*yakhakh*," *NIDOTTE* 2:441–43. The NIV translates the participle as "someone to mediate between us," hence a *mediator*.

for a solution to his problem – a way to speak with God without bringing down on himself God's righteous anger. He longed for an arbiter or an advocate – "someone to mediate between" himself and God so that Job might "speak up without fear" (9:35).

This concept of an advocate finds an echo in the NT, where God in his mercy sent his Son for this very purpose. The apostle John assures believers that "if anybody does sin, we have an advocate with the Father – Jesus Christ, the Righteous One. He is the atoning sacrifice for our sins" (1 John 2:1–2). This is confirmed by the apostle Paul – "There is one God and one mediator between God and mankind, the man Christ Jesus" (1 Tim 2:5) – and also by the writer of Hebrews, who tells us that "Christ is the mediator of a new covenant" (Heb 9:15).

Job, in his response to Bildad, agreed that God does not pervert justice and that no mortal being can contend with the Almighty and survive. Recognizing that he must stand before the God of sovereign power and awesome deeds, Job realized that he could never contend with the Almighty but could only request that he be allowed to present his case.

Earlier, Eliphaz had claimed that God was just while humankind was sinful. Job's response portrays God as unjust but all-powerful and human beings as being too weak to do anything about it. In Job's mind, God was an arbitrary, unpredictable, and terrifying opponent.

Job gave in to self-pity, acknowledging his nothingness and the fact that he was no match for God. He even despised his own life. He felt helpless, especially at the thought that God would not see him as innocent and would destroy him along with the guilty. He became negative toward God and accused him of injustice.

JOB'S MONOTHEISTIC VIEW OF GOD

Chapter 9 is crucial to understanding Job's concept of God. Job was monotheistic. In his time and context, people worshiped many gods, such as the sun, the moon, and the god of the sea. But Job believed that there was a living God, who had created everything and who maintains order in the universe. Let us now consider some attributes of this God in whom Job believed.

God is Omniscient: "His wisdom is profound" (9:4a). As Job acknowledged, this all-knowing God is beyond comprehension. No mortal being can reason with him (9:3). God knew all about Job for he had carefully watched his every step (7:19–20; 10:14). Job believed that God knew that he, Job, was innocent (23:10; 27:6) since God sees everything that is happening both in heaven and on earth. No one can find wisdom or buy it, even with the most valuable precious stones and metals (28:12–19); God alone knows where wisdom is found (28:23). The order in the universe and God's sustenance of creation displays his transcendent wisdom (38:1–39).

God is Omnipotent: "His power is vast" (9:4b). God has control even over earthquakes, landslides, the heavenly bodies, and the waves of the sea (9:5–9). "He performs wonders that cannot be fathomed, miracles that cannot be counted" (9:10), and even Rahab[1] – a reference to the sea at creation – submits to him (9:13).

God is Sovereign: No mortal can go against God without being hurt for he can crush rebellions (9:4b). And no one can turn to him and say, "What are you doing?" (9:12). Job himself acknowledged that he could not confront God (9:14–19) for God was no mere mortal (9:32).

God is Just: While Job did accuse God of being unjust, he actually chose God to be his judge (9:15; 23:1–7), before whom he wanted to unload the pain and injustice that he felt had come from both God and his friends. Recognizing who God is, Job sought his favor, particularly for a chance to present his case. He knew, however, that God is not a human being whom he could confront or manipulate to obtain an instant response (9:32).

God is Almighty: Job frequently used the title "Almighty" to refer to God when describing God's actions, both negative and positive. For instance, Job claimed that the Almighty was the source of the arrows and attacks on him (6:4), as well as the one who had denied him justice (27:2). He also acknowledged that the Almighty was the source of the blessings that Job and his family had enjoyed previously before the calamities came (29:5). It was to the Almighty that Job prayed, hoping that God would answer him and attend to his requests (31:35).

Clearly, the God whom Job worshiped was the all-knowing, all-powerful, and just sovereign. While there is some overlap in these attributes, they all communicate one thing – the living God is the one and only true and powerful God, who knows everything about human beings, including all their losses and pain. And God himself affirmed some of Job's perceptions of him during his self-revelation to Job in chapters 38–41.

---

1. "'Rahab' is identified with Tiamat of the Babylonian creation epic, or Leviathan of the Canaanite myths. It is also used in parallelism to the sea (26:12), or the Red Sea (Ps 74:13), and so comes to symbolize Egypt (Isa 30:7). In the Babylonian Creation Epic there is reference to the helpers of Tiamat. In the Bible the reference is only to the raging sea, which the Lord controlled at creation." See Job 9:13 and note 36 in the *NET* Bible.

Job continued to pour out his complaints before God. Here are a few questions to consider when reflecting on Job 10: What thoughts usually assail a person who is headed toward depression? What are some signs of depression? Is committing suicide the best solution to facing pain and suffering? What purposes may lie behind life's trials?

10:1–3 Job Asked God, "Why?"

Job wanted to know why God was testing him. Pouring out the bitterness of his soul (10:1), Job listed three things that he will tell God: first, that God would not condemn him as guilty (10:2a); second, that he be told what "charges" had prompted God to file this legal case (*rib*) against Job (10:2b); and third, that God explain how it could possibly be good for God to "oppress" one whom he had carefully created and, simultaneously, "smile on the plans of the wicked" (10:3). In effect, Job was saying that the way God was treating him was unjust and that allowing the wicked to go unpunished was unfair.

10:4–7 God Is Unlike Mortal Beings

Job emphasized that God does not have "eyes of flesh" and thus he does not view things as humans do (10:4); nor is time measured for God as it is for human beings (10:5). That being the case, Job wondered why God should "search out" (*baqash*) his faults and "probe" (*darash*) or carry out further investigation concerning Job's sin (10:6). Job used two different terms that carry the same meaning to emphasize how God continuously pursued him even though he knew that Job was innocent and that he could not escape from God's power (10:7).

Job

Job must have wondered if God really loved him. When going through times of undeserved or unfair suffering, have you ever cried, "God doesn't love me!"? Although we tend to connect pain with the idea of a lack of love, pain is often a proof of love – for example, parents who discipline their child do so because they love that child, and the doctor who inflicts pain to cut out a cancerous growth, does so for the good of the patient.

10:8–17 Job Entertained Negative Thoughts about God

Job meditated on the truth that God had created and given him life but struggled to trust that God really had his best interest at heart. Although he recognized that God had shaped and formed him, skillfully as well as intricately, he hastened to add that God was just as ready to destroy him (10:8). Job used three images to describe the process of creation: being molded in clay (10:9), milk poured out to form cheese (10:10), and being clothed with skin and flesh and knitted together with bones and sinews (10:11). This final image is reminiscent of Psalm 139:13–16, which refers to God's involvement in the stages of conception and fetal development. God did not stop there but extended loving loyalty and his providential care over Job (10:12).

The Bible records many instances where God intervened in the lives of people for various purposes: to bless (Ruth 1:6), to test (Job 7:18); or to punish (Exod 32:34; Job 10:14; Jer 6:15). Luke also alludes to this concept in a prophecy concerning what would happen to Jerusalem when God visited to punish (Luke 19:44). In Job, however, the context is not punishment but God's providential care (10:12).

Nonetheless, after this positive note, Job immediately picked up the thread of his earlier accusations regarding God's intention to destroy him (see 10:8). He claimed that just as God had carefully and beautifully created Job, he had also secretly plotted the afflictions that Job was now experiencing (10:13). Job set out to prove this accusation with four suppositions, each beginning with "if" and escalating to show that in every instance, God was against him. First, if Job sinned, God was watching in order to mark him out as a target and would not acquit him (10:14). Second, if Job was guilty, that was woeful (10:15a). Third, even if Job was innocent, he would not be able to lift his head because he would be overwhelmed by shame and affliction (10:15b).[54] And fourth, if

---

54. The next line can be translated either as "drenched with affliction" or "look at my affliction." If we submit to a synonymous parallelism in verse 15 where the adjectives in both lines share similar meaning, then the first option is to be preferred, as in the NIV.

Job held his head high, God, like a mighty lion, would hunt him down with his terrifying power (10:16).

Job also gave three reasons why he believed God wanted to destroy him: first, God was setting him up as a target and overwhelming him; second, God was ready to pounce on him, displaying his awesome power; and third, God repeatedly brought new witnesses, piling up the evidence and intensifying his anger against Job. All this made Job feel as if a whole army of attacks were being directed at him (10:17).[55] We cannot, therefore, blame Job for entertaining the thought that God had carefully created him only to destroy him.

God did not create Job just so that he could hurt him, churning him like milk just to be a spectacle before the world of God's power over humankind. God did not promote and honor Job just to knock him down. Job was, however, justified in seeking answers to these questions: Why did the suffering continue? Why did the suffering increase in intensity? Why would God not speak to him? Against all odds, Job remained stubbornly persevering in seeking some response from God.

10:18–22 Job Preferred Death to Birth and Life

Job wanted to know why God had ever allowed him to be born (10:18a). He wished that he had never been born or been stillborn (10:18–19), which is reminiscent of his lament in Job 3:21–22 (compare 6:8–9; 7:21). Acknowledging that his life was very short, Job wished that God would grant him some reprieve by ceasing his attacks and allowing Job to experience even short-lived happiness before he died (10:20). In concluding this section, Job painted a bleak picture of the realm of death – which he believed he would soon visit – describing it as "the land of deepest night" and a place of "disorder," where light itself seems like darkness (10:21–22). In these verses, Job used four different terms for darkness to signify the inexplicable nature of the realm of death.[56] Nevertheless, Job still preferred death to life, which suggests that he was enduring unbearable pain and was deeply depressed.

---

55. There is a hendiadys here, where "changes" and "army" or "war" are taken as one entity, so that one word describes the other. This then could refer to "successive changes of attack." See E. W. Bullinger, *Figures of Speech Used in the Bible* (Grand Rapids: Baker Book House, 21st printing, 1997), 660.
56. There is double euphemism here to explain about death: Bullinger, *Figures of Speech*, 660.

11:1–20 Zophar Speaks

It was now the turn of Zophar the Naamathite to counsel Job. Zophar rebuked Job for his words and challenged him to repent. These questions will be considered as we reflect on Job 11: Can God forgive and extend mercy? Does repentance necessarily reverse the consequences of sin? What is the right kind of criticism? How should we respond to criticism?

11:1–6 Zophar's Rebuke of Job's Words

Zophar's opening statement seemed to affirm that Job's questions and arguments needed to be heard and to intimate that Job should be vindicated (11:1–2). Then, suddenly, the mood changed as Zophar began to accuse Job of mocking others and claiming to be pure and blameless (11:3–4). Zophar wished (almost demanding) that God would speak and reveal the "secrets of wisdom" – which has two sides to it – to Job (11:5–6). The "secrets of wisdom" probably refer to the "unrevealed dimensions of wisdom – divine mystery. Those are the aspects of wisdom ultimately inaccessible to mortals even when they probe (28:11–13)."[57] As to wisdom having two sides, Walton explains that "competent, responsible thinking has to consider the other side of the equation."[58] The intended outcome is that Job might also realize how God had "forgotten" or forgiven some of his sins,[59] so that "his punishment is less than his guilt deserves."[60]

Zophar entered the dialogue assuming that Job must have sinned. This wrong assumption clouded his judgment, and so it bothered him whenever Job claimed to be blameless or upright. If assumptions are not first tested and validated, both the process of inquiry and its results are often disastrous.

11:7–12 Zophar's Respect for God's Wisdom

Zophar continued speaking about God's wisdom, describing it as unfathomable and limitless, and questioning Job's ability to attain this wisdom (11:7). Through a figure of speech known as "merism,"[61] Zophar described God's wisdom as being "higher than the heavens," "deeper than the depths below" – that

---

57. Seow, *Job 1–21*, 600.
58. Walton, *Job*, 176.
59. In the MT, the particle "mem" on the noun *'avon* (literally, "sin") allows for the rendering, "overlook some of your sins." The *mem* is functioning as a partitive. See Williams, *Hebrew Syntax*, 56.
60. Belcher, *Finding Favor*, 94.
61. Merism states opposite ends – beginning and end to represent a whole spectrum or all of the contents of a thing.

is, lower than *Sheol* – "longer than the earth," and "wider than the sea" (11:8–9). Thus, should God decide to imprison someone or summon an assembly for a court hearing, no one could stop him (11:10). Zophar added that God, knowing the deceitfulness of human beings, would recognize evil immediately (11:11). Therefore, if Job thought that he was innocent, he was mistaken. Even before Job became aware of it, God would have recognized Job's sin.

This section concludes with Zophar's enigmatic statement that the witless cannot become wise any more than the colt of a wild donkey could be born as a human being (11:12). Zophar's use of this proverb was insulting, and might even be termed a verbal abuse. This proverb cites an impossibility that defies both common sense and the law of nature that tells us that living beings only give birth to their own kind. By this, Zophar meant that human beings – and that included Job – could never attain the wisdom of God and that it is impossible and ridiculous to hope to do so!

Having accused Job of mockery (11:3) and of being a deceiver (11:11), Zophar then committed another blunder by coining the name "witless" for Job (11:12). Whether we realize it or not, name-calling causes emotional damage to the recipient. Children who have been subject to name-calling may be adversely impacted in the way they think and feel about themselves well into adulthood. To be called "witless," especially in the presence of his other friends, must have been hurtful for Job.

Zophar was rude, crude, and insensitive in his criticism. He is a perfect example of someone who uses words to abuse others. Arrogant people often try to intimidate others by putting them down and speaking condescendingly to them. Zophar was using sarcasm when he said that he wanted God to answer Job and show him how ignorant he was. Zophar insinuated that Job was just too stupid to understand that God was just, and that Job's suffering was God's discipline because of the "evil" that God saw in Job. Zophar's view of Job was entirely negative.

In shame and honor cultures – such as those found in Southeast Asia – being called "witless" causes loss of face. "Losing face" means a loss of dignity, respect, trust, social standing. Depending on the status of the person and the cause and extent of the loss of face, the adverse effects could range from mild to colossal. The shame that recipients think they have brought on themselves, and especially on their family and clan, may pressure them to do something to restore the lost honor and dignity. It may lead to attempts to get even or, in some cases, even to take their own life. As believers, we must be extremely careful in our use of words and actions as we relate with others.

11:13–20 Zophar's Request for Job's Repentance

Without even assessing the impact of his harsh words (11:1–12), Zophar turned from attacking Job to counseling him. He proceeded to offer a solution to Job's problems, enumerating some steps by which Job could reverse his current situation (11:13–14), and then described the blessings that would follow if Job followed these steps (11:15–19).

Zophar emphasized that Job needed to turn to God in prayer, turn away from sin, and eliminate any evil from his household (11:13–14). Then, forgiven, he would be able to lift up his face without shame or fear, get on with his life and be established once more (11:15), and his pain and suffering would be no more than a vague memory (11:16). Whatever "darkness" Job had experienced because of the calamities would be eclipsed by a brightness comparable to that of the morning (11:17). Zophar suggested that Job would be able to enjoy a long and prosperous life and experience security, hope, and rest (11:18). If Job would just repent, he would be able to settle down without fearing anyone or anything and, moreover, many would seek his favor (11:19), which suggests that the social standing Job had lost would be restored.

The Bible records several instances where a person sinned and suffered immediate and severe punishment from God. For instance, when Achan violated God's ban (Josh 6:17–19) by stealing a robe, gold, and silver, God instructed that he and his family be stoned to death (Josh 7:24–26). The case of King David, however, is different. While David committed adultery and murder, which were deserving of capital punishment (1 Sam 11), God forgave him and spared his life, although he still had to bear the consequences of his sins (2 Sam 12:1–20). Similarly, when the people of Nineveh repented, God forgave them and did not destroy the city as he had indicated to Jonah (Jonah 1:1–2; 3:10).

Zophar then briefly spelled out the consequences of Job not following the proposed steps: "But the eyes of the wicked will fail, and escape will elude them; their hope will become a dying gasp" (11:20). There is emblematic parallelism here, where the second line explains the meaning of the first line. The wicked would fail and not be able to escape; they could only expect and hope for death. In effect, if Job repented, he would have a long and fruitful life, but if he continued in sin, he could expect only death.

Zophar made another false assumption. Building on his previous assumption that Job had sinned, he argued that the only way for Job to be restored to his former life was to repent of the sins he had committed in the past, prior to the calamities. Zophar offered a quick fix to the assumed sin of Job, which even Job did not believe he committed.

Job, if he had complied with Zophar's suggestion and made a confession of sin in order that he might be restored, would have had to (a) confess to sins that did not exist; (b) sin by lying since he was admitting to sins, he had not committed; and (c) lose his integrity by lying for the sake of gaining prosperity.

Zophar rebuked Job for claiming to be pure and blameless, and wished that God himself would speak and reveal his unfathomable wisdom to Job. He then counseled Job to repent, proposing a quick-fix solution that would enable Job to end his sufferings and once more experience security and hope for a brighter future. This chapter emphasizes several attributes of God, including his omniscience, his unfathomable wisdom that cannot be attained by human beings (11:7–9), and his sovereignty to do as he wishes (11:10). God knows the sins of the wicked (11:11), and he punishes them. But God also forgives the sins of those who repent, and he may reverse calamity and grant blessings (11:15, 19).

Like Eliphaz and Bildad, Zophar failed to recognize that sin is not the only reason for pain and suffering, and he, too, started with the wrong premise that Job had sinned. They also thought that Job was proud because he refused to admit to his sin.

CRITICISM: SUBJECTIVE AND OBJECTIVE

Careless criticism may cause someone to lose face. Even well-intended criticism can have the same effect if done inappropriately – at the wrong time, in a wrong environment, or to the wrong person.

Constructive criticism, which considers the merits and demerits of something or someone and judges, accordingly, is a constructive evaluation of a situation or person. The validity and value of criticism depends on the integrity and knowledge – or lack of these qualities – in the one making the criticism. Our aim should always be to give constructive criticism that encourages and builds up rather than tears down.

Anyone can be a critic. Any believer can find fault with another believer. But this is not the Christian way of life. A suspicious type of criticism is not helpful and, indeed, is harmful to any relationship. Subjective emotional criticism often judges based on suspicion and doubt, before all the facts are gathered. In contrast, objective criticism is based on facts.

> While criticism itself is not necessarily a sin, wrong motives make it sinful. A critical nature is often a sign of dissatisfaction and spiritual problems. Such a disposition needs the application of the principles of contentment, appreciation, thankfulness, a willingness to forgive, and confidence in God's plan for one's life.
>
> When we are faced with unfair, suspicious, or angry criticism, the best response is often to remain silent and let some time pass as we place the matter in the Lord's hands. We should take time to evaluate the criticism. If there is any truth to it, we must take action that leads to life transformation. If the criticism is false, the best way to disprove the criticism is often by right living.

12:1–14:22 Job's Response to Zophar

Job had an opportunity to respond to Zophar's scathing attack and accusations. Chapter 12 gives some preliminary answers to these questions: What do God's activities reveal about God himself? What can be known about God through his creations?

12:1–6 Job Argued His Own Case

Job was not only responding to Zophar but also to his other friends (since the pronoun "you" in the Hebrew text is plural). Job addressed them as people who were significant to him and full of wisdom (12:2).

Perhaps Job's friends were like the "council of elders" found among indigenous people groups in Southeast Asia. On account of their age, experience, and wisdom, such groups enjoy the respect of the community. Since they are the guardians of the "customary laws" that are still in place,[62] they are often consulted on these matters. Perhaps the customary laws among these people groups are similar to the collection of wise sayings and teachings that Job's friends often referred to.

Job's initial response to Zophar was disdainful of his friends' wisdom. He maintained that he, like them, also had a mind that could understand and was not inferior to them in any way (12:3). By saying this, Job implied that they should not be so arrogant as to claim the right to sit in judgment on him. Besides, their advice on the issues at hand was common knowledge.

Job tried to respond to his friends who each brought different perspectives to the conversation. Kaiser observes: "Eliphaz had used his dream as his basis

---

62. See the work of C. R. Moss, "Nabaloi Law and Ritual," *American Archaeology and Ethnology*, 15, no. 3 (1920): 237.

for authority but how was Job to refute someone else's dream? Bildad had appealed to what the forefathers taught from their experience, but they were no longer alive, so how could Job answer them? Zophar had chosen to focus on the irrefutable wisdom of God, so how was Job to debate a point with which he agreed in principle anyway?"[63]

Job might have been refuting Zophar's earlier statements (see 11:5–6) when he affirmed, "I called on God and he answered" (12:4b). Sadly, God was not currently speaking to Job, and his silence contributed to Job's present distressing situation. By using the word "laughingstock" (*sekhoq*) twice in the same sentence, Job emphasized how he had become an object of derision to his friends (12:4).

It is likely that the friends were indeed mocking Job because while he claimed to be innocent, the evidence showed that he was suffering. The only conclusion they could come up with was that Job must have sinned. Their question remained unanswered: If Job did indeed have intimate knowledge of God, as he claimed, why had God not done anything tangible to deliver him from his sufferings?

Job observed that it was those who were not experiencing tragedy who showed contempt for the misfortune of others.[64] Underlying the mockery was the belief that those experiencing misfortune must have sinned and, therefore, deserved what came to them. It is no wonder that the friends dished out apathy instead of compassion for Job. Hartley says that those who ridicule Job "strike a mighty blow against him whose feet are slipping"(12:5).[65]

Job's physical, mental, and emotional condition should have evoked pity and compassion from any God-fearing person. But his friends seemed heartless. During the writing of this book, Russia attacked Ukraine. Regardless of our political leanings, does hearing and seeing reports of young soldiers and civilians dying, and of women leaving homes and loved ones behind and fleeing with their small children to become refugees, break our hearts? Do we "mourn with those who mourn" (Rom 12:15b)?

---

63. Kaiser, *Majesty of God*, 82–83.
64. Scholars recognize the difficulty in this verse starting with the word *lappid*, meaning "torch," "lightning." See *HALOT*, s.v. "lappid." In relation to Job 12:5, Koopmans' comment is helpful. He suggests that the word is likely from *pid*, meaning *ruin* so the lamed (*l*) is a preposition. See William T. Koopman, "lappid," NIDOTTE 2:809. Additional meanings include disaster, misfortune, fate. See *HALOT*, s.v. "pid."
65. Hartley, *Job*, 207. A slipping of feet refers to one who is on the verge stumbling or losing faith in the living God on account of the challenges he/she is facing in life. See Psalms 73:2; 94:18–19.

Job also observed that the houses of robbers[66] were tranquil and undisturbed and that those who continued to provoke God enjoyed the security of being led by God's hand or being safe in God's hand (12:6).[67] Job was not referring to ordinary robbers but to professional thieves.[68] Such people do not fear being robbed but remain secure and undisturbed in their homes despite having provoked God by their wickedness. Job seemed to be grappling with the injustice of his own situation, for he was suffering loss of home and security even though he was innocent. This illustration also highlights the flaws in the conventional view of retributive justice. Job, far from being "witless" as Zophar had suggested (11:12), pointed out the obvious: If professional evildoers could experience peace and security, then it is also possible that the righteous and blameless may go through unexplainable pain and suffering.

Job's observation and realization has been the experience of many believers through the centuries, and Christians must acknowledge, and perhaps even embrace, this reality. If Zophar truly believed what he taught – that "true wisdom has two sides" (11:6) – he should have listened to Job's learnings through the experience of his pain and suffering.

12:7–13 Job Pointed to the Basic Truths of God's Greatness

Job instructed his friends to learn about God by turning their attention to God's creation – the animals and birds (12:7), the plants of the earth, and the fish of the sea (12:8). Job pointed to creation for two reasons. First, even these creatures know that it was the power of Yahweh that had "done this" (12:9) – where "this" might refer either to what God had accomplished in creation or to the sum total of everything that had been inflicted on Job. Second, the life of every creature, including the entire human race, is in God's hand, and he is the one who sustains life in all he has created (12:10). More important, people[69] have the inherent capacity to discern and choose what they will and will not accept (12:11). And it is expected that wisdom is to be found among the aged

---

66. Eliphaz used the same term for people of the same profession in 15:21 and suggested that these people attack a wicked person just when he thought everything was at peace and he was living securely.
67. The *NET* Bible has "who carry their god in their hands." The NIV has "those God has in his hands" with the footnote "or those whose god is in their own hand." Alter translates the verse as: "whom God has led by the hand," Writings, 495. Likewise, Seow has "whom God has led by his hand," *Job 1–21*, 632.
68. This participle, *shodedim*, is functioning as a noun, hence a profession.
69. By synecdoche: a part for the whole, where ears that examine words and the palate that tastes food could represent God's creations, particularly human beings.

since a long life brings better understanding (12:12) both about human affairs and about God. Ultimately, "wisdom and power; counsel and understanding" belong to God (12:13). Therefore, neither Job nor his three friends nor even the council of elders have a monopoly on wisdom.

THE CONTRASTING ACTIVITIES OF GOD

Job presented some contrasting activities of God in relation to his creation, along with the corresponding results or effects of these actions. While verses 14–15 center on God's control over inanimate objects, verses 16–24 zero in on God's control over individuals – particularly leaders and judges, and also the nations and their leaders. Participles are used to describe the activities of God and the object of these activities.[1]

In the list below, opposite concepts (and results of God's actions) are in italics, while similar concepts are underlined.

> What he *tears down – cannot be rebuilt*
> Those he *imprisons – cannot be released* (12:14)
> He *holds back the waters – there is drought* (12:15)
> He leads rulers away stripped – makes fools of judges (12:17)
> He *takes off* the shackles – and *ties* a loincloth around their waist (12:18)
> He leads priests away stripped – overthrows officials long established (12:19)
> He silences the lips of trusted advisers – takes away discernment of elders (12:20)
> He pours contempt on nobles – disarms the mighty (12:21)
> He reveals the deep things of darkness – brings utter darkness into the light (12:22)
> He *makes nations great – he destroys them*
> He *enlarges nations – disperses them* (12:23)
> He deprives the leaders of the earth of their reason;
>   he makes them wander in a trackless waste (12:24)
> They grope in darkness with no light;
>   he makes them stagger like drunkards (12:25)

---

[1]. This is significant because when a participle is functioning as a verb, it may indicate immediacy of the action that is in progress, which is the case in Job 12.

In these verses (12:7–9), Job argued that God's creation itself can reveal something about the Creator. Jesus might have been alluding to Job 12:7–9 when he asked his audience to consider "the birds of the air" and "the flowers of the field" and learn from them the principle of not worrying about their daily needs since the Creator himself would provide for them (Matt 6:26–32). Paul also alludes to Job 12:7–9 when explaining that what human beings need to know about God has already been revealed by God in his creation (Rom 1:20).

12:14–25 Job Affirmed that God Is Sovereign over All Humanity

As Job affirmed, all human affairs are under the sovereign control of God. Both the conqueror and the vanquished are under God's command (12:16). God controls the destinies of all people, including the council of advisers and elders (12:17–20), and he reduces the famous and powerful to nothing (12:21).

By interspersing a series of antonyms (opposite concepts) and synonyms (similar concepts) to describe God's activities in maintaining his universe, Job affirmed God's sovereignty. Wisdom can be discerned in these activities. Moreover, Job argued that there is finality in everything that God does. He also observed that in God's management of the universe, there are both positive and negative effects of his actions. From the perspective of human experience, this means that both "good" and "bad things" happen to people. These experiences coexist. As Job had earlier acknowledged, when responding to his wife's criticism, "Shall we accept good from God, and not trouble?" (2:10).

Despite recognizing God's sovereign power, Job still struggled with the question of how God could be just if Job's unjust suffering was God's will. Furthermore, if the theological system proposed by the three friends were to be strictly followed, then all good counselors, judges, kings, priests, advisers, elders, nobles, leaders, and nations would be blessed by God. But the reality is that good people do suffer and fail, and evil people do prosper. Job wanted to know why this was so.

Have you ever felt as Job did? When you are overwhelmed and confused by difficult circumstances:

- Choose to believe that the living God, who creates and sustains the universe is able to bring order into the chaos in your life.
- Hope in the living God.
- Acknowledge that there is so much in life that human beings cannot fully understand.

- Entrust your life and future to the living God. He sees the whole picture and is aware of everything that is happening, including the tensions within you.

The main point that this chapter reveals about God is that he is the omnipotent Creator who has the right and power to do anything with his creations: to destroy and to rebuild, and even to withdraw discernment from the wise and to reveal what is carefully concealed (12:14, 20, 23).

JOB'S EMOTIONAL STATE

Job's initial response to his losses is admirable. He acknowledged that he had owned nothing when he came to this world and recognized the need to embrace both the good and the bad, the blessings and the adversities, that life brings. Once the initial shock had worn off, Job expressed his feelings in a lament, in which he said that he wished he had never been born at all. Thus began his emotional roller-coaster that spiraled downward, going through the five stages of grief identified by Kübler-Ross: *denial, anger, bargaining, depression*, and *acceptance*.[1] In Job's case, these elements did not follow a linear path but happened sporadically. But each element can be detected either in the words of Job or in some of the descriptions given by his friends.

When Job next spoke, he revealed what was in his heart. His lament expressed *anger* and frustration when he cursed the day he was born (3:1–16). He was *depressed* and did enjoy a sense of inner tranquility (3:24–26). He was bitter (7:11–16). Whether he went through bargaining, depression, and acceptance – as modern scholars classify – is unclear. But there were times Job wanted to file a case but doubted that God would even listen to him (9:16). He was unsure of himself (9:20) and felt frustrated with his friends (27:11–12). He accused God of wrong actions against him (30:18–25). He felt isolated and lonely (30:29–30).

Job must have been deeply hurt when Zophar implied that he was "witless" (11:12). In trying moments like this, when his friends' attacks became personal, Job defended himself and refused to accept that he was inferior to them (12:1–2). This reveals self-confidence and a healthy appraisal of himself (12:4–5). Perhaps this is the point when Job started to *accept* the situation. Nevertheless, he went through an emotional roller-coaster of hope (14:7–9; 13–17) and despair (14:18–22).

When Job realized that his friends were "miserable comforters" (16:2) who could not help him, he looked past his situation and asked God for an advocate who would speak for and defend him (16:19–21). If there was someone who could help him, that person had to be from heaven. But Job's ultimate hope was to meet his "redeemer," the living God, face-to-face – that is, to experience him personally (19:20–27). As his self-confidence grew, Job enjoyed greater clarity about his situation. His friends claimed to speak from conventional wisdom, whereas Job argued, correctly, that the reverential fear of Yahweh is itself wisdom (28:28). Job's assessment of himself and his situation in his final defense (29–31) shows that he had made good progress in processing everything that had happened to him. Right to the end, he refuted his friends' accusations and was steadfast in maintaining that he was not conscious of any hidden sin that could explain his suffering.

Like all people, Job also went through pain and suffering – although his suffering was more extreme due to the unusual situation of the dispute between God and *Satan*. Job's body bore the psychosomatic effects of his pain and suffering. Many of his physical experiences are described: sighing and restlessness (3:24–26), insomnia (7:4), inability to catch his breath (9:18), gauntness (16:8), dark shadows under his eyes due to lack of sleep (16:16), "eyes growing dim with grief" (17:7), bad breath (19:17), emaciation (19:20), trembling of the limbs (21:6), and fever (30:30).

In spite of his bad health and constant pain, Job's attitude became more positive as he requested an advocate. His desire for vindication and his ultimate hope of meeting God face-to-face sustained him as he continued to process what had happened in his life. These two factors resulted in a solution to his problem, though perhaps not in the way Job imagined. Elihu entered the scene to serve as Job's advocate. Finally, Job had an encounter with Yahweh, and this experience caused him to realize there is so much more that he needed to know about Yahweh's character, works, and the management of his universe (38–41).

---

1. Elizabeth Kübler-Ross, *On Death and Dying: What the Dying Have to Teach Doctors, Nurses, Clergy & Their Own Families* (New York: Scribner, 1969), ix.

13:1–12 Job's Straight Talk for Dunghill Advisers

Job accused his friends of being worthless advisers. He claimed that he himself had seen, heard, and understood everything about the issues at hand (13:1). He reiterated that he was not inferior to any of them because he also knew what they knew (13:2). Therefore, Job had decided to "argue" (*yakhakh*) his case before God Almighty (13:3). This Hebrew term is used twice in this chapter, albeit having different meanings. In verse 3, it means to "argue a case," whereas in verse 10, it can mean "to chastise" or "reprove." The NIV has "call you to account." Job accused his friends of fabricating lies and being "worthless physicians" (13:4) and suggested that it would have been wiser for them to have remained "altogether silent" (13: 4–5) so he could present his case.

Although Job called his friends' names in this way, he focused on their actions rather than on the core of their being. He accused them of being fabricators of lies because their accusations were false; he labeled them "worthless physicians" because their diagnoses were wrong and, therefore, rejected their prescriptions. Not only had their efforts to comfort Job and bring him relief failed, but they had also added to his mental and emotional stress.

We do not have all the answers to life's questions and problems. But, as believers in the living God, we do know the answers to some vital questions: Who am I? Why am I here? Where am I going? Those who do not have a personal relationship with God go through life without having a clue as to what life is really about. May the Lord use us to point people, especially those who are in pain, to Jesus Christ, who is the way, the truth, and the life (John 14:6).

Job repeated his request to his friends to pay careful attention to his arguments (13:6). He also accused them of acting presumptuously by claiming to be God's messengers while speaking "wickedly" and "deceitfully" (13:7). Job asked if his friends would show God "partiality" or take his side while desiring to "argue [*rib*] the case for God" (13:8). Introducing a slight twist in his interrogation, Job then presented a hypothetical situation: If God were to cross-examine them, would it turn out well or would they try to trifle with God by being deceitful as they had been in their dealings with Job (13:9)? Job gave two reasons why his friends would not be able to deceive God. First, God would definitely call them to account if they showed partiality, even in secret (13:10).[70] Second, God's sovereignty would cause them to be overwhelmed in reverential fear of God and dread of him. (13:11). By likening the "maxims" of his friends to "proverbs of ashes" and their arguments to "defenses of clay" (13:12), Job was saying that his friends' counsel did not carry weight and were faulty and without impact. "Job chides his counselors for being elders and yet so lacking in true wisdom."[71]

Job spoke honestly and openly. He assessed his friends' words and rejected their irrelevant advice. Moreover, he questioned their right to represent God to him when he knew that he himself had a relationship with God. We all

---

70. Deception, partiality, and secrecy are interrelated.
71. Smick, "The Dialogue Dispute," in *Job*.

need to stand against poor advice, especially when it goes against truth and violates our conscience.

13:13–19 Job's Ultimate Hope in God for Vindication

Job resolved to present his case before God. He firmly told his friends to "keep silent" so that he might have a turn to speak and present his case, regardless of the consequences – "let come to me what may" (13:13). It seemed that Job did not care whether he lived or died: "Why do I put myself in jeopardy and take my life in my hands?" (13:14), which Alter says "is an idiom for putting oneself in great danger."[72] Job was saying that he would be risking his life by taking his case before God. But even if God were to kill him, Job would hold on to his hope of being able to argue his case before God (13:15).[73] Since his friends had already condemned him, Job probably felt that an audience with God was his only chance of acquittal.

King David was another man who chose to be under the judgment of God rather than that of men. Toward the end of his career, David had ordered a census of the fighting men in his kingdom. When God, displeased with David's action, asked him to choose between three punishments, David admitted that he would prefer to "fall into the hands of the LORD for his mercy is great" rather than into "human hands" (2 Sam 24:14). The difference between these cases is that while there was definitely sin involved in David's case, Job's friends merely assumed that he had sinned.

On the premise that a godless person cannot approach God and live, Job believed that he could do so and still survive because he was innocent (13:16). He asked his friends to "listen carefully" to what he would say next (13:17). Job reasoned that since he had carefully prepared his case, and since he was in the right, he would be vindicated (13:18). He wondered if anyone dared to file a case (*rib*) against him. If no one took up this challenge, then Job would be vindicated. If, however, there was anyone who could disprove his innocence, Job would "be silent and die" (13:19).[74]

---

72. Alter, *Writings*, 498.
73. The *kethiv* reading in the critical apparatus of the *BHS* has *lo'* (not), but the *qere* reading along with twenty plus Medieval Hebrew manuscripts and the versions have *lô* (to him), a reference to God. The latter is what is adopted here.
74. The term *kharash* express the same meaning as *silent* in 3:11; 10:18; 13:19; 14:10; 27:5; 29:18; and 36:12.

13:20–28 Job's Demands of God

Promising to be transparent before God, Job asked God two questions (13:20–22). First, he asked God to stop terrorizing and frightening him with his overwhelming power (13:21). Second, desiring that there be open communication between himself and God, Job requested that either God "summon" him and he would "answer" or that God let Job "speak" and then "reply" to him (13:22).

Job presented his arguments in the form of a cross-examination (13:23–28), in which he accused God while also revealing how he himself felt. Job's sense of justice demanded that he be told how many wrongs and sins he had committed and be given proof of his offenses (13:23). If God could not show any evidence, this would validate Job's claim that he was innocent. Since he was experiencing God's silence, Job demanded an explanation: "Why do you hide your face?" Job felt that God was treating him as an enemy (13:24). If God could not provide an explanation, then Job might have felt that he was justified in claiming that God had terrorized him without reason. Job used the metaphor of a "windblown leaf" being "tormented" or "driven about" (*nadaf*) by the wind to describe his feeling that God had been terrorizing and "chasing" or "intently pursuing" (*radaf*) him (13:25). Job seemed to have used a play on words – two words that are similar except for the first letter – to emphasize how he felt. Both leaves and straw are light and considered insignificant.

Job asked God so many questions! It is a huge relief for believers who are going through unexplainable suffering to be able to do this and to know that it is alright to ask God questions. God will not be surprised or angry. Perhaps the only parameter is that we guard our hearts so that our questions do not cause us to lose faith but, rather, lead us to a deeper and more meaningful experience of the Lord.

Without even waiting for God's response, Job claimed that God was bringing "bitter things" – that is, strong complaints – against him and formally writing down (*kathav*)[75] these charges, making Job pay for the sins of his youth (13:26). Job never claimed that he was perfect or sinless. "He only maintains that he has committed no such grievous sins as could justify his exceptional

---

75. This is the first time that the term *written* (*kathav*) is used in this book (compare 19:23 and 31:35). The text in 31:35 is significant in that Job wished his accuser wrote down his indictments on a scroll.

suffering. Here he sarcastically suggests that his misfortunes must be a belated requital of the long-forgotten sins of his youth."[76]

The theology of cause-and-effect is again evident here. Job, too, thought that God was holding every past sin or mistake against him and demanding retribution for these wrongdoings. When things go wrong in your life, do you immediately relate them to something from your past, some sin that you committed a long time ago? Did God not forgive you that sin through Christ? Even today, believers are sometimes tempted to think of God as an inconsistent tyrant who keeps bringing up the past simply in order to punish his followers. Nothing could be more insulting to a gracious and loving God!

Sometimes, we may feel as if the wrongdoings that we have confessed are coming back to haunt us. In such situations, taking the following steps may be helpful:

- Choose to believe that God is forgiving.
- Acknowledge the specific sin.
- Repent: Confess and commit not to repeat the sin.
- Ask the Holy Spirit to take control of your life once again.
- Continuously renew your mind by meditating on truths about God.
- Remember that while it is true that God forgives, you may have to bear the consequences of sins you have committed.
- Should Satan keep on reminding you of a particular sin that you know you have already confessed and repented of, take a stand by reminding yourself that God has forgiven that sin.

Job saw himself as being imprisoned, with his feet "in shackles," and devoid of any freedom since God controlled his every step (13:27). Heavily burdened by the weight of all his pain and suffering, Job equated himself to "something rotten, like a garment eaten by moths," signifying his wasting away and ultimate demise (13:28).

To his credit, Job exhibited courageous faith by his total abandonment to God and his determination to trust God and present his case to the Almighty regardless of the outcome. Similarly, in Psalm 44, the psalmist made bold requests of God when God's people were going through a time of great shame and pain (Ps 44:9–16) despite the fact that they had not rejected God, disobeyed

---

76. Rowley, *Book of Job*, 102.

his commands, or been unfaithful (44:17–18). The psalmist argues that the Lord would have known if the nation had rejected him and worshiped other gods (44:20–21) and pleads with God to "awake" and "rise up" and "rescue" his people because of his "unfailing love" (44:23–26).

Here we have a good example of what we can do when we feel wrongly and unfairly treated and could find no help elsewhere. Like Job, we can present our case before God and express fully how we feel about everything, asking him to show us if and how we have sinned against him. Of course, we should do this humbly and reverently, with an honest and open mind, prepared to listen and respond appropriately to what God tells us. He is in control and will hear us when we call upon him.

At this juncture in the discourse, we find that Job was exasperated and agitated because he was not sinful or inferior to any of his friends. So, he retaliated, calling them fabricators of lies and worthless physicians who spoke injustice on behalf of God. Further, Job felt unfairly treated and rejected by God, imprisoned and trapped in his situation with no way out. He compared himself to a dry chaff being blown about by the wind or to a rotten, torn, and worn-out garment that was ravaged by moths. He felt as if he had lost control and was being tossed about on the whims of others. His words convey feelings of insignificance, emotional exhaustion, and burnout.

Job continued to meditate on the deeper matters of life and death, intermittently sharing his thoughts and complaints with God. Contemplating death and the afterlife, Job's mood became more negative, torn between the certainty of imminent death and the uncertainty of what comes afterward. As we reflect on Job 14, we will consider the following questions: What happens at death? Where does a person go after death? Is there consciousness after death? How are the vestigial beliefs about death and the afterlife explained in an Asian tribal context?

14:1–12 The Absurdity of Life, the Certainty of Death

Job waited; but Yahweh did not meet with him. If Yahweh would not appear for the court hearing, how could Job present his case? As hopelessness set in, Job began to reflect on the brevity of life and the certainty of death.

14:1–6 Life is brief

The length of a person's life has been predetermined by God, and Job observed that life was both short and full of trouble (14:1; compare 7:1–2). Using two figures of speech,[77] he likened life to a flower that springs up and then withers, as well as to a shadow that appears and is quickly gone (14:2). So is life! Considering the brevity of life, Job wondered why he would merit so much of God's attention that the Lord would file a case against him (14:3). Job reasoned that no one can produce something pure or clean from something that is impure or unclean (14:4), meaning that no human being is without sin. He added that God knows the length of a person's life because he himself determined its limit and that no one can live beyond the time frame ordained by God (14:5). Therefore, Job implored God to stop watching him and just leave him alone "until he has put in his time as a hired laborer" (14:6). If there is a time limit to the work hours of a laborer to the completion of his task, Job wanted God to just let him complete his.

Pain and suffering tend to make us think more seriously about the brevity and meaning of life. And if ever there was an event during the last 60 years that prompted the whole world to pause and do just that, it was COVID-19. This pandemic leveled the playing field for everyone. Most of us know someone whose life was snuffed out by COVID-19. When this pandemic comes to an end, may our lives continue to be aligned to the purpose for which our God allowed us to survive it.

14:7–12 Death is certain

Using different terms for death and likewise using the imagery related to a tree and to water, Job spoke of the certainty of life in a plant compared to his own life, which he considered futile. A tree dies of old age or, when it is cut down, it leaves behind progeny. In Job's case, however, all his children had died, and he was without any progeny (14:7–10). Just as water evaporates from a lake or river, leaving the riverbed parched and dry, Job's life had come to an end without any progeny (14:11). Job reiterated his point that a person who sleeps and does not wake up or rise is dead (14:12). There is complete cessation of life – no more waking and rising up for that person.

There was a clear change in Job's mood. He grew very pessimistic again, seeing life as brief and fleeting, against the certainty of death. Job asked, "What's it all about?" Life just seemed futile while death could visit anytime.

When death looms on the horizon, it is helpful to give serious consideration to these points:

---

77. A simile – a figure of speech that compares and usually accompanied by the word *like*.

- Death is certain, and it will happen to everyone without exception.
- Jesus offered a glimpse into life after death (see Luke 16:22–26). He taught that after this life, there are only two places for people to go: the presence of God (Abraham's side) or the place of torment (Hades). Moreover, there is no in-between place and no one can cross over from one place to the other.
- The decision on where you are going after this life must be made here and now. To wait until you die is too late (1 John 5:11–13).
- Our only hope, and the solution to the predicament brought about by death, is Jesus Christ, who is the way, the truth, and the life (John 3:16–18; 14:6; Acts 16:31; 2 Tim 2:5), as well as the resurrection and the life (John 11:25).
- Plan to invest the remaining years of your life in doing what is true, just, right, and of eternal significance.
- Setting your house in order may include making your last will and testament, leaving instructions about where you want to be buried, how you want your funeral service to be handled, and other essential details. This can spare your family much unnecessary strife when the time comes.

Job wrestled with the issue of death. Smick reminds us that "a key factor remains a mystery to Job – the presence of power, albeit limited of the Accuser who understandably is not mentioned at all in the Dialogue. In 14:7–22 Job turns again to death as the only way out of his impasse."[78] Following this line of thought, was *Satan* somehow involved in those times when Job sank deeper into depression and contemplated death?

Believers must not discount the spiritual battle that they are plunged into because they belong to God. The enemy, like a roaring lion, is looking for someone to devour, hence Peter's counsel to stand firm in the faith (1 Pet 5:8–9). Paul, too, commands believers to "put on the full armor of God, so that you can take your stand against the devil's schemes" (Eph 6:11). And we do well to remember this promise: "But the Lord is faithful, and he will strengthen you and protect you from the evil one" (2 Thess 3:3).

---

78. Smick, "The Dialogue Dispute," in *Job*.

14:13–22 A Spark of Hope

Job prayed that God would "hide" him in *Sheol* until his wrath had subsided.[79] Until this point, Job had spoken of death as leaving the earth and going to *Sheol*. But here, however, the implication is that God would prescribe a limit to his stay in *Sheol*, after which God would "remember" him (14:13).

Job ventured to ask whether a person who had died would "change," meaning live again. If that were the case, he would endure his plight in life until he was granted "renewal," "relief," or "change" (*khalifa*) that comes at the end of a period of hardship (14:14).[80] The "change" referred to life from this earth to another resurrected life.

Walton, however, understand "change" in a court system, and explain that "in 14:14, Job is hoping that his turn for the court hearing will come."[81] Similarly, others understand this term to mean "*relief* from military service."[82] Most likely, however, Job was referring to his death, where everything would "change" – which captures the root meaning of the word *khalifa*. Bullinger translates this verse as follows: "I wait, till my change come," that is, "till I die: dying being one of the many changes experienced by men."[83]

Job raised important questions about the unknown: When someone dies, will they live again? What happens at and after death? Up to that point in time, people believed that everyone who died, whether righteous or not, went to *Sheol*, the place of the dead.[84] But Job believed that he would live again after his earthly life. It is not far-fetched to say that Job's primary hope was immediate vindication at his court hearing, whenever this happened, while a secondary hope was that death would satisfy his longing for rest.

Job was hopeful that he would be vindicated, claiming that when the appropriate time came, God would summon him for the court proceedings. He described here the first element involved in pursuing a lawsuit – a summons to the offending party.[85] There seems to be a reversal in the format here. Job believed that it was God who had offended him, yet he wanted God to be the one issuing a summons on Job. One reason for this might have been that Job

---

79. The NIV translates *Sheol* as "grave."
80. *Khalifa* can mean changing (like a set of clothes, Judg 14:13, 19 or behavior Ps 55:19) or renewal (NIV) or relief (my translation) (14:14) See Seow, *Job 1–21*, 677.
81. Walton, *Job*, 179.
82. See BDB, s.v. "khalifa."
83. Bullinger, *Figures of Speech*, 621.
84. Refer to Job 7, *Sheol and the Afterlife*.
85. Review Soulen, *Handbook of Biblical Criticism*, 170.

still believed that God continuously longed for his creations, in particular, for Job (14:15).

In verses 16–17, Job presented two scenarios: first, that God would very carefully "count"[86] Job's every step (14:16a) and second, that in the future, God would "not keep track" of Job's every sin (14:16b) since these sins would be "sealed up in a bag" and covered by God (14:17). To seal up sins in a bag means that "God would finally relent, any accusation against Job . . . in effect, expunged from the legal record."[87] God would completely forgive Job, which recalls the psalmist's words: "As far as the east is from the west, so far has he removed our transgressions from us" (Ps 103:12).

Job ended his speech by returning to the melancholy and despair of one who suffers. His pain was eroding his body and washing away his hope for vindication. He likened the destruction of hope to the displacement (*nafal*) of mountains and rocks, the wearing away (*shakhaq*) of stones by water, and the erosion (*shataf*) of soil (14:18–19). What connects these three images is the gradual and then absolute destruction of features that were once markers of stability, strength, and hope. The earlier ray of hope was soon destroyed because God had continuously prevailed until the person simply died.[88] The reference to God altering the person's appearance[89] (14:20) describes death and postmortem or what happens after death, which includes the decomposition of the body. And once a person died, there was no way for the deceased to know if his children would be successful in life or not (14:21). As to the dying person, "nothing matters anymore but the pain of his body and the continual mourning of his soul" (14:22).[90]

In this final speech after the first round of debates, Job refuted his friends' accusations, affirmed God's sovereignty over all his creations, and prepared to present his case before God. He is portrayed as falling into depression and despair, then summoning up a spark of hope, only to give in once more to hopeless distress as he felt his life slipping away. Will Job receive any hope and encouragement from the next round of counseling?

---

86. Literally, "numbering."
87. Alter, *Writings*, 501.
88. *Shelah* can mean "irrevocable disappearance of the man who dies" Alter, *Writings*, 502.
89. Or "his face," or "his countenance."
90. Smick, "The Dialogue Dispute," in *Job*.

15:1–21:34 THE SECOND CYCLE OF SPEECHES

There are three cycles of speeches in the disputation or dialogue section of the book of Job. We have just completed the first cycle, in which we have the speeches of Eliphaz, Bildad, and Zophar, each followed by either two or three chapters that contain Job's response (4–14).

First Cycle	
Eliphaz	4–5
Job's response	6–7
Bildad	8
Job's response	9–10
Zophar	11
Job's response	12–14

We move now into the second cycle of speeches (15–21). In this cycle, Job's response to Bildad and Zophar is just one chapter, while his response to Eliphaz takes up two chapters.

Second Cycle	
Eliphaz	15
Job's response	16–17
Bildad	18
Job's response	19
Zophar	20
Job's response	21

In this second round of speeches (15–21), Eliphaz, Bildad, and Zophar offered little that was new to the debate. They held fast to their flawed doctrine that all suffering is the result of some former or hidden sin in a person's life. One can almost picture the three friends circling Job like a lion that waits for a chance to pounce on its prey. If Job's sufferings were not the result of God's punishment of sin, this would mean that the friends' theological premise was flawed and that their theology was wrong. The friends might also have secretly feared that if the obedience of the greatest man in the East had not guaranteed prosperity and protection, health and wealth, then they, too, might one day suffer just like Job, which was an unthinkable idea!

After the first cycle of speeches, one would have expected the friends to pause and reflect on what they had said to Job. Yet, despite hearing Job's testimony, they were busy outlining their countercharges and failed to hear Job's cry for help or even feel his pain. Job's losses, especially the deaths of his children, did not elicit even an ounce of compassion from them. None of their speeches conveyed any empathy.

As with the first cycle, Eliphaz initiated the second cycle of speeches, which follow the same format, with the friends speaking and Job responding to each one in turn. Although the speeches are shorter than those in the first cycle, each of the so-called friends became more vicious in their attack on Job, focusing on the prospects and future that lay in store for the wicked.[91]

Eliphaz ridiculed Job's wisdom and, like Bildad had done before, appealed to the wisdom of others as he repeated his main thesis: Suffering comes to the wicked and, therefore, Job must be wicked (15:1–35). Job responded to Eliphaz by reproaching his friends and calling them "miserable comforters." He continued to view his suffering as an attack by God for reasons he did not know. As he resumed his complaint, crying out for relief, he wished there was someone who could plead his case. In the absence of wise and meaningful counsel from his friends, Job was losing hope for anything in this life but death (16:1–17:16).

15:1–35 Eliphaz Speaks

Chapter 15 prompts the reader to consider the following questions: What constitutes blasphemy against God Almighty? What is the unpardonable sin? Is it possible for present-day believers to commit this sin?

15:1–16 Rebuke of Job's Attitude

15:1–6 Job's impious speech

While Eliphaz's first speech was delivered diplomatically, this second speech was blunt and biting. Possibly slighted by Job's refusal to admit any sin and his seeming pride, Eliphaz questioned whether Job was really wise. He began by describing what, in his opinion, characterized a wise person. First, the wise do not respond with knowledge devoid of content nor do they "fill their belly with the hot cast wind"[92] (15:2) – that is, they do not accumulate and spew

---

91. Kaiser, *Majesty of God*, 97–98.
92. Hot wind is often referred to in the Bible as a fierce, hot, and dry wind, capable of uprooting a full-grown tree (Ezek 17:10) and even carrying away people (Job 27:21). This wind comes

out destructive words. Second, the wise do not argue with empty and worthless speech (15:3). At this point, Eliphaz became personal, using the pronoun "you" (masculine, singular), and concluded that Job had gone against conventions by undermining or nullifying reverence and hindering or restraining devotion to God (15:4) and adopting the language of crafty people (15:5). Eliphaz asserted that since Job's speech had become misleading and destructive, it was not he (Eliphaz) who condemned Job but, rather, that Job condemned himself (15:6).[93] "Job's staunch defense of his own integrity as well as his challenge to God is taken by Eliphaz as clear evidence that he is an impious liar."[94]

While Eliphaz's expectations of a wise person in relation to speech are valid, applying these criteria to Job without also applying it to himself and his colleagues demonstrated a double standard – saying one thing but doing something else.

15:7–16 Job's pride and sin

Eliphaz began by accusing Job of thinking that he was exceptionally wise and, in particular, wiser than they were. He used rhetorical questions to emphasize that since Job was neither the first person to be born nor existed before creation (15:7), he did not belong among the sages on account of age or experience. Job did not have access to the council of God, enjoyed no monopoly on wisdom, and did not know or understood more than his friends did (15:8–9). While Job also claimed that he knew whatever his friends knew, he did not claim to be wiser than them (compare 12:3; 13:2). But Eliphaz claimed that they had age[95] on their side, which suggests that at least one of them was even older than Job's father (15:10). In short, Eliphaz was saying that since Job was younger than them, had no access to special knowledge from God, and was not as wise as he had claimed to be, he had no right to question the wisdom of the three friends.

Eliphaz accused Job of taking for granted God's "consolations" or encouragement and the gentle words of his friends (15:11). Here, he was being presumptuous in equating God's words of encouragement with their own words in their earlier speeches.[96] Eliphaz went on to accuse Job of getting carried away by his emotions and becoming angry with them and with God

---

"specifically from the deserts of Arabia, Mesopotamia, and Babylon," Vicchio, *Book of Job*, 122.
93. The words "mouth" and "lips," when used as metaphors, stand for "words" or "speech."
94. Alter, *Writings*, 503.
95. Literally, "gray haired" and "aged."
96. "God's encouragement" is "a gentle word."

(15:12–13). Repeating a claim made in his earlier speech (compare 4:17–19), Eliphaz reaffirmed that no one can be regarded as "pure" or "righteous" (15:14). For if God could not even trust his angels[97] and if even the heavens are not pure in his sight (15:15), how much less would he trust a person who is thoroughly corrupt,[98] with a propensity to sin continuously (15:16).[99] Eliphaz's reasoning was that Job was guilty as charged because no mortal is blameless before God. The fact that Job was angry with God only confirmed Eliphaz's negative view of Job.

A cursory reading of the first cycle of discourses is anything but encouraging. Each of the friends started with a flawed assumption. Instead of testing their assumptions, they asked rhetorical questions to emphasize and impose their own definition of retributive justice on Job. They also misrepresented God to Job. In this chapter, Eliphaz equated their words with God's encouragement. Perhaps we need to pause at this point and think of the last time we counseled or offered advice to a friend in pain. Was the friend encouraged? Did we speak truth with empathy? Did our words help transform the person's life for the better? What was one thing we did or said that we can be proud of? Looking back, what did we learn from the experience? What should we not repeat the next time we have a chance to encourage someone?

15:17–35 Reminder of the Fate of the Wicked

Eliphaz had not yet finished his speech. He demanded that Job listen to him so that he could tell him what he had observed and learned from the teachings of the wise. These sages are described as those who had inherited the land before any strangers had intruded – implying that they were of pure stock and, therefore, that their teachings were unadulterated (15:17–19).

Eliphaz spoke about the terrible fate that awaited the wicked. The wicked person "suffers torment," is disturbed by "terrifying sounds," and, even in peaceful times, is attacked by marauders or professional robbers (15:20–21). He remains without hope for only death awaits him (15:22). "He wanders about for food like a vulture," living with the knowledge that judgment[100] is imminent (15:23) and with the constant pressure of distressing threats and troubles that threaten him "like a king poised for attack" (15:24). All this happens

---

97. Eliphaz reiterates a protasis statement in 4:18.
98. "Abominable and corrupt" is taken as a hendiadys.
99. Literally, "drinks iniquity like water."
100. Literally, "day of darkness."

because "he shakes his fist [*natah* + *yad* = literally, 'stretch hand'] at God"[101] – in other words, he defies or "vaunts himself against the Almighty" (15:25).

The OT uses the image of God stretching out his arm in power to create the heavens (Jer 10:12; Zech 12:1), to punish (Exod 7:4–5; Isa 5:25; 9:21), and to deliver his people (Deut 4:34; Jer 32:21). In this context, Eliphaz used the phrase "shakes his fist" (15:25) to signify a wicked person's hostility and defiance toward God. The parallel line adds that he "vaunts himself" against God, suggesting a continuous and repeated act of arrogance toward God (15:25–26), which could well be termed blasphemy.

Did Job however, actually commit the sin of blasphemy? These words (15:25–26) are merely Eliphaz's criticism of Job and do not describe Job's actions. Admittedly, Job had been brutally honest before God about how he felt and what he wanted, but, as he claimed later, he did not commit blasphemy as Eliphaz insinuated. If he had done so, God would have destroyed him. Toward the end of the book, when God revealed himself to Job, he did not accuse Job of blasphemy. On the contrary, God was angry with Eliphaz and his other friends for not speaking the truth about God (42:7–9).

It is alright to ask God questions and be transparent before him about how we feel without fear of committing blasphemy. The psalmist did so in various situations. For example, the psalmist asks, "How long?" (Ps 13:1–2), admits his depression (Ps 42:6), and blames God for the nation's defeat in battle because he thought God had not gone with them (Ps 44:9). But while we may bring all our questions to God, we must ensure that these questions are not motivated by unbelief, by the desire to pass the blame onto someone else – maybe even God – or by a stubborn unwillingness to hear the truth. If you find yourself in a situation you cannot handle, talk to God about it and seek a trusted friend to help you process your thoughts and emotions.

A related theme in the NT is "blasphemy against the Holy Spirit." Three of the Gospel writers record the incident where the teachers of the law explained Jesus's miracles by claiming that he was possessed by Beelzebul[102] and that he had an unclean spirit in him. Jesus warned his disciples that all sins and slander could be forgiven except the sin of blasphemy against the Holy Spirit, which makes a person guilty of an eternal sin (Mark 3:22–30).[103] Uytanlet argues

---

101. Dreytza explains that the metaphorical use of *yad* covers a wide range of meaning that is centered on the concept of power related to God or humankind. See Manfred Dreytza, "yad," *NIDOTTE* 2:403.
102. Literally, "Lord of flies" and a reference to Satan.
103. The parallel passages are Luke 12:10 and Matthew 12:32.

that "blasphemy against the Holy Spirit happens when a person says that the work of the spirit is the work of the devil, and in the process, calls the Holy Spirit 'Beelzebul.'"[104]

Referring to the statements of the teachers of the law, Evans explains that "their malicious misidentification of the work of the Holy Spirit as the work of Satan constitute a serious form of blasphemy for which there can be no forgiveness (3:28–29). Instead of saying, 'He has the Holy Spirit,' as they should have, they made the absurd and potentially misleading statement that 'he has an unclean spirit' (15:30)."[105] Stated another way, "it consists in either (1) willfully continuing to deny the Gospel when the Holy Spirit has made clear to you that it is true or (2) attributing the works of the Holy Spirit to the Adversary (Satan)."[106]

If you are wondering whether you have committed this unpardonable sin, that is something that only you and God can know. The very fact you are concerned about this possibility is an assurance that you are probably not guilty of this sin since this does not indicate either a persistent defiant attitude toward God or a refusal to acknowledge him in your life. If you find that the pain you are going through is nudging you toward unbelief and losing faith, there is forgiveness in Jesus Christ (Matt 9:1–8; Eph 1:7–8; Col 1:13–14; 1 John 1:9). God is compassionate and forgiving; but if we continue to rebuff his loving-kindness and refuse to trust in him, Jesus Christ's statement should serve as a stern warning and an urgent corrective to us.

Eliphaz acknowledged that while the wicked man looks robust and fat – indicative of a good life – after his "presumption in assaulting God, he is doomed to a fate of misery."[107] He will be compelled to live in a devastated town, in an uninhabited house that is destined to become rubble. He had no prospect of becoming rich since any wealth gained would not last and his properties would not prosper. Neither would such a person escape punishment for God, in his anger, would destroy him (15:27–30).

Eliphaz offered this advice to the wicked: "Let him not deceive himself by trusting what is worthless, for he will get nothing in return" (15:31). Eliphaz

---

104. Samson Uytanlet with Kiem-Kiok Kwa, *Matthew: A Pastoral and Contextual Commentary*, ABCS (Carlisle: Langham Global Library, 2017), 133.
105. Craig A. Evans, "Mark," in *Eerdmans Commentary on the Bible*, eds. James D. G. Dunn and John W. Robertson (Grand Rapids: Eerdmans, 2021), 1075.
106. David H. Stern, *Jewish New Testament Commentary* (Clarksville: Jewish New Testament Publication, 1992), 46.
107. Alter, *Writings*, 505.

compared the wicked to a plant whose branches do not flourish because they wither before their time, to a vine that has been stripped of its unripe grapes, and to an olive tree that has shed its flowers (15:32–33). What is common to all these plants? The growth and production process had been cut short just when they were showing signs of being fruitful.

Eliphaz added that the company of the godless brings no gain and that a fire would consume the homes of those who engage in bribery (15:34). Whether intended to be a literal or figurative fire, the message is that destruction awaits the wicked and their wealth. The reason for the harsh punishment is found in the next verse: "They conceive trouble and give birth to evil; their womb fashions deceit" (15:35).[108] Their purpose, plans, and actions is to do evil.

Had this chapter ended at verse 30, it would have been easier to conclude that Eliphaz was simply describing the life and demise of a wicked person in general, simply as a warning to Job. But the verses that follow indicate that Eliphaz's words were directed at Job. The similarities between Eliphaz's description of the hypothetical wicked person and the experiences of Job show that this is not a far-fetched idea (see the comparative chart below). It appears that Eliphaz had Job in mind all along when he was describing the wicked person.

In response to Job's defense (13:1–6; 17–19) this chapter is full of scathing allegations against him. Eliphaz made vicious accusations against Job, charging him with having argued with empty words without substance and claiming to be wise while he was guilty of speaking crafty and destructive words (15:1–6). He added that Job had turned against God and was corrupt and sinful (15:7–16), and he even suggested that Job had committed blasphemy by shaking his fist at the Almighty (15:25), concluding with the remark that Job should be counted among the company of godless people who conceived mischief and produced iniquity (15:34–35).

There is no question that the wicked will be punished and destroyed. The argument put forward by Eliphaz – visionary, theologian, philosopher, and leader of the group of friends – can be summarized like this: You deserve to suffer because you have sinned against God, and you are reaping what you have sown. This is the *presumptive theology* that assumes guilt based on observation, vision, dreams, or tradition. Eliphaz attacked Job, rebuking his behavior and ridiculing his wisdom. He did not affirm that Job was innocent;

---

108. The MT has "belly," but there is a figure of speech, a metonymy. Thus, "belly" is put for heart and thoughts.

instead, he claimed that Job's worthless talk and his own mouth condemned him. His accusation that Job claimed to have "a monopoly on wisdom" (15:8) while disregarding the wisdom of others was a direct reference to Job's refusal to accept the allegations of the three friends. As a result, his verdict – which was shared by the other two friends – was that Job could not be as pure and righteous as he claimed. The chart below compares the words and actions of the wicked person (as described by Eliphaz) with Job's words and actions.

The Wicked	Job
1. All his days the wicked man suffers torment (15:20a).	1. Job had said that his flesh pained him (14:22).
2. The ruthless man through all the years stored up for him (15:20b).	2. Job had spoken of his days and months being determined (7:3; 14:5).
3. Terrifying sounds fill his ears (15:21a).	3. Job may have expressed fear of sounds.
4. When all seems well, marauders attack him (15:21b).	4. The Sabeans made an attack and carted away Job's oxen and horses and killed his servants except one of them (1:13–14).
5. He despairs of escaping the realm of darkness (15:22a).	5. Job could not sleep as darkness brought no peace (7:4)
6. He is marked for the sword (15:22b).	6. Job's servants were murdered (1:15, 17).
7. He wanders about for food like a vulture. He knows the day of darkness is at hand (15:23), which he could not escape (15:30a).	7. Job believed that death was imminent (6:7) and his days or life on earth were almost over (7:6–10).
8. Distress and anguish fill him with terror; troubles overwhelm him, like a king poised to attack (15:24).	8. Job had said that God terrified him (7:14; 9:34; 3:21).
9. He will no longer be rich, and his wealth will not endure, nor will his possessions spread over the land (15:29).	9. Job had lost all of his wealth and property (Job 1:14–17).
10. Let him not deceive himself by trusting what is worthless, for he will get nothing in return. Before his time, he will wither (15:31–32a).	10. According to Eliphaz, Job was reaping what he had sown (4:8).

The Wicked	Job
11. And his branches will not flourish. He will be like a vine stripped of its unripe grapes, like an olive tree shedding its blossoms (15:32b–33).	11. Job relocated at Dung Hill after the calamities came (2:8). It can be said that like a plant, he was not flourishing at that time.
12. For the company of the godless will be barren, and fire will consume the tents of those who love bribes (15:34).	12. Job lost his children (1:18–19).
13. They conceive trouble and give birth to evil; their womb fashions deceit (15:35).	13. Job, as a wicked man, he was born to trouble (5:7).

16:1–17:16 Job's Response to Eliphaz

When Eliphaz accused Job of blasphemy against God, it only added salt to Job's emotional wound. As we reflect on Job's response in this chapter, this question will be addressed: What is a godly way to settle a grudge or conflict?

16:1–5 Job's Disgust at His Three Friends

Commenting that he had heard many similar arguments before, Job called Eliphaz and his companions "miserable comforters" (16:1–2), as indeed they were, for although they had originally come with the intention of comforting Job (2:11), they ended up contributing significantly to his misery. Commenting on verse 3, Seow observes that "Job is here quoting the friends. They are the ones who ask him if there is no end to his windy words. Job understands the friends to mean as well that his need to speak up amid his pain is born of some sickness."[109]

In his speech, Eliphaz had described what was expected of a wise person (15:2–3). Job responded – not only to Eliphaz but also to his other friends – by asking them to consider a hypothetical scenario in which their positions were reversed. If they were in his situation, Job, too, could argue as they had done, stringing words together to form impressive speeches and scornfully shaking his head at them (16:4). However, Job said that he would not do any of these things – which would have made him no different to his friends – but, instead, he would "encourage" them with words of "comfort" and hope that would

---

109. Seow, *Job 1–21*, 732. The "you" in verse 3 is 2ms, referring to Job; whereas verses 2, 4, and 5 has "you" as 2mp, referring to the friends.

bring them "relief" from their burdens (16:5). A Christian community is expected to minister to and comfort each other in times of pain and suffering.

In a contemporary Asian setting, it is often hard to follow Job's example. The natural instinct is to get even if necessary to save face and redeem lost honor or respect. However, as we allow the indwelling Holy Spirit to fill us, he gives us the strength to resist the temptation to get even with anyone (Gal 5:22–23). Moreover, we will also receive the ability to extend compassion and the wisdom to act appropriately in such a situation.

16:6–17 Job's Distress at the Hand of God

Job complained about God's mistreatment. In his previous complaints, Job had never referred to God by name but only as "he" or "you;" but here, for the first time, he addressed *El* – which is a name of God – as his assailant (16:11). Job shared that whether he spoke or refrained (*khasakh*) from speaking, his physical and mental pain could not be "relieved" (16:6). While Job had used the same word *khasakh* (relief) in verse 5, in verse 6, this term conveys a different meaning. Job accused God of having weakened him by his sufferings and pointed out that it was God who had wiped out his "entire household" (16:7). He also added that the fact that God had afflicted him was itself a witness against God (16:8).

Job compared God's angry actions against him with the way a ferocious animal attacks its prey. But here, the normal process of watching the prey, attacking it, and then feasting on it is reversed: God, in his anger, was already attacking and tearing Job apart, gnashing his teeth, and glaring at him like an adversary (16:9).

The expression "gnashes his teeth at me" (16:9) is echoed in the NT, where Luke records that the members of the Sanhedrin, upon hearing Stephen's speech concerning Jesus Christ, "were furious and gnashed their teeth at him" (Acts 7:54). In both Acts and Job, gnashing teeth at someone expresses the same emotion: extreme anger, as the action itself suggests. In Acts, it describes the fury of the Sanhedrin against Stephen; in the book of Job, it depicts Job's perception of God as harboring sustained anger against Job himself.

Having described what God had done to him, Job then described the activities of a group of people who had jeered,[110] scornfully struck, and attacked him (16:10). Job believed that it was God who had turned him over to these ungodly people (16:11).

---

110. Literally, "opened wide their mouths against him."

Prior to God's attacks, all had been well with Job. But then, God had "shattered," "seized," and "crushed" him, and set him up as a shooting target (16:12). Job accused God of mercilessly piercing Job's kidneys and allowing the bile to just spill out on the ground (16:13). The kidneys and the gall bladder are delicate internal organs; when these are damaged, other organs, and indeed the whole body, are affected.

Job also compared God's attack on him to the actions of a warrior breaching the security of a walled city and breaking through swiftly to attack (16:14). The phrase "again and again," coupled with "burst" and "rushes," expresses the speed and intensity with which God attacked Job. God's actions caused Job to sew sackcloth to cover his "skin." Then he thrust his "brow" in the dust (16:15). Job had bloodshot eyes from weeping so much and shadowy rings under his eyelids (16:16). The Hebrew term *qeren*, which the NIV translated as "brow," but which the NASB translated as "horn," usually refers to the literal horn of an animal (Gen 22:13; Ps 22:21). It is sometimes used in the OT as a symbol of strength or power (1 Sam 2:10; Jer 48:25).[111] Job used the term to signal his humiliation, loss of strength, and total abandonment to the situation. That he thrusted his "brow" in the dust (16:15) signifies defeat. These descriptions (16:15–16) present a picture of the extreme pain of a person who had not committed any sin (16:17).

Job had accused God of many things: God had emaciated him, torn him apart, hounded him, handed him over to the wicked, set him up as a shooting target, and attacked him from all sides – physically, emotionally, spiritually, and socially (16:8–16). Yet, Job continued to maintain his innocence (16:17). He "does not claim to be pure, but he does assert that his prayer has been so. His problem is not that he is wicked, as one might take Eliphaz to have claimed in his previous speech; his problem is God's hostility against the innocent."[112]

This section (16:6–17) presents the anatomy of a broken person with a broken body. Of his journey to this point, Job was able to identify the cause of his problem. From the start, its origin was spiritual in nature involving the wager by God and *Satan*; but it affected his physical, mental, and emotional faculties. In this section, Job acknowledged that God was the cause and source of his pain and suffering. He also refuted his friends' accusations, knowing that these were not true, and he refused their counsel because it was flawed.

---

111. *HALOT*, s.v. "qeren."
112. Seow, *Job 1–21*, 737.

As for God, Job seemed to focus only on the negative aspects, forgetting God's gracious attributes and the blessings Job had experienced in earlier years.

16:18–22 Job's Desire for an Intercessor

Job appealed to two types of witnesses: the "earth," which was an inanimate witness, and a divine witness from heaven. Addressing the earth, Job requested that it not cover his blood or muffle his cries for justice (16:18). In the OT, it was common to call on "the heavens and the earth" as witnesses to agreements, as was done in relation to the formulation of the Mosaic covenant (Deut 4:26; 30:19; 31:28). Mendenhall acknowledges instances where even the mountains, rivers, sea, heaven and earth, the wind, and the clouds are called upon to witness a covenant or a treaty.[113]

As to the divine witness, Job used the words "witness"[114] and "advocate"[115] to refer to some entity in heaven (on high).[116] Although some scholars still hold to the traditional view that God is the referent in these verses,[117] this may not be the case. It seems contradictory that Job, who presented God as the source of his afflictions (16:7–14), would now call him his advocate (16:20–21).

A Recap of a Court Scene

Earlier chapters showed Eliphaz (4:17–19; 15:25–26), Bildad (8:2–3), and Zophar (11:3, 11) bringing serious accusations against Job. Job disputed these accusations, maintaining that he was innocent. Upon realizing however, that he could not convince his friends of his innocence, Job requested a hearing before God. Rejecting his friends as witnesses, Job attempted to assemble the following players in the courtroom:

> Judge: God
> Advocate-mediator: A friend who pleads on behalf of the accused
> Complainant: Job
> Witness: Earth and the One who is in heaven

---

113. George Mendenhall, "Covenant Forms in Israelite Tradition," in *BAR* 3 (1970): 33.
114. Heb. *'ed* – witness, testimony.
115. Heb. *sahed* – an Aramaic loan word, meaning *advocate*, which is also used in Genesis 31:47. See note on Job 16:19, *NET* Bible.
116. The synonymous parallelism indicates that the "witness" in heaven is equal to the "advocate" on high.
117. Rowley, *Job*, 120–21; Hartley, *Book of Job*, 264; Kaiser, *Majesty of God*, 105. Alter does not think that the witness here refers to God, but to the "impartial mediator or judge for whom Job has already expressed a longing," Writings, 508.

In a regular court hearing, a judge would not serve as both judge and advocate-mediator at the same time for the same case. In some instances, the accused may choose to represent himself or herself (especially if he or she is a lawyer) but being both advocate and judge of one's own case is invalid since the goal is to have an impartial hearing and decision on the case. Job requested that God be the judge in his case and that someone from heaven – which could be any member of the heavenly council – be his mediator.[118] He did not trust any of his friends to fulfill this role although, later, Elihu offered to be Job's mediator.

As this related to a *rib* (a lawsuit or controversy) the three elements of a lawsuit – as outlined by Soulen[119] – were already in place: a summons to the offending party (13:22; 14:15), charges against the offender (16:7–17), and a call for witnesses (16:18–21).

Job was innocent, yet he suffered many adverse effects of various calamities. He referred to an "intercessor"[120] (*melits*) as his friend who would come to his aid as his "eyes pour out[121] tears to God" (16:20). Job wanted someone to argue his case (16:21; see also 9:33); but if God were to be the judge in the court hearing, it is unlikely that he would also serve as the intercessor. Walton proposes a member of the heavenly council: "If we combine information from the context of Job, the Old Testament, and court documents from the ancient Near Eastern cultural background, we can infer that Job hoped for a member of the divine council to call on God to account on his behalf."[122] The pericope concludes with Job acknowledging that he would soon die (16:22).[123]

Job was not asking for too much in requesting for an intercessor-mediator. This was part of the culture of the time. The concept of a mediator is as old as time and humanity. The Bible records that judges, priests, or prophets served

---

118. People in ancient world believed that what happens on earth is a replica of what happens in the heavens. Just as there are council of elders on earth, there is also a council in heaven. It is possible that Job was looking at the whole council in heaven and asking if any one of the members would have compassion on him, take the role of an advocate, and help him plead his case. He used different terms for a role that an advocate, mediator, or intercessor could do for him. Refer to "A Typical Tongtong Process" below (page 115).
119. See Soulen, *Handbook of Biblical Criticism*, 170.
120. As a participle, this Hebrew term is used only four times in the OT and could be translated as "interpreter" (Gen 42:23), "spokesperson" (Isa 43:37), "intercessor" (Job 16:20) or "mediator" (Job 33:33).
121. The Hebrew term *dalefah* has a cognate in Arabic, *dalafa*, which also means "to drip through." See *HALOT*, s.v. "dalaf."
122. Walton, *Job*, 215.
123. Literally, "Go on a journey and will not return" is a euphemism for death.

as mediators between God and the people. For instance, Moses mediated between God and Israel. The prophets spoke to God on behalf of the people and also spoke to the people on behalf of God.

A mediator helps resolve an issue wisely, using strategies appropriate to the situation. For instance, Nathan used a parable to confront David about his sin with Bathsheba (2 Sam 12:1–13). Abigail pacified David by giving him the supplies that his army needed so that he did not kill Nabal (1 Sam 25:18–35). There is no single, rigid, quick-fix solution for all issues. In addition to the process Jesus laid down for resolving conflict (see Matt 18:15–35), contemporary believers should also examine and reflect on other biblical principles that can be usefully applied in such situations and, wherever possible, doing so in ways that are consistent with cultural norms and mores.

Job rejected the counsel of all three friends (16:1–2). His language communicates his outrage at their cruel words. They offered nothing new, and Job dismissed their words. He felt no sense of obligation to listen to them for, in reality, they offered no comfort.

Job acknowledged that he was in constant pain, that he felt humiliated, weak, and tired of weeping, and that he was ready to eventually surrender to defeat. Job longed for a person to whom he could pour out his heart. Burdened, and in tears, he reached out continuously to God.

MEDIATION IN THE ASIAN CONTEXT

In Asia, particularly Southeast Asia, the concept of a mediator or mediation is not new. As it was in Job's time, so it is now – mediation is expedient in day-to-day affairs, whether religious or non-religious in nature.

In non-religious settings, whether domestic or cross-cultural, the need for a mediator – a "third party" to act as a "go-between" – is recognized. On the family level, a parent often mediates altercations between siblings; when one of the children wants to get married, parents may invite a matchmaker to negotiate the marriage proposal. On the level of a clan,[1] the head of the clan – or its leaders – is consulted, and at community level, the wise men or members of the council of elders are consulted to settle petty issues as well as business and social disputes. The goal of such meditation is to maintain peace and harmony in the community. On religious matters, the priest or "shaman" of a religion mediates between the worshipers and their God, local deity, or ancestral spirits.

Barkai writes that in Japan, "mediation was the primary, traditional method of resolving village disputes, with village leaders serving as mediators. This country has a long history of compromise, mediation, and conciliation."[2] He goes on to suggest that "the three most effective tools for mediating cross-cultural disputes are pre-mediation meetings (joint or private); caucus during mediation; and the Socratic method of questioning."[3] Avruch reviews the work of Lee and Hwee and highlights some elements that help to ensure good mediation: trust in mediation, an open exchange of information, and the mediator's active participation by authoritatively directing the process rather than just facilitating it.[4]

These key elements of the mediation process are still evident in the *tongtong*[5] – a mediation process used by people groups in the northern part of the Philippines. The derivative *tongtongan* can refer to the place of negotiation or to the negotiation process itself. What follows is a verbatim excerpt from a typical *tongtong* process among the *Kankana-ey*[6] people group, taken from the work of Malanes.[7] Malanes presents the process as prose. This author however, presents the process in an outline form.

---

1. Larger than a family unit, a clan would include the grandparents, aunties, uncles, and cousins.
2. John Barkai, "A Cross-Cultural Mediator To Do? A Low-Context Solution for A High-Context Problem," *Cardozo Journal of Conflict Resolution* 10 (2008), 50–51.
3. Barkai, "A Cross-Cultural Mediator," 52.
4. Kevin Avruch, Review of *An Asian Perspective on Mediation*, eds. Joel Lee and Teh Hwee, *Peace & Conflict Review* 4, Issue 1: 2.

5. *Tongtong*. As a noun, a free translation of this term is "a conversation, a negotiation." As a verb, a free translation would be "to converse," or "to negotiate." The term however came to refer to "a justice system that is based on consensus." See Maurice Malanes, *Power from the Mountains: Indigenous Knowledge Systems and Practices in Ancestral Domain Management* (Geneva: International Labor Union, 2002), 11.
6. There are three main people groups in Benguet Province, northern part of the Philippines: *Kankana-ey*, *Ibaloy*, and *Kalanguya*. They follow the same cultural practices, customary laws, norms, and mores.
7. Malanes, *Power from the Mountains*, 11–12.

A TYPICAL *TONGTONG* PROCESS[1]

Part One: Hearing of the Case and Decision

1. Both the contending parties go to the *tongtongan* or community court.

2. An elder may start the session by presenting the background and explaining the bone of contention in the case or by immediately calling the complaining party to present its case. A complainant who cannot speak for himself or herself may appoint a relative to present the complaint.

3. The other party is then called to argue, deny, or admit the complaint. While both contending parties are permitted to argue freely, any of the elders may speak up to guide and direct the arguments when these seem to be going nowhere or when the arguments become heated.

   - The council of elders and any of the ordinary folk of the community gathered there may reprimand anyone who stands or points fingers at somebody.

   - Every elder (man or woman) who joins in the discussion actually helps to interpret the custom law under the *tongtong* system.

   - Anybody who joins in the *tongtong* deliberations essentially acts as a moralist. As such, he or she advises the disputing parties or mediates with tact and diplomacy.

   - The *tongtong* system is participatory, and no one is assigned beforehand to pass judgment.

> - The *tongtong* system covers all aspects of behavior, and its decision-making process is participatory. Under this system, no one is judge and no one presides.
> 4. An agreement or decision is reached only after both parties have presented their side of the case.
> 5. An elder may call for a break. The elders and representatives from both parties huddle in a corner to arrive at a common decision. The decision has to be unanimous because voting is not the norm. Once it reaches a decision, the group meets again.
> 6. An elder, speaking clearly and loudly, announces the verdict.
>
> **Part Two: Decision on the Penalty**
> 1. The second part of the *tongtong* is to decide the penalty.
> 2. The second stage continues to be participatory, and the party to be penalized may bargain until a decision is made.
> 3. Only once a decision about penalty is made can the *tongtong* rest the case.
>
> ---
> 1. Malanes, *Power from the Mountains*.

Job bemoaned his situation and expected that death would be imminent. In his helplessness, he longed for an intercessor. Job 17 prompts us to consider two questions: May a person refuse the advice of a counselor? In what situations might it be appropriate to do so?

17:1–2 Job's Desperate State

Job lamented his pitiful plight. His spirit was broken, and he resigned himself to the fact that his life would soon be over and that all he had to look forward to was the grave (17:1). This was the honest admission of a person on the brink of giving up all hope. Unfortunately, even as he awaited death, Job continued to be an object of derision, forced to endure hostility (17:2). There seemed to be no letup for Job, who continued to experience pain from all sides – the loss of his properties, his wealth and his health, the insensitivity of his friends, and now derision by "mockers" surrounding him.

17:3–5 Job's Disclaimer of His Friend

Job made a request of God: "Make a pledge with me" (17:3, my translation).[124] A pledge is a commercial item given as security to ensure that a debt will be paid, or an obligation met by the agreed time and date. For instance, in the OT, Judah handed his seal, cord, and staff as a "pledge" (*'eravon*) to Tamar pending delivery of the young goat that he had promised her (Gen 38:17).

In a court of law, a pledge could be cash bail for the defendant to ensure that he or she appears in court for the hearing of the case. Although Job had no debt, he stood accused of sinning against God. Since he had also lost everything except his life, he had nothing to offer as a pledge to God apart from himself and his claim to innocence. If Job won his case, he would lose nothing but had everything to gain. If he lost his case, he could lose everything. Regardless of Job's pitiful situation, he abandoned himself to the mercy of the living God – who was Job's only recourse and hope – crying out for vindication and justice. Sadly, as the next line affirms, there was no one to put up "security" or serve as a guarantor for Job.

Job stated that no one would agree to serve as his guarantor because God had closed the minds of his friends – and any bystanders – so that they failed to understand that Job was innocent (17:4). And though innocent, the reason why Job was suffering has not been revealed, and no one had any inkling why God had allowed all these things to happen to Job. Job then cited a proverb: "If anyone denounces their friends for reward, the eyes of their children will fail" (17:5). Clines explains, "The best interpretation of this obscure verse is to take it as a popular proverb of the boastful man who calls his friends to a banquet when his larder is so empty that his children are starving."[125] Andersen comments, "The failure of the eyes of his children would be a fit punishment for a person who gives false eyewitness testimony in order to defraud his friends' children of their inheritance. This is a grave charge to fling at the friends, who have not betrayed any such motive for discrediting Job."[126]

Job 17:5b is sometimes viewed as a declaration by Job that because his enemies had betrayed him, their children would become blind.[127] Although

---

124. The lexical form *'arav* means "to stand surety," "to barter," "to enter into a wager." See *HALOT*, s.v. "'arav." The noun form and derivative *'aravon* refers to "a pledge" or "a surety" as in Genesis 38:17, 18.
125. David J. A. Clines, *Job 1–20*, WBC 17 (Dallas: Word, 1989), 395.
126. Andersen, *Job*, 184.
127. The term *kalah* may contribute in isolating the meaning of 17:5b. The word means "to come to an end," "be completed," or "to perish." In some cases, it can also mean *to fail*, which is how the word is used in several texts when referring to the eyes. An analysis of select verses

this interpretation may seem viable, Job did not subscribe to the principle that children should suffer the consequences of their parents' sins (21:19–20). Another approach is to explain and take this line to mean "not being able to see or experience what is hoped for" (17:5b). Job was warning his critics that any plans they had to gain something out of his situation would not succeed and their children would not be able to possess and enjoy whatever gain they might have expected.

When we reach a stalemate in a counseling situation, we may need to evaluate the effect and relevance of our ministrations. This may involve the following:

- Consider that true theological statements can be wrongly applied. Many of the statements of Job's friends, taken on their own, sound like good theology; but their application was shallow and insensitive, as well as destructive. As the book of Proverbs says, "Like a thornbush in a drunkard's hand is a proverb in the mouth of a fool" (Prov 26:9).
- Realize that suffering and prosperity are not distributed in the world in proportion to the evil or good that a person does. Job was right in commenting that the wicked are spared from the day of calamity (21:30), while the just and blameless become a laughingstock (12:4). Therefore, let us refrain from judging one another.
- A good counselor does not arrogantly preach theology but, rather, suffers together with the one in pain and offers love and truth from God's word. Such a counselor also drinks deeply from the fountain of God's truth when trying to help others and let love stand as a watchman at the gate of his or her mouth.
- When all hope is lost, and when God seems far off, hold fast to him and trust him to help in some way.

---

carry these nuances: of eyes being tired of weeping (Lam 2:11), strained in looking for food (Jer 14:6), tired in looking for God (Ps 69:3 [MT Ps 69:4]), and not being able to see or experience what is hoped for (Job 11:20; 17:5; Lam 4:17).

Job 4:1–27:23

17:6–16 Job's Despair before His Friends

Continuing the thought of verse 2, Job declared that God had made him a "byword" (17:6). This expression – also used in the Psalms (44:14) and in the blessings-curses section of Deuteronomy (28:37) – depicts the experience of a person whose sufferings on account of affliction are compounded by the insults of those around. Job claimed that those who mocked him (17:2) also spat on his face (17:6) – an expression of outright contempt of Job as a person. As a result, Job's eyes had "grown dim with grief" and his whole body had become like a "shadow" (17:7). There are three ways to interpret "shadow" here: a transitory life, a life that is near its end, or an emaciated body.[128] The latter seems most likely since Job had become weak and emaciated. Job observed that "the upright are appalled at this; the innocent are aroused against the ungodly" (17:8). Hartley gives a plausible explanation: "An upright person is so appalled at the abuse borne by an innocent victim that he, also an innocent person, stirs himself to oppose this kind of behavior from the godless. He defends the innocent and condemns the guilty. But Job's friends have not followed this standard of conduct. Instead, they have sided with the scoffers and added to his suffering."[129] Regardless, Job declared that "the righteous will hold to their ways" (17:9a). Since the "righteous" person in verse 9 is referred to in the singular (as opposed to the plural usage of "upright" in 8a), the referent here is Job, who was committed to keep doing what was right and maintain his integrity, despite his situation.

A God-fearing person is more concerned with integrity than with rewards of wealth or good health. *Satan's* charge was that Job worshiped God only because of God's protection and blessings. Yet, up to this point, Job had not sought the restoration of his health and wealth as rewards, and although he poured out his complaints to God, he did not curse him.

Job invited his friends – those who claimed to be upright – "to come . . . try again" but hastened to add that he would not "find a wise person" among them (17:10). Job was either taunting them by inviting them to continue sparring with words in the hope that they would change their minds and be sympathetic to his plight and perhaps help resolve his problem.

Job believed that his end was near,[130] and this prospect of death caused his plans, and even his heart's desires, to be "shattered" (17:11). But Job had not

---

128. See BDB, s.v. "tsl."
129. Hartley, *Book of Job*, 269.
130. Literally, "days allotted to him were over."

lost hope. His night would turn into day. Although he was staring darkness in the face, he knew that light was near. Job was hopeful because he still believed in his God.

Just as Job did not lose hope, he also did not side with "corruption" (17:13–16). He would die[131] and face darkness (17:13), but if he were to resort to calling corruption his father, mother, or sister, he would lose sight of his hope and others would not see him as a person of hope (17:14–15). Job would choose to go down to the gates of death and descend to the dust rather than lose hope or side with corruption.

Job was physically, emotionally, and spiritually worn out. As his once healthy body wasted away, his mind began preparing for death. He endured the pain of social isolation and rejection and, worse, the sense that even God had abandoned him. Job was a man without hope, looking forward only to death. The chapter ends on a strong note of despair.

18:1–21 Bildad Speaks

In this chapter, it is once again Bildad's turn to speak. Bildad's speech raises important questions for our consideration: What are the warning signs that we are about to cross the line between helping and hurting a person who is going through pain? Are there limitations to the power of positive thinking?

18:1–4 The Denunciation of Job

Bildad dismissed Job's arguments, clearly regarding them as baseless since he told Job to "be sensible" in order that they might discuss the issues (18:1–2). Probably responding to Job's earlier challenges about the friends' lack of wisdom (12:1–3, 7–9), Bildad questioned why Job regarded them as stupid beasts (18:2–3). Job had complained that God was tearing him apart (16:9), but Bildad accused Job of being self-destructive in his anger and tearing himself to pieces (18:4). Implying that Job had been irrational with his words, Bildad argued that irrespective of what Job said or did, neither the earth nor the rocks would be moved from their place (18:4). By this he meant that Job could not change the traditions and precepts of their forefathers, which had been set in place long ago (compare Eliphaz's earlier claim in Job 15:9–10).

Like Eliphaz, Bildad was also defensive. The three friends were no longer focused on Job's suffering but on their own words and their own doctrinal positions. They were protecting themselves and their reputation as wise men.

---

131. Literally, "spread my bed."

Job 4:1–27:23

The doctrine of cause-and-effect that had operated in the universe since creation began should not be set aside just for Job. Bildad likened rejecting his counsel to asking God to change the form and order of the earth (18:4; compare 14:18).

Christians often lose the opportunity to make an impact on a suffering friend because they choose to defend their doctrines rather than show practical compassion. This could easily happen if, even before hearing a friend's full story, we consciously or subconsciously start with the premise that suffering is the result of sin.

When we are about to cross the line between helping and hurting someone in pain, we may tend to:

- Lose sight of our primary purpose in such a situation, which is to help our hurting friend.
- Take personally the statements of a hurting friend when, in truth, these statements may spring out of the person's pain.
- Forget to speak the truth with love.
- Insist on solutions that do not really address the issue the person is facing.
- Believe that only we could solve the problem and fail to ask the person concerned how we could best help in a way that is meaningful to them.
- Dispense an overdose of positive thinking that prevents the real issues from being dealt with realistically. This may happen when exaggerated statements – verging on lies – are made with the intention of encouraging the person. This may lead to the person entertaining false hopes, which then results in additional pain.
- Insist to almost coercing to lead a person in the Sinner's Prayer when he or she may not be ready yet to discuss spiritual matters.

18:5–21 The Downfall of the Wicked
18:5–10 The wicked themselves become trapped

Bildad cited a proverb: "The lamp of a wicked man is snuffed out" (18:5). Specifically, "the light[132] from his flame stops burning" (18:5, my translation). Since light can represent both life (compare 3:20) and prosperity (compare

---

132. The NIV has "lamp," but I retain "light," which is the rendering in the Hebrew text.

22:28), Bildad was saying that the wicked would not enjoy long life, progeny, or prosperity. Even the light in his house was dim and the light "along with him"[133] "goes out" (18:6, my translation).[134] The life of the wicked would certainly be cut short.[135]

Bildad added that the wicked were restricted and trapped by their own schemes (18:7–8). Their fall is depicted as being their own fault. The entrapment process is described in reverse order: a trap seizes the wicked man by his heels, a snare takes hold of him, and a rope hidden in the ground and a trap on his path lie in wait for him (18:9–10).[136]

18:11–21 The wicked perish without descendants

The wicked man is attacked by terrors on all sides (18:11) and more calamities awaited him (18:12). The references to "parts of his skin" being eaten away and "death's firstborn"[137] consuming his limbs (18:13) seem to be an oblique reference to Job. "The description speaks not of a slowly progressing disease; but of the total destruction of the body in the grave."[138] Unprotected, he would be marched off to "the king of terrors" – a reference to death (18:14).[139] He would lose everything, for even his house would be strewn with sulfur and destroyed by fire (18:15). The wicked man is likened to a tree whose roots dry up and whose branches wither (18:16), leading to death. Consequently, any remembrance of him would be erased (18:17) as he would be driven away from the land to wander in darkness (18:18) and left without any descendants (18:19). People everywhere[140] would be "appalled at his fate" (18:20) – which was also the reaction of the three friends when they first saw Job. Bildad concluded his speech by reiterating that such desolation and destruction would

---

133. Most translations have "light above him" taking the particle *'al* in the Hebrew text as locative, but the particle can be taken as accompaniment. See Williams, *Hebrew Syntax*, 52.
134. This translation is therefore adopted: The light "along with him" goes out.
135. The phrases *snuffed out* and *goes out* plus the synthetic parallelism – the second line expands or completes the main idea of the first line – in verses 5 and 6 emphasize the certainty that the life of the wicked would be cut short.
136. This is the second time that this style of presentation – reversing the order of the process (compare 16:9) – was used to capture the attention of the recipients and thus draw them to the message of the text.
137. Bullinger thinks that "first born of death" is a euphemism for the cruelest and most calamitous death *Figures of Speech*, 687.
138. Walton, *Job*, 216.
139. Seow, *Job*, 787.
140. "East and west" represents a merism.

come on the dwelling places of the wicked, identified here as those who do not know God (18:21).

Bildad seemed to have enjoyed listing the disasters that would fall on the "wicked one."

While he spoke generally about the plight and destiny of the wicked, his description seemed to zero in on Job's situation – note Bildad's reference to skin disease and the loss of everything, including children who would have carried on a man's family name. Since Bildad had insinuated that Job was the wicked one, we can infer that his concluding verse implied that Job did not know God, which is far from the truth.[141]

Going by Bildad's statements, it seems that he persisted with the premise that only the wicked suffer calamities. He believed that Job's unparalleled suffering could only have been caused by his sin. Bildad's philosophy did not take into account the possibility that the upright do sometimes experience suffering, too.

Nothing new is said about God in this chapter. Bildad's statements imply that the lives of the wicked are in God's hand and that it is God who brings calamities, and even death, on the wicked. His speech merely reiterates the view of a stern and punishing God, a God without mercy.

19:1–29 Job's Response to Bildad

Job had just heard Bildad's insinuation that he, Job, did not know God. We need to address the following questions: What do you do when everyone, including God, seems to be against you? What does it mean to wait on God?

19:1–6 The Hostility of the Friends

Job accused his friends of causing him grief by repeatedly crushing him with their words (19:1–2). He charged them with shamelessly attacking him "ten times" (19:3). Earlier, Zophar had accused Job of idle talk and mockery (compare 11:3), and Job was now countering these accusations. "Ten times" may be symbolic for "often," or Job might have had in mind ten specific accusations that were particularly shameless. Job experienced no compassion, only condemnation, arrogance, and criticism, from his friends turned counselors.

---

141. Regarding the end of chapter 18, Vicchio explains: "Much of contemporary scholarship agrees with C. D. Rodd's conclusion when he writes, 'All we find in this chapter is stern theology passionately defended.' Driver and Gray say the meaning of verse 20 is, 'The whole world is horrified at the wicked man's fate.'" *Book of Job*, 139.

He stated that if he had erred, he would take responsibility for his error but desired to be left alone to deal with it himself (19:4). He reminded them also that they had acted rudely in using his shame to build their case against him (19:5). And Job did not leave God out of the picture. Using the same term (*'avat*) that Bildad earlier used to argue that God does not pervert justice (8:3), Job rebutted Bildad's claim and reasoned that God had wronged him and done him an injustice by entrapping him with his net (19:6). "The interesting point, however, is that both the accusing trio and Job all agreed that all of Job's afflictions and suffering were coming from God; nevertheless, they disagreed on the reason for all these trials. The three men attributed this affliction to retribution for Job's sin, while Job attributed it to God's unfair treatment of him!"[142]

These friends refused to share Job's pain. Their judgmental responses demonstrate that they did not even attempt to understand what Job was going through. Their speeches reveal that they were useless counselors.

19:7–12 The Hostility from God

Job felt that God had made him an adversary. Although Job cried out for help, God had been deaf to Job's cries (19:7). Moreover, God had "blocked" Job's movements (19:8), "stripped" him of honor (19:9) and uprooted his hope (19:10). In his anger, God had treated Job as if he were an enemy (19:11), marching against Job and surrounding his house (19:12).

Although Job spoke as if God was angry with him, in truth, Job was angry with God. He charged God with ignoring him and remaining deaf to his cries for help. He was convinced that God could do whatever he wanted and that nothing happened unless God willed it. Therefore, he was sure that God was directly responsible for his suffering. On account of these offenses that God had supposedly committed against him, Job had grown bitter. He saw God as an unpredictable tyrant, an enemy general enjoying his supremacy over his weak subjects.

Have you ever been angry with God? Have your circumstances been so harsh and merciless that you turned on God in resentment and shouted, "Why?" God's silence is one of the most difficult periods in a believer's life. Like Job, we all want to know why difficult things that we do not understand happen to us. It is during these hard times of God's apparent silence that we

---

142. Kaiser, *Majesty of God*, 117.

must learn to wait. When God seems distant and silent in the face of your cries, remind yourself that:

- God's delays and our waiting is part of our progress in walking life's journey with God.
- The real strength of our faith comes from waiting on the Lord! Those who have faith are not in a hurry; when in doubt, they wait.
- Waiting means depending, in total abandonment, on the Lord, with no human attempts to take over and make things happen.
- Waiting means faith plus patience in times when we are tempted to worry and be impatient; impatience is the opposite of waiting in faith.
- Waiting is a test of our patience, our endurance, and our inner strength.
- Waiting is the ability to face mental torture, verbal abuse, and sessions of soul pain on the world's stretching rack.

Waiting on the Lord is not a waste of time but is the best time to be still, know, and have a deeper experience of God.

19:13–22 *The Hostility from Others*

Job's family and friends abandoned him.[143] Although they should have been the first to help in times of adversity, they failed to do so. Job claimed that his relatives and friends had either maintained their distance or forsaken him (19:13–14). In fact, members of his household treated him as an outsider. Even his servants refused to obey him (19:15–16).

Job might have had halitosis, making his breath repulsive and foul-smelling to his wife and family (19:17). Even the youngsters had become disrespectful toward him, probably turning their backs on him when he spoke (19:18). This had not been the case before the calamities came for then Job had been treated with respect and people had valued his opinion. When troubles came, Job's inner circle – his close friends and loved ones – became hostile toward him and even detested him (19:19). The psychosomatic effect of these multiple betrayals

---

[143]. This section is riddled with participles that are functioning as nouns (when referring to people) and with synonymous parallelisms to emphasize the strong emotions of betrayal that Job felt from the people closest to him.

was that Job felt as though his bones were clinging to his skin (19:20a) and claimed that he had "escaped only by the skin of my teeth" (19:20b). Alter gives this plausible explanation: "Because teeth don't have skin, some scholars have tried to emend the text. But poetry need not be bound by anatomical logic. The verse should be read as a vivid hyperbole: I was so ravaged by disease and deprivation, turned into mere skin and bones that all I came away with was the (essentially nonexistent) skin of my teeth."[144] It is also possible that Job was referring to the enamel on his teeth, which, being the hardest part of the body, was the only part that was not affected in any way by the malignant skin disease.

Indeed, everything around Job was collapsing, and his relationships, as well as his physical, emotional, and mental faculties, were affected. Job issued a personal plea to his friends to be gracious and have pity on him because he was experiencing the brunt of God's punishment[145] (19:21) and, knowing how much he was suffering in his body, not to pursue him as God had done (19:22).

19:23–29 The Hope of Seeing God

Job listed his wishes (19:23–27). By expressing the wish that his words be written on a scroll, inscribed with an iron stylus on lead, or engraved for all time on a rock (19:23–24), Job was saying that his experiences should be recorded in a manner that time could not erase so that others might see how unfairly and unjustly he had been treated by God and by others.

Verses 25–27, probably the best-known verses in the book of Job, are considered a key turning point in Job's journey of faith and understanding of God's sovereignty. Job made an important statement: "I know that my redeemer [*go'el*][146] lives" (19:25a).

The term *go'el* may refer to a relative who marries a childless widow to continue the family name of the deceased (Ruth 4:5–6), an avenger of blood, seeking justice for a slain relative (Num 35:12, 19, 21; Josh 20:3–9), one who buys back a property that was mortgaged (Lev 25:25; Ruth 4:2–4), or one who stands as witness with a family member during litigation (Prov 23:11). Although Job needed someone to defend him in his imminent court hearing, his family, relatives, and friends had forsaken him when he needed them most.

---

144. Alter, *Writings*, 514.
145. Literally, "the hand of God touched me." There is a figure of speech, *anthropopatheia*, to indicate punishment. See Bullinger, *Figures of Speech*, 879.
146. This term *go'el* is an active participle, serving as a noun from *ga'al*, meaning to "redeem," "avenge," "reclaim."

While Saadiah thinks that this *go'el* refers to a human being,¹⁴⁷ Habtu argues that Job was not thinking of a human redeemer.¹⁴⁸ Clines explains that Job's "deposition of character" and himself would be his own *go'el*.¹⁴⁹ This means that Job's character would be the very thing that would vindicate him. Kaiser clarifies: "This 'Redeemer' seemed to be parallel with the earlier 'Witness' mentioned in 16:19. How could this be a lesser figure than the Messiah Himself, given his task and names?"¹⁵⁰

The "redeemer" that Job referred to (19:25a) could only be the divine Redeemer, God (19:26). Several OT passages present Yahweh as *go'el* (Isa 41:14; 43:14; 47:4; 48:17; 49:26; 63:16; Jer 50:34). Since the term "redeemer" is used frequently of God, "it is difficult to believe that the poet is not gesturing toward God in some way."¹⁵¹ Verse 27 affirms this since, despite everything that Job had gone through at the very hands of God, he said of God: "Whom I have beheld¹⁵² personally; whom my eyes will see; whom my innermost being is spent in longing for."¹⁵³

Although Christians believe in the resurrection of the body and affirm that Jesus Christ is our only mediator (1 Tim 2:5; Heb 8:6; 9:15), it seems quite early in that time and dispensation to argue that Job had Jesus Christ in mind when he referred to his redeemer.¹⁵⁴ Longman comments that "the equation between Jesus and Job's redeemer is the result of an all too hasty reading of an OT text from the perspective of the NT . . . Job's hope for a redeemer bears little semblance to the type of redeemer the NT describes."¹⁵⁵ It seems safe to say that Job had the living God in mind when he referred to his redeemer.

---

147. Saadiah Ben Joseph Al-Fayyumi, *The Book of Theodicy: Translation and Commentary on the Book of Job*, trans. Lenn Evan Goodman, YJS 25 (New Haven: Yale University Press, 1988), 116.
148. Tewoldemedhin Habtu, "Job," in *ABC*, ed. Tokunboh Adeyemo, (Grand Rapids: Zondervan, 2006), 583.
149. Clines, *Job 1–20*, 459.
150. Kaiser, *Majesty of God*, 121.
151. Seow, *Job 1–21*, 807. Consider the work of Andersen, *Job*, 194 and Rowley, *Book of Job*, 138.
152. Literally, "and my eyes have beheld." There is a figure of speech: heterosis of tenses, to indicate that the action is as good as done. See Bullinger, *Figures of Speech*, 518–19.
153. This is a literal rendering of the MT.
154. See also the discussion of Walton on the "mediator" and "resurrection," *Job*, 225–29.
155. Tremper Longman III, "Job's Fifth Response" in *Job*, BCOTWS (Grand Rapids: Baker Academic, 2012), https://www.perlego.com/book/2050908/job-baker-commentary-on-the-old-testament-wisdom-and-psalm.pdf.

Job maintained that his redeemer "will stand[156] on the earth" (19:25b), meaning that this redeemer will appear to exercise justice for Job. There are three possibilities as to when Job expected this to happen: (a) *Vindication at his court hearing before he died*[157] – which would have been at the height of Job's suffering.[158] Having assembled the key players in a courtroom, Job expected God to listen to his plea and come to the hearing. Claiming innocence, he hoped for God to intervene and vindicate him before he died. (b) *Vindication after his death*[159] – for this view to be valid, the phrase "in my flesh" (19:26) has to be translated "apart from my flesh" or "without flesh." And (c) *Vindication at his resurrection*,[160] when he would see God with his "own eyes" as he stood face-to-face with the redeemer. Although many scholars believe that Job did not really expect that he would be resurrected, there is evidence that people in OT times have a concept of resurrection, but this "remained marginal to Old Testament belief, whether chronologically or theologically"[161] – it was not fully developed yet.

Habtu explains that verses 26–27 suggest that Job believed that there was someone who would vindicate him in the future and also that he foresaw the atonement, the incarnation, and a personal resurrection.[162] Job believed that "after he dies, he will be resurrected and will himself see the one who will vindicate him (19:26–27). This is Job's final hope and what his *heart yearns* for."[163]

On one hand, it is not far-fetched to say that Job was looking primarily for *immediate vindication* – that is, before Job's death, when the Lord appeared at his court hearing and when their fellowship would be restored. On the other hand, if Job should die without being granted a court hearing, then he

---

156. The verb *qum* can mean "to rise," "get up," "stand up," "to appear in a lawsuit," "to come to fruition," "to stay fixed," "to endure," "to fulfill." See *HALOT*, s.v. "qum."
157. See the works of Hartley, *Book of Job*, 296; Walton, *Job*, 220.
158. LongmanIII, "Job's Fifth Response," in *Job*.
159. Refer to *Jubilees*, 28–31. Described here are the spirits of those who died, freed and in the presence of God. See also Andersen, *Job*, 194.
160. See the work of Kaiser, *Majesty of God*, 123.
161. Philip S. Johnston, *Shades of Sheol: Death and Afterlife in the Old Testament* (Downers Grove: InterVarsity Press, 2002), 227. The following passages in the Old Testament do or may refer to resurrection: 1 Samuel 2:6; Job 14:10–14; 19:25–27; Psalms 16:9–11; 17:15; 49:15; 73:23–26; Isaiah 3:10–12; 25:8; 26:19–21; Ezekiel 37:1–14; Daniel 12:2, 13; Hosea 6:1–4; 13:14. The doctrine of the resurrection was not fully developed in the OT, but there is clear evidence that by the time of Jesus Christ the Pharisees, the more conservative branch of Judaism, believed strongly in a resurrection after death.
162. Habtu, "Job," 583.
163. Rao, "Job," 599.

expected *vindication after his death*, when *he had been gathered to his people*[164] and would see God "in his state of death. This points not to bodily resurrection after death but to conscious awareness after death."[165] Job believed that he would live again to meet the living God.

The convention at that time in the Ancient Near East was that a person who died would live again. In Egypt, for instance, people believed that after death they would live again, enjoying the same status they had at the time they had died. Hence, pharaohs were buried with their slaves and with some essential items that they would need in the next life. On display presently is a large boat beside the Great Pyramid of Giza in Egypt. According to the tour guide, the boat was used to ferry Pharaoh Khufu to his next destination *via* the Nile River.[166]

It is significant that Job's ultimate goal was to meet his redeemer face-to-face. Psychologically, and from the standpoint of logotherapy,[167] the "important thing is that Job has thought about doing something through engaging in this image, even imagining that his case could be won against all odds. The passion that flows from 'the defiant power of the human spirit,' such as Job's statement that 'I will see Eloah' (19:26) argues that he is emerging from his turmoil, that meaning is returning to his existential vacuum."[168] Out of the depths of his pain, Job found something concrete to live for, a goal and purpose that was larger than himself.

Job reminded his friends about judgment (19:28–29). Placing himself in his friends' shoes, he imagined them saying, "How we will hound him, since the root of the trouble lies in him." Job reminded them, by way of a command,

---

164. This is a phrase for death and joining one's ancestors – Isaac (Gen 35:29), Jacob (Gen 47:30; 49:29), Aaron (Num 20:24), Moses (Num 31:2; Deut 32:50). Smick also thinks that Job's vindication is after his death at the end of his life, but not at the eschaton. Smick, "Dispute Dialogue" in *Job*.

165. Roy B. Zuck, "A Theology of Wisdom Books and the Song of Songs," in A Biblical Theology of the Old Testament, ed. Roy B. Zuck (Chicago: Moody Press, 1991), 228–29.

166. This author saw the boat and heard the tour guide's explanation during an educational tour that she participated in May 2005. See also the chart in chapter 7 of this work, *Sheol and the Afterlife*.

167. Logotherapy was developed by Victor E. Frankl. It is "an approach to psychotherapy that focuses on the 'human predicament,' helping the client to overcome crises in meaning. The therapeutic process typically consists of examining three types of values: creative (e.g., work, achievement); experiential (e.g., art, science, philosophy, understanding, loving); and attitudinal (e.g., facing pain and suffering). Each client is encouraged to arrive at his or her own solution, which should incorporate social responsibility and constructive relationships." See *APA Dictionary of Psychology*, s.v. "logotherapy," http://www.dictionary.apa.org.

168. Lewis, *Victor Frankl*, 80.

to fear death[169] since even wrath is a sin worthy of death. Therefore, they needed to realize that there would be a judgment to come. It is far too early at this point in the progress of revelation to think of judgment as referring to the eternal white throne judgment. The idea here would have been the immediate punishment of sin. In effect, Job communicated that the three friends would be judged for the way they had been treating him. They were the guilty ones, not Job.

Like most people who suffer, Job felt alone, isolated, and in need of sympathy and compassion. People who are suffering need our help, our encouragement, perhaps even our tears. We all need praying and concerned friends to come to our aid and help us maintain a proper perspective both about God and about what we are going through. Job experienced hostility from his friends, God, and even his family and relatives. Yet, he kept hoping for vindication – either here on earth or in the afterlife. He believed he would meet his Redeemer face-to-face, and he refused to tarnish his integrity by giving in to the temptation to admit sins he had not committed.

Job felt abandoned by his loved ones and experienced painful rejection by his friends, and even God. When he cried out about the injustice and the violence done to him, he received no answer, and no one was willing to help him. He was emotionally drained, as he so movingly expressed in his cry, "How my heart yearns within me!" (19:27). Yet, Job rose above all his troubles to confess his trust in God – his redeemer whom he was ready to meet – and held fast to the belief that he would be vindicated.

20:1–29 Zophar Speaks

As Zophar takes up the baton in this chapter, a question worth thinking about is this: How do you respond to someone who is angry?

20:1–3 The Expression of Outrage at Job

Zophar felt insulted by Job's statement that the friends would one day be judged for what they had done. While Zophar's words about the fate of the wicked are true, he rejected Job's faith affirmation and continued with his painful assault. The rambling style of Zophar's speech reflected the traditional way of arguing in ancient times.

The structure of Zophar's speech is quite simple. Verses 1–3 contain a typical response that arises from hurt feelings due to Job's previous speech.

---

169. Literally, "the sword."

Verses 4–29 are about the doom of the wicked. Clines observes that Zophar's speech dealt almost exclusively with the fate of the wicked.[170] He also notes the different purposes of each of the three friends in bringing up the issue of the fate of the wicked: Eliphaz portrayed what Job was not (Job 15), Bildad portrayed what Job might become (Job 18), and Zophar portrayed what Job could not avoid without making some radical changes.[171]

We sometimes encounter people who are angry and difficult. How should we respond to such people? While a person is still spewing angry lava, we should keep calm and listen to what is being said. If we do have to say something, we should be guided by this proverb: "A gentle answer turns away wrath, but a harsh word stirs up anger" (Prov 15:1). As we listen carefully, we should examine the merits of what is said and consider if it is true, relevant, and appropriate. When the person has finished talking, we must assess whether it is the best time to discuss or respond to what has been said. In an Asian context, it is also important to be mindful of the age and status of the person and, since confronting is not helpful in this part of the world, a mediator may sometimes be needed.

20:4–11 *The Explanation of the Brief Prosperity of the Wicked*

Destruction awaits the wicked. Zophar based his argument on supposedly ancient maxims, which he claimed had been there since the creation of humankind (20:4). "The mirth of the wicked" – who are identified in the next line as the "godless" – "is brief" (20:5). Regardless of what these people had achieved, Zophar declared that their lives would soon perish – like their own excrement that is flushed out and gone forever (20:6–7). He also pointed to the brevity of life by comparing their lives to a fleeting dream or vision that dissipates with the night (20:8). The parallelism emphasizes the transitory quality of a man's life and achievements: He would soon be gone, no longer seen by his acquaintances and those in his own household (20:9). With regard to his wealth, his children would have to use it to pay off[172] the poor[173] (20:10). When the wicked die, it is payback time for the poor. The wealth and other possessions that they had accumulated and so greatly valued during their

---

170. Clines, *Job*, 482.
171. Clines, *Job*, 482.
172. The verb is in the piel stem that allows the rendition that is adopted.
173. An alternative translation is, "his children will seek the favor of the poor," meaning, be dependent on the poor. The parallel line however speaks about returning wealth, which is basically what the children will do in paying off the poor.

lifetime would be returned to the poor through their children. The wicked man's body,[174] which had once enjoyed youthful vitality, would be buried in the ground (20:11).

Zophar's first point, argued in 20:4–11, was that the joy of the wicked or godless is temporary and short-lived. All the blessings they had enjoyed would be taken away because of their wickedness, and this sudden end to their happiness would be a clear signal that they had sinned grievously. Verses 6–9 suggest that the higher a person rises in this world, the quicker they would disappear when their wickedness is discovered. Whatever heights the wicked may attain, they will still be destroyed. Zophar's message to Job was that if there was any arrogance in him, the "eye that saw him" – referring to people in this chapter – would no longer see him since he would have been destroyed (20:9).

A similar thought is expressed by the Filipino proverb "Kung gaano kataas ang lipad, gayon din ang lagapak pagbagsak," which can be freely translated as "However high a person flies, that's equally the height from which he will fall."

The book of Proverbs gives many warnings about pride:

> "He mocks proud mockers but shows favor to the humble and oppressed" (3:34).

> "When pride comes, then comes disgrace, but with humility comes wisdom" (11:2).

> "The Lord detests all the proud of heart. Be sure of this: They will not go unpunished" (16:5).

> "Pride goes before destruction, a haughty spirit before a fall" (16:18).

These verses clearly teach that God is against the proud but is pleased with a humble spirit and disposition (Ps 51:17; Isa 57:15), and Paul also counseled believers to pursue humility (Phil 2:3–4).

The root cause of pride is sin and could stem from love of self or poor self-esteem. Signs pointing to the presence of pride include moral superiority, narcissism or undue love of self, a know-it-all attitude, being overly critical of others, a desire to control, and boasting about wealth, a good life, beauty, or accomplishments. Ultimately, God knows when a person is prideful, and so it is important that we be aware of pride in our lives. When offended, a proud

---

174. Literally, "bones."

person often seeks revenge and immediate vindication, whereas the humble person seeks reconciliation and restoration.

20:12–18 The Evident Punishment of Sin

Zophar used images drawn from the digestive system and its processes to illustrate the points he made in this section. Commenting on a wicked person who loved evil,[175] he likened evil to a morsel of food that is carefully chewed in the mouth,[176] signifying the enjoyment of evil (20:12–13). However, that very "food" or meat,[177] once digested, would become poisonous within, like a serpent's venom (20:14), and he would be compelled, by God, to vomit out the wealth he had accumulated by his wickedness (20:15). In other words, God himself would divest the wicked of this wealth – if not in their lifetime, then after death. Zophar added, "He will suck the poison of serpents; the fangs of an adder will kill him" (20:16). If the sucking of poison represents the illegal accumulation of wealth, then whatever it was about wealth that attracted the wicked could well be the cause of their destruction. Continuing the theme of the achievements of the wicked, Zophar explained that such people "will not enjoy the streams, the rivers flowing with honey and cream"[178] (20:17), meaning that they will not gain any profit or benefit from their wickedness (20:18).

Zophar made an important point in this section: The punishment for sin is a slow process because God often permits the consequences of sin to work themselves out in a person's life. We would do well to be firm but gracious to those who are going through some form of "discipline" by God.

---

175. Literally, "evil is sweet in his mouth."
176. Literally, "like a morsel of food his tongue hid it in the middle of his palate." By synecdoche, tongue and palate can represent the whole mouth.
177. Literally, "bread." It is a figure of speech, synecdoche of the species: bread is put for all kinds of food, including fish. See Bullinger, *Figures of Speech*, 627.
178. There is a figure of speech, synecdoche of the species: honey is put for whatever is sweet and delicious. See Bullinger, *Figures of Speech*, 626.

GOD'S DISCIPLINE AND PUNISHMENT

The idea that suffering is the result of sin did not begin or end with Job. This idea was prevalent even in the time of Jesus Christ, when the automatic explanation for infirmities seemed to have been that these were the consequence of sin – either the sin of an individual or that of the person's parents. In John 9, we read about a man who was born blind. On seeing this man, the disciples asked Jesus if his infirmity was due to the man's sin or that of his parents. It seemed that they knew of no other explanation for such a disability. Jesus clarified the situation by declaring that the man's blindness had nothing to with sin but had "happened so that the works of God might be displayed in him" (John 9:3). Jesus then healed the man.

Pain and suffering are not always related to sin or punishment; but where sin is the cause of suffering, this is sometimes accompanied by punishment or discipline. It is important to understand the difference between the concepts of punishment and discipline. Punishment is a penalty for breaking the law or offending someone, which usually ends once the penalty is paid. Discipline, on the other hand, is a corrective process, which focuses on the development and transformation of the individual concerned.

It is often difficult to discern whether a person is suffering due to punishment or discipline. Sometimes, punishment and discipline may overlap. Sometimes, God has some specific purpose in view when he permits suffering. For instance, Yahweh acknowledged that he had let his people, who came out of Egypt, experience famine and thirst in order to humble them and test them to know what was in their heart, adding that these bitter experiences were meant to discipline them because he loved them (Deut 8:2–5).

When going through pain and suffering, and if you are wondering whether this is punishment or discipline, consider the following:

- The living God does not allow pain and suffering without a purpose.
- Where God allows pain and suffering, it is for his purpose and glory.
- A personal spiritual assessment—where is your heart?
- Sin may be one cause of suffering, but it is not the *only* reason for pain and suffering.
- Should you become aware of sin in your life – perhaps because someone who cares for you pointed it out – confess it immediately.
- Whether it is punishment or discipline, ask the Lord to help you discern his purpose and submit to this.

- If the trials persist, even though there is no sin involved, perhaps the Lord might be trying to teach you something or to call your attention back to himself.
- Whenever the Lord disciplines, he has your best interest at heart (Deut 8:5; Heb 12:4–11).

Someday, we maybe tasked with conducting a disciplinary process in relation to another person. In such a situation, we must make sure that the penalty is commensurate with the offense committed, that the disciplinary action is restorative in its purpose and nature, and that it does not do injustice to or degrade the person in any way, which could lead to the person losing face and even faith. The Deuteronomic law limited punishments such as beatings to 40 lashes so that the offender was not humiliated (Deut 25:1–3) – this illustrates the importance of being mindful of the context of the person under discipline and sensitive to what is acceptable within the person's culture. Southeast Asia is an honor-shame culture.

20:19–29 The Exasperation of Overlooking Repentance

Zophar gave two main reasons for the calamities experienced by the wicked man. First, the wicked man had grievously oppressed the poor, seized their houses, and left them destitute (20:19). Second, his "craving" was endless (20:20), and he used any means to satisfy his craving until there was nothing left for him to devour, whereupon the accumulation of wealth had to end. As a result, his fortune would not last (20:21) and, suddenly, he would find himself in great distress (20:22).

If Zophar had Job in mind as he spoke, then he was insinuating that Job had become rich through illegal means and by abusing the poor and the marginalized, and that what had happened to Job was the just consequence of such sin.

Zophar then offered an imprecatory prayer (20:23–29). In the Semitic world, imprecation "is still an honorable rhetoric device. The imprecation has a juridical function and was frequently a hyperbolic means (Pss 109:6–15; 139:19–22) of dealing with false accusation and oppression. Legally the false accusations and the very crimes committed are called down on the perpetrator's head."[179] An imprecation is a cry for justice and a call on God to address an injustice done, especially in the case of those who have no one to defend them.

Zophar declared that God would vent his burning anger against the wicked person (20:23). Even if he should escape the sword, he would not be able to escape the bronze arrow (20:24) that would penetrate his liver[180] (20:25). Death and poverty awaited the wicked man since the destruction[181] of his treasures was certain and fire would consume whatever was left of his house and also himself (20:26).

When Zophar said, "The heavens will expose his guilt; the earth will rise up against him" (20:27), he was using a figure of speech to explain that heaven and earth and everything in between would cooperate to bring about the destruction of the wicked person. God's anger would be poured out like a flood that washed away his house (20:28). God's inheritance for the wicked is the loss of life and accumulated wealth (20:29).

Zophar's speech focused narrowly on the terrible consequences of the sin of the wicked. While what he said is true, what he left unsaid is very dangerous. His speech gives no hint of the possibility of repentance or mercy and includes no evidence of compassion. Zophar seemed just as materialistic as the wicked people he had condemned since he viewed the loss of prosperity as the worst that could happen to a person under God's judgment (20:28).[182] Job, however, despite his great material losses, was tormented mainly by the loss of communication with God and his insufficient understanding of God's purpose in his suffering. Zophar "does not call Job to repentance and does not have a speech in the third cycle of speeches. This is his final word to Job, and he does not leave him with any hope, because he believes his fate is certain."[183]

Feeling insulted by Job's words, Zophar issued tirades about the plight of the wicked, claiming that he was citing ancient maxims. While there is some truth in what Zophar said – for instance, that the joy of the wicked was momentary (20:5), and that they would not enjoy the fruit of their labor (20:18) – his statements were observations about a typical wicked person. Seow argues that the "offenses of the wicked, especially when stated plainly (as in 20:19) are generic . . . while it is an exaggeration to say that Zophar has Job in mind throughout the poem, it is also difficult not to read Zophar as

---

179. Smick, "The Dialogue Dispute" in *Job*.
180. Literally, "gall bladder."
181. Literally, "total darkness."
182. Andersen, *Job*, 197.
183. Belcher, *Finding Favour*, 95.

responding at least indirectly to Job here and there."[184] If Zophar did indeed have Job in mind when he made some of these pronouncements (20:6, 9, 12), he was cruel and in error for counting Job among the wicked.

An important aspect of retributive justice is that God will definitely punish the wicked. In this chapter, this judgment takes the form of the premature death of the wicked and the inability to enjoy the fruit of their labor and their accumulated wealth.

Job did not disagree with Zophar's basic theological premise that the joy of the wicked is momentary. Job was already convinced that all human life is temporary and that the wicked would, ultimately, be judged by God. The difference between Zophar and Job was that Zophar – because he believed that God's judgment was immediate and, in this life – assumed that Job must have sinned and was suffering the consequences of it, whereas Job maintained that he was innocent of any such sin. Zophar assumed that suffering was always the result of God's punishment of sin, while Job believed that suffering could happen for unknown reasons and that, sometimes, the righteous suffered and the wicked did not.

Zophar was a good example of someone with correct theology in one area – the ultimate judgment of God on the wicked – but applied it wrongly, in this case, to an upright person. Zophar was a one-dimensional and small-minded person, who viewed Job's losses as nothing more than evidence of Job's wickedness and God's vengeance.

21:1–34 Job's Response to Zophar

Job called for silence so that he could share his own observations about the wicked, who were, in fact, prosperous and living a good life. He continued to address his friends as a group.[185] At the end of his speech, after refuting their arguments, Job rejected their counsel. In reflecting on Job 21, the following questions will be addressed: How does Job's description of the plight of the wicked differ from that of Zophar? Is there justice in children bearing the consequences of their parents' sins?

---

184. Seow, *Job 1–21*, 835.
185. In 21:2, the pronominal suffix of the noun is 2mp = "the consolation of you" or "your consolation." After a speech from a friend, Job responded. He would not only address his friend who just delivered his speech, but each of them in the group. This was first noted in 6:21 and observed in the chapters that followed: 12:2, 13:2, 16:2, 17:10, 19:2.

Job

21:1–6 Job's Appeal for His Friends to Listen

Job appealed to Eliphaz, Bildad, and Zophar to pay close attention to his words. If they would just give him the courtesy of listening, this would be more comfort and encouragement than any they had provided so far. He urged them to bear with him before they may continue to mock him (21:1–3) when they saw what had happened to him (21:5). Even Job admitted that when he remembered his shocking situation, he himself was terrified and physically shaken (21:6). Job was not being arrogant. He was simply trying to understand God's purpose in his situation.

21:7–16 Job's Claim that the Wicked Prosper

Job opposed and questioned Zophar's view that the wicked do not prosper and voiced his views concerning the wicked that they actually continue to live, grow old, and even become rich (21:7). Job refuted Bildad's claim that the wicked do not have children (18:19)[186] and asserted that the wicked do see their children and descendants prosper (21:8), their houses are secure and free from God's punishment (21:9), and their livestock give birth without miscarriages (21:10). The full-term development in the offspring of their livestock resulted in prosperity, and their children were happy and content for "they sing to the music of timbrel and lyre; they make merry to the sound of the pipe" (21:12). The ungodly had everything they needed and had no cause for concern, and, having finished their earthly life in prosperity, they went down to *Sheol* in peace – without experiencing the pain that normally accompanies death (21:13).

Job's reflection is reminiscent of the words of the psalmist who once envied the prosperity and success of the wicked but changed his perspective when, on visiting the temple, he realized the final destiny of the wicked (Ps 73:3–17).

Have you faced – or are you experiencing – a situation similar to that of the psalmist? Consider the following: (a) Since the living God is your loving heavenly Father, ask for what you need. If it is meant for you, he will give it to you; if it is not, and it will not ultimately benefit you then he will not give it to you. (b) Choose to enjoy what you have presently. (c) Refuse to entertain the idea that you can only enjoy life if and only if you can also have the material

---

[186]. Miscarriage, the natural loss of an embryo or fetus, and infertility, the inability to reproduce, are not the result of sin. It is therefore wrong to automatically accuse a person of sin when a miscarriage occurs or when there is infertility. Either two is part of the mystery in the creation of life. Also, embrace the reality that it is the living God alone who opens or closes the womb (Gen 30:22).

things that your neighbor owns. (d) Trust the Lord that he knows your needs and will provide in a timely manner.

From a limited and purely human perspective, many wicked people do seem to prosper and enjoy life. They do not want God in their lives and do not delight in knowing God's ways (21:14). Job himself quoted the questions the wicked might ask: "Who is the Almighty, that we should serve him? What would we gain by praying to him?" (21:15) Since the ungodly do not know God, they do not see their need of him and find no reason to serve or pray to him. They prosper in all areas of their lives without God and live to enjoy life. Under such conditions, who indeed would see their need for God?

Job was saying that it is rare, even unusual, that the wicked are suddenly judged and swept away. In fact, many wicked people seem to die happy, and many upright people die difficult and painful deaths. A person's character cannot be judged by the prosperity they enjoy – or lack – on earth. The Bible tells us that some of the greatest saints in history have been hungry, hunted, tortured, poor, jobless, murdered, and considered failures by those around them. The author of Hebrews simply states that "the world was not worthy of them" (Heb 11:38).

Job also added, "Their prosperity is not in their own hands" (21:16a), which must mean that it was in God's hands since the previous verse refers to the Almighty (21:15). "God controls the prosperity of the wicked, and that is what makes it an enigma when the 'counsel of the wicked' is so far from God (compare Ps 1:1)."[187] As if jolted back to reality, Job concluded by stating that he would not listen to the advice of the wicked (21:16b), and rightly so, for reasons that he would enumerate in the verses that follow.

21:17–21 Job's Claim that God Will Punish the Wicked

Having discussed the prosperity of the wicked, Job reflected on what happens when death or calamity come to the wicked: their life and prosperity is cut short by God and they become "like straw before the wind, like chaff swept away by a gale" (21:17–18). Both "straw" and "chaff" are light and combustible materials, and using these to describe the fate of the wicked implies that the wicked would soon perish (compare Ps 1:4).

Job cited his friends' belief about what would happen to the children of the wicked – that is, that God was storing up the punishment for a person's[188]

---

187. Smick, "The Dialogue Dispute" in *Job*.
188. Literally, "man."

iniquity for his children.[189] This recalls God's commandment: "I, the LORD your God, am a jealous God, punishing the children for the sin of the parents to the third and fourth generation of those who hate me" (Exod 20:5).

Job, however, paused here to voice a prayer: "Let him repay the wicked, so that they themselves will experience it!" (21:19). Job thought it more fitting that the eyes of the wicked should witness their own destruction and that they themselves should "drink the cup of the wrath of the Almighty" (21:20) – meaning that they themselves would suffer the consequences and punishment of their sins. He added that once the wicked were gone, they would not know what happened to those they left behind (21:21). We see here Job's uprightness in recognizing the injustice of children being made to suffer the consequences of the sins of their fathers. We find this same principle in Ezekiel: "The one who sins is the one who will die. The child will not share the guilt of the parent, nor will the parent share the guilt of the child. The righteousness of the righteous will be credited to them, and the wickedness of the wicked will be charged against them" (Ezek 18:20).

Although it often seems as if the wicked prosper and enjoy life on earth, at some point, there will come a time of reckoning. Job believed that if the wicked did not experience punishment during their lifetime, they would do so after death.

21:22–26 Job's Claim that Death Spares No One

The answer to Job's rhetorical question – "Can anyone teach knowledge to God?" – is obviously "no!" since God himself would be the one to judge "even the highest" or the angels (21:22).[190] Job's wisdom is evident in his recognition that no one can teach God anything since he alone is judge over all. Job observed that while one person "dies in full vigor" – perhaps at a young age, when strongest and most prosperous (21:23–24) – another may die "in bitterness of soul," with a broken heart and without having tasted the best of life (21:25). The common factor here is that both would be dead, buried, and rotting in the grave (21:26).[191] Truly, death is a leveler of everyone, whether young or old, rich or poor, beautiful or ugly, happy or sad.

---

189. Literally, "sons."
190. Literally, "the ones on high."
191. Literally, "consumed by worms."

21:27–34 Job's Perception of the Treachery of Friends

Job recognized his friends' treacherous thoughts and schemes to do him harm (21:27). He argued that any traveler could tell them that the wicked nobles, who were thriving everywhere, seemed to be spared judgment (21:29–30). In this context, judgment refers to immediate punishment of personal sins, which could include death. There seemed to be no one denouncing the wrongdoing of the wicked and repaying them for what they had done (21:31). Moreover, the wicked were carried peacefully to their graves, which were watched over by guards, and they were given a grand funeral, with a large procession following and preceding the coffin (21:32–33).

Job observed that the wicked had everything – a good life and, at the end of their life, a lavish funeral. Job concluded this chapter by saying that his friends could not really "console" him (21:34), just as he had earlier labeled them "miserable comforters" (16:2). Although Job had expected his friends to console him and ease his pain, they had failed miserably. Job considered their advice and responses and concluded that "nothing is left of your answers but falsehood" (21:34).[192] Neither their presence nor their words helped Job. If anything, they made things worse for him. Job not only experienced their lack of empathy but also their betrayal, and he rejected both their counsel and their definition of retributive justice.

Job's rebuttal of Zophar brings the second cycle of speeches to a close. After appealing for a sympathetic hearing (21:1–6), Job adopted the form of wisdom disputation to raise questions about the traditional view of predictable and immediate retribution (21:7–33) and concluded his speech by declaring that his friends could not help or console him in his pain (21:34).

Several features set this speech apart from Job's previous speeches. First, this is the first speech which is directed completely at his friends and not at God. Second, Job specifically responded to several accusations of his friends, and there are more direct connections to their previous speeches. And, as he addressed these issues, Job appears more rational and in control than he did in his earlier speeches. Third, the structure of this speech is more narrowly focused than the earlier speeches.

22:1–27:23 THE THIRD CYCLE OF SPEECHES

This cycle represents Job's friends' final attempt to make him admit his hidden sins. The speeches are shorter and include repetitions of some of the earlier

---

192. The Hebrew term can also mean "treacherous acts," "betrayal."

accusations. Eliphaz became more personal, directly identifying Job's assumed sins; Bildad focused on the transcendence of God and the finiteness of human beings; and Zophar did not even deliver a third speech.

Third Cycle	
Eliphaz	22
Job's response	23–24
Bildad	25
Job's response	26–27
Zophar	-
Job's response	-

22:1–30 Eliphaz Speaks

Eliphaz started off the third cycle of speeches. In his first speech, he had counseled Job to seek God (5:8) and accept the discipline of the Almighty (5:18). In his second speech, he indirectly accused Job of blasphemy against the Almighty (15:25–26). In this third speech, Eliphaz, using the second person "you," directly charged Job with sins he had not committed.

The questions to be addressed in relation to this chapter include the following: What did Eliphaz assume about God? What accusations did he dump on Job? How should we respond to false accusations?

22:1–5 Eliphaz Asserted that God Was Disinterested

Responding to Job's claim that the wicked go through life without being held accountable for the evil deeds they have committed, Eliphaz implied that God does not benefit from a person's virtue, innocence, or blamelessness (22:2–3). At first, his questions – emphatic on account of their repetition – were general. But then, beginning with verse 3, Eliphaz used "you" and "your" to directly address Job, asking sarcastically if Job really thought that God would judge him for his piety (22:4). Through a rhetorical question, Eliphaz suggested that Job's wickedness was great (22:5). Unlike his earlier oblique accusations, these were direct and blunt statements.

Eliphaz presumptuously spoke for God and misrepresented him by saying that Job's piety did not matter to the Almighty. He implied that it would be useless to bring a case before God since Job had committed grievous sins. This marked a change in Eliphaz's approach. In his first speech, he had encouraged

Job, citing himself as an example in speaking about presenting a case to God (5:8). In his second speech, as a warning to Job, he had presented the state of the wicked (15:20–24; 27–35). When Job decided to bring his case to the Almighty (compare 13:3, 13–18), Eliphaz – in this third and final speech – seemed to be blocking him.

From the start, Eliphaz misrepresented God in two ways. First, he claimed that the Almighty did not care whether or not Job pursued a godly life. However, it does matter to God that his children "be holy" (Lev 20:7, 20; Deut 23:14; 1 Pet 1:15) and live in reverential fear of him. As Smick points out, "Eliphaz does not know of God's contest with the Accuser over Job's former, blameless life."[193] Second, Eliphaz declared that God would not attend to Job because of his grievous and unnumbered sins; yet, God is a forgiving God (Pss 86:5; 103:12; 130:3–4; Isa 43:25; Dan 9:9; 1 John 1:9).

We are to represent the Lord, our heavenly Father, well. The apostle Paul called believers "Christ's ambassadors" (2 Cor 5:20) and acknowledged he was an "ambassador in chains" (Eph 6:20). In our contemporary settings, too, we may be misrepresenting God and Jesus Christ. For example, like Eliphaz, we may present an angry God who punishes the wicked, while forgetting to acknowledge that he is also a loving God who cares for his people (Deut 7:9; Pss 86:15; 136:26; Rom 5:8; Eph 2:4–5). And sometimes, we may try to "play God" in the lives of others, perhaps by taking it upon ourselves to police the sins of fellow believers in order to condemn and ostracize them, without any intention of seeking their restoration. Closer to home, we may misrepresent God when we make promises to our children and then break those promises.

Introducing the concept of God as our heavenly Father to children is good and necessary, but our behavior is even more important because children are greatly impacted by the way their earthly parents treat and raise them – and this can lead to their growing up either trusting God or staying away from anything related to God. Therefore, parents and others who are in a position of influence over children have a grave responsibility (Matt 18:6).

22:6–20 Eliphaz Accused Job of Disobedience

To prove that Job was not innocent as he had claimed to be, Eliphaz cited a long list of sins that, according to him, Job had committed (22:6–9) – a list without material evidence. First, he charged that Job had taken pledges for no

---

193. Smick, "The Dialogue Dispute" in *Job*.

reason and, thereby, "stripped people of their clothing, leaving them naked" (22:6).[194] In the ANE, there was a general command to do what was just.

The Mosaic legislation affirmed this and made specific provisions for marginalized groups in society. For instance, while garments could be taken as a pledge, the creditor had to return these items before sunset (Exod 22:26–27; Deut 24:10–13). Failure to follow this statute incurred God's wrath. Second, Eliphaz claimed that Job had failed to provide water and food for the weary and hungry (22:7), thereby neglecting this most basic form of kindness that characterizes an upright person. Third, Job, in his position of authority as a powerful landowner, had either oppressed widows and orphans – both marginalized groups – or failed to help them obtain justice (22:8–9).

Luke 1:53 is probably an allusion to Job 22:9. While Eliphaz accused Job of failing to respond to the needs of widows and orphans, Luke presents God as satisfying the needs of the hungry, but sending the rich away empty-handed. Those who neglect or abuse the helpless will find that they are denied God's mercy. On account of these assumed sins of omission, Eliphaz envisioned dire consequences for Job: traps, sudden terror (22:10), darkness surrounding him, so that he could not see, and flood waters, representing destruction (22:11). A common theme here is the suddenness with which these calamities would come and the totality of the destruction that they would bring. In the midst of these, Job would not experience God's mercy.

Acknowledging that God knows all that happens (22:12–20), Eliphaz brought God into the center of the discussion. He emphasized the sovereignty and exalted eminence of God – whose places is in the highest heavens, high above the stars (22:12) – as well as the fact that nothing escapes God's notice so that he judges fairly in spite of any perceived hindrance of darkness and thick clouds (22:13–14).

Since God is the all-knowing judge, Eliphaz counseled and warned Job not to follow the traditional path of sinners, which leads to destruction (22:15–16). In describing these sinners as those who commanded God to stay out of their lives, insisting that he had no involvement in their lives (22:17), Eliphaz seemed to be alluding to Job's earlier statement (compare 21:14). Eliphaz pointed out that it was God who had provided for the needs of these sinners (22:18) and added that their riches would soon be gone, and the upright

---

194. There is a figure of speech, a synecdoche where the whole is put for one of its parts. In this situation, it can refer to one who is scantily clad. See Bullinger, *Figures of Speech*, 637. The MT has "You take a pledge from your brother for nothing and strip the naked of their clothing."

would then have an opportunity to witness their "ruin" and "mock" their plight (22:19), saying, "Surely our foes are destroyed, and fire devours their wealth (22:20)." This suggests that the wicked will be totally destroyed, along with the possessions they have accumulated during their lifetime. Eliphaz, if he had Job in mind here, was suggesting that Job, if he repented, would have a chance to gloat over the misfortunes of his opponents.

God invites believers to rejoice when justice is served; but to rejoice over the misfortune of another – even an opponent or one who has offended us – is not pleasing to God: "As surely as I live, declares the Sovereign LORD, I take no pleasure in the death of the wicked, but rather that they turn from their ways and live" (Ezek 33:11). Proverbs counsels, "Do not gloat when your enemy falls; when they stumble, do not let your heart rejoice, or the LORD will see and disapprove and turn his wrath away from them" (24:17–18).

22:21–30 Eliphaz Appealed for Job to Repent

Following his presentation of God as the all-knowing judge, Eliphaz advised Job to be reconciled (*sakhan*)[195] to God by accepting and heeding the Lord's instructions (22:21–22). Eliphaz even made promises on behalf of God: If Job repented and returned to God, his prosperity would be restored (22:23). The proof of repentance would be for Job to "remove wickedness far from [his] tent" (22:23). This meant that any possessions that he had acquired by devious means would have to be returned – for instance, items that the marginalized had given him as pledges or the withheld wages of workers. Several consequences would flow from Job's repentance and obedience: the Almighty himself would be Job's prized treasure and reward (22:24–25), and Job's delight would be in him alone (22:26); God would listen to Job's prayers (22:27); and Job would be enabled to make good and successful decisions (22:28). Eliphaz concluded with two examples of situations in which Job's intercession would be effective: When Job prayed for the downcast, God would save them (22:29), and even a person who was "not innocent" would be delivered (*malat*) on account of Job's intercession (22:30). This is exactly what the Lord asked Job to do at the conclusion of the book – that is, to intercede for his friends, including Eliphaz (42:7–8). This chapter requires us to consider this question: Should Job repent simply in order that his possessions, power, and influence be restored to him?

---

195. *Sakhan* in the hiphil stem can mean "to have the habit of," "to get acquainted," "to reconcile." See *HALOT*, s.v. "sakhan."

JOB

23:1–24:25 Job's Response to Eliphaz

In response to Eliphaz's final appeal for repentance, Job persisted in his attempt to bring his case before God, seeing this as his only chance since his friends had pronounced him guilty even without a trial. Here are two questions to reflect on as you read Job 23: What was Job's foremost desire at this point? Can we be brutally honest with God?

23:1–7 Job's Longing

Job started by admitting that he still had a "bitter" (*meri*) complaint against God. This is the only time that the term "bitter" is used in the book, but this one word aptly summarizes how Job was feeling. The parallel line explains the reason for the bitterness: "his hand[196] is heavy in spite of my groaning" (23:2). The "hand" here refers to punishment,[197] and Job felt that God's punishment or chastisement – as he perceived this – was too severe. If he could just locate where God was, he would go there and present his case, backed up by many arguments (23:3–4). Job anticipated that God would not argue against Job's innocence (23:5–6). He was confident that God would not contend with him nor using his power, press charges against him (23:6). Job believed that "there" – that is, in the place where God is – the upright would be able to plead their case, and he also believed that if he could present his case "there," he would be acquitted: "I would be delivered forever from my judge" (23:7).

23:8–12 Job's Innocence

Job acknowledged that in whichever direction he went, he could not find God (23:8–9); consequently, his case could not be tried. But, reasoning that God knew how to handle him, Job was willing to be examined and "tested" by God so that he might be refined like gold (23:10). He claimed that he had closely and doggedly followed the path that God had laid, "without turning aside" (*natah*) from it (23:11) and that he had not "departed" or wandered (*mush*) away from God's commands[198] but claimed, "I have treasured the words of his mouth more than my daily bread" (23:12). In making these claims, Job denied that he had sinned – as his friends had insisted – and continued to assert his innocence.

---

196. The MT has *yadi* ("my hand") while the LXX and Syriac has *yado* ("his hand"). The latter is adopted in this work with the referent as God.
197. Bullinger, *Figures of Speech*, 879.
198. Note that two different Hebrew terms (*natah* and *mush*) are used but carry the same meaning.

23:13–17 Job's Frustration

Job stood in awe of God's presence (23:13–17). He affirmed that God is unique, that no one can oppose his plans (23:13), and that God would fulfill what had been prescribed for his own life (23:14). God is indeed sovereign over the hearts of all people and in every area of their lives. This was why Job repeatedly said that he was "terrified" in the presence of God. When Job contemplated the greatness of God, reverential "fear" (*pakhad*)[199] took hold of him and he gained confidence over the darkness (23:15–17). The Hebrew term used, which the NIV translates as "fear" in verse 15, refers to "awe" or "reverential fear." Job was terrified but, equally, felt a reverential fear of God. He then concluded and said: "Yet I am not silenced by the darkness, by the thick darkness that covers my face" (23:17). Indeed, Job would not be silent, but would present his case before God despite the seeming hindrances that he foresaw.

While Job was brutally honest before God, expressing what he thought and how he felt, in all this, he never cursed God – which was exactly what *Satan* had wanted in the first place (compare 1:11; 2:5). If you are wondering whether you can be brutally honest with God, here are some points to ponder:

- Open your heart to God, pouring out your concerns, telling God how you see things and what you feel and sense about your relationship with him.

- Remember that while the living God is personal, we must still approach him with reverential fear.

- Commit everything to the Lord, regardless of the situation that you are in, and determine that you will never curse God.

- Refuse to allow your pain and suffering to deteriorate to the point of bitterness and rebellion that moves toward unbelief.

- Always maintain fellowship with the living God.

What does this chapter tell us about God? According to Job, God is sometimes the author of calamities (23:2). The upright can reason with God, who is their judge, and expect a fair trial and vindication (23:7). From a human standpoint

---

199. The Hebrew word *pakhad* in the Qal stem simply means "be in awe." In the Piel stem, it is "to be in great dread." In the Hiphil stem, "to be filled with dread." The word is in the Qal stem in 23:15b, which hence allows for the rendering "in awe" or "reverential fear."

however, God can seem distant and elusive (23:8–9). Nevertheless, even calamities and difficult situations are often used by God to work something good (23:10). God is sovereign, and no one can influence or oppose his intentions (23:13). God inspires awe in people, as he did in Job (23:16).

In the next chapter, Job's frustrations increased because of God's apparent indifference to the acts of social injustice that abounded. Questions to be answered as we read Job 24 include the following: What are the social injustices addressed in this chapter? What are their manifestations in present-day situations? How can a church help to address these issues?

24:1–17 Job's Exasperation

Job started this pericope with a question: "Why from the Almighty are not the times hidden and they that know him not see his days?" (24:1).[200] Job was making the point that his friends could not perceive God's plans and purposes and that even those who knew God would not always witness the punishment of the wicked for the injustices they had committed.

Job proceeded to list some of the injustices that he had observed. First, wicked people "move boundary stones" to deceitfully obtain additional land, which they then used as pasture for stolen flocks (24:2). In the ANE, moving boundary stones was a common occurrence, which carried a corresponding punishment. Under the Deuteronomic law, a person who did such a thing was cursed (Deut 19:14; 27:17). Second, wicked people deprived orphans and widows of their work-animals by driving away the orphan's donkey and taking the widow's ox as a pledge (24:3). Today, in some parts of Southeast Asia, both donkey and ox continue to be used for farming. Taking away these animals would mean that their owners lose their primary means of eking out a living. Third, the actions of the wicked thrust the poor and needy into even more difficult situations (24:4). Job equated these marginalized people to wild donkeys who were compelled to scavenge for food wherever they could find it (24:5). The next verse, which repeats the message of verse 5, has two possible readings: "They reap their corn in the field" or "They reap their corn in a field that is not their own" (24:6a).[201] Bullinger reasons that there is a "case for ellipsis of the accusative, which must be supplied. The verse may then read,

---

200. This is a literal rendering of the MT. Bullinger recognizes a figure of speech, metonymy of the adjunct: the day is used for what transpires during it and the context dictating what it is *Figures of Speech*, 594. The NIV has "Why does the Almighty not set times for judgment?"
201. These are the literal renderings of the MT.

'They reap [their corn] in a field not their own. They glean the vintage of the wicked.'"[202] Poorly clothed and exposed to the elements, they were forced to huddle close to a rock for shelter (24:7–8). Fourth, a child without a father is taken away from the mother while he is still breastfeeding. And worst, if the infant in the next line refers to the same child, that infant is taken to pay a debt because the family is poor (24:9). Injustice is done on the child, on the mother, and on the marginalized family. This is a heart-wrenching situation. And sad to say, this type of injustice still happens in some parts of the world today though the cases are not often reported. Fifth is the abuse of slaves and laborers (24:10–11). Even in their utter poverty – no food or clothing – they were forced to work in the olive groves and vineyards (24:10–11). These descriptions imply that the poor and needy had become slaves of the landowners under whom they had suffered abuse – working without proper clothing to protect them from the elements and being denied the privilege of eating and enjoying what they had harvested. These wounded souls "groan and cry out for help; but God has not charged the perpetrators of injustice" (24:12, my translation). The parallelism emphasizes the agony of the poor, who cried out to God for help without receiving immediate answers.

The social injustices that are identified in this chapter include land-grabbing, kidnapping, ill-treatment of widows and orphans, and abuse of slaves and laborers. The Deuteronomic law includes several provisions intended to protect the poor and the marginalized: slavery is limited to seven years (Deut 15:12–18); kidnapping is a capital offense (24:7); pledges taken by creditors are to be returned by sunset (24:10–13); poor laborers are to be paid their daily wage by the end of the day (24:15); foreigners, orphans, and widows are to be treated kindly (24:17); landlords are to provide for the poor and needy (24:19–22); and a curse is incurred by those involved in land-grabbing by moving boundary stones and those who withhold justice from the marginalized (27:17, 19).

Extending kindness is a legacy that we can leave to future generations. In the 1940s, slavery[203] was still in place in some parts of the Philippines – for instance, in the province of Benguet. Either the masters had inherited slaves

---

202. Bullinger, *Figures of Speech*, 8–9.
203. "There was no more slavery in the 1960s. It was in the late 1950s that owners were ordered to release their *baga-en* (slaves)" (Belinda Myerson, interview by author *via* Messenger, October 22, 2022). Refer also to Proclamation No. 397, s. 1965, which was signed by then President Diosdado Macapagal on May 15, 1965. This proclamation made public "the supplementary convention on the abolition of slavery, the slave trade, and institutions and practices similar to

from their parents or they had personally bought them. A family had a slave that they inherited. This slave took care of a person we shall call Mr. X, the eldest of seven siblings. When the slave was set free, Mr. X became very ill and longed for the slave to come back, but this was not possible anymore due to the declaration that all slaves must be set free. Years passed. Then before Mr. X passed away, he instructed his daughter to locate the former slave's grandson and help him receive education. Mr. X could not undo the abuses that his grandparents had done to these precious people, but when he was able, he tried in some simple ways to extend kindness to their families.

Postmodern forms of slavery include human trafficking, child sex trafficking, child labor, indentured slavery, forced labor, and forced marriages, which are common in Southeast Asia, as well as in many other parts of the world. Many are forced into these miserable situations in order to survive or to pay off inherited debts, while many others are victims who have been lured into such situations under false pretenses.

Overseas Filipino Workers (OFWs), especially domestic helpers (DHs), could easily fall into such situations if some or all of the following conditions occur: (a) they live in the same house as their employers and are subject to exploitation; (b) they do not have a day off and are not free to leave the house; (c) they are not paid on time, and their wages are often withheld; (d) they are not provided with decent meals; (e) their passports and identification papers are confiscated by their employers on arrival; (f) they are unjustly accused and beaten by their employers; and (g) they are not allowed to communicate with their family members. What can be done in such cases? If you are aware of someone in this situation, you could pray for that person and ask the Lord to guide you on how to help in practical ways.

Job went on to describe the wicked as those who defy even the law of nature by doing their work at night – stealing and robberies when they should be sleeping as the rest (compare 24:16) and engaging in evil deeds at all times (24:13). He cited the example of murderers, adulterers, and thieves, who not only do their evil deeds under cover of darkness (24:14–16) but have become accustomed to and welcome the "terrors of darkness" (24:17).

The friends had insisted that God punishes the wicked immediately. To disprove this claim, Job observed that the wicked prosper and enjoy life, while

---

slavery, done at the European Office of the United Nations at Geneva, on September 7, 1956." See "Proclamation No. 397, s. 1965," *Official Gazette of the Republic of the Philippines*, http://www.mirror.officialgazette.gov.ph.

their wickedness knows no bounds. If these people were indeed being judged immediately, as the friends had claimed, how could the injustices described in the farms and plantations ever be reconciled? There was a discrepancy between the friends' claims and Job's experiences.

Job 24:13–17 seems to connect with this verse: "Everyone who does evil hates the light, and will not come into the light for fear that their deeds will be exposed" (John 3:20). The wicked love darkness and do not want to come into the light because they do not want their evil deeds to be exposed. The light, obliquely referred to in John, is Jesus Christ. From a spiritual standpoint, people do not want to come to Jesus because doing so involves admitting their spiritual bankruptcy and commitment to Jesus Christ means staying and continuing to walk in the light.

24:18–25 Job's Confidence

Because of Job's belief that the wicked are punished immediately, scholars disagree about whether or not verses 18–25 were spoken by Job, and some wonder if these verses should be added to Bildad's speech (Job 25). Longman asserts that there is no textual indication that these words are not Job's and suggests that Job might have been anticipating the ultimate fall of the wicked.[204] Smick reasons that these verses should be viewed as Job's wish list.[205] These need not be moved elsewhere for they are a continuation of Job's observations on what becomes of the wicked and express his belief that there is an end to wickedness.

Job pointed to the plight of the wicked. First, their inheritance, which includes land, will be cursed so that it does not yield any produce (24:18). Second, *Sheol* will receive them as readily as heat absorbs water from the snow (24:19). Third, they will be forgotten even by their own mothers, and maggots will feast on their corpses (24:20a). Finally, they will be like trees that are cut off (24:20b). Both evildoers and their deeds – which included preying on barren women and widows (24:21) – will, therefore, cease since God will destabilize proud evildoers (24:23). Although momentarily exalted, the wicked will ultimately be "brought low" and "cut off like heads of grain" (24:24) – they could be destroyed anytime, just as a tree is cut off at the appointed time or corn is plucked and gathered when it is ready for harvest.

Any form of injustice must be avoided for it violates the image of God that is inherent in the victim (Gen 1:26–28). This image of God does not

---

204. Longman, "Job's Seventh Response" in *Job*.
205. Smick, "The Dialogue Dispute" in *Job*.

only cover the ability to rule over creation but includes the mental, moral, and social aspect of a person (Eph 4:24; Col 3:10). Mentally, human beings were created as rational beings with the capacity to think and reason. Morally, humans were created to reflect the holiness of God, and they continue to bear this moral image of God even though this is corrupted by sin on account of the fall. Socially, human beings were created to have fellowship with both God and others (Gen 2:18; 3:8) and have the capacity to relate to each other with love and respect. To mistreat a person or act unjustly toward him or her is to sin against both God and the other person.

If there is any agency or organization that should take the lead in social reform, it is the church. But is the church doing its duty? Is it truly a place where social injustice is not tolerated? Is your local church free from social injustice? Is it fulfilling its role in furthering reforms that would eliminate unjust practices and create a better social environment for all people?

When there is social injustice, here are some things that we, as believers, should consider or do:

- Identify the form of injustice.
- Determine the cause of the injustice.
- Assess the effect of the injustice on a family, clan, local church, or at a national level.
- Are the responsible parties aware of the injustice?
- What has my local church done to rectify this problem?
- Seek the Lord's will about what should be done to help alleviate or rectify an injustice.
- Make viable proposals to the appropriate authorities and agencies.
- Commit to be part of the solution instead of contributing to the cause of an injustice.
- Remember that we stand accountable to God for our words and actions for nothing is hidden from him.

After his lengthy explanation about the fate of the wicked, Job concluded by challenging his friends to disprove his observations and arguments. If they could prove that his words were "false," then whatever Job had said would be nullified (24:25).

25:1–6 Bildad Speaks

Bildad's final speech is a short one. It is also the last of the speeches of the three friends. Some scholars attempt to use some material from Job 26–27 to add to Bildad's final speech or to create a third speech for Zophar. But, as Belcher suggests, to "accept the incomplete third cycle as evidence that the debate has collapsed."[206] Here is a question to consider as we reflect on this chapter: If a person is just like "a worm," what value does that person have according to Bildad?

25:1–3 God Is Infinite

Bildad argued that dominion and awesome power belong to God, who "establishes order in the heights of heaven" (25:2), meaning that it was God who had set in place the laws of nature to maintain order in the universe. Moreover, in every spiritual conflict, too, God is in control and has at his disposal a whole army – "forces" or a host (*gedud*) – that cannot be numbered.[207] In the immediate context, this is a reference to angels. That God's light shines on everyone (25:3) seems to "suggest that God's searching scrutiny holds all beings, terrestrial and celestial to account."[208]

What does this final speech of Bildad reveal about God? God is sovereign over the universe, having "dominion and awe" (25:2a). He is omnipotent in that he is the one who establishes order in heaven (25:2b). His forces cannot be numbered and his light shines on everyone (25:3).

25:4–6 Human Beings are Finite

Bildad claimed that no human being can be upright before God and that no one "born of a woman" can be "pure" (*zakhah*). He argued that if even "the moon is not bright" and "the stars are not pure" (*zakhakh*)[209] in God's eyes (25:5), how much less could a mortal being – whom he likens to a "maggot" or "a worm" (25:6)[210] – be pure! Apart from the wordplay, the parallelism equates the worm with the maggot, and both images emphasize the insignificance of

---

206. Belcher, *Finding Favour*, 109.
207. This Hebrew term is used three times in the book of Job (19:12; 25:3; 29:5) and can mean either a military troop or angels.
208. Alter, *Writings*, 530.
209. This word is used only four times in the entire *Tanakh* and three of these are in the book of Job (9:30; 15:15; 25:5). The other is Lamentations 4:7.
210. There is a word play here. Bildad used two words (*zakhah* and *zakhakh*) of the same meaning, yet slightly different in the root word by one letter, ending with either "h" or "kh."

humankind before God. "These terms symbolize a wretched, lowly existence, and they have the smell of death about them."[211]

If God is morally perfect and no human being is upright before him, then this included Job himself, along with the rest of the human race. Bildad was directly refuting Job's claim to be innocent (9:15; 10:7; 23:11–12). In the same way, when Bildad correctly asserted that God is upright in the execution of justice, he was refuting Job's accusation that God is not just!

Imagine a person sitting through several counseling sessions and hearing the kinds of things that Job's friends said to him: You are witless (Zophar); your blameless life does not matter to God (Eliphaz); you are insignificant before God (Bildad). Is there anyone whose self-worth would not be affected by such statements? As a believer in the Lord Jesus Christ, when you are inundated with lies and false accusations from the enemy, reaffirm these truths in your life:

Who I Am?
- I am a child of God (John 1:12).
- I am a joint heir with Christ, sharing in his inheritance (Rom 8:17).
- In Christ, I am a new creation, a new person (2 Cor 5:17).
- I am reconciled to God, and I am a minister of reconciliation (2 Cor 5:18–20).
- I am a saint, set apart for God (Eph 1:1).
- I am a fellow citizen with the rest of the people in God's family (Eph 2:19).
- I am chosen and dearly loved by God (1 Thess 1:4).
- I am born of God, and the evil one cannot touch me (1 John 5:18).
- I am not the great "I AM" (Exod 3:14; see also John 8:24, 28, 58) but, by the grace of God, I am what I am (1 Cor 15:10).[212]
- Since I am in Christ, by the grace of God, I have been justified – completely forgiven and made righteous (Rom 5:1).
- I have been bought with a price; I am not my own; I belong to God (1 Cor 6:19–20).

---

211. Hartley, *Book of Job*, 357.
212. These were selected from the list of Neil T. Anderson, *Victory Over the Darkness* (Ventura: Regal Books, 1990), 45–47. It is also part of the materials he gave during a seminar in San Juan City, Philippines in the 1990s, of which he instructed the participants to share to others.

- I have been crucified with Christ, and it is no longer I who live, but Christ lives in me. The life I am now living is Christ's life (Gal 2:20).
- I have been blessed with every spiritual blessing (Eph 1:3).
- I was predestined – determined by God – to be adopted as God's son or daughter (Eph 1:5).
- I may approach God with boldness, freedom, and confidence (Eph 3:12).
- I have been rescued from the domain of Satan's rule and transferred to Christ's kingdom (Col 1:13).[213]

One of Job's requests was that his friends just listen to what was in his heart. But he received only accusations and – when he decided to present his case before God – discouragement. Bildad, pointing to God's transcendence, insisted that God would not bother to listen to a sinner, an insignificant creation such as Job. Since Bildad's intention in emphasizing humanity's insignificance was to discourage Job from bringing his case before God, his statements were quite forceful. Yet, there was nothing new in them, and he was merely reiterating the view already expressed by Eliphaz that no human being is upright and innocent before God (4:17–19; 15:14–16). Although this is true, by focusing so much on God's transcendent attributes, Job's friends ignored the fact that God also chose to be gracious and extend mercy to his frail creatures. This aspect of grace is what is missing in the retributive justice that they espoused. Bildad "believes in an ordered world . . . that is founded on RP"[214] or the so-called Retribution Principle.

26:1–14 Job's Response to Bildad

Bildad had argued against Job's claim to be innocent, insisting that no mortal being is righteous before God. Three questions can usefully be addressed as we read Job 26: Did Job accept Bildad's counsel? What did Job think about it? How did he feel about it?

---

213. Anderson, *Victory Over the Darkness*, 57–59.
214. Walton, *Job*, 249.

JOB

26:1–4 Job Questioned Bildad's Counsel

Job responded to Bildad with a series of statements in which he used a particle that, in this context, is best translated "how"[215] to add force to the contempt he felt toward his friends' actions. Bullinger recognizes irony in verses 2–3 in the way that Job responded.[216] He singled out Bildad and, while acknowledging that Bildad had "helped," Job saw it as "pretending to help when the one offering help is powerless to do so."[217] Since there is irony here, Job's statements actually denied that Bildad had been able to deliver the helpless, counsel the unwise, or offer insights that helped to understand Job's own situation. Bildad had failed to deliver profitable words of advice to Job (26:4). It is obvious that Bildad's source of counsel was not God.

26:5–14 Job Acknowledged God's Creative Power

Bildad had tried to inform Job of the supremacy of God and the relative insignificance of humankind. It was now Job's turn to inform Bildad of what he knew about God. Although God is only referred to by the pronoun "he," the "chapter is full of activities that can only be attributed to God."[218] God has knowledge, power, and control over the realm of the dead (*rephaim*)[219] and is aware of how the inhabitants in that place writhe in pain or are "in deep anguish" (26:5). God also knows all about *Sheol*, the place of the dead – which is identified in the parallel line as "Destruction" (=*abaddon*) – for it is "uncovered" or laid bare before him (26:6).

In the next few verses (26:7–10), Job portrayed God's control over the whole earth (above the subterranean waters) and his ongoing actions in maintaining the universe, the effects of which can be observed by humankind.

> "He spreads out the northern skies over empty space;
>   he suspends the earth over nothing" (26:7).
> "He wraps up the waters in his clouds,
>   yet the clouds do not burst under their weight" (26:8).

---

215. Williams, *Hebrew Syntax*, 24.
216. Bullinger, *Figures of Speech*, 813. Literally, "an arm without strength."
217. Alter, *Writings*, 532.
218. Walton, *Job*, 249.
219. Literally, "shades," "ghosts" = "departed spirits." Walton identifies the Rephaim with the "shades of perhaps deified royal ancestors," *Job*, 250.

"He covers the face of the full moon,[220]
    spreading his clouds over it" (26:9).
"He marks out the horizon [*khag*] on the face of the waters
    for a boundary between light and darkness" (26:10).

The Hebrew term *khag* pertains to a "circle."[221] The same word is used in Isaiah 40:22, where the earth is conceived of as a disk,[222] and also as a reference to the vault of heaven (Job 22:14). Long before Job and his friends were born, Yahweh God existed. He alone is worthy of our worship and praise. This same God is alive today and continues to invite people to come to himself in Jesus Christ (Matt 11:28). Job refused to accept Bildad's counsel and his friend's attempt to enlighten him about what God could do. Job's speech reveals that he knew more about God than his friend and, thus, it was he who informed and enlightened Bildad.

In this chapter, Job acknowledged God's omnipotence in creating the heavens and the earth (26:7). God is ruler of everything that he created, including the rain and the clouds (26:8–9), and is sovereign over earthquakes (26:11), tidal waves, the sea monster (26:12), and the gliding serpent (26:13). In referring to these animals, Wilson suggests, "This is an anticipation of the second Yahweh speech (chs 40–41) and shows the possibility of Behemoth and Leviathan being creatures of mythology at that point."[223] Their significance is that "God has control over the forces that might cast fear into the human heart."[224] All these things represent just a fraction of God's power and majesty.

Any person can know the living God through the Scriptures. For example, the book of Exodus reveals many dimensions and attributes of God, including God's own self-revelation: He is the God who keeps his promises (2:23–25); the personal and eternal God who is the great "I am" (3:12–15); omnipotent (7:14–29; 11:1–10); Yahweh Rophe[225] (15:25–26); Yahweh Nissi[226] (17:8–15); Yahweh Eliezer[227] (18:4); greater than all gods (18:11); most holy, and awesome God (19:9, 12–13, 18); who forbids idolatry (20:4–5); whose presence

---

220. Walton translates the sentence as: "the one edging the surface of [his] throne by spreading his cloudbank over it," *Job*, 255.
221. See *HALOT*, s.v. "khug."
222. *HALOT*, s.v. "khug."
223. Lindsay Wilson, *Job, Two Horizons Old Testament Commentary* (Grand Rapids: Eerdmans, 2015), 129.
224. Wilson, *Job*, 129.
225. "Yahweh, the one who heals," or "The Lord heals."
226. "Yahweh, my banner" or "The Lord, my banner."
227. "Yahweh, my helper" or "The Lord, my helper."

is like a consuming fire (24:17); who spoke to Moses "face to face" (33:11); who is patient, kind, faithful (34:6–7); and a transcendent yet personal God (40:34–38).

27:1–23 Job's Closing Disclosure

Taking a personal inventory of our lives is not easy. It is a hard, tiresome, time-consuming, and a painful process, but doing so usually places us in a better position to love and serve God. Suffering often drives us to self-examination and to critically evaluate our spiritual life. As we reflect on Job 27, here are two important questions to address: To what does the "breath of God" refer? Are believers supposed to use imprecatory prayers?

27:1–6 Job's Assertion of Innocence

Job began chapter 27 with an oath: "As surely as God lives" (27:2a). He "is not simply making a serious statement but is delivering an ultimatum to his friends – further debates will be useless."[228] Wilson sees this as Job's first oath of clearance or innocence.[229] An oath that is "based on the existence of God is the most extreme (the last resort) in Job's society for a condemned person to plead innocent."[230] This oath is also Job's final step. "He speaks of an oath to the court as if it were in session. In his oath, he refers to the hearing whether one is listening or not."[231]

Job pointed out that God had "denied" or withheld justice from him (27:2b), by which he probably meant that "God has denied him the right to defend himself in court."[232] The parallel line describes God as the Almighty (*Shadday*) who had made his life "bitter" (27:2c). Despite these complaints, however, Job affirmed that he would maintain his integrity "while my breath[233] is still within me and the breath from God is in my nostril" (27:3, my

---

228. Walton, *Job*, 259.
229. Wilson, *Job*, 130. Job gives another oath in chapter 31.
230. Smick, "Dialogue Disputes" in *Job*.
231. Vicchio, *Book of Job*, 188.
232. Walton, *Job*, 259.
233. *HALOT*, s.v. "nshm." The Hebrew word *neshama* by itself means "air." When it is attached to other words, however, it will carry different meanings. For instance, it may refer to the plain movement of air (2 Sam 22:16; Ps 18:16), breath of a person (1 Kgs 17:17; Isa 2:22), the act of breathing life onto a person as was the breathing of life on Adam and Eve (Gen 2:7), the breathing of God (Job 4:9, 32:8, 33:4; Isa 30:33), or simply a living being (Deut 20:16, Isa 57:16).

translation).[234] Job was saying that while he had breath – the same breath that God had breathed on Adam and Eve at creation – he would not speak or utter evil or anything deceitful (27:4).

The NT affirms that God is the source of this "breath of life." For instance, the apostle John, in a vision, saw that "the breath of life from God" entered the two prophets killed by the beast from the abyss (Rev 11:11). Just as God gives life, it is also God who takes back this life from those to whom he has given it – whether the wicked or the upright. Job promised to tell only the truth. He would be totally transparent and open with his assessment of himself. The parallelism emphasized Job's desire not to sin with regard to his speech. Facing his friends, Job issued an oath that began with a strong negative interjection, "I will never" or *far be it* – that he would ever declare his friends to be upright. Job affirmed that as long as he lived, he would not let go of his "integrity"[235] (27:5) but would maintain his "innocence" (27:6). Job refused to accept the accusations of his friends and confess to sins he had not committed merely in order to restore his former status in life.

27:7–10 Job's Prayer against His Enemies

Who was Job's enemy? He described such a person as "one who rises or takes a stand against him" (27:7, my translation).[236] Job uttered an imprecation[237] against his enemies, asking that God would cut them off or take their life and not listen to their cry when distress overwhelmed them (27:8–9). This was because they did not take delight in the Almighty and did not call on God at all (27:10) – here, Job used the same term that Eliphaz had earlier used when encouraging Job to return to God and delight himself in the Almighty (22:26). Was it right for Job to make this imprecatory prayer? Perhaps not, but he was expressing his thoughts about people who claimed to be his friends and yet brought accusations against him. He was being human. This, however, does not justify his or our desire to pray such imprecatory prayers.

---

234. The NIV has: "As long as I have life within me and, the breath of God in my nostril." There is synonymous parallelism here where *neshama*, meaning "breath" is parallel to the word *ruakh*, which can also mean "spirit", "wind", "breath".
235. Smick, "The Dialogue Dispute" in *Job*.
236. This is a literal rendering of the Hebrew Hithpolel participle from *qum*.
237. Refer to the explanation of an imprecatory prayer in Job 20:23 of this work.

27:11–23 Job's Desire to Educate His Friends

Job said to his friends, "Let me teach you concerning the power of God. I will not hide who the Almighty is. Behold! All of you have seen this, so why have you become so vain?"[238] (27:11–12, my translation).[239] What Job meant was that this "smug assumption that the speaker knows what God knows about good and evil, reward and punishment, is characteristic of the friends."[240] As he had been compelled to do throughout the debates, Job once again defended himself. In the ancient world, affirming one's innocence in words was not enough. Often, this had to be accompanied by calling on God – both as a witness and to punish the guilty one. Job's three friends, and all who agreed with them, had become Job's enemies. Convinced of his innocence, Job would not give in to their unfounded accusations (27:12).

Although some scholars see Job 27:13–23 as the words of Zophar, this section is consistent with Job's imprecation against his enemies in verses 7–10. Moreover, Job did not deny that the wicked would *"eventually* be punished; he only questioned why they continued to prosper."[241] Scripture is full of instances where God causes the evil intended or done to backfire as a punishment on the evildoers themselves. The evil done by Pharaoh in ordering that the infant Hebrew boys be drowned ended with the drowning of the Pharaoh who was ruling at that time,[242] along with the Egyptian army, in the Red Sea (Exod 1:15–22; 14:5–10; 23–31). Haman built gallows to hang Mordecai but, instead, he himself was hanged (Esth 7:10). Daniel's enemies plotted to murder him but, ultimately, it was they who were thrown into the lions' den (Dan 6:24).[243]

Job acknowledged that his friends were witnesses to the power of God. Yet, their actions spoke otherwise. The parallelism in verse 13 emphasizes that

---

238. This is a literal rendering of the MT. The NIV has "I will teach you about the power of God; the ways of the Almighty I will not conceal. You have all seen these yourselves. Why then this meaningless talk?"
239. The Hebrew term used for "to teach" is in the cohortative mood (parsed: imperfect, first person, singular, a request or command) indicating a request of the first person. It allows therefore for verse 11 to begin with "Let me." There is a sense in which Job was asking permission before he could do what he was planning to do (teach). Asking permission in that context would be very appropriate.
240. Alter, *Writings*, 533.
241. Zuck, *Job*, 121.
242. The Pharaoh who ordered the infanticide is not the same as the Pharaoh at the time of the exodus.
243. Wiersbe, *Be Patient*, 105.

while the "wicked" – who are also described as being "ruthless" – might enjoy progeny, wealth, and life, they will ultimately lose all these blessings.

Although the wicked might have numerous children, these children would die by the "sword" and "never have enough to eat" (27:14). The wicked man would not be mourned for by his widows (27:15). The plural form "presupposes polygamy. Presumably the widows will not mourn because they have no use for their good-for-nothing husband."[244] Upon his death, these wives became widows. In ancient times, a widow – unless she had adult children to look after her – was in a very vulnerable situation, just like other marginalized groups such as orphans and foreigners. In the time of Moses, God made statutory provisions for the care of these groups (Exod 22:22–25; Deut 10:18; 24:17–19). Since the widows referred to in Job had lost their provider and protector, we would expect them to be mourning for him; yet, Job declared that "their widows will not weep for them" (27:15). It is possible that the wicked husband only brought these women shame and pain, and, hence, they did not mourn for him but welcomed their freedom at his death.

POLYGAMY IN THE OLD TESTAMENT AND IN ASIA

Beginning with Adam and Eve, the first husband and wife, God designed marriage to be monogamous (Gen 2:21–24). The fall, however, disrupted that design.

Old Testament Context

Lamech, from the line of Cain, was the first man to have two wives (Gen 4:19). The patriarch Abraham had a legal wife and a concubine. Although Isaac had one wife, his son Jacob had two wives (Leah and Rachel) and two concubines (Bilhah and Zilpah). Leah had six sons and a daughter (30:20–21), Rachel had two sons (30:23–24; Gen 35:17–18), Bilhah had two sons (Gen 30:4–8), and Zilpah also had two sons (Gen 30:9–13). Genesis offers no explicit condemnation or endorsement of these polygamous unions. Polygamy is a general term for marriage to more than one wife or husband concurrently.[1]

During the time of Moses, the Deuteronomic law included a regulation for the king, who was God's representative for the people: "He must not take many wives, or his heart will be led astray" (Deut 17:17). Disobedience to this

---

244. Alter, *Writings*, 533.

statute had dire consequences. For instance, Solomon had seven hundred wives and had acquired three hundred concubines, and these women turned his heart away from God to worship other gods (1 Kgs 11:3–4).

An examination of polygamous unions in the OT reveals that most of these men had the means to support additional wives. They had their own reasons for choosing polygamy. For Jacob, it was to marry his first love; for David, it was usually for political alliances – although, in one instance, it was to provide for and protect Abigail (1 Sam 25:39–43). The women who married these men had the security of a home, provision, and protection. An unmarried woman in those days was under the protection of her father or a male family member; once she married, that responsibility was taken on by her husband. A woman who had been widowed was vulnerable to exploitation. This was one reason why Naomi decided to send her daughters-in-law home to their families in Moab after they were widowed (Ruth 1:8–11); and when Ruth chose to go with her to Bethlehem, Naomi took upon herself the responsibility to find a husband for Ruth (Ruth 3:1).

Polygamy caused many problems. There was often jealousy among the wives – for instance, Elkanah's wife Peninnah made life difficult for Hannah, his other wife (1 Sam 1:1–8). There was sibling rivalry, as in the case of Joseph and his brothers (Gen 37:3–4). There was also the question of who would receive the double portion of the inheritance: the firstborn of the first wife or the firstborn of the second wife, if she was the favorite wife? In the case of Jacob, would the double portion go to Reuben (Leah's firstborn) or Joseph (Rachel's firstborn)?

Jesus Christ on Polygamy

Jesus Christ did not condone polygamy. His response to the Pharisees – when they asked him whether it was lawful for a man to divorce his wife for any reason – made this clear. Jesus pointed them back to God's original design for a monogamous marriage – one man, one woman (Matt 19:5–6; see also Gen 2:24). To divorce a wife to take on another wife constitutes adultery – which violates the seventh commandment (Exod 20:14) – and can lead to a polygamous relationship. Although Moses permitted divorce, "Jesus' reply implies that it was not what he wanted."[2]

This teaching of Jesus Christ on monogamy was revolutionary because it meant that a married man could not marry a widow. In societies where polygamy is practiced, widows can be the second wife of a married man, but Christians are not permitted to do so. With the expansion of the church in Jerusalem, caring for widows was one of the problems that the apostles had to address (Acts 6:1–7). When they discovered that the Hellenistic Jewish widows were being neglected, the apostles assigned deacons to attend to their needs. The problem of caring for widows was not limited to Jerusalem but was also found in other places. Paul encouraged women to minister to widows so that the church could focus on those who had no one else to take care of them (1 Tim 5:16). Paul, in his epistles, also affirmed Christ's teaching on monogamy. One of the requirements he specified for church leaders was that they be "the husband of one wife" (1 Tim 3:2, 12; Titus 1:6 ESV).

The Asian Context
Some cultures, communities, and people groups in Asia continue to practice polygamy. How do we counsel a man who comes to faith in Jesus Christ and is concurrently living with two or more wives? An elderly pastor, working among minority people groups who were coming to Christ, counseled his clients in this way:

- Pray and seek the Lord's will on how to go about this matter.
- Choose, from among the wives, the one with whom you would like to live for the rest of your life.
- Renew your marriage vows with her.
- Talk to the other wives. If they can be independent and live on their own, send them off peacefully, with gifts that they can use as capital to start a new life independent of you. If you think that they cannot survive independently of you, let them live in another house and provide for them, but refrain from sleeping with any of them. If, one day, they choose to leave, set them free peacefully, with gifts to be able to start a new life elsewhere.[3]

---

1. The more specific term "polygyny" is the marriage of a man to more than one wife while "polyandry" is the marriage of a woman to more than one husband. Polygyny appears to be more common in the OT narratives.
2. Uytanlet and Kwa, *Matthew*, 200.
3. I acknowledge that other more mature believers have differences of opinion with this assessment.

Although the evildoer had heaped up wealth – both "silver like dust"[245] and "clothes like piles of clay" (27:16) – the upright would end up wearing these garments and inheriting the wicked person's money (27:17). Hence, the wicked would not be able to enjoy the fruit of their labor. Even "the house he builds is like a moth's cocoon, like a hut made by a watchman" (27:18),

---

245. Literally, "silver like dust." Proverbially and by metonymy "dust" refers to an immense amount. See Bullinger, *Figures of Speech*, 758.

meaning that the house was made of flimsy and combustible materials, which would soon be lost along with his wealth (27:19).

As to the life of the wicked, Job explained that natural catastrophes[246] will overwhelm them and, like a flood or whirlwind, suddenly snatch them, sweeping them away and mercilessly uprooting them (27:20–22). Any attempt to break free or "flee" (27:22b), will be met with derisive "claps" (*sapaq*) and "hisses" (*sharaq*) (27:23).[247]

The use of the "s" sounds in these verses help to bring out the utter helplessness of the wicked when the calamities come. Of course, this is not evident when the words are translated into another language, but if one could listen to these words read one after the other in Hebrew, one could almost hear a hissing sound – a sound of derision. More importantly, who or what is the referent in verse 23? The nearest antecedent is the "east wind" in verse 21. There is a personification in these verses, with the east wind depicted as having hands to seize and carry off the wicked person. Consequently, even if the wicked person tried to hold on to something, the force of the east wind would sweep him away and, in the end, he would be totally destroyed. Smick observes an *inclusio* in verse 23 and argues that the referent is God (compare 27:13) and that it is God, and not the storm, who hisses from his abode in heaven.[248]

Job had accused God of denying him justice and making his life bitter (27:2). While continuing to maintain his innocence (27:3–6), Job uttered an imprecatory prayer against his enemy, the wicked person (27:7–23).

---

246. Literally, "terrors."
247. There is an apparent play on words here. Both words start with a sibilant (s sounding letter) and only the letters "p" and "r" are different.
248. Smick, "The Dialogue Dispute" in *Job*. Pulling and hissing are natural "actions" of the wind. We therefore retain the wind as the referent here.

ASIAN PERSPECTIVE ON IMPRECATORY PRAYER

The Psalms – which contain the prayers of God's people in the OT – are replete with imprecatory prayers. For instance, King David prayed this about his enemies: "May those who seek my life be disgraced and put to shame; may those who plot my ruin be turned back in dismay. May they be like chaff before the wind, with the angel of the Lord driving them away; may their path be dark and slippery, with the angel of the Lord pursuing them" (Ps 35:4–6).

An analysis of imprecatory psalms (such as Psalms 7, 55, 58, 59, 69, 109, and 139) shows that while imprecatory prayer invokes curses and judgment on the enemy's personal life and family, this is not necessarily for revenge. Even in David's prayers, the overriding purpose was so that the enemy might recognize that there is a living God who hates evil and injustice but will stand for and protect his people. On David's part, these prayers were also a cry for justice.

The practice of imprecatory prayers is not new for people in Asia. Their customary law requires showing respect to elders. Since one who intentionally and grievously offends an elder may incur his curse, it is best to be cautious with our words and actions when relating or dealing with them in our day-to-day affairs.

Should believers today pray imprecatory prayers? Consider the instructions of Jesus: "Love your enemies, do good to those who hate you, bless those who curse you, pray for those who mistreat you. If someone slaps you on one cheek, turn to them the other also. If someone takes your coat, do not withhold your shirt from them. Give to everyone who asks you, and if anyone takes what belongs to you, do not demand it back. Do to others as you would have them do to you" (Luke 6:27–31).

I asked a colleague about the practice of imprecatory prayer in his country. He said: "We do sometimes utter imprecatory prayers though it is not a common practice. As Christians, we pray to God and believe that our prayer should be in agreement with God's will. We also believe we have to pray for our enemies, but this is an area where we often fail. Instead of praying for them, we tend to curse and pray to God for judgment."[1]

What, then, accounts for these imprecatory prayers? The examples from the psalms show that these prayers were uttered by people who had been hurt because of an injustice done to them. These were cries for justice, not necessarily for revenge. We do well to examine the prayers that we pray about people who have hurt us.

---

1. Thangbiakmuang Guite, interview by author *via* Messenger, April 18, 2022.

JOB 28:1–28
INTERLUDE ON WISDOM

Chapter 28 may seem like an intrusion to the whole disputation, but it is not. It serves as an interlude, which, "as the literary apex of the book anticipates the theophany but does so without creating a climax."[1] This hymn is supremely unique in that it explains the superiority of God's wisdom over human wisdom. It also reveals Job's skepticism of the ability of human beings, however wise, to fully understand the wisdom of God, a concern that is shared by Elihu.

To whom do we attribute Job 28? Wilson mentions two reasons why Job may not be the speaker: first, Job is not identified as the speaker in chapter 28, unlike in other chapters (see 26:1; 27:1; 29:1), and, second, the sudden change in genre and the ironic tone adopted in chapter 28 signal that it was unlikely to have been part of the debate.[2] These are valid observations. But chapter 28, while it is not part of the dialogue, "functions as a bridge between the dialogue and the groups of speeches that are coming."[3]

This beautiful poem, which falls into the category of "wisdom literature," comes from the heart and mouth of Job himself. Disappointed with the three counselors, Job shared some of his own beliefs about wisdom. He exclaimed, "Where can wisdom be found? Where does understanding dwell?" (28:12) and acknowledged that "it cannot be found in the land of the living" (28:13). Furthermore, even someone who owned all the precious metals and jewels of the earth could not purchase true wisdom (28:15–16). In light of all his troubles and the suffering he was enduring, Job's presentation and conclusions are amazing. As in Job's case, God often gives us great insight into himself and his attributes when we have faithfully endured a great trial.

---

1. Smick, "Interlude on Wisdom" in *Job*.
2. Wilson, *Job*, 133. He also mentions other scholars who take Job as the speaker, continuing his words in chapter 27 (J. G. Janzen, Childs, Good, Whybray, Greenberg, Lo, G. Wilson); who sees it as an interlude or authorial comment (Westermann, Andersen, Sawyer, Hartley, Habel, Walton); and equally see it as inauthentic (Driver and Gray, Dhorme, Geller, Pope). Smick, "Interlude on Wisdom" in *Job*.
3. Hartley, *Book of Job*, 373.

Chapter 28 seeks to answer the following questions: What is wisdom? Where can it be found? What has wisdom to do with suffering? What does the reverential fear of the Lord involve?

While the issue of underserved suffering remains unresolved, we – like Job – can take comfort in our caring, loving, and all-knowing God, whose ways – though often incomprehensible to us – are always just, fair, and meant to make us holy. As brilliant as the three wise friends were, they were unable to give a theological explanation about how to live in perfect harmony with the living God in a non-harmonious world, especially when undeserved and unexplainable pain and suffering were also introduced.

This poem can be divided into three sections, each defining a group of people: first, those who find wealth at great effort and cost (28:1–11); second, those unable to find true wisdom (28:12–22); and, third, those to whom true wisdom is revealed in and through God alone (28:23–28).

28:1–11 HUMAN BEINGS' ABILITY TO FIND WEALTH

This passage tells of the process involved in mining precious stones. Job affirmed that while there are places where riches such as silver, gold, copper, and iron are found, locating and accessing such places – which are often uninhabited and unknown – is a difficult and dangerous process (28:1–4). Once the exact mining spot has been identified, intentional digging and continued turning over of soil reveals the place where "lapis lazuli" and "nuggets of gold" can be found (28:5–6). This place is below the ground, where even the falcon cannot see, and lions dare not go (28:7–8).

Job described the painstaking work involved in unearthing precious stones.[4] The miner digs down toward the lowest stratum of the earth (28:9), cutting through rocks to make mining shafts that reach down to where the precious stones lie (28:10), and then deliberately controlling the flow[5] of underground rivers so that they can bring out the stones (28:11).

Crude and small-scale mining – whether by creating small tunnels in the ground or panning by the riverside – is a difficult job. It involves skill, physical strength, and courage to dig underground in darkness, go through the process of extracting gold dust from the ore, melting the gold dust in acid concentrates, and then heating this to purify and solidify it. Today, of course, it is easier to mine precious stones on account of current technological innovations, but Job

---

4. The MT has "secret, hidden things."
5. The MT has "weeping."

lived in a completely different age. Nevertheless, minerals and precious stones still enjoy a high value today. For example, the buying price of one gram of high-quality gold – usually the result of 2–4 days of work through gold panning by a riverside – is around $46 USD for 15.7 karat gold in January 2024.

Gold, also known in olden times as "yellow iron," is expensive, but it can be found. How about transcendent wisdom?

28:12–22 HUMAN BEINGS' INABILITY TO FIND WISDOM

Job went on to compare the value of wisdom with the value of the precious stones already described. He asked: "Where is wisdom to be found?" and "Where is the source[6] of understanding?" (28:12, my translation).[7] Job then answered his own questions: Humanity does not know the value of wisdom, which cannot be found either in the land of the living (28:13) or in the seas and oceans of the world (28:14). There is a "merism" here – "land" and "sea" – indicating that wisdom is not found anywhere on the surface of the planet earth.

Wisdom is priceless. It cannot be bought with gold or silver, not even with the gold of Ophir or precious gems such as onyx or lapis lazuli (28:15–16). Wisdom has incomparable value, far surpassing that of the finest gold or any other precious stones – gold, crystal, coral, jasper, rubies, or topaz (28:17–19). Three types of gold are identified here: finest gold, gold of Ophir, and purest gold. But wisdom is of greater value than gold and all these precious stones. This brings to mind King Solomon. When Yahweh invited him to ask for whatever he wanted, Solomon chose wisdom and knowledge over wealth and honor. This pleased the Lord so much that in addition to wisdom, he also gave wealth and honor to Solomon (1 Kgs 3:5–13; 2 Chr 1:7–12).

Job then repeated what he had already said in verse 12. Wisdom is carefully hidden from every living being (28:21); although "Destruction" (*Abaddon*) and "Death" – personified here as living creatures – claim to have heard of knowledge and wisdom, they do not really know much about it (28:22). "This probably means that those who reach that place have a belated understanding they have missed in life (compare the rich man in Luke 16:19–31)."[8] Regardless, there is a recognition that wisdom does exist.

---

6. Literally, "place."
7. The NIV has: "But where can wisdom be found? Where does understanding dwell?"
8. Smick, "Interlude on Wisdom," in *Job*.

JOB

28:23–28 GOD'S ABILITY TO REVEAL WISDOM

God is central in this section, which answers the question posed earlier (28:12, 20) about the whereabouts of wisdom: "God understands the way to it and he alone knows where it dwells" (28:23). It is only God who truly understands how wisdom works and where it is found. He knows the source of wisdom because he himself is its source and because he is omniscient. Instead of a direct and lengthy definition of wisdom, Job described how wisdom operates. Wisdom is discerned in creation and in the maintenance of the heavens and the earth and everything in it (28:24) – this is a figure of speech, a merism, where the heavens and the earth include everything that happens between heaven and earth. Wisdom was operative when God created and established the force of the wind and measured out the "huge mass of the primordial waters" (28:25),[9] as well as when he prescribed limits to the rain and laid out the path of a thunderstorm (28:26). "Even if humans can never have divine wisdom, they still receive the benefits of the good and just cosmic order, as it reflects God's hidden wisdom."[10]

God himself evaluated, examined, and confirmed wisdom (28:27) and made this a permanent fixture in his management of the universe. The final verse is vital to Job's whole argument: "The fear of the Lord – that is wisdom, and to shun evil is understanding" (28:28). The name of God used in verse 28 is *Adonay*,[11] which is translated Lord. One implication of this is that this instruction is for everyone, and not just for the nation Israel, to whom God revealed his personal name as Yahweh. The fear of the Lord is not just the beginning of wisdom but is equivalent to wisdom. Likewise, to shun evil is equivalent to understanding. In other words, "man must reverentially acknowledge that he and his world are subject to their Creator. A man begins to be wise when he ceases to strive for wisdom independently of God. He advances through the attainment of wisdom through the laws of God and the observations of nature."[12] And humans may share in this wisdom "only through knowledge of the revealed mind of God."[13]

---

9. Alter, *Job*, 536.
10. Wilson, *Job*, 138.
11. *Adonay* is used here as one of God's names, and not as a substitute for Yahweh. The other names of God in the book of Job are: *El, Elohim, Eloah, Shadday*, and *YHWH*. See discussion on page 22.
12. Vicchio, *Book of Job*, 194.
13. Smick, "Interlude on Wisdom" in *Job*.

God himself answered the question – asked twice in this chapter – regarding where wisdom could be found: Wisdom and understanding are found only in a relationship with the Lord, a relationship characterized by worship and obedience.

This chapter makes three things clear. First, wisdom evades man's search for it, both in "the land of the living" and in the place of the dead. Second, God alone knows "the way" to wisdom since it resides in him alone, even before creation itself. Third, human beings cannot find wisdom through their own investigation but can experience it through developing a relationship with God and living in the fear of the Lord (Prov 9:10). This reverential fear of the Lord includes loving and serving God with all our being, observing his commandments, holding fast to him (Deut 10:12, 20), and worshiping him "acceptably with reverence and awe" (Heb 12:28). Wisdom requires living in the presence of God, according to his will. While we can never claim to be in total possession of wisdom, its presence or absence can be discerned in the day-to-day experiences of life.

Wisdom: James and Job

James counseled the early believers, exiled in various parts of the Roman Empire: "If any of you lacks wisdom, you should ask God, who gives generously to all without finding fault, and it will be given to you" (Jas 1:5). The context here was one where these believers found that multiple trials were continuously coming their way. In such times, believers must seek God to gain insight into his purpose in allowing these trials.

Even though Job had reverentially feared God and shunned evil, he was not spared suffering, calamities, and pain. But, in his times of suffering, Job sought for an answer beyond what the naked eye could see. From the depths of his despair came this gem – the realization that God is all-wise and that fearing him is the *beginning* of all wisdom.

This should encourage us to evaluate any situation and include God in the picture for he is the all-wise God, who sovereignly created and maintains a universe that is both complex and amazing. Yet, this awesome God is also personal and caring and will see us through the perplexities of life, including every kind of problem and pain.

JOB 29:1–42:6

THREE SETS OF SPEECHES

Chapters 1–28 concern the debates between Job and his friends. The debates were now over and neither Job nor the three friends had won. After declaring that wisdom rests only with God (Job 28), Job seemed to feel the need to explain how he had reverentially feared God and shunned evil. His speech is the first of three speeches, which can be presented as follows:

The Speeches	
Job's Speech	Chapters 29–31
Elihu's Speech	Chapters 32–37
Yahweh's Speech	Chapters 38–42

Job's monologue follows the A-B-A' pattern, which can be presented in this way: A – proof of what his life exemplified (29); B – an account of his losses and his suffering (30); A' – proof of what his life exemplified (31). Job also issued a final challenge to God to explain his case (31:35–37).

29:1–31:40 JOB'S SPEECH

Chapters 29–31 present Job's testimony, his final attempt to defend his integrity and refute the charges brought against him. Before proceeding, however, it is in order to give a recap of the charges – more accurately, the trumped-up charges – that Eliphaz, Bildad, and Zophar brought against Job.

Eliphaz accused Job of wrongly claiming to be innocent (4:17–19; 15:14), spewing useless speech and destructive words (15:3, 5–6), undermining piety and hindering devotion to God (15:4), expressing anger toward God (15:12–13), rebellion against and defiance of the Almighty God (15:25–26), injustice and oppression of the poor (22:5–7), abuse of widows and orphans (22:8–9), and accusing God of injustice and inattention (22:13).

Bildad accused Job of using empty words without substance (8:2), accusing God of perverting justice (8:3), being angry (18:4), and claiming to be upright and pure before God (25:4–6).

Zophar accused Job of mocking without shame (11:3), claiming to have pure beliefs and to be innocent (11:4), deceit (11:11), oppressing the poor (20:19), and avarice (20:20).

The common accusations the three friends brought against Job were that he claimed to be innocent, spoke uselessly, accused God of injustice, and oppressed the poor. Their underlying accusation was that Job had not only sinned but was guilty of hidden sins that he refused to confess. In the previous chapters, Job had tried to rebut some of these accusations, consistently claiming his innocence. In chapter 29, Job affirmed his relationship with God and his experience of God by looking back and recapitulating the good times when he had enjoyed security and God's blessings before these experiences of being overwhelmed by pain and suffering.

29:1–25 Job's Past Honor and Blessings

Chapter 29 describes the life of a person who enjoyed a relationship with the Almighty during the patriarchal period. Job's relationship with God permeated his whole life, including his family life and social dealings. He was unusually blessed with a large extent of land, as well as livestock, like the patriarchs Abraham, Isaac, and Jacob.

The questions to be addressed as we read Job 29 include the following: What was life like for Job before the calamities came? Why was he known as the greatest man in the East? Why was he known as upright?

29:1–6 God's Kind Dealings

Job recalled how things had been before the calamities came upon him, a time when God had "watched" (*shamar*)[1] over him. Since "lamp" and "light" signify God's blessings, these verses convey that he had felt tremendously blessed (29:2b–3): he was in the prime[2] of his life, his entire household enjoyed God's intimate fellowship, the Almighty was with him, and his children were a joy to him (29:4–5). Job was also blessed materially: "My step was bathed with cream and the rock poured out abundant olive oil for me" (29:6, my translation).

---

1. *Shamar* was the same term that God used in 2:6 to allow *Satan* to do anything with Job; but he must preserve Job's life. It is used nine other times (eleven in all). In four of these, Job had accused God of carefully watching him and checking on him to mark his sin (10:14; 14:6) and restrict his movements (13:27; 33:11).
2. Literally, "autumn."

Bullinger recognizes that hyperbole[3] is used to emphasize the prosperity and affluence that Job had enjoyed.

This section tells us that God watches over believers and that – contrary to the idea that God is distant and has no interest in his creations – intimate fellowship with God is possible. Although expressed in different terms, this kind of deep and special fellowship with God was also the experience of Enoch, Abraham, Moses, and David. Enoch "walked faithfully with God" (Gen 5:22); Abraham is called God's "friend" (2 Chr 20:7; Isa 41:8); Yahweh spoke to Moses openly[4] "as one speaks to a friend" (Exod 33:11) and knew Moses intimately "by name" (Exod 33:17); and David is called a "man after [God's] own heart" (1 Sam 13:14; Acts 13:22), which implies that he was loyal to God and to God's purposes. This fellowship with the living God is possible today for those who put their trust in Jesus Christ because of who Jesus is and what he has done. He is God's final word (Heb 1:2), the radiance of God's glory and representation of his essence (Heb 1:3), the faithful and merciful high priest who reconciled people to the living God (Heb 2:16–18), the source of eternal salvation (Heb 5:9–10), the Savior (Heb 7:25), the one who secured eternal redemption for us (Heb 9:12), and the perfect mediator between humanity and the living God (Heb 9:15; 12:24) who tasted death for every person (Heb 2:9).

Verses 2–6 are also parallel to the second element of a *rib* (case) in Soulen's outline. In this case, Job reviewed God's kindness to him and his family before the calamities came. This second element now completes what is still missing in the elements of a lawsuit (along Soulen's outline):[5] summons to the offending party (13:22; 14:15), recitation of beneficent acts bestowed on the offender in former times (29:2–6), accusations against the offender (16:7–17; 19:7–12), and a call for witnesses (16:18–21). Until this point, Job had believed that God was the offending party. Therefore, he had requested a hearing. With regard to benefits, Job's case was different since he was the recipient of the benefits, whereas according to the typical format, God, as benefactor, should have enumerated his blessings on Job. Job had also identified the witnesses, which did not include his three friends. Therefore, he now had all the players – whom he had been trying to assemble since he had first resolved to bring his case before God (13:13–19) – and was ready to present this.

---

3. Bullinger, *Figures of Speech*, 424. Clarify Job 22:17 and Micah 6:7.
4. Literally, "face to face."
5. Soulen, *Handbook of Biblical Criticism*, 170.

29:7–10 Job's Respected Position

That Job had been well-respected is evident from the description of what took place at the city gate (or plaza): Job had a reserved seat (29:7); the young men humbly stepped aside when they saw Job and even the elders rose to their feet (29:8); and both leaders and nobles were silent[6] or tongue-tied[7] in Job's presence (29:9–10), which suggests that they paid careful attention to his words. Here is a picture of a person who commanded the utmost respect from young and old alike, whose wisdom was such that his audience felt they need not add more to what he had said.

This section describes the typical way elders were respected during Job's time and in his culture. This kind of deference is still observed in conservative circles in Southeast Asia, which is an honor-shame culture. In such cultures, identity is defined not just by the individual's own persona but by the status of their family and clan in the community. In Indonesia, for example, a person is known by their family and the status the family enjoys in the community. A person who cannot trace their ascendants back to the seventh generation does not receive as much respect as someone with a good ancestry. A similar situation exists in many other Asian countries.

People respected Job because of his age, wisdom, and the kindness that he extended to others. He was as good with his words as he was with his actions. There is consistency in his life. He was a man of integrity.

29:11–17 Job's Own Acts of Kindness

Those who heard what Job said spoke well of him, and those who witnessed his deeds commended him (29:11). Job then went on to list some of these praiseworthy deeds:

- He had "rescued" the "poor" and "fatherless" (29:12).
- He had "made the widow's heart sing" (29:13).
- He had "put on righteousness as clothing" and justice as his "robe" and "turban," meaning he performed the role of a judge[8] who decides cases fairly (29:14).
- He had become "eyes to the blind" and "feet to the lame" (29:15).

---

6. Literally, "they put their hands to their mouths." This is usually done in the presence of a respected person.
7. Literally, "their tongues clung to their palates."
8. The MT includes the objects that represent the function of a judge: "robe and a turban."

- He had been "a father to the needy" who "took up the case of the stranger" (29:16).
- He "broke the fangs of the wicked and snatched the victim" (29:17).

By listing some of these good deeds, Job was actually refuting some of the charges against him. For instance, he denied Zophar's and Eliphaz's accusations that he had oppressed the poor (20:19; 22:6–9) by declaring that, like a father, he had helped the poor, widows, orphans, and strangers. Job embodied the character and behavior of one who fears God, is just, and has compassion on the marginalized (Deut 10:18; 4:17–19).

Smick observes that "Job did not concentrate on ritual righteousness (though see 1:5) nor other ethical or religious responsibilities but on that area where humans most often fail – in their response to the sufferings of others."[9] One underlying reason for this is what Walton observes about an honor-shame culture: "Corporate identity takes precedence over individual identity, with the result that selfhood is shaped primarily by social interaction, not private inward perception."[10]

29:18–20 Job's Wish to Die Peacefully in His Old Age

Job recalled a time when he had wished to die peacefully at home, in the presence of his family, after having enjoyed a long life (29:18).[11] He equated himself to a tree, referring specifically to its roots and branches, indicating his desire for a life of vitality and prosperity, which would also leave behind a good legacy that would help keep the respect and honor that was rightfully his (29:19–20).

Even in Asia, most people desire to have a long life, especially if they are healthy and have good family support. Those who have children long to see their great-great-great-grandchildren, which is possible if someone lives to be about 100 years old. In the Philippines, House Bill 10647, which was approved in January 2022, mandates that "those who reach the age of 101 years old shall receive cash gifts worth PHP1 million on their birthday, as well as a letter of felicitation from the President."[12] This is an incentive for senior citizens to try

---

9. Smick, "Monologues" in *Job*.
10. Walton, *Job*, 313.
11. The MT can be translated literally as "the number of days be as the grains of sand."
12. Filane Mikee Cervantes, "House Raises Centenarian Cash Gift to P1-M," *Republic of the Philippines: Philippine News Agency* (January 31, 2022), http://www.pna.gov.ph.

to live longer. The bill also provides that "all Filipinos who reach the age of 80, 85, 90, and 95 years old shall receive PHP25,000 and a letter of felicitation from the President."[13]

29:21–25 Job's Position as a Respected Elder

Picking up the theme of his respected position (29:7–10), Job remembered that whenever and wherever he had spoken, his audience had listened to him and received his counsel without question or argument (29:21–22), and he likened their response to the ground that readily receives the spring rains (29:23). When Job would smile – perhaps in approval or acknowledgment – people appreciated this, even though they did not expect this of him (29:24). Job had been a wise and respected leader – like a commander or a king – who was compassionate and caring to those who mourned (29:25).

Job 29 contains at least sixteen different references to Job's past goodness and prosperity. The chapter gives the reader information about Job's evaluation of himself and supports the claim of the writer that Job was a man "who reverentially feared God and shunned evil" (1:1; 2:3; my translation). It also supports the statement that Job was "the greatest man among all the people of the East" (1:3) and God's statement that "there is no one on earth like him; he is blameless and upright" (1:8b).

Job had enjoyed an intimate friendship with God. He had been blessed with children, and was prosperous, respected, and enjoyed a good reputation. He had helped strangers, orphans, widows, and the handicapped, and had prosecuted those who acted unjustly. Job was honored and loved by family and friends. He was like a king or a commander-in-chief of an army, yet also a comfort to mourners.

If the friends had truly listened to Job earlier, as he had requested, they might have realized the error in their premise and their erroneous application of retributive justice to the questions and the issues that Job had raised.

When Job lost everything, including his social standing, the people who had once respected him treated him with disdain. As a person of stature in an honor-shame culture, his status in the community mattered greatly and gave impetus to his need for God's vindication.

Job desperately wanted a hearing before God so that he could defend himself, and he was hopeful that God would vindicate him. Having maintained throughout that he was innocent, in this chapter, he provided strong

---

13. Cervantes, "House Raises Centenarian Cash Gift."

evidence of his righteousness and appealed to his standing in the community to counter and refute his friends' charges against him.

30:1–31 Job's Present Dishonor and Suffering

Having recalled God's past blessings, Job then went on to describe his present situation. Questions to consider in relation to Job 30 include: Can God himself be the cause of our suffering? Does God remain silent to the cries of the innocent? Can we be honest about our thoughts concerning God when he does not respond or seems late in responding to our prayers?

30:1–15 Job Was Mocked by Young People
30:1–8 Job identified his mockers
Shifting the focus away from himself, Job described the people who were mocking him. These were young men of no consequence, whose fathers Job held in great disdain. Sheep dogs are trained to help guide the sheep. Job would not even have dreamed of allowing these fathers to associate with his trusted sheep dogs. These mockers – people of ill repute, who enjoyed no standing in society – were emaciated and "haggard" for they survived on herbs and roots (30:3–4), hardly appealing or substantial nourishment. They had been rejected by the community and were treated with disdain like professional thieves. Their living quarters included ravines and holes in the ground (30:5–6). They brayed like animals as they huddled together (30:7) and were regarded as sons of nameless people (30:8). Verses 1 and 8 serve as bookends for this section. Job's mockers were introduced as having fathers whom Job despised (30:1); now, in verse 8, he described them as morally base, unknown, and outcasts of society.

30:9–15 Job described the actions of his mockers
These young men taunted Job incessantly with their songs, scorned him, and spat on his face (30:9–10). Job, however, viewed the actions of these mockers from a different perspective, seeing God himself as the architect of these afflictions (30:11). His mockers rose against Job, laying traps, planning his destruction, and advancing fast against him, taunting him by saying that no one would help him (30:12–14). Not only did terrors overwhelm Job, but he was also stripped of the honor due to him and the security that came with it (30:15).

30:16–23 Job Felt Abandoned by God

Job felt as if he was being emptied of life and just about to die. Extreme suffering and pain enveloped his life (30:16–17). Yet again, Job pointed to God as being behind his suffering, picturing God as grabbing him and throwing him to the ground (30:18–19). Job then addressed God directly, saying "you," accusing God of being inattentive to his cries for help (30:20). Job concluded that God had turned against him cruelly, attacking and tossing him powerfully in the wind (30:21–22), and even seeking Job's death (30:23). The parallelism in these verses (30:20–23) emphasizes how Job tried in vain to attract God's attention in the face of God's continuous mistreatment.

Was Job right in accusing God of silence? We will respond to this by looking at the book of Psalms, which records the honest confessions of believers. Job 30:16–23 has the marks of a lament psalm. For instance, the statement "my life ebbs away" which the ESV translates as "my soul is poured out" (30:16), is an expression frequently used in the psalms to picture the extreme pain of the righteous sufferer, who then likens his life to a liquid that is being emptied out of the container of his body (Pss 22:14; 42:4). Similarly, the phrase "I cry out to you, God, but you do not answer" (30:20) finds parallels in many psalms, where the psalmist expresses frustration and consternation over God's silence and pleads with God to respond to his cries and not remain silent (Pss 35:22; 39:12; 83:1).

As believers, how should we respond when God seems silent?

- Recognize that God's silence might perhaps be his answer for the present moment.
- During God's perceived silence, evaluate your request and allow God the freedom to respond according to his will (Matt 6:10).
- Ask God to help you discern whether his answer is "yes," "wait," or "no."
- While the Lord honors persistence in prayer, once he has already said "no," be warned against persisting in your request for he may let you have your way, if only to show you your folly as he did with Israel's request for a king, which was both premature and wrongly motivated (1 Sam 8:4–22).
- Since God promises to answer us when we call on him, ask with an expectant heart and thank him regardless of the answer (Matt 7:7; John 14:13).
- Review and meditate on God's promises (Matt 6:33; 7:11).

30:24–31 Job Was Wracked by Pain

Job had hoped for better days. Surely God would not hurt[14] someone in distress, who cried out for help (30:24). Job recounted what he had done for others – he had wept and grieved with those who were poor or in trouble (30:25) – hoping that this would convince God to relent. Unfortunately, even when he had hoped for good and light, only evil and darkness came his way (30:26). The contrasting parallelism stresses how Job received the exact opposite of what he had hoped for. Using a double figure of speech,[15] Job described the restlessness he experienced because of his continued afflictions (30:27). His skin had been "blackened" by his malignant skin disorder and his cries for help went unheeded, leaving him feeling isolated – like "a brother of jackals and a companion of owls"[16] (30:28–29); Job's cries of pain might even have sounded like the howls and hoots of these animals.

Job was experiencing discomfort, a burning fever, and extreme pain on account of his malignant skin disorder and other diseases that cannot be accurately or fully identified (30:30). "My lyre is turned to mourning and my pipe to the sound of wailing" (30:31) is a figure of speech, a personification to express the melancholy and depression that Job was experiencing. Where once there was festive music, now there is only the sound of weeping and mourning.

Suffering, even among the saints, is universal, something that was experienced by Job as well as other believers in the OT. God's silence is often seen as the withdrawal of his favor. While this may result in dejection, humiliation, and defeat, this chapter shows that believers can be honest with God about their feelings, even asking God why he does not answer their prayers or asking how long he will remain silent and unresponsive to their cries.

In this chapter, Job described the young people who were mocking him and concluded that they were people of no consequence (30:1–8), who acted wickedly toward him (30:9–15). Although Job cried out to God, he felt that God was deaf to his cries (30:16–23). While he had nurtured hopes of better days, his hopes had been dashed; his sufferings had increased and intensified so much that he had reached the brink of despair.

Job was sick, melancholic, depressed, and hurting – both physically and emotionally. The insults and mockery of people he had helped in the past was an additional source of pain. He felt ostracized since people avoided him like

---

14. Literally, "stretch his hand."
15. Synecdoche: inward parts for the whole body and hyperbole: inward parts boiling.
16. The *NET* Bible has "ostriches."

the plague. He felt as if even God was afflicting and persecuting him, and not responding to his cries for help. Although Job nurtured the hope that God would have mercy and answer him (30:24), he felt isolated and alone, and deeply mourned his situation (30:29–31).

31:1–40 Job's Confession and Final Oath

Chapter 31 is parallel to chapter 29, almost forming a chiasm with an A-B-A' structure. These chapters mirror each other with respect to Job's life before the calamities, his relationship with Yahweh, and his kind dealings with others as an offshoot of that relationship.

In chapter 31, Job affirmed his innocence one last time, speaking of several different areas: his personal character (31:1–12), his treatment of his servants and the poor (31:13–23), his relationship with God (31:24–28, 33–37); his attitude toward his adversary (31:29–32), and his care of the farm workers and the land (31:38–40).

These questions will be addressed in this chapter: What were the charges against Job? Was he able to refute each of these charges? What characterizes a person who is "broken" before God?

31:1–4 Job Was Not Guilty of Lust

Job had avoided lust. He had made a covenant with himself not to "look"[17] lasciviously or "lustfully" at a virgin (31:1), a lady of marriageable age, so that he might avoid sin. Truly this greatest man in the East, was also a man of integrity even in his private life.

This verse finds a connection in the NT, where Jesus Christ warned that a person who looks at a woman with lust has already committed adultery (Matt 5:28). Jesus "strongly denounced a lustful gaze because it is the starting point of an adulterous relationship."[18]

Job then posed some rhetorical questions that communicate important truths: First, everyone receives an inheritance from God Almighty (31:2); second, calamity and misfortune are the portion of the unjust and sinners (31:3); and, third, God knows every step that a person takes (31:4). Job felt that God would have known that Job lived with integrity, as he had been asserting ever since the visit of his three friends. He did not feel that he deserved the suffering that he was experiencing, and he could not understand why God was allowing it.

---

17. Figure of speech, synecdoche: the eyes for the whole person.
18. Uytanlet and Kwa, *Matthew*, 60.

31:5–8 Job Was Not Guilty of Falsehood and Deception

Job had avoided lies and deception. From verse 5 right up to the end of the chapter, Job presented a series of hypothetical situations dealing with specific sins that Job had already claimed he did not commit. The argument takes an "if-then" form, where Job boldly declared that if guilty of these particular sins, he was ready to face the due punishment. "If" Job had been guilty of "falsehood" or "deceit" (31:5), then he invited God to weigh his deeds "in honest scales" so that God might recognize his integrity (31:6). "If" Job had "turned from the path," by allowing his heart to be led by his eyes, so that "his hands have been defiled," (31:7), "then" he would gladly bear the consequences, which would entail others eating what he had planted and even uprooting his crops (31:8). Having clean hands is a requirement for a person to be able to enter into God's presence (Ps 24:4). When Job claimed that his hands had not been "defiled," he meant that he had not sinned by his actions such as deceiving others. And implied in verses 7 and 8, he did not covet and steal the produce of others.

31:9–12 Job Was Not Guilty of Adultery

Job had not committed adultery. He confidently declared that "if" his heart had been "enticed by a woman" or if he had "lurked" or lain in wait (*'arav*)[19] at his neighbor's door, "then" he was ready to face the consequences, which included his wife being involved in grinding for another man and having sexual relationships with other men (31:10). Job's argument – about giving our spouse to immorality because we had been guilty of immorality – sounds strange to us. But Job was operating on the "an eye for an eye" (commonly called *talionic*) principle that was common in the ANE. So, if he had abused someone else's wife, then, according to this principle, someone else should abuse his wife. This principle is not biblical but cultural, and Christians must not practice immorality or the *talionic* principle. The Lord told us to forgive our enemies.

Every sexual sin has a domino effect on other areas of life such as livelihood, which, in Job's case, would have meant that his agricultural produce would be affected (31:11–12). Had Job committed adultery, his words would have been practically a curse upon himself; but because Job knew that he was innocent, he was confident that his wife and his produce would not be taken from him.

---

19. This term is used three times in the book of Job (31:9; 37:8; 38:40). Its nuance in other chapters is of animals waiting to suddenly pounce on their prey.

Job

31:13–23 Job Was Not Guilty of Social Injustice

31:13–15 Job did not abuse his servants

Verse 13 continues the pattern of the previous sections. "If" Job had rejected or failed to address the complaints of his servants – both male and female – then God would have the right to call him to account and punish him for such an injustice (31:13–14). "Even a slave has legal rights and may bring a suit against his master, and Job says that in the days of his prosperity he always honored those rights"[20] because Job recognized that the same God had created both Job and his servants (31:15).

Entering the workforce as a domestic helper involves a great risk, hard work, and an act of faith that the employer will be a kind and just person. Sadly, at least half – if not more – of the stories we hear these days are about acts of injustice and cruelty rather than kindness to domestic helpers. If you do have domestic servants in your household, what stories would they tell? Would they speak of your injustice and cruelty or of your kindness? Perhaps we could reflect on some reasons for extending kindness to those who work for us: the plight of the servant, our reverential fear of God, the fact that we are all, equally, creations of God, and the knowledge that we are accountable to God for the way we treat others.

31:16–23 Job did not abuse the poor

Job listed some possible acts of injustice that, if he had committed them, would make him liable to experience the consequences. Such injustices include:

- Refusing the requests of the poor (31:16a)
- Oppressing widows (31:16b)
- Refusing to feed orphans (31:17)
- Denying clothes to his workers who were dying from cold (31:19–20)
- Raising his hand against the fatherless in court (31:21)

If Job had committed any of these injustices and specifically made a threatening gesture to the fatherless in court, he was willing to allow his whole arm[21] to be incapacitated (31:22). "This would be a measure-for-measure justice, retaliation for raising one's hand against the orphan."[22] Job however, had not

---

20. Alter, *Writings*, 544.
21. Literally, "side."
22. Alter, *Writings*, 545.

done any of these things, both because he was mindful of the consequences and because God's majesty rendered him unable to do such things (31:23). Here indeed was a man of integrity. His reverential fear of the Almighty controlled how he related to and treated his workers and the marginalized in society.

31:24–28 Job Was Not Guilty of Idolatry

Job had not trusted in wealth, nor had he worshiped the sun or the moon. This section lists more hypothetical statements. It would have been idolatry "if" Job had put his "trust in gold" or relied for "security" on the "great wealth" he had accumulated (31:24–25) or been "enticed" into offering "a kiss of homage" – which is an outward sign of worship[23] – to "the sun in its radiance or the moon moving in splendor" (31:26–27). Such sins deserve God's judgment since they represent unfaithfulness to God (31:28). When our appreciation and awe of created objects lead us to worship the creature instead of the Creator, this is sin.

We must appreciate Job's steadfast faith in God, despite everything that had happened to him. In that time and context, how easy it would have been to worship what could be seen with the naked eye – such as the sun, moon, and stars. Yet, despite his altercations with God, Job refrained from doing so and remained monotheistic. When temptations come our way, may we remain faithful to the living God and may our trust in him deepen.

31:29–30 Job Was Not Guilty of Exacting Vengeance on Others

Job had refused to rejoice over the "misfortune" and "trouble" that came on his adversary (31:29). He affirmed that he had not sinned by cursing such a person (31:30). While he did pray an imprecatory prayer against his enemies (27:7–10), there was no hint of rejoicing on Job's part; he was crying out for justice, not revenge.

31:31–34 Job Was Not Guilty of Selfishness and Hidden Sins

As further proof of his integrity of heart, Job described the atmosphere in his home, which was probably the place where he was most highly respected. He claimed that no one in his household could ever say that they had "not been filled with Job's meat" (31:31).[24] He had even opened his doors to provide shelter for traveling strangers (31:32). Job had a heart for the needy and had

---

23. Bullinger, *Figures of Speech*, 605.
24. This is stated as a rhetorical question. "Job's meat," literally "animal flesh," represents the food that he provided for his household and others.

not neglected to minister to the less fortunate. Verse 32 – which speaks of Job's hospitality to strangers – may have a conceptual connection with Matthew 25:35, where Jesus taught that hospitality to strangers and those in need is a mark of those who belong to God's kingdom. Job added another condition to this section but without mention of consequences: "If" he had covered or "concealed" his sin, this might have been because he feared the crowd or the contempt of his family or clan (31:33–34). Such a fear would have resulted in Job remaining silent, not daring to go outside (31:34). Yet, before the calamities, Job was constantly seen at the city gate and regularly sacrificed burnt offerings for his children. Such actions do not point to guilt or hiding to cover up sin.

31:35–37 Job Longed for Hearing Before God

Job expressed his longing for a formal hearing in a court. He was ready to sign his "defense" statements. He also named the other participants in the court case: the Almighty (his judge) and Job's accuser (the plaintiff). The latter would "put his indictment in writing" (31:35). Then Job would carry this indictment and wear it proudly like a crown (31:36). "So confident is Job that the accusations against him are baseless that he would proudly wear the writ of indictment as an ornament."[25]

31:38–40 Job Was Not Guilty of Abusing the Land or Tenants

The final "if" in this chapter concerns the land. There is personification, with the land described as crying out and its furrows as being "wet with tears" (31:38) – that is, a cry for justice. The next verse sheds light on this. If Job had "devoured" the produce of the land "without payment" and mistreated the tenants (31:39), then the consequences would be that thorns and weeds would infest the land (31:40).

Verse 40 completes Job's testimony and his monologue. His words seem to echo what a character witness from among his family and friends might have testified to in vouching for his integrity. Job was prepared to face a court hearing – if only the Almighty would grant his request.

---

25. Alter, *Writings*, 546.

Chapter 31 offers an impressive list of Job's moral attributes:

- He was not guilty of lust (31:1–4).
- He was not guilty of falsehood and deception (31:5–8).
- He was not guilty of adultery (31:9–12).
- He was not guilty of social injustice (31:13–23).
- He was not guilty of idolatry (31:24–28).
- He was not guilty of exacting vengeance on others (31:29–30).
- He was not guilty of selfishness and hidden sins (31:31–34).
- He longed for God to hear him (31:35–37).
- He was not guilty of abusing the land or tenants (31:38–40).

Remembering every accusation that had been brought against him, Job refuted these one by one. His accusers had judged him harshly, maligning and condemning him relentlessly. They had posited assumptions without any foundation or validation and drawn unfounded conclusions about Job's life.

Chapter 31 represents Job's final testimony. True to his word, he had prepared his case and his arguments (13:18; 23:4). As he considered his friends' accusations against him, he used hypothetical questions to refute these, mustering all his courage and strength to defend himself and argue his innocence. He was brutally honest about his current experiences with God, and complained that no one, not even God, was listening to him.

How do we approach God during times of suffering? The Bible clearly wants us to approach the Lord with a humble and penitent heart. The psalmist prayed, "The sacrifices of God are a broken spirit; a broken and contrite heart, O God, you will not despise" (Ps 51:17 ESV). This is the attitude of a heart that God recognizes. But what does Scripture mean by brokenness? Brokenness is an act of the will; or rather, it is the shattering of self-will. It is not a one-time experience but a lifestyle of unconditional and absolute surrender to God. It is obedience to the sovereign will of God and his direction for our lives. The chart below compares and contrasts the characteristics of unbroken and broken people.[26] Reflecting on this list may give us an idea on whether or not we have covered some distance in our faith walk with God.

---

26. This is based on a presentation by Nancy L. DeMoss at a Campus Crusade for Christ gathering in 1996.

Comparing Unbroken and Broken People	
Unbroken People	**Broken People**
1. Preoccupied with the failures of others	1. Preoccupied with their own spiritual need
2. Look down on others and judge	2. Look up to Jesus and give compassion
3. Independent, self-sufficient spirit	3. Dependent spirit, recognize the need for others and the need for Jesus. They do not have to prove themselves; they yield the right to be right.
4. Claim rights and have a demanding spirit	4. Yield their rights and have a meek spirit
5. Self-protective of their rights, time, and reputation	5. Self-denying, surrender of rights, time, and reputation for the sake of others
6. Motivated by the desire to be served	6. Motivated to serve
7. Motivated to be a success	7. Motivated to be faithful and make others a success
8. Desire for self-advancement	8. Desire to promote others
9. Desire recognition and are envious, angry, and jealous when they are overlooked	9. A sense of their own unworthiness and are eager for others to get the credit and be lifted up
10. The attitude that, "This ministry is privileged to have me and my gifts."	10. Have nothing to offer but the life of Jesus flowing through their broken spirits
11. Confident in how much they know	11. Humbled by how much they have to learn
12. Self-conscious	12. Not concerned with self at all but are Jesus-conscious
13. Holds others at arm's length	13. Takes the risk of loving others intimately and give of themselves even when it is not returned
14. Quick to blame others	14. Quick to take responsibility and admit wrong
15. Unapproachable	15. Easy to approach
16. Defensive when criticized	16. Receive criticism with a humble and open spirit

Comparing Unbroken and Broken People	
Unbroken People	**Broken People**
17. Concerned with what others think, with respectability and reputation	17. Concerned with being real, with what God thinks, not with what others think
18. Do not like to share their inner self	18. Are transparent and open
19. They engage in coverup and are afraid of exposure	19. Not afraid of being honest; once exposed, they are open and honest about it
20. Do not like to say, "I was wrong, please forgive me."	20. Easily admit wrong and accept forgiveness
21. Tend to deal in generalities when confessing sin	21. Deal with specifics as the Holy Spirit directs
22. Concerned about the consequences of their sins	22. Grieved about the broken relationship with God and people
23. Remorseful over sin	23. Genuinely repentant and will forsake sins
24. Wait for others to come and ask for forgiveness	24. Race to the cross to forgive and reconcile
25. Compare self with others	25. Compare self with the holiness of God
26. Blind to real heart condition	26. Walk in the light
27. Do not think they have anything to repent of	27. Have a continual heart attitude of repentance
28. Do not think they need revival and renewal of heart	28. Continually sense their need for a fresh encounter with God and with the Holy Spirit

Broken people are God-centered; they do not usually think just of themselves but consider the welfare of others, too. *Unbroken* people tend to focus on themselves most of the time.

A Recap of Job's Monologue

Job took three chapters to declare his innocence and make a final appeal to God to respond to him. As in the case of his three friends, Job's traditional understanding of wisdom took over, and he fell back on the belief that who he was and what he had done was the basis of his relationship with God. This flood of information about his goodness (Job 31) is the grand finale – the climax of a long series of oaths – and a challenge to God to take his life if what Job had declared was not true. In these verses, Job boldly and shamelessly hurled his claims at God. Job wanted God to write an indictment against him so that he could refute it. Job's hope was that he had boxed God into a place where God would vindicate him according to the claims that Job had made in these chapters (29–31). God, however, did not take the bait. Instead, he remained silent and waited for his representative, Elihu, to speak (32–37) and prepare Job for God's ultimate encounter with Job (38–42).

A Recap of Chapters 1–31

When Eliphaz, Bildad, and Zophar had arrived, they could not even recognize their friend Job because his face was so disfigured on account of his malignant skin ulcers. They found him on a dunghill. He had lost everything except his wife and his own life. The friends concluded that Job must have greatly sinned, hence the unexplainable calamities that had come upon him. None of them had any idea that, behind the scenes, *Satan* had challenged God to a duel with Job as the wager. The battle of words (dialogue-disputation style) that ensued between Job and his friends revealed their different views of God and suffering.

THE PERSPECTIVES ON SUFFERING			
Character	God's Purpose in Suffering	God's Character in Suffering	God's Stance in Relation to Suffering
Eliphaz, Bildad, and Zophar	Discipline	An exacting judge	Compensation
Job	Destruction	A despotic, harsh enemy	Injustice

Each friend's case against Job revolved around the principle of retribution. Before the supposed arraignment and hearing of the case – and even though Job insisted that he was innocent – his friends had condemned Job as guilty. Job, however, persisted in arguing that he was innocent and, for a long time, kept on asking God to intervene. Although Job denied the charges against him and tried to explain himself, his friends refused to listen. They were bent on imposing their preconceived notion that Job must have sinned greatly to merit the suffering he was experiencing.

Job appealed for a hearing and made the necessary preparations for his case. The players in the courtroom – excluding his three friends – and the elements necessary to pursue a *rib* (as suggested by Soulen) were in place: summons – Job as the offended party repeatedly appealed for a hearing (13:22; 14:15); benefits – Job listed the blessings that he had received from God earlier (29:2–6); accusations – Job had listed his main accusations against God, which were that God had caused Job's suffering and had been inattentive to his cries (16:7–17; 19:7–12); and witnesses (earth) – Job had called on witnesses (16:18–21).[27]

Having made his final appeal for innocence (Job 31), Job felt ready to meet and face God for the confrontation. Job sought answers to several questions: Why was he suffering, despite being innocent? What was the reason for God's deafening silence? When would God respond? Would God grant him a fair trial? Was there any benefit to the disputation? Did the disputation yield any benefits? The disputation revealed the conventional view of the time concerning retributive justice and the friends' view of God in relation to pain and suffering. Measured by the standards of today's counseling models, the process followed by Job's friends was flawed. Nevertheless, they unknowingly helped Job to process what was happening in his life, thereby enabling him to get out of his "pit of despair," hope anew, and set new goals – such as the determination to bring his case before God. Through the disputations, Job had a chance to reveal his view of God – what it was like to be in fellowship with God and, equally, what it was like when God seemed distant and inattentive to his cries. More than anything else – even more than the restoration of the wealth and honor he had once enjoyed – Job longed for the restoration of fellowship with God. While Job remained patient even after he had lost almost everything, during the disputations, he became impatient. At that point, Job was brutally honest about his emotions, accused God, and became vindictive toward his friends. In addition to helping Job to process his emotions, the friends kept him company.

32:1–37:24 ELIHU'S SPEECHES

Following Job's monologues, we have Elihu's speeches (32–37), which are the second of the three sets of monologues in chapters 29–42.

Yahweh had already granted each request of *Satan*, and the sufferer had responded appropriately (Job 1–2). It would seem that allowing undeserved

---

27. See Soulen, *Handbook of Biblical Criticism*, 170.

suffering to continue (7:3) – even after Job had been tested and had proven his loyalty (1:21–22; 2:10) – supported Job's claim that Yahweh was a whimsical and capricious God. If Job's initial responses are taken as disproving *Satan's* accusations (1:9–11; 2:4–5), then why was the suffering allowed to continue? Did Elihu perceive that God had something more to reveal to Job? Was there some attitude or theological belief that had to be corrected? If so, then continued suffering would certainly bring it to light.

For Elihu, it was not so much the "why" but the "what" that had become the issue. What was God doing? What was the reason for continued suffering? What should have been Job's proper response to continuous undeserved suffering? What sins were associated with Job's misunderstanding of God and his false theological assumptions?

Chapters 32–37 contain Elihu's speeches, in which he scathingly rebuked his friends for failing to respond appropriately to Job's statements and questions. Elihu also rebuked Job for insisting on his innocence. Nevertheless, Elihu assumed the role of an advocate for Job when he asked Job to reply, set his arguments in order, and take a stand (33:5). In the contemporary setting, this pictures a lawyer, who is preparing a case and his client for an arraignment.

Elihu[28] presented a unique perspective on Job's suffering and the dilemma he was facing as a result. These six chapters – covering five separate speeches[29] attributed to this young wise man – occupy an exceptionally important position in the overall argument of the book, specifically in our attempts to understand Job's struggle with undeserved suffering.

If it can be demonstrated that Elihu's speeches are genuine and that they are an integral part of the book of Job, then the reader may confidently conclude that Elihu's message is vital to the purpose and argument of the book. It is important to deal with the question of the genuineness of Elihu's speeches because of the extent of the textual material that is allotted to Elihu, the placement of the Elihu speeches in the book, and the reaction the speeches have drawn from critical circles on the question of authenticity.

---

28. The proper name *'elihu'* means "He is my God" or "My God is He." The latter is adopted by E. W. Bullinger, *The Book of Job* (Grand Rapids: Kregel, 1990), 161. Elihu is similar to the name Elijah, "Yahweh is my God."
29. Job 32:6–22; 33:1–33; 34:2–37; 35:2–16; 36:2–37:24. Scholars differ in their opinion on the division of the speeches. For a detailed representation of this five-part division, see David Allen Diewert, "The Composition of the Elihu Speeches: A Poetic and Structural Analysis" (Ph.D. diss., University of Toronto, 1991), 576–79.

Job 29:1–42:6

A number of scholars defend the speeches of Elihu as an original part of the book of Job. Early proponents considered Elihu as exalted above Job and his friends and as representative of the authentic Jewish view of providence.[30] The early church historians and the Reformers generally accepted the authenticity of Elihu's speeches.[31] John Calvin was complimentary toward Elihu and "there are few people in the Bible Calvin admires more."[32] Reacting to the early nineteenth-century opposition, Umbreit and Stickel[33] were among the first to maintain Elihu's authenticity.[34] Cornill refers to the Elihu speeches as "the summit and crown of the Book of Job" and says that they provide the only solution to the problem of suffering.[35]

Zuck offers four answers to the major critical objections: (a) Elihu was not mentioned earlier in the book as he was a silent observer, not yet involved in the disputation; (b) Elihu's style differed from that of the other four debaters – for instance, he used *El* for God 19 times compared with Job who used it 17 times; (c) Elihu's view of suffering differed from that of the three – while they had claimed that Job was suffering because he had sinned, Elihu said that Job was sinning because he was suffering – and Elihu also put his finger on Job's wrong attitude of complaining against God (33:13; 34:17); and (d) while it was true that Job did not answer Elihu, this might have been because Elihu silenced him.[36]

Alter expresses a "plausible consensus" that the speeches of Elihu are "an interpolation, the work of another poet."[37] Vicchio mentions nine reasons

---

30. Moses Maimonides, *Guide to the Perplexed*, trans. M. Friedlander (New York: Dover, n.d.), 296. Maimonides lived from AD 1135 to 1204. See also Solmon B. Freehof, *Book of Job: A Commentary* (New York: Union of American Hebrew Congregations, 1958), 205.
31. Although they accepted his authenticity, they were not always complimentary to Elihu. Thomas Aquinas believed that Elihu's knowledge was superior to the opinion of the other friends, but that he was moved by "vainglory" so that he misinterpreted Job's words and did not express the whole truth. Calvin, on the other hand, would not accept this criticism. See Susan E. Schreiner, *Where Shall Wisdom Be Found? Calvin's Exegesis of Job from Medieval and Modern Perspectives* (Chicago: University of Chicago Press, 1994), 131–34.
32. Schreiner, *Where Shall Wisdom Be Found?*, 131. For Calvin, Elihu's teaching was essentially the same as the truth declared in God's whirlwind speeches.
33. Johann Gustav Stickel, *Das Buch Hiob rhythmisch gegliedert und übersetzt mit exegetischen und kritischen Bemerkungen* (Leipzig: Weidmannische Buchhandlung, 1842), 195–219.
34. Friedrich Carl Umbreit, *Das Buch Hiob: Uebersetzung und Auslegung* (Heidelberg: Mohr, 1832), xxvi–xxvii.
35. Carl Cornill, *Introduction to the Canonical Books of the Old Testament*, trans. G. H. Box, Theological Translation Library 23 (New York: Putnam's Sons, 1907), 428.
36. See Zuck, "Job," 754–55.
37. Alter, *Writings*, 547.

why some scholars claim the "Elihu speeches were an addition to the book."[38] Some of these reasons are summarized below (in italics), along with a response that counters the objection.

(1) Elihu was not mentioned when the friends were introduced (2:11–13)
It seems unlikely that Elihu would be mentioned in the prologue (Job 1–2) since Yahweh, *Satan*, and Job are the major focus of these chapters. Neither the wife nor the three counselors are mentioned until chapter 2. Moreover, it also seems unlikely that a young bystander would interrupt the serious discussions found in the dialogue (Job 3–31) between three elderly "wise men" and a prominent Near Eastern person. Elihu was drawn into the conversation because of his frustration with the inadequate answers the three "wise men" offered in response to Job's dilemma.

(2) Elihu was not included when God spoke to Eliphaz and his two friends (42:7)
The epilogue is reserved primarily for Job's response to the speeches of Yahweh and Yahweh's response to Job's repentance. The epilogue also voices a condemnation of the false representation of God by Eliphaz, Bildad, and Zophar. It was not necessary for Yahweh to praise Elihu because Yahweh's speeches,[39] Job's response, and Elihu's correction of the three friends strongly suggest that Elihu was correct and that his views were compatible with those of Yahweh. Therefore, it is not surprising that God was silent with regard to Elihu.

(3) Elihu's speech is written in prose (32:1–6)
Since Elihu is a new character, and one with a youthful personality, a different vocabulary and style would naturally be expected.[40]

(4) The final words of chapter 31: "The words of Job are ended" (31:40b)
While this is true of Job's monologue, he still had a few words to say in response to Yahweh's interrogation (40:3–5; 42:1–6).

---

38. Vicchio *Book of Job*, 212.
39. Dhorme asks, "If it is Elihu who expounds the author's thesis, why is it that Job, who is constantly rebuked by Elihu, should receive the praises of the Epilogue?" (*A Commentary on Job*, cviii). It should be remembered, however, that Job was rebuked by Yahweh in chapter 38 and that Job expressed initial repentance in chapter 40 and final repentance in 42, which preceded any praises on the part of Yahweh. That is, Job was rebuked, he repented, and *then* he was praised. It would seem logical to conclude that Elihu had no need to repent because he was not rebuked by the Lord.
40. Andersen states that "style is also a quality whose assessment can be highly subjective," *Job*, 51.

(5) None of the characters referred to Elihu

Perhaps, as the youngest among them, none of the friends expected Elihu to make a speech or even chime in with his ideas about the theological discussion of these sages. Elihu seemed to have assumed the role of *advocate-mediator* for Job. Since it was Job who had suffered the losses, it was he who sought an answer to the question of why he was suffering despite his innocence. Elihu wanted to guide Job toward a resolution of the issues he was facing and prepare him for a confrontation with Yahweh. Nevertheless, when Elihu spoke to Job, he also included the rest of the friends.[41]

(5) Job responded to the three friends but not to Elihu

When Elihu joined the conversation, he acknowledged that he was young. Part of the reason for his earlier silence had been to show respect for his elders (32:4–6). But, having grown frustrated as he had watched the debates drag on and witnessed Job's painful rebuttals, he had decided to speak out for Job's sake. Elihu believed that it was the Almighty who gives understanding and that it was the spirit within him who had prompted him to speak (32:8). This admission, along with the manner in which Elihu conducted himself humbly and patiently, commanded the respect of Job and the three friends. Elihu had not gone far in his speech and already the friends felt "dismayed and have no more to say, words failed them" (32:15). Perhaps Job, by then, had perceived that Elihu would speak truth to him.

Chapters 32–37 are an authentic part of the text and not just an addition. These chapters play a significant interpretive, explanatory, and theological role in understanding Job's suffering and his relationship with Yahweh. Elihu's speeches revealed Job's misconceptions about God and corrected these wrong ideas, thereby preparing Job for his confrontation with Yahweh. Elihu also fulfilled the role of an advocate for Job.

32:1–33:33 Elihu's First Speech

This chapter attempts to answer these questions: Are the elderly necessarily wise? What are the attributes of a wise person? What is the key difference between the speeches of Elihu and those of Eliphaz, Bildad, and Zophar? What qualified Elihu to serve as a defense attorney for Job? What is the relevance of chapter 32 to Elihu's view of suffering?

---

41. Elihu uses "you," parsed as masculine plural in the Hebrew text.

JOB

32:1–5 Elihu's Introduction

The three friends had stopped responding to Job because he had claimed to be upright in his own eyes (32:1). But it was Job's claim to be upright in the sight[42] of God that made Elihu "very angry" with Job (32:2). "Job constantly, but improperly, in his view, insisted on 'justifying himself rather than God.'"[43] Elihu was also angry with the three friends because they had not given a satisfactory response to Job's arguments but, instead, had condemned him (32:3).

The text tells us that this was the first time Elihu had spoken with Job. He was the last in a line of four to speak and sympathize because the other three were older than him (32:4). However, when he perceived that the three did not really answer Job's questions, "his anger was roused" (32:5). The repeated use of "angry" or "anger" (32:2–3, 5) may indicate the intensity of Elihu's anger.

Elihu followed the protocols of the time, waiting until silence and custom allowed him to speak. To interrupt would have been a major breach in ancient Near Eastern etiquette. This respect of authority and elders is also found throughout the OT, specifically in the commandments in relation to parents (Exod 20:12; Lev 19:3; 20:9; Deut 5:16). Therefore, Elihu's right to speak could not just be presupposed; the offering of respect to elders remained a necessity even though, as in this case, their wisdom had failed.

Deference to elders continues to be practiced in Asia. In the Philippines, children and grandchildren practice *mano po* – a practice of taking the hand of their parents or grandparents and placing it on their own forehead as a way of showing respect and affection. Where there are family or business meetings facilitated by the elders, younger members let the elders speak first; and when they wish to say something, if not already called upon to do so, they respectfully request a turn to speak. Here is another example, which is a true story. At a wake, where relatives were asked to share their memories of the deceased, the facilitator called on an engineer from among the clan to be the first to share. But a much older lady stopped her, saying, "Let me be the one to share first because I am older." This awkward moment illustrates how, regardless of educational attainments, elders are respected. The older person had the right to speak first before the engineer could share her thoughts.

---

42. The *mem* on the Elohim indicates relationship: "before" or "in the sight of." See Williams, *Hebrew Syntax*, 56.
43. Kaiser, *Majesty of God*, 177.

32:6–10 Elihu's Respect for the Three

Elihu admitted that since he had been exceedingly fearful to share his knowledge because of his youth (32:6), he had allowed his friends to do the talking. He had thought that with their age, they would have gained more wisdom (32:7). But he subsequently realized that "it is the spirit in a person, the breath of the Almighty, that gives them understanding" (32:8). Elihu used two different words – "spirit" (*ruakh*) and "breath" (*neshamah*) – in this verse. The latter refers only to the "breath" God breathed into Adam when he made him into a living being (Gen 2:7). Elihu, by referring to both "spirit" and "breath," was acknowledging that people became wise only because they had God's breath (*neshamah*) in them.[44] This is "pivotal to the entire argument and occupies the central position of this section, and . . . severs the exclusive bond between old age and wisdom."[45] Elihu acknowledged that God is the source of all true wisdom, who gave him a position and a legitimate right to be heard. He also claimed, "It is not only the old who are wise, not only the aged who understand what is right" (32:9).

"Right" in verse 9 translates the Hebrew term *mishpat*.[46] Throughout the debate, Job had defended his integrity by maintaining that he acted according to *mishpat* (29:14; 31:13) – that is, what is just and right. Job's inaccurate concept of retribution theology led him to believe that his legal privileges had been breached by Yahweh. Because Job viewed God as violating his legal rights, he took the unprecedented step of challenging God to enter into litigation with him (9:32; 13:18; 23:4). Job, as well as the three friends, had failed to understand *mishpat* in its correct sense, and it was their misunderstandings and Job's impertinence that kindled Elihu's anger and prompted him to enter into the debate.

Elihu demanded a hearing to reason with his friends. Having said that old age does not guarantee wisdom, Elihu asked his friends to listen to him so that he might disclose to them what he knew (32:10). The crux of Elihu's words was to establish that age does not guarantee wisdom, and that youth can be wise is a common scriptural axiom.[47]

---

44. See note on Job 32:8, *NET*.
45. Diewert, "Composition of the Elihu Speeches," 76, 78.
46. This word can mean "judgment," "justice," "ordinance," "right," "privilege," "legal due." See Herman J. Austel, "mishpāt," in *TWOT* 2:947.
47. See Genesis 37:2; 41:12; 1 Kings 3:7; 1 Chronicles 22:5; 29:1; Jeremiah 1:6–7; Daniel 1:1–7. Qoheleth holds that gray hair does not ensure understanding (Eccl 4:13), nor does the prosperity of wise men guarantee wisdom (Eccl 9:15).

32:11–14 Elihu's Evaluation of the Three Friends

First, Elihu claimed to have waited patiently and listened attentively to the arguments of his friends (32:11). Second, although he had paid close attention so that he could understand what his friends had said, none of them had been able to convincingly refute Job's arguments (32:12). Third, Elihu warned them against claiming that they had found wisdom. Only God could refute Job, not a human being (32:13). Since Job had not argued with Elihu, Elihu would not respond to Job's words using his friends' arguments (32:14). In the preceding section, Elihu had claimed authorization and qualification to speak. In this section, he justified his intervention, gave his assessment of the arguments of the three, and then announced his intention to address the problems created by their faulty theology and Job's final erroneous verdict against God. The sequence of verses 11 and 12 show Elihu's patience and attentiveness in listening to the words of the three and the failure of their search for wise answers during the arguments. This was Elihu's justification for his intervention. The arguments of the three may have sounded convincing to the others and to themselves, but they had failed to persuade Job to accept their logic.

The tone of verses 13 and 14 is one of sarcasm[48] and correctly describes the attitude of the three. Elihu was anticipating some objection on the part of the three when he said, "Do not say, 'We have found wisdom.'" This is the same as saying, "Do not say to yourselves, 'We are the wise ones.'" This was doubtless the mood of these three counselors, who were contending that they had done their best. Their silence may not have been totally related to their defeat. Ultimately, on all moral matters, God is the final judge of all actions and motivations of a person (32:13).

32:15–22 Elihu's Desire to Address the Three

Elihu had observed that his friends had ceased to reason with Job. The earlier lively and wordy speeches had suddenly stopped (32:15–16). Elihu chided the three on the deficiency of their theology and concluded that their silence obligated him to speak on behalf of Yahweh. Since they had stopped speaking, Elihu was free to offer his solutions to the problem. Elihu had many things to say, and he declared that he was compelled to speak by "the spirit within me" (32:17–18). To stress the urgency of this compulsion, he used a figure of speech in which he likened the need to speak to the kind of pressure that

---

48. Norman C. Habel, *The Book of Job: A Commentary*, OTL (Philadelphia: Westminster, 1985): 453.

"bottled-up wine" exerts on "new wineskins" and sought permission to speak out and be relieved of this pressure (32:19–20). Elihu promised not to display "partiality"[49] or "flatter anyone." While implying that he was not "skilled in flattery," he hastened to add that if he did engage in flattery, his Creator would soon intervene in judgment (32:21–22). There is an important principle here: Anyone seeking to counsel others and deliver God's message is accountable to God to speak the truth without using flattery.

Elihu's external justification for entering the debate – the silence of the other characters –was followed by internal justification. Verse 18 is similar to Job 32:8. The implication is that Elihu spoke out from the depths of his own being and with the Almighty who gives understanding, offering wisdom that was "spiritual" rather than traditional.

The failure of the three friends convinced Elihu that they were not led by God and, hence, unable to minister to Job. For Elihu, the ineffectiveness of their arguments shattered any pretense of wisdom. Yet, the three friends stayed, even after losing the debate. This suggested that they were waiting, like Job, for God's intervention – but while Job was waiting for his exoneration, they were waiting for their vindication through Job's condemnation. The failure and the silence of the friends created a vacuum in the debate, a vacuum that anticipated Elihu's entrance.

Elihu's objectives in his first speech were to establish that he was a legitimate and consequential character in the discourse, whose anger was appropriate since he was a defender of God's justice (32:6–10); to demonstrate that wisdom was not limited to those of advanced age and experience (32:11–16); to assert that God is the only source of all true wisdom (32:8, 18); to disassociate himself from the wisdom tradition of the three counselors (32:13–14); to align and identify himself with Job and his struggle (32:14); to reveal that the three friends – by their silence and their failure to convince Job – had demonstrated that the aged are not always wise (32:15–16); and to explain that he was pressured into speaking not only by his passionate commitment to justice but also to the truth and to God, his Maker (32:17–22).

---

49. Literally, "lift the face."

> ## THE RELEVANCE OF JOB 32 TO ELIHU'S VIEW OF SUFFERING
>
> Chapter 32 is crucial to Elihu's view of suffering because it authenticates and identifies the person and message of this new character. For Elihu to be introduced as a new and unique character with a distinct message, he had to be disassociated from the three, as well as from the tedious cycles of accusation and self-justification that had preceded his arrival.
>
> Elihu's message, if it was to be separated from traditional wisdom, had to show evidence of authenticity. As a legitimate, Spirit-controlled messenger, Elihu's view of suffering had to carry authentication and authority. Elihu's affidavit of authenticity was his relationship with Yahweh's Spirit and his devotion to the impeccability of God's justice. So resolute was his allegiance that Elihu even alluded to a death sentence if he failed to flawlessly represent the Spirit's message: "For if I were skilled in flattery, my Maker would soon take me away" (32:22; compare Deut 18:20–22).
>
> Chapter 32 establishes the essential components that govern Elihu's decision to intervene: (a) he had a right to speak; (b) he was different from the others and equal to Job; (c) the assumptions of the three and Job concerning God's character and justice were inadequate and flawed; (d) his message was Spirit-inspired, not tradition-induced; and (e) he dared not speak deceitfully.

33:1–33 Elihu's First Speech Answering Job's Charges

This speech was Elihu's response to Job's charge that God was his enemy (33:10). This chapter invites us to consider these questions: How does God communicate with humankind? Had God really become Job's enemy? What is the relevance of chapter 33 to Elihu's view of suffering?

In this chapter, there is a change in the addressee. In chapter 32, Elihu was preoccupied with justifying his entry into the debate, and he concentrated mainly on the three antagonists, directly addressing the three in 32:6–14 and speaking to an unspecified group in 32:15–22. In chapter 33, Elihu turned his attention exclusively to Job (33:1). He used Job's name often in his speeches (33:1, 31; 34:5, 7, 35–36; 35:16; 37:14), thereby consistently disassociating himself from the three and claiming affinity with Job.

33:1–7 The Appeal to Job

Addressing Job, Elihu told him to listen to his every word (33:1) since he was about to make a lengthy speech[50] and would do so with integrity and insight (33:2–3).

The Elihu speeches contain four references concerning the spirit or Spirit (32:8,18; 33:4; 34:14). Two references are almost identical and "may complete an *inclusio*,"[51] where the major parallel terms are "the Spirit (of God)" and "the breath of the Almighty." These four statements reveal three crucial points: Elihu asserted that the Spirit and the breath of the Almighty are the only source of true wisdom (32:8); he claimed a personal relationship with God's Spirit, where he could draw on Yahweh's wisdom (32:18; 33:4); and he maintained that it is the Spirit of God who gives and sustains all life on earth. Elihu's intention, in verse 4, was to state that since both he and Job had been created by God's life-giving Spirit, this affirmed and underscored their common origin and equality. Elihu then called on Job to answer him, prepare his case, and take a stand (33:5); but he also reminded Job that he was his equal – "I too am a piece of clay" (33:6) – and that, therefore, Job had no need to fear him and that the pressure on him would not be heavy (33:7). Harsh as Elihu's words sometimes seem, his affinity with Job was genuine and his concern for truth was central to his message. For Job, truth would be a light burden to bear after the numerous false accusations of the three.

Although Elihu had earlier stated that he was fearful about speaking his mind because he was younger than the rest (32:6), his manner of speaking and his actions negated this. He spoke strongly and with authority as he affirmed Job by claiming to be on equal footing with him before challenging him to prepare his case.

33:8–12 Elihu Quoted Job's Words

Elihu claimed that he had carefully listened to the verbal exchanges between Job and the three friends. We see evidence of this in his second, third, and fourth speeches, where he quoted Job at length (33:8–11; 34:5–9; 35:2–3). For instance, Job had earlier made these claims: "I am pure, I have done no wrong; I am clean and free from sin" (33:9); "Yet God has found fault with

---

50. Literally, "open the mouth." See Bullinger, *Figures of Speech*, 842.
51. Johns, "The Literary and Theological Function of the Elihu Speeches" (PhD diss., Saint Louis University, 1983), 154. See also Robert V. McCabe Jr, "The Significance of the Elihu Speeches in the Context of the Book of Job" (PhD diss., Grace Theological Seminary, 1985), 86.

me; he considers me his enemy" (33:10); and "He fastens my feet in shackles; he keeps close watch on all my paths" (33:11).

Verse 9 is an allusion to Job 13:23, verse 10b quotes Job 13:24b, and verse 11 quotes Job 13:27 and also alludes to Job 14:16. These verses are a fair summary of Job's arguments and accurately reflect the central tenets of his claims, showing that Elihu had tried to understand where Job was coming from and, in so doing, demonstrated that he was qualified to be Job's defense attorney. Elihu affirmed that God does respond to human need and pointed out what he perceived as errors in Job's speeches and actions. Elihu's overriding goal was to lead Job to a deeper relationship with Yahweh. To achieve this goal, he had to help Job to comprehend the purpose behind his present suffering.

Briefly, the first quotation advanced three contentions that Job had previously offered in his own defense: he was innocent (33:8–9; compare 9:20–21); God's persecution was arbitrary, capricious, unjust, and an abuse of his power and justice (33:10–11); and God's silence meant that Yahweh had passed over Job's case, neglecting and overlooking him (33:12–13). In relation to the first assertion, Job did not deny the possibility that he had sinned (7:21; 10:5–6; 13:26; 14:17); but if he did, that was his concern alone (19:4).

The prepositional phrase "in this" in verse 12 is a reference back to verses 9–11. It would seem very awkward if, after elaborately presenting Job's position, Elihu would ignore Job's statements, and move on to something completely new (33:13). The contention that "God is greater than any mortal" did not originate with Job but with Elihu. God's greatness is a continuing theme in the Elihu speeches (36:5, 22, 26; 37:5, 14–18, 21–23) and form the theological foundation of Elihu's arguments. He did not issue a blanket condemnation of Job but only declared him incorrect on specific points. Elihu pointed out that since God is greater than humankind, Job was wrong to maintain that his argument was without fault and that God was guilty of injustice. The core of Elihu's speech consisted of a refutation of Job's untenable position and a defense of God's greatness. Elihu specifically defended God against Job's charge of hostility by arguing that divinely inflicted suffering can be ultimately redeeming, and that God acts fundamentally for, not against, humankind.

From this we can discern some practical principles for a counselor: identification with clients and their problem, specifying the wrongs committed, and leading clients to discover other aspects of God and his redeeming purpose.

33:13–28 Elihu Refuted Job's Words

33:13–18 God speaks through dreams. Elihu presented his initial defense of Yahweh and gave a general response to the inconsistencies of Job's position. He did not attack Job's claim to innocence in relation to the suffering he had experienced but, instead, concentrated on Job's faulty view of God. Elihu rebuked Job for contending (*rib*) that God had not responded to him (33:13) and had been inattentive to his cries (compare 30:20). He pointed out that although God speaks to people in various ways, unfortunately, people do not always perceive that he is doing so (33:14).

Elihu's first argument was that God continually communicates with people through dreams or night visions when they are asleep (33:15–16), warning them to turn them from wrongdoing and pride so that they might be spared from death[52] (33:17–18). This countered Job's accusation that God was apathetic and silent. While God's testing and discipline may be painful, it is proof that God is active even in silence.

People in the ANE believed that their gods could communicate to them through dreams and visions. Gnuse produced a work that listed dreams from Sumerian, Akkadian, Assyrian, Babylonian, and West Semitic reports. For instance, under Sumerian dreams, he listed Sargon's dream that foreshadowed the death of his superior and his eventual rise to power.[53] Even the living God made use of this medium of dreams to communicate to his people.[54]

Although Eliphaz's description of his own experience with dreams points to the wisdom tradition that divine messages came in night visions (4:12–13), Job saw dreams as divine cruelty (7:14). Elihu, alluding to and responding to Job's statement (7:14), presented dreams as a legitimate context for divine revelation and receiving messages from God.

---

52. Literally, "the sword."
53. Robert Karl Gnuse, *Dreams and Dream Reports in the Writings of Josephus: A Tradition-Historical Analysis* (Leiden: Brill, 1996), 47.
54. See Genesis 20; 31:24; 41:1; Numbers 12:6; Judges 7:13–15; 1 Samuel 28:6; 1 Kings 3:5; Daniel 2, 4, 7; Joel 3:1. The classical methods of OT communication included dreams, lots, Urim and Thummim, angels-messengers, and the prophets. These media of communication from God ceased to be the norm with the completion of the Holy Scriptures. There are exceptions however, especially in the last days prophesied by Joel (Joel 2:28–29). We must be discerning. Prophesies from God in our time would stand God's test, his word (Deut 18:20–22), and time itself. In the NT, Peter was instructed to visit the household of Cornelius through a vision (Acts 10:9–47). Even Paul received his Macedonian call through a vision (Acts 16:6–10). As to the contemporary setting, we hear stories of Jesus Christ revealing himself to individuals through visions in countries which are not open to Christianity. We must be open to similar claims; but be discerning.

33:19–22 God speaks through distress. In Elihu's second argument against Job's claim of God's indifferent silence, he argued that Yahweh chastens humankind through pain and suffering, which may take the form of rheumatism or arthritis, constant body aches, a loss of appetite, and emaciation until one is on the brink of death (33:19–22). The parallelism in these verses indicate the extreme pain that the person concerned suffered. This also describes what Job was experiencing.

In this particular context, the ultimate purpose of suffering is presented as being to lead people to deliverance, a deeper relationship with God, and restoration to God. Elihu did not present this as a negative principle but as a positive one. Sometimes, the seeming inattention of God is because we fail to perceive what God is doing even though, in fact, he is responding to our cries. As C. S. Lewis, a world-renowned British scholar and writer, so aptly put it, "God whispers to us in our pleasures, speaks to us in our conscience, but shouts in our pains: it is his megaphone to rouse a deaf world."[55]

33:23–28 God speaks through angels. Elihu's third argument posits that God speaks through an angel, a messenger-mediator, who serves as a gracious guide to correct and point a person to what is right. In verse 24, the first line contains a request for deliverance while the second line states the reason why the request should be granted. This messenger would be gracious and would speak to God to "spare people from going down to the pit" because he "found a ransom for them" (32:23–24). The messenger-mediator, under instruction from Yahweh, is the one acting on behalf of the sufferer. The problem is that the components of the ransom are not explained. Pope relates the concept to "doctrines of intercession by righteous men and vicarious expiation."[56] Habel views the term as a ransom paid in a court of law by a mediator for one in need.[57] Johns suggests a "bribe" or a monetary "ransom" since Job's position and wealth were completely lost.[58]

Elihu continued to attack the premise of the three that Job was suffering on account of sins committed. He clearly maintained that suffering was not always evidence of divine animosity. It is here that Elihu developed his first

---

55. Jana Harmon, "C. S. Lewis on the Problem of Pain," C. S. Lewis Institute, Fall 2012, https://www.cslewisinstitute.org.
56. See Pope, *Job*, 252. See also Johns, "Literary and Theological Function," 190.
57. Habel, *Book of Job*, 179. Driver and Gray interpret ransom to mean the price paid in lieu of forfeiting life, *Book of Job*, 291.
58. Johns, "Literary and Theological Function," 190.

clear proposal regarding Job's suffering. Indeed, deliverance from the grave and renewal of health are the result of the gracious intervention of Yahweh through a messenger-mediator. McCabe explains that verses 25–28 describe the results of the efficacious work of the intermediary angel. The sufferer will be restored physically (33:25) and also spiritually to a proper relationship with God (33:26). Those who are healed in this way will then publicly declare their sinfulness and the graciousness of God in delivering them from death (33:27–28).[59]

Throughout verses 23–25, the person played no active role in the process of restoration. But in verse 26, the sufferer took action. This section has two parts: the description of the person's prayer to God and God's acceptance and restoration of the person (33:26), and a declaration of thanksgiving that sin has been confessed and God has delivered.[60] The person addresses God in verse 26 and gives a testimony in verses 27–28.

In contrast to the physical renewal of verse 25, verse 26 is a reference to spiritual restoration: "that person can pray to God and find favor with him." The term *ratsah*, which translates "favor," is a cultic term that often refers to God's acceptance of a sacrifice.[61] The kind of sacrifice God accepts is spiritual brokenness and humility (Ps 51:17). Elihu was saying that the person's confession and repentance would constitute a sacrifice that would be acceptable to God. The sufferer, instead of being punished for his sin, would receive gracious restoration. The sufferer who receives this truth "sings out"[62] to others and announces that even though he had sinned, God had not withdrawn from him or given him what he deserved.[63] Once the relationship with God is renewed, the sufferer becomes a witness to God's mercy and glorifies God before the whole community.

This is the true message of divine retribution: The messenger-intercessor acts on behalf of the person who sinned, revealing his fault and then finding a ransom for his deliverance. God's admonition is always accompanied by the provision of grace. If Elihu's assumption was correct – that Job had sinned since the beginning of the debate – then Elihu was not only pointing out Job's faults of pride, anger, and bitterness but, as a faithful messenger-advocate, boldly

---

59. McCabe, "Significance of the Elihu Speeches," 125.
60. Diewert, "Composition of the Elihu Speeches," 206.
61. The term means "pleased" or "satisfied" (2 Sam 24:23; Ps 51:18; Jer 14:12; Ezek 20:40, 41; Hos 8:13; Amos 5:22; Mic 6:7; Mal 1:8, 10, 13).
62. See Gordis, *Book of Job*, 379.
63. McCabe, "Significance of the Elihu Speeches," 128.

asking for Job's deliverance⁶⁴ and, at the same time, encouraging Job to offer prayers to God. The messenger-advocate speaks to humanity for God and for God to humanity, guiding the person toward the right path of conduct,⁶⁵ a role that Elihu would do for Job.

What can be learned from this section? The true counselor speaks truth, not overlooking sin when it is there but also giving space for the Spirit of God to be the one to convict the person of any sin. Thus, the counselor leads the client toward God, who cares, so that there might be a restoration of fellowship.

33:29–30 The Purpose of God – to Instruct

Elihu continued that God delivers a "person" or people "to turn them back from the pit that the light of life may shine on them" (33:30). The expression "twice, even three times" in verse 29 suggests that God does so repeatedly. Indeed, the Lord "holds back mortals from going down to the pit so they could experience the 'light of life.'"⁶⁶ He is not always the God of immediate compensation, who can be held to assumed boundaries, but a gracious and loving God who works for his creation. Pain and suffering are also meant to keep a person from sinning and self-destruction for, in the process, God vindicates and restores a person – emotionally, spiritually, and physically.

33:31–33 The Plea to Job to Listen

Elihu reiterated his instruction to Job to listen carefully and remain silent (33:31; see also 33:1) so that Elihu could teach him wisdom. Job was only to speak if he had an answer (33:32). By repetition, Elihu emphasized the need for Job to be silent and listen (33:33).

Elihu's demeanor, however, was not one of arrogance but of humility, and he offered Job the opportunity to interact with Elihu's first speech (33:32). Reyburn paraphrases "For I want to vindicate you" as "I am anxious to find you innocent," or "I want to prove you right."⁶⁷ Such a sentiment is not found in the lengthy speeches of the three counselors. Elihu was genuinely concerned about clearing Job's name and desired to see him vindicated of the false charges against him, without, however, affirming Job's accusations against God's justice and righteousness.

---

64. This principle is often seen in the Psalms (Pss 25:16; 27:7; 30:11; 86:16; 119:132).
65. See 1 Kings 9:4; Proverbs 2:13; 4:11; 14:2.
66. Kaiser, *The Majesty of God*, 185.
67. William David Reyburn, *A Handbook on the Book of Job* (New York: United Bible Societies, 1992), 622.

The "wisdom" that Elihu would teach (33:33) probably referred to the content of his next three speeches where, among other things, he would remind Job of God's mysterious ways and his power in creating and sustaining the universe, present retribution wisdom and explain how it applies to suffering, and sketch how God rules the world and deals with wickedness. Elihu's desire for Job's vindication was not an arrogant statement but an assertion drawn from Job's own failure to distinguish between compensation wisdom and the wisdom described by Job himself (see 28:12, 20, 28). These are proverbs with which Elihu would later concur (37:24). Wisdom and understanding dwell with God alone, not with people; by definition, "The fear of the LORD – that is wisdom, and to shun evil is understanding" (28:28).

In his second speech, Elihu had several objectives: to identify himself with Job (33:1–7); to maintain that the source of any wisdom he offered was the Almighty God (32:8); to establish – by quoting Job – that Job had drifted toward arrogance and bitterness (33:8–11); to respond to Job's insistence that he was innocent and his charge that God was arbitrary, unjust, and abusive, and that Yahweh's silence meant noninvolvement in Job's life; to provide evidence that God does speak (33:12–30); and to offer Job an opportunity to respond to Elihu's first speech and to prepare him for the next speech (33:31–33).

Elihu assumed the logical position that Job was suffering undeservedly *before* he sinned by the statements he made during the debate, and he addressed the issue of the *continuation* of Job's sufferings. He offered explanations that would help Job to deal with this lengthy period of suffering without falling into serious sin. He also answered Job's charge that God's apparent silence meant that he was uninvolved in Job's agony. Job's later statement of repentance (42:5–6) demonstrates that his understanding of Yahweh was inadequate and needed correction. Elihu, then, was pointing to specific areas that needed correction; once these were presented and understood, Job would be ready to hear from Yahweh.

Elihu saw himself as the divine messenger sent by God to graciously point out Job's sin that had developed since the initiation of Job's original undeserved suffering. His major concern was to solidify the relationship between Job and Yahweh since this relationship had become strained by Job's misunderstanding of God's actions. If, in fact, repentance was needed, then Job's prolonged suffering could be shortened if he would respond to the mediatorial ministry of the messenger-interpreter. Job had to let go of his prideful stance and humble himself before a gracious and merciful God. Verses 26–28 describe a situation that will, in fact, take place later (see Job 42:1–6). In addition, there is a striking contrast between Elihu's view of suffering and that of the three friends. Even when his people fail, God responds with mercy and patience, offering grace to the offender. The doctrine of immediate compensation for sin is, once again, overthrown. Suffering only becomes evil if it is used to justify rebellion against Yahweh. Elihu emphasized that it was time for the sufferer to come to his Lord for healing, comfort, and restoration.

Continuing the thought of 32:21–22, where he had promised to refrain from flattery and partiality, Elihu assured Job of his personal integrity – his words corresponded to his heart. The knowledge that Elihu was about to impart sprang from a pure heart. His wordiness originated from a deep desire to assure Job of his integrity and his lack of malice and deception.[68] Although Elihu's verbosity[69] is often criticized, his abrupt intrusion into the debate was incompatible with ancient custom and traditional wisdom. His caution in addressing these men is understandable since their status as wise men also included political and societal power.[70] To have insulted someone of Job's prominence[71] – a standing that the three friends also probably shared – could have had injurious results for the youthful Elihu. Elihu was simply seeking to establish himself as a newcomer whose presence was legitimate and whose words were worthy of attention.

Elihu pleaded with Job to listen. Although the three advisers had also urged Job to listen, they were interested in defending their system, while "Elihu was interested in the restoration and justification of Job."[72] Elihu challenged Job to either speak up or remain silent. For the first time in the debate, the grief-stricken and expressive Job made no defense. His silence, however, was not due to boredom caused by a repetition of previous arguments, as Alden suggests.[73] Job had been attentive for several months, interacting at will with the three friends. The statement that "the words of Job are ended" (31:40) did not mean that Job could not or would not speak again (40:3–5; 42:1–6). Instead, Elihu's plea was a desire for the sufferer to carefully weigh what had just been said. He was also making a proper announcement that he had something further to add and that, if Job did not wish to enter the discussion, Elihu would go on with his monologue.

---

68. Similar expressions are found in Isaiah 29:13 and Psalm 12:3.
69. See Job 32:10–11, 17–20; 33:1–3.
70. For an example, see 29:7–17.
71. He was the greatest of all the men of the east (Job 1:3).
72. Michel, *Job's Real Friend Elihu*, 31.
73. Robert L. Alden, *Job*, NAC 11 (Nashville: Broadman & Holman, 1993), 331.

It is important to establish here that Elihu did not simply replicate the arguments of the three friends. O'Connor observes, "If Elihu is simply repeating what is found in the speeches of the Friends and of the Lord, how could a great poet (or intelligent editor) include them in his work?"[74] The original premise of the three that Job was suffering because he was a clandestine sinner was the theory that Elihu was seeking to disprove. Furthermore, if Elihu was saying that Job's initial suffering was due to his present sinful attitudes, then his view would have been equivalent to the three in attempting to justify God by condemning Job and rejecting his claim to innocence. The only difference would be that the focus would change from past sin to present sinfulness. This is a crucial point: The present sin of Job was because he was suffering; he was not suffering because of his present sin.

THE RELEVANCE OF JOB 33 TO ELIHU'S VIEW OF SUFFERING

In Job 33, Elihu's attitude was one of gentleness and sympathy. Unlike the three counselor-friends, Elihu identified himself with Job as a fellow sufferer and not just an observer. He made a great effort to meet Job on the same level, sympathizing with his suffering and focusing on what he and Job shared in common – that is, that suffering is the destiny of all people. In fact, Elihu saw that any attempt to escape from suffering was doomed to disappointment and failure.

Job had been intent on pursuing a relationship with God and was grieved because his suffering seemed to indicate that his former relationship had been lost and God's silence seemed to demonstrate his indifference to Job's cries for deliverance. Elihu wanted to demonstrate the fallacy of Job's theology and, in so doing, to try to make God's purpose in suffering clearer to Job. Job's suffering was not a punishment for some past or hidden sin. Rather, Elihu viewed suffering as, among other things, a preventive measure that kept Job from perpetuating sin or false perceptions of God and his purposes. Job's

---

74. Daniel J. O'Connor, "The Hybris of Job," *ITQ* 55 (1989): 125.

flawed concept of God's justice and providence were challenged and put in a new and correct perspective.

Elihu wanted to help Job to realize that a relationship with God was not based on deeds or even attitudes of loyalty, purity, or righteousness but, rather, on grace. God rewards the righteous on the basis of grace, never because of some human action seeking a "deserved response." Although Elihu did not minimize Job's sin during the debate, he did not view sin as the primary cause of Job's suffering as the three friends did. When Elihu cautioned, "God is greater than any mortal" (33:12), he was reminding Job that this was the reason why Job – and indeed we – did not always understand and sometimes misunderstood God's intentions. Elihu also emphasized that God is the source of true comfort and that he sometimes allows suffering – not as an act of rejection but to train the sufferer to rely on God rather than on human righteousness.

God was not silent, as Job had thought, but actively working in ways that Job could not perceive. Elihu explained that God speaks to us in many ways: in dreams, in pain, and through his messenger-mediator. Bode comments that suffering, as a teacher, drew Job closer to God by his grace because God's sovereign control over the affairs of Job's life was not limited by the restrictions of a theological system of recompense but were acts of grace and mercy. Elihu laid down the requirements on Job's side: humble submission, confession of sin, and joy[1] toward Yahweh, in contrast to pride or stubborn insistence that God is unjust in his dealings, leading to bitterness. Through Job's suffering, God was helping him to gain a new understanding and drawing him into a closer relationship with himself. God's objective was to keep Job from destroying himself by tenaciously holding on to a false belief system that not only attempted to regulate Yahweh but caused Job to become prideful. In everything, even in suffering, God has a good, gracious, and healing purpose for us – to save us from destruction and bring us closer to him.

---

1. William Bode, *The Book of Job and the Solution of the Problem of Suffering it Offers* (Grand Rapids: Eerdmans-Sevensma, 1914), 135.

34:1–37 Elihu's Second Speech

Elihu continued with his response to Job's questions about God's apparent injustice and silence. There are several questions to be addressed in relation to this chapter: Is God fair? How is God's justice manifested in his intervention in human affairs? Why did God continue to test Job? What is the relevance of chapter 34 to Elihu's view of suffering?

Elihu, in chapters 33 and 34, did not attempt to speak out of his experience but claimed to speak out of what God had taught him. Chapter 34 is a response to the main tenet of Job's complaint – that is, that God was unfair and unjust.

34:1–9 Elihu Rejected Job's Quotations

Calling on the wise to learn from him and listen to him, Elihu compared the sensory reception of words with tasting food as he urged his audience to consider what was good and right (34:1–4). He reviewed Job's complaint that God was unjust and tried to summarize and rephrase what Job had been trying to say (34:5–9):

> "I am innocent, but God denies me justice.
> Although I am right, I am considered a liar;
> Although I am guiltless, his arrow inflicts an incurable wound."

This section and the defense that follows alludes to *Satan's* claim: "Does Job fear God for nothing?" (1:9; compare 34:9). Elihu began by summarizing the core of Job's complaint, rather than using Job's exact wording. He presented Job's position using four "interrelated axioms:"[75]

1. "I am innocent" or "just" (compare 9:15, 20; 10:7, 15; 13:18).
2. "God has taken away my rights" (compare 6:28–29; 9:7; 27:2) – God refused to hear Job's case.
3. "I am considered a liar" (compare 6:28) – Job viewed his suffering as evidence against his claim to innocence and righteousness.
4. "'My wound is incurable' even though I am 'without transgression'"[76] (compare 6:4; 9:17; 6:13).

Elihu examined the kind of person that Job was. In his evaluation, Job "drinks scorn like water" (34:7). "The scorn or derision mentioned here is not against Job, but against God. Job scorns God so much he must love it."[77] The parallel line elaborates on this, stating that Job had enjoyed the company of evildoers (34:8). These two verses, however, are quotations from Eliphaz (15:16; 22:15). Regardless of his disdain for the three, Elihu used their quotations to include

---

75. Hartley, *Book of Job*, 451–52.
76. The Qal passive participle of the Hebrew term *'anash* refers to an "incurable wound" or "illness." See BDB, s.v. "'anash."
77. See *NET* Bible.

the friends as objects of his monologue and utilized their words in formulating his own position.

Eliphaz had charged Job with lapping up iniquity like water. But Elihu, while he accused Job of sinful, mocking speech, did not suggest that he was guilty of perpetrating wicked deeds. This subtle but unmistakable difference is crucial for understanding Elihu's position – Job's suffering was not necessarily the result of terrible wrongdoing, as Eliphaz, Bildad, and Zophar had suggested. In Elihu's view, Job's suffering was primarily preventive, not punitive.[78]

On this issue, McCabe is critical of Gordis, Feinberg, and Zuck, maintaining that chapter 34 presents suffering as *punitive* not preventive. But he fails to differentiate between the view of the three advisers – that Job was being punished for some illusive sin committed before the calamities – and Elihu's view of the potentiality of Job continuing to suffer even more because of present attitudes and sins committed *in* his suffering.[79] Zuck maintains that Elihu was not dealing with past sinful actions but with present sinful attitudes and that "Elihu viewed suffering as protective, rather than retributive."[80] Elihu's full separation from the doctrine of the three advisers and his passionate concern with Job's present, not past, sin is not always accepted. For instance, Zuck suggests that "Elihu's attitude matches that of Satan; hit a man hard enough and he will break" and that Elihu "failed to take into account the possibility that Job was suffering *without* due cause in specific sins."[81] Elihu's attitude was preventive and corrective, not punitive, and his focus was present faults, not past sins.

Even in verse 9, Elihu rephrased the argument of Eliphaz (22:2) – that a person does not benefit when he finds favor with God – and presumed that this was Job's belief as well. This verse actually helps to clarify the use of Eliphaz's quotations. Elihu used these quotations to state his conviction that Job was on his way to becoming one of the wicked because his present speech showed certain similarities to theirs. He then took one of Job's own statements concerning the actions of the wicked – "Who is the Almighty, that we should serve him? What would we gain by praying to him?" (21:15) – and turned it against him. "Elihu was afraid of the place to which Job's doubts were beginning to

---

78. Gordis, *Book of Job*, 387.
79. McCabe, "Significance of the Elihu Speeches," 157–58.
80. Zuck, *Job*, 141, 148.
81. Zuck, *Job*, 151–52 (italics his).

lead him. Job had not cursed God, as Satan had wagered, sure enough, but he was getting perilously close to falling into Satan's trap and doing just that."[82]

34:10–37 Elihu Refuted Job's Theology
34:10–12 God Is Just

Fact One: God acts in accordance with his nature. Elihu urged his audience, whom he called "men of understanding," to listen as he spelled out several attributes that pointed to the justice of God:

- God Almighty does no evil (34:10).
- God repays people according to their deeds (34:11).
- God does not pervert justice (34:12).

One reason this pericope was directed toward the sages was that it was a proper statement of retribution theology or the Almighty's administration of his world in contrast to the fixed formula of compensation theology proposed by the three. This definition, however, is also used in the distorted theology of compensation: the bad are judged, the good prosper. The principle here, however, is not a fixed, totally predictable system, as the three would have had Job believe, but a relational principle between a human being's deeds and consequences such as receiving a just reward in accordance with the character of the Almighty. The difference between the compensation theology of the three and the true doctrine of retribution that Elihu maintained throughout the remainder of his speeches is that God has all the facts, knows what is "good" and "right," and administers justice in accordance with his own nature rather than in accordance with humanity's assumptions regarding that nature. If judgment or blessing is delayed, then God is still just and good.[83]

The three tried to explain this seeming incongruity by accusing Job of past sin and guilt, while Job tried to explain it by insisting on his own innocence and accusing God of unfairness. For Elihu, this was tantamount to accusing God of acting wickedly and perversely toward his creation. In his view, the three friends and Job had all perverted God's retributive justice.

---

82. Kaiser, *Majesty of God*, 188.
83. This same positive principle of just retribution is taught in the New Testament in such passages as Romans 14:10 and 2 Corinthians 5:10 in relation to believers, and Revelation 20:11–15 in relation to unbelievers.

34:13–15 God Is in Control

Fact Two: God is not accountable to any being. With verse 13, Elihu began a series of rhetorical questions. The first question asked who gave God the right to rule the universe. The answer, of course, is no one, and it was upon this truth that Elihu based his conclusion. There are two implications of verses 13–15. First, if God is sovereign over the universe, he is not accountable to anyone. Second, as the sovereign Sustainer, he demonstrates his grace every moment through his life-giving Spirit, who nourishes and supports life on earth. If God so willed, he could remove all life from earth, and humanity would cease to exist. Termination would be immediate and final.

The point is that God has complete control over all life and no life could exist were it not for his grace. Furthermore, to be qualified to question God's administration of justice over his creation would require that the critic of God's justice be entrusted with the administration of the world, making him equal to God. So, one would have to usurp God's authority and place oneself above the Lord in order to question God's actions. This, for Elihu, is absurd. Also, the indirect implication of these three verses is that God is clearly involved in his creation and is actively concerned for and sustains all life generally and his human creation specifically. God is absolutely sovereign over the world, possessing total control over life and death, answerable to no one. But if power and authority corrupt people, can the same be true of God? This question is answered in the next section (34:16–20).

34:16–20 God Is Impartial

Fact Three: God cannot be corrupted because he is perfectly impartial. Elihu urged his audience to listen, if they had "understanding," as he identified some facets of justice in the character and actions of God. In doing so, Elihu used figures of speech, synthetic parallelism, and rhetorical questions. He began with a rhetorical question, "Can someone who hates justice govern?" which can be re-stated to say, "Someone who hates justice cannot govern" (34:17). He then introduced the "just and mighty One,"[84] who treats everyone equally because they are his creation and whose lives are in his hands (34:18–19).

The point of the pericope (34:18–19) and the recollection of Job's former words (34:5–9) is that God proves that he is just through his impartial dealings

---

84. This is one of the titles of God. However, instead of seeing two separate attributes ("just" and "mighty"), one can combine them into a single attribute: "righteous mighty One" or "mighty righteous One," using a figure of speech called a *hendiadys*.

with all people of the earth – rich and poor, powerful and weak, leader and outcast – "for they are all the work of his hands" (34:19). Death is not deferred for the great on account of their greatness nor hurried for the poor on account of their poverty. The purpose in making this point is to warn those who think God administers death unfairly and to encourage those who are experiencing suffering and poverty that God is aware of their circumstances. God, in his sovereignty does not act indiscriminately or show favoritism. He is not corrupt in the use of his own principles of justice but uses them perfectly to administer his world.

Job was preoccupied with the continued prosperity and power of the wicked (21:7–16). But Elihu asserted that the wicked do not get away with anything (34:17–20). God's impartiality is demonstrated by the inexplicable and sudden nature of the death of poor and rich alike (34:20). Elihu used these verses to gain Job's agreement since Job had essentially made the same point earlier on (12:17–21; 21:19–20). Elihu was dealing with contradictory statements in Job's former declarations, proving that he had paid close attention to Job's words during the debate.

34:21–25a God Is Knowledgeable

Fact Four: God is the omniscient judge. Elihu had already portrayed God as the just rewarder (34:11), the sovereign authority (34:13), the sustainer of life (34:14–15), and the impartial ruler (34:16–20).[85] Now he declared that God could not be biased in his administration since it is guaranteed that all his actions are just because his omniscience frees him from the temptation to show partiality.[86]

Elihu stated that God's omniscience – the ability to see and comprehend all activity and thoughts on earth – substantiates his justice. Elihu was offering a defense based on statements already made by Job. For instance, the wording of verse 21 is similar to Job's earlier statements (see 24:23; 31:4). If Job were truly innocent, Elihu's contention in verse 21 has a positive application: Because of God's knowledge of Job's ways, there was no need for God to "examine" and "to come before him for judgment" (34:23). Job, however, had earlier applied this fact in a negative way, insisting that Yahweh was watching him with a view to persecuting him (13:27). Verse 22 denies the possibility

---

85. In addition, the next section points to God as the omniscient Judge (34:21–25a) and the absolute Executor (34:25b–30). See Zuck, *Job*, 150.
86. Diewert, "Composition of the Elihu Speeches," 288.

of hiding from God. "Darkness" and "deep shadow" do not hinder God from seeing the evil that people do. This corresponds with Job's earlier statements (24:13–17), especially the reference to the adulterer who thinks that no eye will see him because of the "dusk" (24:15). But God, in his omniscience, sees the works and thoughts of all human beings, and he will administer just and fair punishment according to their deeds.

God's omniscience will not allow him to make any mistakes when punishing evildoers. Since God sees all, a court appointment is not necessary (34:23–24). Job had been demanding a court appointment since the beginning of the debate; but a trial is unnecessary, either for condemnation or for blessing, because God knows the thoughts of humankind, even before they form in the heart.[87]

34:25b–30 God Is Sovereign

Fact Five: God is just in condemning the wicked. Elihu stressed the punishment of the wicked and answered Job's complaint about God ignoring the plight of the poor (24:1–12). Sin may be privately committed, but retribution will be publicly administered (34:26). On this basis, God can judge people publicly and openly "without inquiry" (34:24), and his punishment will always be just and expeditious. This judgment is based on their failure to follow God and, specifically, for their cruel treatment of the poor (34:27–28). When the cries of the poor reach God, he will act on behalf of the afflicted. Although the wicked do not know God's ways and oppress the humble and needy, God knows the ways of all people and will address the plight of the poor. The wicked will be "shattered" (34:24a), overturned (34:25b), "crushed" (34:25c), and punished (34:26a). Contrary to Job's assertion (24:1), God does punish the wicked, but Elihu made it clear that God is not bound to act within the time limits or boundaries dictated by human theology.

God carefully watches people, destroying the wicked for their disobedience but attentive to the cries of the poor and afflicted (34:21–28). But it is his prerogative to either respond or to refuse to act when his people call on him to ask that the godless do not take advantage of others. Elihu concluded that God is not obligated to speak and is justified in remaining silent. In verse 29, Elihu strikes out again at the fixed formula of compensation theology.[88] So,

---

87. See Psalm 139.
88. Hartley admits that verses 29–30 are difficult to interpret, for they are "replete with textual problems." After discussing these difficulties, he concludes that "no reconstruction has won a

"even if God chooses to be silent and hide His presence, His justice is never in question."[89]

Like Job, Elihu clearly understood that even though God does judge the wicked, violent and oppressive people do frequently prosper. Elihu also admitted that even when God hears the cries of the afflicted, he is sometimes silent, hiding his face from those who suffer. Job regarded the hiding of God's face as an act of hostility (13:24); but verse 29 also recalls Elihu's earlier argument, where he asserted that God's silence does not imply noninvolvement or inactivity on the part of Yahweh (33:12–30). Just as God spoke again and again to humankind, using different methods, so he acts silently as the "absolute Executor"[90] to perform his will "over individual and nation alike." And as the Sovereign, God "keeps the godless from ruling" and "laying snares for the people" (34:30). Where evil seems to reign supreme, Gordis explains, "God permits evildoers to hold sway in order to punish men and nations that have themselves been guilty of seeking to snare the innocent."[91]

Elihu was honest and he agreed with Job's perplexing observation that the wicked do sometimes prosper, while the righteous are often oppressed. Unlike Job, however, Elihu did not agree that this contradicted God's just rule over earth and humankind. God's silence is neither arbitrary nor a violation of his justice. God's slowness does not deny his goodness, justice, or omnipotence. Once again, Elihu corrected Job's misconceptions about God. Verse 29 "harks back to Elihu's opening statement to Job" (34:17) and concludes that "accusations of injustice brought against God by human beings (i.e., Job) are absurd."[92] Contrary to what oppressed people often believe, God's silence in the face of oppression does not mean that God hates justice.

34:31–37 God Is Free

Fact Six: God is not manipulated by human beings or their theology of compensation. Elihu then went on to describe the hypothetical case of someone who says to God, "I am guilty but will offend no more. Teach me what I cannot see; if I have done wrong, I will not do so again" (34:31–32). Elihu asked Job whether God should repay this hypothetical sinner according to

---

consensus and it is best to work with the MT." (*Book of Job*, 459). See also Dhorme, *Book of Job*, 523–24; and Gordis, *Book of Job*, 392–93.
89. Alter, *Writings*, 555.
90. Zuck, *Job*, 150.
91. Gordis, *Book of Job*, 381.
92. Diewert, "Composition of the Elihu Speeches," 318.

Job's terms or in accordance with God's own justice (34:33). Should God be dependent on Job's opinion in governing the world and the individuals in it? The problem with the confession of verses 31–32 is that the sinner has not admitted to questioning God's right to act in accordance with his own nature. This was the position that Job had maintained throughout the debate (6:24; 9:20, 29–31; 10:2, 15; 33:9–10) and he had not changed either his declaration of innocence or his charge of injustice against God. He was simply willing to admit that he had had enough and that if God would answer him in a courtroom setting, revealing to him that he had done wrong, he would make the necessary corrections and reform.

In this final pericope of the chapter (34:34–37), Elihu's remarks were no longer directed to Job (34:33) but appeared to address his audience since his wish for Job was expressed in the third person (34:36–37).[93] From the outset, Elihu had called on the wise to listen to his arguments (34:2) so that, together, they could come to an equitable assessment (34:4). Either Elihu was calling on Job to rebut what Elihu had said about Job in previous passages or urging him, as the defendant in the case, to give Elihu the facts that he needed to adequately defend Job.

Verse 34 introduces the findings which follow in verses 35–37. Elihu commanded the "men of understanding" and any "wise men" present to agree with him in issuing the verdict that "Job speaks without knowledge; his words lack insight" (34:34–35). The phrase "without knowledge" recurs in the Lord's first discourse (38:2) and in Job's own admission and response to Yahweh (42:3). The triple occurrence – with Elihu, Job, and the Lord all in agreement on this point – emphasizes the importance of this statement.

Elihu's verdict emphasizes two important points: first, Job spoke without knowing all the facts (34:35; 37); second, the more Job spoke, the more his sin of false accusation against Yahweh was multiplied (34:37). Essentially, Job presented his arguments against God without a full understanding of God's nature or character.

Elihu uttered an imprecation against Job, that he be tried for answering like an evildoer (34:36). To be "tested to the uttermost" or "to the limit" or "to the end" represented a wish that Job would get to the end of himself so that he might recognize the seriousness of his situation. Elihu was not uttering a wish that Job would die but, rather, that he be tested to the point where he would finally respond to Yahweh by letting go of his insistence that he had a

---

93. McCabe, "Significance of the Elihu Speeches," 156.

case against him and renewing his relationship with Yahweh before his sinful attitude resulted in the ultimate discipline. Elihu also presented another cause for alarm (34:37). In this verse, "rebellion," "conspiracy," "obstinacy," or "transgression" translate the Hebrew term *pesha'*.[94] Job had reversed his original statements of loyalty and trust in God's justice and seemed to have verbally defected to the side of wickedness. Elihu viewed Job's words as disloyalty to the ways of God for, as Johns explains, "noting Job's dissatisfaction with God's justice, Elihu detected an attitude of rebellion in Job."[95] Elihu was sincerely concerned that if Job continued in this vein, he would suffer even more for rebelling against God. The conclusive evidence that influenced Elihu's assessment of Job's drift toward rebellion was that "he claps his hands among us." This term *safaq* appeared earlier on with reference to the east wind that "claps its hands in derision" against the wicked (Job 27:23). The clapping of hands can also refer to the following: (a) silencing others, thereby treating their counsel with contempt;[96] (b) an expression of joy (2 Kgs 11:12; Ps 47:1);[97] or (c) an expression of spiteful triumph (Lam 2:15; Nah 3:19).[98] In this context, it would be best to understand this term as an act of contempt or scorn. Whichever way the gesture of clapping is perceived – whether toward the wise men, Elihu, or God – this was a confirmation to Elihu that Job was moving in a direction synonymous with derision and contempt toward God and his justice. Elihu, like Job, did not agree with the oversimplified premise of the three.

Job's initial response to suffering had been that God was just (1:20–22; 2:10); in the course of the debate, however, his position shifted, and he began to accuse God of injustice, even adding rebellion to his sin by refusing to alter his stance (34:37). As Elihu defended God's justice and the operation of his righteous rule against Job's inflammatory accusations,[99] his words became more intense. Elihu "quite accurately capsuled Job's position."[100] The core of Job's position was that Yahweh, by allowing Job's suffering to continue proved that Job's claim of innocence was false and that Job was a liar. Based on his belief in compensation theology, Job's suffering remained the deciding evidence to all but Elihu and Job himself that he was guilty. Seemingly, Job's only recourse

---

94. Eugene Carpenter and Michael A., Grisanti, "peshah'," *NIDOTTE* 3:710.
95. Johns, "Literary and Theological Function," 120.
96. Zuck, *Job*, 152.
97. Zuck, *Job*, 152.
98. R. L. Mixter, "Hand" in *ZPEB*, ed. Merril C. Tenney (Grand Rapids: Zondervan, 1975), 28.
99. Clarify Job 9:14–24; 16:11–14; 19:7–13; 21:17–18; 24:1–12; 27:2.
100. Hartley, *Book of Job*, 452.

was to declare God guilty for refusing to grant him an audience and for allowing him to continue to appear a liar even though he was righteous. Job's conclusion was that God's actions toward him were unjust.

As demonstrated above, Elihu had a clear understanding of the seeming contradiction between reality and the claims of retributive justice. While he was well aware of wicked rulers, corrupt judges, and deceitful leaders, he maintained that their existence did not nullify God's justice. There are apparent exceptions to God's administration of this justice when wicked continue to prosper and the poor are oppressed. Even though God sometimes uses the wicked as his tools of judgment – as he used the Chaldeans to punish Israel (see Hab 1:6–11) – this does not mean that the wicked are exonerated or that their wickedness is justified. In Israel's history, God often allowed wickedness to develop and prosper significantly for the purpose of using wicked people as instruments of divine judgment on other nations who then turned on themselves and self-destructed.[101] In addition, the context of verses 31–33 bring to light a fact that is often overlooked: "The exploited and oppressed are seldom completely innocent themselves."[102] Therefore, God's silence and his seeming detachment are means used by his justice to express his will in dealing with all levels of humanity.

THE RELEVANCE OF JOB 34 TO ELIHU'S VIEW OF SUFFERING

Elihu's desire to see Job vindicated (33:32b) intensified in chapter 34. Elihu wanted to prevent Job from being punished by God for making false accusations against Yahweh and his administration of justice. Elihu's sternness with Job resulted from these concerns and not from the conviction shared by the three friends that Job's suffering was caused by previous sins. Elihu's arguments can be summarized as follows:

---

101. See the book of Habakkuk and the discipline of evil within Judah and the eventual self-destruction of neo-Babylonians or Chaldeans.
102. Johns, "Literary and Theological Function," 117.

> First, God allowed undeserved suffering to continue in Job's life for the purpose of revealing Job's struggle with accepting God's justice. Nevertheless, God is just and good in allowing Job to suffer (34:5–9).
>
> Second, God does not have to explain why he allowed Job to suffer. God is impartial, and his justice will ultimately prevail.
>
> Third, if Job refused to listen, punitive and disciplinary suffering would surely follow (34:21–28). Elihu was attempting to protect Job from God's disciplinary action.
>
> Fourth, God's delay, silence, and seemingly allowing evil people and nations to grow are often part of his plan to discipline or bring people to himself (34:29–30).
>
> Fifth, suffering is part of his plan to redeem humankind.
>
> Elihu's argument was to establish that God is fair and impartial in the administration of his justice. Accordingly, Elihu's fourth speech (Job 35) is a continuation of this defense and addresses Job's specific accusation about God's silence and his position that "there is no profit in trying to please God" (34:9).

35:1–16 Elihu's Third Speech

This chapter responds to these general questions: Why is God sometimes deafeningly silent to people's cries for help? What is the relevance of chapter 35 to Elihu's view of suffering?

35:1–3 Elihu Quoted Job's Words

Elihu challenged Job's claim to integrity (35:1–3), questioning if Job really believed that his claim of being upright before God[103] was correct and reminding Job that he had questioned whether being upright was of any benefit in God's sight (21:15; see also 34:9). The "evident sense is that he feels it makes no difference whether he is virtuous or sinning, and he has no special motive to offend because he gets nothing from it."[104]

Elihu addressed Job as well as the three antagonists (35:4). Addressing the three indicated that he was continuing to defend his argument and that his counsel was not the same as theirs (32:14; compare 35:4). Job, however, was still the primary focus of Elihu's argument demonstrated by the fact that

---

103. The particle *mem* on God connotes relationship and can be rendered "before" or "in his presence." See Williams, *Hebrew Syntax*, 56.
104. Alter, *Writings*, 556.

he quoted Job in verses 2–3 and by his repeated use of the second person masculine singular form in verses 5–8.

Elihu quoted Job for the third time, setting Job's words within the framework of a rhetorical question directed specifically at Job. Verse 2a is a legal question: "Do you think this is just?" Of course, this rhetorical question demands a negative answer since no human being, regardless of their righteous acts and pious standing, could be more righteous than Yahweh. Nevertheless, Elihu contended that Job had answered, "I am in the right, not God" (2b).

The quotation in verse 3 clearly demonstrates Job's conformity to compensation theology. Job, like the three, assumed that the reward for obedience and godly living was guaranteed by God's own rule of action. When Job's faith in that assumption was shattered by his own experiences, instead of casting off his obvious misinterpretation of God's retributive justice, he turned on God and the operation of his justice with a cynical question: "What profit [is it] to You?" and "How am I better off than if I had sinned?"[105] This rendering would indicate that Job believed that his righteous deeds affected God's treatment of him. Johns rephrases what he thinks Job tried to say: "If it matters to God what I do, then God will express that by a difference in the way he treats me. I have been righteous. It has not made a difference in the way God treated me. Therefore, it does not matter to God what I do."[106]

35:4–16 Elihu's Refutation of Job's Words

35:4–8 God is not influenced by the sin or righteousness of human beings

Elihu did not mince his words as he emphasized that God's justice remains unsullied (35:4–8). In effect, he said that Job should recognize that God was exalted high above him (35:5). Verses 6–7 convey a single thought, expressed from the negative influence of "sin" – based on an earlier speech by Job (7:20a) – and the positive influence of "righteousness" – based on what Eliphaz had said (22:2–3). The main thought of these verses is that it is impossible for a person to influence the operation of God's justice through either sinful actions or righteous deeds. "Elihu uses the image of giving and receiving; what can Job possibly give to God, and what can God possibly receive from Job?"[107]

---

105. The NIV renders 35:3 as: "What profit is it to me and what do I gain by not sinning?"
106. Johns, "Literary and Theological Function," 121.
107. Johns, "Literary and Theological Function," 122.

But while Job's transgressions or righteous deeds would not impact God, such deeds would affect Job himself and other people (35:8).

Elihu maintained that God's perfect retributive justice was still in force even though Job had attempted to define that retributive justice on his own terms. Although Job observed that the wicked prospered while the poor were oppressed, he did not possess the ability or right to conclude, on the basis of that observation, that God was unfair or unjust.

35:9–16 God does not answer those who do not acknowledge his existence

Elihu described how the oppressed cry (*za'aq*) for help against the abuses of those in power (35:9). Sadly, they do not cry to God, seeking him: "Where is God my Maker who gives songs in the night" (35:10). By failing to address God directly as their "Maker," they show that they are no different to the animals and birds who do not know God as God (35:11). The birds continually sing and the animals cry in pain, but they are not wise enough to address God as their "Maker;" yet, even people fail to seek God and cry out to him (35:10). Why does God not answer the prayers of such people? Because they are arrogant. God's silence may *appear* to be cruel and whimsical, but understanding the circumstances – that is, these people's arrogance in failing to acknowledge him as their Maker – will confirm God's justice.[108] The point is that God's silence is justified and does not imply that he is uninvolved with humanity's suffering.

Elihu said that the attitude of the wicked is not humility but pride. That is why God does not answer them. Johns explains, "If the reason for crying out is pride and not a desire for God's presence, God's refusal to answer makes excellent sense."[109] While human suffering should call forth God's compassion, it does not mean that God is unfair in allowing suffering, especially when human beings arrogantly refuse to turn to him. "God cannot be coerced or pressured by such pleas into acting in a set way."[110]

Job, when he said that he did not see God, was entering the realm of the arrogant wicked. Since he, too, failed to acknowledge God's existence by saying that he did not see him, God would not listen to him either (35:14a). Job lamented his situation but had not yet advanced to the stage of singing

---

108. Diewert, "Composition of the Elihu Speeches," 370.
109. Johns, "Literary and Theological Function," 128.
110. Hartley, *Book of Job*, 466.

the praises of Yahweh amid his suffering; he did not turn to God to be taught the purpose for his suffering but continued to complain and lament his condition;[111] he was demanding an audience with God based on a prideful need for vindication rather than the simple desire for God's presence in his suffering. He was in danger of being among the arrogant wicked who deny God's existence. On account of this, God's silence was justified.

Neither the multitude of words that gushed from Job's mouth nor his rebellious spirit in reprimanding God for his silence (13:24; 23:3) and demanding that he be allowed to march into God's presence as a proud defendant (13:15; 31:35–37) were acceptable responses to suffering. Even his complaints that God had failed to consider his case and that he had to wait to have an audience with God (35:14b) and his accusation that God never punishes the wicked or takes notices of wickedness (35:15) were arrogant complaints which God did not have to respond to.

In short, Job was guilty of speaking empty words and multiplying arrogant words against God (35:16). Therefore, God was not answering him. Verses 15–16 were Elihu's response to the view Job had expressed earlier (21:7–21), where he charged God not only with failing to hear and deliver the oppressed but also with allowing the wicked to live on in prosperity without being punished. Elihu saw such talk as "empty talk" and "without knowledge" or at best, uninformed.

In comparison to the arguments of the three, Elihu's words made far more sense, getting to the heart of the matter by giving a meaningful response to the question of why God is sometimes silent in the face of people's cries for help. Moreover, Elihu recognized God's justice and emphasized that God alone is just and that he alone can vindicate Job. Elihu then explained possible reasons for God's seeming inattention to the cries of people in distress.

Elihu insisted that it was incorrect to imagine that the actions of humankind – based on their limited knowledge and insight – would influence God to alter the just administration of his creation. Elihu maintained that God is transcendent and accountable to no human being. Divine silence is the right of transcendence. Therefore, it is human beings, not God, who are benefited or cursed by the good and evil of human actions. This does not mean that faithfulness and righteous living are unimportant to God.

---

111. Zuck, *Job*, 155.

THE RELEVANCE OF JOB 35 TO ELIHU'S VIEW OF SUFFERING

One of the most common reactions to suffering, especially when it is undeserved, is to become bitterly judgmental about God's goodness and justice. Verses 2–3 reveal that this was Job's attitude, which led to Elihu's first principle of suffering in this chapter: Suffering can often become an excuse to abandon a righteous lifestyle. Experiencing suffering for no apparent reason, while observing the prosperity of the sinful, puts righteousness under pressure, as in Job's case. Nevertheless, suffering is not an excuse for sin and must not discourage righteous living.

The second principle is related to God's purpose – to bring the sufferer to a deeper knowledge of him and his purposes, which requires that the sufferer focus on God and his purposes (35:5–7). Verse 5 calls Job to refocus his attention away from compensation theology and consider God's preeminence and transcendence. Here, Elihu seemed to have been anticipating what he would say in his final speech, and these words may also be a preview of the Yahweh speeches. The key point here is that suffering, when rightly received, is designed to turn the sufferer away from an anthropocentric perspective to one that is theocentric. Job focused on his vindication and on his desire to witness the immediate punishment of the wicked (35:6–7). Elihu however, maintained that neither exemption from suffering for the righteous nor immediate suffering for wickedness could be guaranteed in this world.

The third principle related to suffering is that since God is omniscient, he knows and understands everything and acts justly and caringly at all times – even when he is silent. And God's silence does not mean that he is uninvolved or detached from the sufferer. Suffering may cause a person to lament and expose their inner fears and anger, but God is present and can turn a sufferer's lament into "songs in the night" that praise God's goodness (35:9–11). The danger, as demonstrated by Job's response, is that people may give in to frustration and anger and "cry out" from hearts filled with bitterness and pride (35:12–14) instead of a desire to be in the presence of God.

The fourth principle is that a wrong focus, attitude, and actions in suffering can delay God's help and restoration. The expression of Job's pride and anger against God only caused a delay in relief for his multiplied words were "without knowledge" and could not help him (35:15–16).

36:1–33 Elihu's Fourth Speech

In these two chapters (36–37), Elihu's strong defense takes on a more compassionate tone as several themes are brought together. The essence of these themes could be described like this: Whatever else may be said about the problem of suffering, we must maintain that God is just (36:3). He is fair and cares for his people, and bitterness and anger are not acceptable responses in situations where God allows suffering – it is only the "godless in heart who harbor resentment" in this way (36:13). Elihu, concerned for Job's precarious position, continued with warnings to Job not to pursue his destructive path.

The questions that will be answered in this chapter include the following: Is there a difference between God's treatment of the wicked and his dealings with the upright? What is the basis on which God acts? What is the relevance of chapter 36 to Elihu's view of suffering?

36:1–15 Elihu's Explanation of Suffering

36:1–4 God is the source of knowledge

Since Job had made no reply, Elihu resumed his final speech. In these first verses, he affirmed his source of knowledge and therefore instruction. He started by requesting his audience to be patient with him a little longer so that he could instruct them on God's behalf (36:1–2). In ascribing justice to his Creator (36:3), Elihu was pointing to God's just administration of the world. Since the phrase "I get my knowledge from afar" is parallel to "my Maker," Elihu was claiming that the knowledge he was about to share was from God. Therefore, his words, unlike those of the three adversaries, were "not false" but true (36:4). The "one who has perfect knowledge" (36:4) could be God or the Spirit of God whom Elihu was representing (compare 37:16).[112] The idea was that God or God's Spirit was in their midst, guiding both Job and Elihu. Early on, he acknowledged that it is the Almighty who gives understanding (32:8).

36:5–12 God uses suffering for instruction

Elihu described God as "mighty but despises no one" and "firm in his purpose" (36:5). He reasoned that although God is powerful, he does not reject or despise anyone. He is not internally weak, indecisive, or vindictive in his actions. God is not afraid of confrontation "but is stouthearted, characterized by inner

---

112. Alter thinks that "Elihu is referring to himself, with characteristic lack of modesty." Writings, 557.

resolve and courage."[113] Therefore, God acts justly and is never indifferent or biased toward anyone (compare 9:16; 27:2; 30:20).

Elihu presented two kinds of people in verse 6 — the wicked and the oppressed. In the verses that follow (36:7–14), he contrasted God's actions toward them and their corresponding response to God's intervention in their lives. Elihu compared God's punitive acts against the wicked with his execution of justice (*mishpat*) for the poor (36:6). He then expanded on this thought, maintaining that God's dealings with humanity are in accordance with his character and justice. The wicked would ultimately be punished (21:7–9, 30), while the afflicted would be vindicated (19:23–25; 42:10–16). Job's question as to why the wicked are allowed to live a long life is the focus of Elihu's statement (compare 21:7): God does not forsake the righteous even in suffering but, like kings, he establishes them on thrones (36:7; compare 1 Sam 2:8; Job 29:25; Ps 113:7–8). Those who trust in him are sometimes exalted in this lifetime (36:7, 11) but always and fully in eternity (Rev 5:10; 22:5).

If God treats the righteous with justice and goodness (36:6–7), how can one explain the sudden reversal of fortune in which blessing collapses into misery? Elihu was dealing with the question "Why do the righteous suffer?" His focus, however, was not the suffering of the righteous *per se* but the activity of God within the context of their misery. Elihu suspended the issue of *cause* and focused instead on the *divine response*.

The point that Elihu was attempting to make was that Job had enjoyed prosperity in the past as a result of God's gracious dealings and had, therefore, been able to fulfill the obligations that went with his position in society. If God had done this for him in the past, and if Job had done this for others, then God would surely exalt Job again. Therefore, Elihu's warnings were aimed at encouraging Job to wait patiently for God's deliverance.

Contrary to the doctrine of the three counselors, Elihu acknowledged that the righteous frequently suffer great affliction and oppression (36:8). While suffering is not evidence of wickedness, God may use times of affliction to point out and correct a person's transgressions (36:9–10). God's justice does not change; it stands firm and can be anticipated and depended on. What cannot be anticipated is God's timing, purpose, and methodology, which are governed by his sovereign will. We cannot assume that people going through afflictions are sinful or wicked. God's purpose in permitting suffering may be revelatory, preventive, pedagogical, directive, or some other purpose that is in

---

113. Diewert, "Composition of the Elihu Speeches," 468.

accordance with his will. Elihu proposed that there is a corrective function to suffering: "He tells them what they have done – that they have sinned arrogantly" (36:9). Suffering is preventive and disciplinary in that it is designed to reveal unnoticed transgressions and prevent arrogant behavior. God may communicate to the sufferer the reason, purpose, and response required within that situation – making them listen to correction and commanding them to repent of their evil (36:10). Two choices and their consequences are presented. A person may choose to "obey and serve" God or not to "listen" to God. The consequence of obedience (listening) is "prosperity" and "contentment" (36:11) while refusing to listen leads to certain death (36:12).

36:13–15 God responds to the penitent

Elihu went on to explain that the refusal of the godless to call on God for help would result in their dying young. Was this an indirect warning to Job? Ruin awaits those who do not respond to God's disciplinary action. They grow angry and bitter under affliction because "even when he fetters them, they do not cry for help" (36:13b). God is the explicit agent of their binding or suffering. Instead of humble prayers to God during suffering, the disobedient express only their bitterness so that they die before their time or turn to sinful practices among cult prostitutes [*qedeshim*] (36:14). The Hebrew word *qadesh* refers to cult personnel, a class of priest, or a consecrated cult or temple prostitute.[114] Verses 13–14 deal with what happens to the disobedient and godless. Rowley explains that these temple prostitutes usually die untimely deaths due to debilitating sexual excesses and abuses.[115] The term is graphic, painting a picture of the terrible death that awaits those who have chosen to be disobedient. It is important to note that since verse 5, Elihu had been speaking in generalities, using words like "they" and "them." He was not implying that Job was guilty of this particular category of wickedness. In fact, in verse 15, Elihu offered positive encouragement to Job, giving him hope by affirming that God's purpose in suffering is to deliver the sufferer "through," "by," or "in" the affliction. Alter

---

114. See *HALOT*, s.v. "qadesh." The NIV however, translates the term as "male prostitutes." Similarly, the *NET* Bible has "male cultic prostitutes" while the NKJV has "perverted persons." The plural masculine which is the case in Job 36:14 is used three other times (Deut 23:18; 1 Kgs 15:12; 2 Kgs 23:7) while the feminine plural is used three times (Gen 38:21; Deut 23:18; Hos 4:14). It is also used in the singular as a collective twice (1 Kgs 14:24; 22:47). With the other possible usage of the word, context will dictate which would be the appropriate translation to use for each case.
115. See Rowley, *Book of Job*, 229; Driver and Gray, *Book of Job*, 311; and Dhorme, *Book of Job*, 544.

explains that "the experience of suffering leads to a new liberating insight in the sufferers – into what they have done and how they must change."[116]

Suffering is the package and the context through which the voice of God comes.[117] This forms a good conclusion to the preceding argument: The arrival of suffering (36:8) begins the process of deliverance. Suffering constitutes the means, the instrument, or the process by which God delivers the sufferer. Suffering is designed to make the afflicted listen to what God is saying. Once again, Elihu showed that God is not silent.

36:16–33 Elihu's Exhortation to Job
36:16–21 Remember God's past ministrations

Elihu reminded Job that God had delivered him from the brink of distress and settled him in a restful place, to a "table laden with choice food" (36:16). Indeed, once the sufferer hears and responds to God's voice, he will most likely experience the blessings that God has prepared for him. Elihu maintained that God is humankind's most patient, compassionate, and persistent teacher. Perceiving that Job's mind was on the punishment of the wicked, Elihu assured him that justice would be served (36:17). He counseled Job not to be enticed – either by riches or by bribes – into following the ways of the wicked (36:18).

Verse 19 is a warning against self-dependence and seeking deliverance from suffering from anything beyond the humble submission required by God's justice. With reference to Job's continual plea for death, Elihu appealed to him not to "long for the night" (36:20). "Night" refers to Job's eagerness for divine judgment because he believed that it would bring vindication. But Elihu wanted Job to focus on God instead.

Verse 21 demonstrates, yet again, that Elihu's view was different from that of the three antagonists. Job was not suffering because of past sin. The clause "beware of turning to" indicates a condition that has yet to take place but is only potentially possible. Although Job's initial suffering was undeserved, in the process of his struggle with undeserved suffering, flaws and potentially devastating tendencies had been exposed. Job needed to recognize that this test

---

116. Alter, *Writings*, 558.
117. Since the preposition (Heb. *be* – "in," "with," "by") can be taken either way, is suffering the context or the vehicle for the divine message? Diewert sees the options as minimal and perhaps he is correct. If suffering is the vehicle, it is the context in which God works. If suffering is the context, then God is using that context as a vehicle for opening the ears of the sufferer. Suffering "functions as the locus and the vehicle of the divine warning." "Composition of the Elihu Speeches," 493.

would disclose whether he would remain true to God or seek relief through sinful means. Elihu's compassionate warning against Job's possible attempt to evade suffering was consistent with God's purpose in sending the affliction. Job was to view his suffering not as a sign that God is unjust and capricious but as a means by which unperceived tendencies toward sin can be recognized, "its consequences averted and the restoration of righteousness and its rewards experienced."[118]

36:22–25 Extol God's awesome works

These verses assert the supremacy of God in his incomprehensible activities. Elihu's first question introduced and summarized his contention that God is the supreme teacher who uses suffering to direct and instruct (36:22; see also Pss 25:8–14; 94:12). As a loving and caring teacher, God uses suffering to move his students along the right path, in contrast to a capricious, tyrannical god who would simply be indifferent or would direct his subjects for self-amusement. Elihu's second question asserted that God cannot be swayed by human accusations or traditional prescriptions (36:23). His dealings with humanity are free of manipulation and coercion. Therefore, no one – including Job – could accuse him of error. Since God is above all in knowledge and no one can accuse him of error, his wisdom is superior to that of humankind for he is "exalted in his power."[119] He is an exceptional teacher, self-sufficient and beyond reproof. For Elihu, suffering was indispensable to a deeper relationship and understanding of God and "may even be viewed as forming part of the price to be paid for ransoming the sufferer from disaster."[120]

Having affirmed God's superiority, Elihu exhorted Job to remember that he was to exalt the work of God, not criticize and question its fairness. Elihu wanted Job to abandon his present anger and mockery and simply declare the greatness of God (36:24). God has revealed his works to humanity so that people are rightly overwhelmed by the marvels of nature and the universe. Elihu's believed that once Job abandoned his complaint, he would praise God and begin to reap the benefits of the suffering he was undergoing.

36:26–33 Acknowledge God's wise governance

Elihu asserted that God is unquestionably "great" and "beyond our understanding" (36:26). The way in which God uses his power to bless or afflict, to

---

118. See Diewert, "Composition of the Elihu Speeches," 507–8.
119. McCabe, "Significance of the Elihu Speeches in the Context," 203.
120. Diewert, "Composition of the Elihu Speeches," 503.

save or destroy, is beyond human understanding (36:26, 29; 37:5; compare Ps 139:6; Eccl 8:17; Isa 55:9; 1 Cor 13:12). Job's problem was that he was seeking to comprehend the workings of the incomprehensible God.

The use of verbs (36:27–31) in the imperfect indicate God's continuous actions in maintaining the universe. To answer the question whether God is just, Elihu pointed out that God's justice can be discerned in his control over events in the heavens – for instance, the precipitation and evaporation of water (36:27–28), the roar of thunder (36:29), and lightning that reaches the depths of the sea (36:30) – and in God's use of these elements to govern his moral order on earth and execute justice among people (36:31–33). Surely, no human being can fully understand the power that controls this cycle and keeps it operating year after year!

This section finds a connection with Jesus's words in Matthew 5:45: "He causes his sun to rise on the evil and the good and sends rain on the righteous and the unrighteous." God is just in his dealings with people and in his operation of the world and, so, everyone has a chance to experience the effect of his care and provision.

God actually used thunder to defeat Israel's enemies – for instance, when the Philistines attacked Israel "the LORD thundered with loud thunder" against them so that, in the ensuing confusion and panic, they were defeated (1 Sam 7:10). Equally awesome in Elihu's description of the atmosphere is the fact that long before the science of astronomy or meteorology had been developed wise men during Job's time had observed some of the consistencies in phenomena in the heavens and drawn conclusions that were to be tested through time. For instance, we now know that lightning and thunder are interrelated.

Indeed, the living God, whom we serve, is awesome. The glimpses of his power and wisdom that we see in nature are just the fringes of who he is.

Elihu gave a brief synopsis of who God is and his dealings with humankind: He punishes the wicked but is sympathetic to the upright, although he may also punish them when they disobey; God continues to watch over and care for the upright (36:7); he instructs and corrects them and, when they repent and obey him, he blesses them (36:10–11); when they disobey him, they are judged and punished (36:12); God is exalted in power (36:22); his justice is seen in the fact that he decides independently, without letting anyone influence his decisions (36:23); he is beyond human comprehension and is eternal (36:26); and he provides for the righteous (36:31).

THE RELEVANCE OF JOB 36 TO ELIHU'S VIEW OF SUFFERING

In chapter 36, Elihu presented suffering as having both a disciplinary and instructive purpose. He developed this principle extensively, in contrast to the three who did not accept that Job was being disciplined or instructed but insisted that he was being punished as an evildoer. According to their strict, inflexible theology, the only reason for suffering was sin, which meant that anyone suffering must be a sinner. In contrast, Elihu introduced Job and the reader to a new concept of suffering as a means to prevent disciplinary action for sins that were "potential and latent."[1] Elihu introduced this idea in Job 33:16–30 (compare 5:17) and dealt with it again in 36:7–15.

Elihu specifically identified the righteous as the sufferers and then narrowed his focus to Job. Even the righteous, and Job in particular, were not exempt from faults and erroneous beliefs. According to Elihu, "God's purpose in allowing suffering is to gain the attention of the sufferer and communicate to him the folly of continuing along his present path, at the end of which lies harm."[2] Suffering, then, is a means of delivering the sufferer (36:15).

There are several corollaries to this principle:

First, regardless of the deferment of the punishment due to the wicked and despite the suffering of the righteous, God's justice is guaranteed. God's perfect use of retributive justice will balance out in spite of the seeming inconsistencies observed by limited human understanding (36:6–14). While God may defer judgment of the wicked, his justice is never arbitrary or unfair (36:23b). "Man's worst imperfection is his propensity to project his standards of conduct and his knowledge onto the Almighty."[3]

Second, Elihu differed from the three friends on the issue of the initial *cause* of Job's suffering. However, he did indicate that Job, during his suffering, was no longer entirely blameless in his attitude toward God. Nevertheless, Elihu maintained that God acts for the benefit of humankind by using suffering as a catalyst for introspection (36:8–12). While humans may not understand God's reason, timing, or purpose, suffering can be revelatory, preventive, pedagogical, or directive (36:9–10, 15b–16, 21–23).

Third, Elihu pointed to the mercy and majesty of God that should lead human beings to acknowledge that God is "beyond our understanding" (36:26) for he is the supreme God.

Fourth, if Job had recognized God's purpose in allowing suffering in his life – instead of complaining and demanding a court hearing – he would have glorified God and magnified his works (36:22–24). Suffering was the voice by which God spoke to Job. Such periods of suffering are times to exercise patience and faith, knowing that God is present in, during, and through the suffering (36:15). The well-known "patience of Job" and his faith – which were evident when his suffering began, before the long series of monologues – both needed renewal so that Job might await the execution of God's perfect justice.

Job's suffering was a price worth paying if it fulfilled God's purpose in correcting a dangerously faulty view of his justice and inaugurated a new relationship between God, Job, and the three counselors. This would also serve as a pattern and guide for future believers who struggled with God's sovereign expression of his justice.[4] Suffering is not designed to encourage suicidal death wishes (36:20; compare Job 3) or vindictiveness against those who appear to be wicked (36:17; compare 21:7–33; 24:1–24); rather, it is intended to be an experience that is beneficial both to the sufferer and to those related in some way to the sufferer.[5] As will be seen later, suffering may also result in a closer relationship with Yahweh (42:5–6).

---

1. Gordis, *Book of God and Man*, 113–14.
2. Johns, "Literary and Theological Function," 189.
3. Bakon, "The Enigma of Elihu," Dor le Dor 12 (1984): 226.
4. As evidenced throughout the history of Israel, and even into the times of the New Testament.
5. Johns, "Literary and Theological Function," 192.

37:1–24 Continuation of Elihu's Fourth Speech

Continuing from the previous chapter – where Elihu described God's dealings with both the wicked and the righteous and encouraged Job to listen to God's voice – Elihu now concluded his speech with a description of God's power in the heavens. Here some questions we can reflect on in relation to this chapter: What are the qualities of a good defense attorney? What gave Elihu the edge to present himself as mediator for Job before God? What is the relevance of chapter 37 to Elihu's view of suffering?

37:1–5 God's Voice in Thunderstorms

Elihu continued to express his amazement at God's control over the rain and lightning (compare 36:27–33) and also admitted to being nervous (37:1) at the prospect of being in the presence of God or an experience of this. His declarations reveal his great emotional involvement. Elihu commanded Job to listen to the Lord's loud rumbling voice (37:2). Here Elihu used a figure of speech – *anthropopatheia*[121] – to describe a facet of God's power that included releasing as opposed to restraining lightning, followed by loud thunder. He equated the whole process to God's "voice" that no one could trace when God "sends it to the ends of the earth" (37:3–4). The essence of verse 3, much like 36:30, communicates the reality that when there is a thunderstorm, God's lightning permeates the ends of the earth and dominates the whole landscape. The deafening sound that follows the flashes of light is like the unexpected roar of a lion. God's voice thunders and he does awesome deeds that no one can understand (37:5). Diewert suggests that God's ways, like the lightning-bolt, are unfathomable (36:26; 37:5). There is the concept of both power and mystery here that should instill in people a sense of awe and amazement toward the Creator.[122] This entire unit then serves as a fitting introduction to other incomprehensible things that are controlled by God's power (37:6–13).

37:6–16 God's Control over Snow and Rain

Elihu listed how God controls various atmospheric elements and their effect on the people and animals once these processes are set in motion. For instance, when God commands the snow to "fall on the earth" and the rain "to shower" to create a "mighty downpour" (37:6), these intervene in people's work and activities. And these occurrences force people to recognize that these are God's activities (37:7).

The power of the weather confines and restricts human activity on earth. This is important to Elihu's argument since confined people are forced to at least consider their dependence on the power of the Creator, who is the source of such storms. The desired result is that they would acknowledge God's creative work. Animals are forced to take cover, and even the strongest of animals are confined to their dens and lairs, where they hibernate for survival (37:8). Truly, God reveals himself to his creation through the elements. When people and animals seek cover however, they are not always protected from the "tempest" and the "driving winds" that bring on the ice storms (37:9–10). Elihu maintained that God uses the elements fairly and justly in his administration of justice and moral order and that all the elements of nature are obedient to God's command. It is God who chooses whether or not the rain will be a

---

121. *Anthropopatheia* (*anthropos* – man + *pathos* – affections, feelings) is a figure of speech that ascribes human passions, actions, or attributes to God (Bullinger, *Figures of Speech*, 871).
122. Diewert, "Composition of the Elihu Speeches," 537.

life-giving shower (37:6b; compare Isa 55:10; Amos 4:7) or whether it might even be a destructive torrent (compare Ezek 13:11).

Elihu turned to the clouds to illustrate the power and majesty of God (37:11–12). Once the clouds are loaded with moisture, God moves them to their designated location (37:12). The point that Elihu continued to stress was that God's sovereign control over the weather implies that he is sovereign over everything and everyone on earth. Therefore, God is totally involved with his creation. He wisely and masterfully charts the course of the clouds, and, unlike Job, they obediently go wherever he commands.[123]

Verse 13 serves as a summarizing statement that connects with Job 36:31: all the activities of the normal weather cycles and the unexpected storms serve God's purpose for good or affliction and demonstrate his greatness and justice. God can use the weather as a rod of discipline on the disobedient (Gen 6:17; Exod 9:18; Josh 10:11; 1 Sam 12:17) or as a blessing to the obedient (Jer 5:24; Zech 10:1; Acts 14:17). Elihu presented Yahweh as all-powerful but always acting with a purpose, which he narrowed down to either *correcting* or *showing love* (37:13).[124] Therefore, God is worthy of praise, not criticism and accusation; and God is not defined or restricted by human assumptions or tradition.

Elihu then commanded Job to "stop and consider God's wonders" (37:14) so that he might gain insight into his own situation and acknowledge God's superior wisdom and power. Elihu resumed his earlier speech about the lightning and clouds and directed several rhetorical questions at Job, asking if he could do or even understand the things God does. There are many similarities between this unit and God's speech in the next chapter. Elihu made a concerted effort to bring Job to a place of acknowledging God's justice and sovereignty.

Certainly, Job did not know how God controls the clouds, the storms, and the lightning (37:15), nor did he understand how God layered[125] or balanced the clouds in the sky (37:16). Even modern-day meteorologists cannot predict the weather with certainty. It was crucial that Job grasp the significance of these rhetorical questions, the purpose of which was to humble Job by highlighting his limitations.

---

123. Hartley, *Book of Job*, 481.
124. Bullinger recognizes a homonym (words of the same spelling but different meaning) in the word *chesed*. Depending on the context, it can mean "mercy," "goodness," or "grace." At other times, it can mean the opposite, which are "shame," "disgrace," or "blasphemy" (*Figures of Speech*, 1009). The author of Job used homonyms in other instances as in Job 23:15, 34:19.
125. Bullinger, *Figures of Speech*, 1009.

37:17–24 Elihu's Conclusions

God controls the hot south wind (37:17), which, when it blows, causes life to come to a standstill and clothing clings to the body. On such a day, the sky is like a "mirror of cast bronze" that reflects the heat of the sun (37:8; Deut 28:23). Ancient mirrors were cast of bronze and had to be hammered out and polished to a finish that could reflect an image. Elihu was asking Job if he could assist God in hammering out a molten sky. Of course, he could not!

Having humbled Job by revealing his insignificance before God, Elihu's sarcasm gave way to compassion as he charged Job to "tell us what we should say to him" (37:19). Adopting the stance of a lawyer, Elihu asked Job to tell him what he wanted to relay to God because they – Elihu and the three friends – could not prepare Job's case without his input. Although Elihu would not call for a confrontation with God as Job had done, his inclusion of himself in drawing up "our case" implies that he, too – like all of us – had struggled with the same questions as Job. It is significant that God's first question to Job was this: "Who is this that obscures my plans with words without knowledge?" (38:2). How can an ignorant person teach the inscrutability of God's ways? And how can any case – however, well it is prepared – prove that the Creator and Sustainer of the universe is wrong?

Elihu followed with two other questions (37:20): "Should he be told that I want to speak?" and "Would anyone ask to be swallowed up?" Elihu wondered if God had been informed that Job wanted to speak to him. Earlier, Elihu had said that Job must be "tested to the utmost" (34:36–37). Elihu included himself in these hypothetical rhetorical questions that demanded a strong negative answer. No one, no matter how confused or disturbed would wish to place himself before the Almighty God and be consumed. Elihu strongly advised against any course of action that would place Job in a position where he would be defeated or destroyed by God.

Returning to the wonders of God's work in the heavens (37:21), Elihu likened the presence of God to the brightness of the sun, which the human eye cannot tolerate, especially on a bright and clear day. In verse 22, instead of describing the sun, Elihu presented the "golden splendor" of God coming out of the north in awesome majesty. This corresponds with ancient Ugaritic mythology that refers to the north as the residence of the gods.[126] "Elihu sees that God is about to appear. The word 'awesome' emphasizes terror that a

---

126. Alden, *Job*, 365n158; and Zuck, *Job*, 161. See also Pope's account of Baal's golden palace in the northern mountains of the sky, (*Job*, 286–87).

display of divine power arouses in earthly creatures, and the word 'majesty' represents the splendor that attends the holiness of God."[127]

Verse 23 was Elihu's response to Job's statements that he could not find God to present his case before him (9:11; 23:3–4, 8–9). God is truly incomprehensible, but "Shaddai will never violate justice – he will not *oppress* the people capriciously. That is, when God reveals himself to Job, Job will be reduced to silence as God will convince him that he has been treated fairly and justly."[128] Zuck points out that although Job was aware of God's sovereignty and power (9:4–12; 10:16; 12:13–25; 23:13–16; 26:5–14; 28:23–28), he continually accused God of being unjust or exercising that power and sovereignty capriciously (7:20; 9:17, 20–24; 10:2–3; 13:24; 16:9, 12, 17; 19:6–12; 27:2; 30:19–23).[129]

The last two lines of verse 23 succinctly restate the two major motifs in Elihu's speeches: God is omnipotent and his justice is exercised perfectly.[130] There is no contradiction between God's sovereign use of his power and justice either in nature or in human affairs. Elihu affirmed a divinely balanced equilibrium that was central to his argument.

Hartley understands verse 24b positively and takes it to mean that "men fear him; indeed, all the wise of heart see him,"[131] while most other commentators include the negative particle *lo'* and translate the last line in this way: "All the wise of heart cannot perceive him" or "he does not regard any who are wise of heart."[132] This line is a reference to a concern expressed by Job in his second speech (9:2–13). Elihu's response was that no one could be wise enough to challenge God in a legal dispute (compare 9:4). Agreeing with Job that "the fear of the Lord . . . is wisdom" (28:28), Elihu humbly included himself and the three in this final statement. No wise man knows all there is to know about God. The reverential fear of God is the foundation of all true wisdom, but even this cannot result in a full understanding of God and his ways. True wisdom for human beings is not, therefore, knowing all that God knows. Elihu never claimed that he superseded God; instead, he stood in reverence before God's power, justice, and transcendence.

---

127. Consider Psalm 18:8–16 and Habakkuk 3:2–15. See Hartley, *Book of Job*, 484.
128. Hartley, *Book of Job*, 484 (italics his).
129. Zuck, *Job*, 162.
130. See Job 34:12–15, 17, 19–20; 36:3, 5, 22.
131. Hartley, *Book of Job*, 484. Gordis renders the verse as: "Yes, all the wise-hearted stand in awe." (*Book of Job*, 410, 434).
132. Diewert, "Composition of the Elihu Speeches," 399; Habel, *Book of Job*, 497.

Elihu was faithful to his presentation of God's power and justice, throughout his speeches. From his first response to Job's quotation (33:12) to this final verse, he held that God was just even in allowing suffering to come to Job. Now, as Yahweh approaches, Elihu has sufficiently prepared the way for God's complete answer to the question of Job's suffering and his doubts. After his final words, "Elihu disappears from the book of Job. His entrance and exit from the story are as seemingly random and mysterious as his identity."[133]

In light of the fact that Job could neither understand nor do what God does, Elihu offered to represent him as his lawyer before the God who "thunders with his majestic voice," and "does great things" which humans cannot comprehend (37:4–5). Elihu presented God as the all-powerful sovereign, who had established the laws of heaven regarding the skies, lightning, and the clouds (37:15–16), was awesome in majesty (37:22), and never acted unjustly (37:23). God the Almighty is beyond the reach of human beings, yet he intervenes personally in their affairs, especially to teach, to correct, and to extend mercy.

Elihu's fourth and final speech "is clearly designed to prepare for the theophany that will follow . . . the material is still an integral part of the book, consciously performing a literary purpose that appears to be twofold: to give another human perspective free from the heat of the debate and to prepare the reader (and Job) for the theophany."[134]

Elihu desired to represent Job before God. The question is, was he really qualified for this job? We need to investigate the qualifications of a good lawyer, especially that of a defense attorney. Such a person must possess the following traits and attributes: the heart, the head, and the hands for their profession and client. As to the *heart*, Elihu was committed to his client, he had the passion to prove that his client was innocent, understood where the client was coming from, and had the persistence to pursue the case to obtain justice. As to the *head*, Elihu possessed the intelligence and an analytical-critical mind to evaluate the arguments and respond accordingly. As to the *hands*, Elihu had the *skills* to be able to articulate and communicate his thoughts effectively and persuasively in his speech and to handle the case strategically. Moreover, he had the social skills necessary to negotiate when required and the confidence to defend his client with integrity.

Elihu was more than qualified! After carefully listening to the arguments of Job and his friends, he had acquired full knowledge of all the accusations

---

133. Rao, "Job," 608.
134. Smick, "The Monologues" in *Job*.

lodged against Job and was passionate enough to speak up in support of Job, arguing his case well. Elihu was honest, fair, confident in his bearing, and knowledgeable about the procedure involved. He had the courage to boldly confront both Job and his three friends, and to tell them when they were at fault. Elihu's speeches prepared Job for his confrontation with Yahweh.

THE RELEVANCE OF JOB 37 TO ELIHU'S VIEW OF SUFFERING

Chapter 37 (along with chapter 36) demonstrates Elihu's determination to convince Job to concentrate on the positive aspects of his suffering rather than being preoccupied with his personal pain. This chapter also shows how suffering can be a lesson in humility. In describing God's supreme control over all aspects of the weather (37:2–13), Elihu sought to convince Job of God's power not only to destroy but to care for everyone, including Job himself (37:12–13).

Elihu then used a series of rhetorical questions that challenged Job to carefully consider God's power and infinite wisdom in contrast to Job's own limited strength and knowledge (37:14–18). Based on Job's ability to understand the inexplicability of God's ways (37:19–22), this contrast demonstrated the "futility of expecting to have a hearing with the Almighty" in the way Job had in mind.[1] In view of God's transcendent might and justice, all humankind should be humbled before him.

The proper response to suffering, as presented in this chapter, is not to arrogantly mount a defense of our own rights and righteousness (37:19–20) but, instead, to stand in awe of God's power, recognizing that even though we cannot always understand the cause of our afflictions, these afflictions fulfill God's just purposes in the individual life of the sufferer and in the collective lives of all humanity (37:23–24). Viewing God's handiwork should have challenged Job's "error of egocentricity" and humbled him,[2] enabling him to stand before God with a right attitude as he dealt with the question of his suffering.

---

1. McCabe, "Significance of the Elihu Speeches," 224.
2. Bakon, "Enigma of Elihu," 221.

A Recap of Elihu's Monologue

The three rounds of debate between the three friends and Job had revolved around their accusations that Job had committed some unknown, hidden sin *prior* to his suffering and their insistence that this was the only explanation for his suffering, which they viewed as a punishment from God.

Elihu observed that Job, during the debates, committed sins that involved questioning the justice and goodness of God. He presented ten possible reasons for suffering, nine of which had little to do with sin, thereby discounting the claims of the three that Job's suffering was connected to sin and sin alone. However, even though Elihu pointed to many reasons for suffering, he did not claim to have the final answer for Job's dilemma. Instead, he directed Job to God, the source of wisdom and justice, who has the ultimate answer to all questions about suffering. One important question that needs to be answered is whether Job did indeed sin during the debates. Contemplate Job's four theological errors:

1. God is silent: He is not listening to me or involved in my life (30:20; 34:29).
2. God is unjust: He is not fair and good (33:10–11; 34:5).
3. God is not merciful: He won't forgive me (9:27–31).
4. God does not care: He does not care whether my lifestyle is holy or sinful (34:9; 35:3).

Elihu responded to Job's flawed theology by demonstrating that:

1. God is not silent: He is listening and actively involved in my life (33:14–33).
2. God is not unjust: He is fair and good (34:10–12).
3. God is merciful: He will forgive me (33:23–28; 6:5a, 15–16).
4. God does care: He does care if I have a holy or sinful lifestyle (34:11, 21; 36:8–16).

The following statements serve as evidence of Job's sin during, but *not before*, the debates:

Job's desires and requests in light of his pain and suffering:
- "Why did I not perish at birth and die?" (3:11).
- "That God would be willing to crush me" (6:9).
- "Let me alone" (7:16).
- "Turn away from me so I can have a moment's joy (10:20).

Job's complaints and accusations against God:
- "I know you will not hold me innocent (9:28).
- That "no one can rescue me from your hand" (10:7).
- "God assails me and tears me in his anger" (16:9).
- "All was well with me . . . but he shattered me" (16:12).
- "Without pity he pierces my kidneys and spills my gall on the ground (16:13).
- He "rushes at me like a warrior" (16:14).
- "God has wronged me" (19:6).
- "I call for help; there is no justice" (19:7).
- "His anger burns against me; he counts me among his enemies" (19:11).
- The "hand of God has struck me" (19:21).
- "God . . . has denied me justice; the Almighty who has made my life bitter" (27:2).

Job did not sin *before* the calamities. While going through pain and suffering, however, his complaints and actions verged on rebellion. Elihu offered himself as an advocate for Job. Was he able to serve that purpose? This seems unlikely since he is not mentioned again. Nevertheless, what Elihu did was significant for he prepared Job for his confrontation with God by pointing out Job's theological deficiencies and reminding him of God's attributes and awesome works.

38:1–41:34 YAHWEH'S SPEECHES

Yahweh's speeches center on revealing his wisdom in creating and maintaining the universe and in the exercise of his justice as he relates to his creatures. These speeches were interrupted briefly on two occasions by Job's confessions (40:3–5; 42:1–6). God spoke of his sovereignty and omnipotence as demonstrated in the creation of the earth, the heavens, and the underworld (38:4–38). Animate creation also testifies to God's sovereign power and providential compassion on them (38:39–39:30). Then God asked Job, "Will the one who contends with the Almighty correct him? Let him who accuses God answer him!" (40:2). Of course, Job could give no satisfactory answer (40:3–5).

Job

38:1–39:30 Yahweh's First Speech

Elihu briefly introduced who the Almighty God is in chapter 37 by presenting his activities in the heavens and on the earth. Then suggesting several possibilities and reasons for suffering, he pointed Job toward God. Neither Job nor any other wise person could satisfactorily explain why God does what he does. The main difference between Elihu's observations and the views of the three friends were that Elihu said that Job's suffering was not the result of any past or hidden sin. While Job sinned during the debates, this was in no way the cause of his suffering. In his speeches, God would seek to correct Job's false theological views and his wrongful attitudes.

38:1–38 The Marvels of the Inanimate World

The Lord revealed himself to Job by his name, Yahweh, which is used in the prologue, the Yahweh speeches, and the epilogue. It is God's personal and covenant name.[135] This chapter deals with cosmogony (38:4–21), meteorology (38:22–38), and zoology (38:39–41).[136] These questions will be addressed: What can be known today about the atmosphere, the rising and setting of the sun, the vast underworld, and the heavenly bodies? What do native religions in Asia believe about the heavenly bodies?

38:1–3 Yahweh's introductory statements

Yahweh reached out to Job in a theophany,[137] speaking with Job out of a whirlwind.[138] We can feel and see the effects of a whirlwind, but we cannot see the whirlwind itself. Centuries removed from Job, the prophet Elijah was taken up to heaven in a whirlwind (2 Kgs 2:1, 11); in Job's case, however, Yahweh communicated with him out of the whirlwind.

Yahweh's objective was to bring Job to the place where he understood the difference between God's wisdom and human wisdom. He challenged Job, whom he described as one who "obscures my plans with words without knowledge" (38:2), to a showdown. Davy explains that, from Yahweh's perspective, Job had obscured God's design – his principles for administering creation – by viewing this through the lens of a retribution principle.[139] He adds, "Job has erred because he presumes to know how the universe works, or should work,

---

135. Refer to the discussion on page 22.
136. Alter, *Writings*, 564.
137. Theophany refers to the manifestations of God to his people.
138. The NIV has "storm." *Se'arah* itself can mean: "storm," "high wind." See *HALOT*, s.v. "s'r."
139. Davy, "A Missional Encounter with Cultures" in *Job*.

even though his knowledge is limited. It is this limited perspective that Yahweh exposes that ranges around creation."[140]

Yahweh then commanded Job to prepare – to "brace" himself – like a man to be interrogated by God (38:3). During this discourse, God did not address Job's suffering directly or respond to Job's attacks on his justice. After attempting to find answers to complex questions and problems, Job was now compelled to listen to God.

Yahweh continued with a series of rhetorical questions to test Job's knowledge of the natural world: the earth, the seas, the elements, oceans, land, the climate, the solar system.

38:4–7 The earth

God's first few questions concern the construction of the earth. God asked Job whether he had been there when the earth was established, whether he knew who had measured and determined the earth's boundaries, and whether he knew on what its bases were set and who had laid its cornerstone (38:4–6). Since these were rhetorical questions, Job was not expected to answer; and even if he had tried to, he would not have been able to answer accurately since he had not been present at the creation of the earth when "the morning stars sang together" and the angels[141] "shouted for joy" at the wonder of it all (38:7).[142]

Since Job had not been present at earth's creation, he knew nothing about how God had created the world nor about his moral governance of it; neither did Job understand the invisible and spiritual world over which God exercised his sovereign rule. So, if Job could not explain creation or the actions of the Creator, how could he explain God's actions in his own life?

38:8–11 The seas

The rhetorical questions in this case were not intended to gather information but to make Job aware of his own position. Yahweh was the one who had shut up the waters of the sea behind doors when it emerged like a baby from its mother's womb (38:8). He had made the "clouds its garment and wrapped it in thick darkness" (38:9) and also fixed "limits" for it (38:10) so that its

---

140. Davy, "A Missional Encounter with Cultures" in *Job*.
141. The MT has "sons of God," which Bullinger explained is a Hebrew idiomatic expression for angels. *Figures of Speech*, 844. He also recognizes an irony in verses 4–5, *Figures of Speech*, 808.
142. A similar expression is in Psalm 148:3 where the stars are commanded to praise God.

majestic waves were confined, and it could not go beyond what Yahweh had decreed (38:11).

God, as Creator, is pictured as the one who set the boundaries in the coastlines and seashores. He alone controls the oceans, the process of condensation, and the clouds that bring water to the earth. Job remained silent.

38:12–15 The elements

Yahweh asked Job if he had ever "given orders to the morning" (38:12). Showing "the dawn its place" would necessitate exercising control over the sun. Yahweh then described the effect of the rising of the sun on the earth using a figure of speech known as "personification," presenting the light of the sun as slowly taking hold of the edges of the earth to shake off the wicked (38:13). He then likened the transformation of the earth to "clay under a seal" as its features slowly take form and "stand out" (*yatsav*)[143] like a garment (38:14). As for the wicked, their light would be withheld so that their "upraised arm is broken" (38:15). The "upraised arm" here refers to acts of violence or rebellion that would be stopped at the coming of dawn.

As commander-in-chief over his creation, God orders the sun to rise and set at the times he allots. In the ancient world, and even among some tribal groups in Southeast Asia, the sun was an object of worship; here in Job, God is portrayed as controlling the sun and its life-giving rays. If God's light exposes the evil of human beings, how can God's fairness and justice be questioned? Job remained silent.

38:16–18 The oceans

Yahweh asked Job if he had been to the main springs of the sea or walked about in the "recesses of the deep" (38:16). Had Job visited that place, he would have discovered "the gates of death," also described as "the gates of the deepest darkness" (38:17). Job obviously had no knowledge of the source or boundaries of the primeval ocean with all its tributaries.

We have only recently begun to understand the subterranean waters below the earth's surface.[144] God was asking, "Job, do you understand the deep things under the earth and how they operate and add to the balance and function of life?" If Job could not understand these things, how could he understand the deeper things of God? How could he understand the mysterious workings of

---

143. Alter emends the verb to *titstaba'* – meaning "to take color," Writings, 160.
144. That portion that has land, water, vegetation, and air, allowing life to exist.

God's creation? Job did not understand the deep things of the physical planet, and he certainly did not understand the deep secrets and mysterious ways of the Creator. In addition, Yahweh asked if Job could even comprehend the "vast expanse of the earth" (36:18).

38:19–21 Light and darkness

Yahweh questioned Job about the origin of both light and darkness, concluding with a biting remark: "Surely you know, for you were already born! You have lived so many years!" (38:21). If Job had indeed been born at that time of creation, he would have been able to trace the path of light and darkness back to their respective dwelling places. Clearly, he could not do so because he was not there.

38:22–30 The climate

Yahweh continued to question Job about matters related to climate and weather: snow and hail (38:22–23), lightning, east winds, rain, and thunderstorm (38:24–27), dewdrops, ice, frost, waters hard as stone, and the frozen surface of the deep (38:28–30).

Using the military image of war and battle, Yahweh asked if Job had visited the storehouses[145] of snow or hail, both of which God had reserved for "times of trouble," specifically described as "days of war and battle" (38:22–23). In biblical history, God used hail to destroy Israel's enemies – for instance, in Joshua's time, most of the Amorite coalition was destroyed when "the LORD hurled large hailstones down on them" (Josh 10:11),[146] and more soldiers died from the hail than by the sword. God also asked Job whether he knew the way to the places where lightning and the east winds were "dispersed" or "scattered" over the earth (38:24).

Yahweh also asked who had "cut a channel for the torrents of rain, and a path for the thunderstorm," to bring the rain that watered[147] uninhabited lands so that vegetation would sprout (38:25–27). Even if Job had traversed the Arabian deserts, he would not have known what we now know about other deserts and uninhabited places around the world.

Continuing with his rhetorical questions, Yahweh wanted to know if the rain and dew had a father or if ice and frost had a mother (38:28–29). In the

---

145. This is a reference to the skies.
146. See also Isaiah 28:17; 30:30.
147. Literally, "satisfy."

next verse, he referred to water becoming solid and the surface of the ocean reaching freezing point (38:30)[148] – both processes which Job would not have been able to explain.

Yahweh's questions about the earth's atmosphere were meant to make Job aware of how little he actually knew about these elements and, even more importantly, how little he knew about their Creator under whose continued control they functioned so well.

38:31–35 The solar system

Yahweh went on to ask Job if he could control the heavenly bodies by binding or loosing "Pleiades" or "Orion" (38:31) or leading out "the Bear with its cubs" (38:32) – references to major constellations that have clusters of their own. The appearance of these constellations in the hemisphere may indicate seasons in the year. God asked Job if he knew the laws of the heavens, how things were held together and moved in their orbits and, similarly, how God ruled over the earth (38:33).

How does God control the millions of stars so that they do not collide? Could Job steer the planets across the sky? Of course not! Can the human mind fully understand the workings of the divine? It cannot. Yahweh asked Job if he could command the clouds to release water to drench him (38:34) or control the lightning as it speeds along (38:35). This is almost comical.

Today, we do not know as much as we would like to about the weather, which seems so unpredictable, but we do know a great deal more than the people of Job's time. We have instruments to predict variations in temperature and oncoming rain and storms, so that people can prepare for changes in the weather. In Job's time, people could only know that a storm was coming when they saw clouds forming and felt the cool breeze around them.

38:36–38 The creation

One would need supernatural wisdom to create the laws of nature and the inanimate world.

Instead of asking Job if he has the wisdom to develop this, Yahweh next asked who gives wisdom to the ibis and understanding to the rooster (38:36). God was referring to animals and birds that he created on earth. Similarly, he referred to rain and clouds (38:37) and dust (38:38) – all a part of his original

---

148. Literally, "from whose womb did the ice and frost come?"

creation (Gen 1–2). If Job could not understand earthly matters, how will he understand heavenly matters (compare John 3:12)?

Yahweh asked if Job could command the clouds, the lightning bolts, the rain, or any other element in the natural world. Each time, Job gave no answer. Only God controls nature and all the elements that bring life and order to the physical world. God's message to Job was that he has control of Job's life, including what he had allowed to come into Job's life by way of adversity. Job failed the examination on the physical world, demonstrating his lack of knowledge about how all these things work together for God's glory, in the way God determines.

Thematically, chapter 38 ends with verse 38, and verses 39 to 41 really belong in the next chapter, which is the arrangement followed in this commentary.

Through rhetorical questions, Yahweh showed that Job knew nothing about how Yahweh had brought the earth into being (38:4–7) and set limits on the sea (38:8–11), and about his control over the sun, the vast underworld (38:12–21), and other phenomena in the heavens and the atmosphere (38:22–38). It was only through Yahweh's informative descriptions that Job learned some of the finer details concerning these phenomena in the heavens. These rhetorical questions, however, were not primarily for the purpose of informing Job but, rather, to demonstrate his ignorance regarding the Creator, who had every element of creation under his perfect control.

Yahweh's disclosures correspond to Elihu's declarations about God. The chart below shows the similarities.

| The Similarities between Elihu's and Yahweh's Statements ||
Elihu's Statements	Yahweh's Statements
His thunder announces the coming storm (36:33).	Then the LORD spoke to Job out of the storm (38:1).
Job speaks without knowledge; his words lack insight (34:35).	Who is this that obscures my plans with words without knowledge? (38:2)
Who appointed him over the earth? Who put him in charge of the whole world? (34:13)	Where were you when I laid earth's foundation? Tell me, if you understand (38:4).
He says to the snow, "Fall on the earth," and to the rain shower, "Be a mighty downpour." (37:6).	Have you entered the storehouses of the snow or seen the storehouses of the hail? (38:22)

| The Similarities between Elihu's and Yahweh's Statements ||
Elihu's Statements	Yahweh's Statements
He draws up the drops of water, which distill as rain to the streams (36:27).	To water a land where no one lives, an uninhabited desert (38:26).
The breath of God produces ice, and the broad waters become frozen (37:10).	From whose womb comes the ice? Who gives birth to the frost from the heavens? (38:29)
He fills his hands with lightning and commands it to strike its mark (36:32).	Do you send the lightning bolts on their way? Do they report to you, "Here we are"? (38:35)
The animals take cover; they remain in their dens (37:8).	When they crouch in their dens or lie in wait in a thicket? (38:40)
Can someone who hates justice govern? Will you condemn the just and mighty One? (34:17)	Would you discredit my justice? Would you condemn me to justify yourself? (40:8)
His thunder announces the coming storm (36:33).	Do you have an arm like God's, and can your voice thunder like his? (40:9)
If you are righteous, what do you give him, or what does he receive from your hand? (35:7)	Who has a claim against me that I must pay? Everything under heaven belongs to me. (41:11).

38:39–39:30 The Marvels of the Animal World

The previous chapter informed Job about the natural world and the wisdom with which Yahweh governs and sustains the universe and his creations. Job failed that first examination, which focused on the physical world. Yahweh then administered the next examination, related to the animal world, beginning with lions and ravens (38:39–41). In relation to each creature, Yahweh asked a few questions about Job's knowledge, understanding, or experience with these animals before moving on to describe some characteristics and behavior of the animal.

In this section, the following questions will be addressed: What was God's purpose in asking Job so many questions? What was special or unique about wild goats, deer, hawks, eagles, and the ostrich?

38:39–41 Lion and raven

Yahweh asked if Job could hunt prey for the lioness to feed her hungry young as they crouched in their dens or lay in wait, ready to pounce on their victim

(38:39–40). Did Job know who prepared food for the raven's young when they "cry out to God" for food (38:41)?

Job could not catch prey to satisfy the hunger of the lion, but God can and does so. God's providence supervises all of creation, and he makes sure that his creatures are cared for. God's provision even for the raven is a concept that is carried over into the NT. Jesus Christ affirmed that although the birds – specifically, ravens – do not work, God provides food for them (Matt 6:26; Luke 12:24). If God values these tiny creatures and provides their food, then how much more will he provide for the needs of people, who are so precious to him, especially those who believe in him and pray sincerely to him for their "daily bread."

39:1a The mountain goat

Yahweh went on to question Job about the mountain goat. As a wealthy landowner, Job must have possessed many goats, but he would not have known the exact due date for one of these goats – much less for a mountain goat – to deliver its young.

39:1b–4 The deer

Did Job know how many months it takes before a doe (female deer) gives birth (39:1b–2)? Yahweh explained that the doe crouches down as she births her young, after which her labor pains end (39:3). The young fawns quickly grow strong, only to go away and never return (39:4). This is also true of the mountain goat and its young. It is God, not Job, who helps these animals bring forth their young. Only God understands the intricacies of pregnancy, labor, and delivery, not just in relation to humans but also for animals in the wild. His plan behind all this is not always understood by humanity.

39:5–8 The wild donkey

Yahweh described the wild donkey as free (39:5), living in the desert (39:6), scorning the noisy city (39:7), and preferring to scout the mountains for green grass (39:8). It was God who had made the wild donkey free to roam in the wilderness. Job could not explain why God made the donkey this way – swift and wild and free. Although Job once owned "five hundred donkeys" (1:3), he did not know much about them; but God knew every detail about these creatures.

39:9–12 The wild ox

Turning to consider the wild ox, Yahweh asked if Job was able to tame this animal so that it would serve him. God listed three ways to know if someone had been successful in taming the wild ox: the ox would choose to stay near its feeding troughs (39:9), it could be held to the "furrow with a harness" to "till the valleys" (39:10), and its great strength would be used to accomplish the task of bringing in and gathering grain onto the threshing floor (39:11–12). Job would have been able to relate to these ideas since he had once owned five hundred yokes of oxen; but to domesticate a wild ox would have taken many hours and required special skills that Job probably did not possess.

If Job could not tame the wild ox, how could he possibly question God's justice and his management of the universe? Job had demanded that God should act in a way acceptable and understandable to him, but God cannot be manipulated and controlled by his creations. Like the wild ox, God does not obey the demands of human beings. God is God. He is independent and sovereign in all that he does.

39:13–18 The ostrich

Yahweh went on to relate several amusing facts about the ostrich. Even though the ostrich – whose feathers are not comparable with those of the stork – cannot fly, it flaps its wings joyfully (39:13). The female lays her eggs on the ground, forgetting that they may be trampled and crushed (39:14–15), and she mistreats her young, even though this means her labor would then be in vain (39:16). She is devoid of wisdom and good sense (39:17). Yet, "when she spreads her feathers to run" (39:18), she mocks the horse – probably because she can outrun it. The ostrich is a strange animal. It is a huge bird with feathers, but it is one of the few birds that cannot fly. The female cannot even remember where she laid her eggs. Yet, despite its poor memory, it is capable of running faster than a horse – an advantage when fleeing from predators.

Although it might have seemed to Job that there was no reason for God to create the ostrich, this creature had a purpose and a part to play in God's creation. It might also have seemed to Job that God, like the ostrich, was forgetful – but this thought is almost blasphemous. God is not forgetful but cares for his creation, even for such a comical species as the ostrich, and especially for Job. While it might have seemed to Job that there was no purpose for his life and that it made sense to hide his head in the sand, as the ostrich is proverbially said to do, God's master plan included a place and a purpose for Job.

39:19–25 The horse

Yahweh questioned Job about the horse, asking whether Job had given this animal its strength, clothed its neck with a flowing mane, or made it "leap like a locust, striking terror with its proud snorting" (39:19–20). Yahweh then described the horse as having strong paws that enable it to charge into battle with no fear of weapons such as the sword, arrows, or the flashing spear and lance (39:21–23). Clearly, God was not referring to an ordinary horse but to one trained for battle. This warhorse impatiently beats on the ground when it hears the sound of the trumpet, which is the commander's battle cry (39:24–25). Who made the warhorse so brave? How can an animal be so courageous as to run into battle with no concern for its life? Only God could give it such courage. In the heart of all his creatures, including Job – who is especially in view here – God can instill the ability to face life courageously and fulfill their purpose in life.

39:26 The hawk

Yahweh asked whether it was Job's wisdom that gave the hawk the ability to fly high and to be able to discern when it was time to migrate south (39:26). It was God, not Job, who had given the hawk this ability.

39:27–30 The eagle

Yahweh asked if Job could command the eagle to soar and build its nest high on a rocky crag (39:27). This rocky crag is the stronghold from which the eagle searches for food for its young ones to feast on (39:28–30). Who gave the eagle the instinct to protect its young by building its nest high on a cliff, where it could keep them out of sight of predators? Who made this bird powerful enough to attack and feed on other animals? God did. Like the eagle, whose keen eyes detect everything from afar, God looked down on Job and saw all that he had been through. From the very beginning of the book, God had been keenly aware of Job – an upright man, the greatest man in the East, and one who had consistently shunned evil.

Some of these animals and their characteristics are known to human beings, but not all of these can be known by any one person. It takes time and diligence to observe these characteristics and draw intelligent conclusions. Yahweh's speech in chapter 39 highlights the uniqueness, intricacy, and beauty of each of God's creations, as well as God's creative and sovereign power over all living beings.

It is disturbing and grievous that so many people continue to worship creatures above the Creator, the living God. For instance, Hinduism claims to have *330 manifestations* of gods, where everything with or without life is, in the understanding of most people, a god or a goddess.[149] For this reason, in Nepal, there are as many temples as there are houses. In Nepal and India, some animals, such as the cow, are especially revered, and there is even a specific festival during which Hindus pay respect to the cow.[150] People bathe their cows, place garlands on their necks, and pay tribute to them. This is also true of the dog and the crow.[151] Moreover, there are gods and goddesses for abstract ideas – for example, Sheba, the Hindu goddess of wisdom.[152]

Chapter 39 is the second part of God's examination for Job. In this examination, which deals mainly with animals in the world, God scored one hundred percent while Job scored zero percent. Yahweh answered his own questions and then educated Job about some of the finer details of the animals he had created. God alone is both Creator and Sustainer of the universe and our world. Human beings may observe how the universe functions and how animals live and survive, but only God knows fully why each of these creatures exist. Because he created all living beings, God knows the nature, characteristics, and abilities of each one.

When introducing God to someone within the context of a multiplicity of gods and goddesses, consider the following principles:

- Identify a common concept (biblical and local-cultural) to serve as common ground to start the conversation.
- Analyze the concept within the cultural context – how do the locals understand it?
- Analyze the concept within the biblical context – how does the Bible explain it?
- Identify what is absolute and nonnegotiable in relation to God and his revealed truths.

---

149. If we apply that theory to Christianity, even Yahweh has many *manifestations*, including the whirlwind in Job, which we call "theophany."
150. Cows are not worshiped as gods but as (1) transporters for gods (Vishnu travels on cows) and (2) providers of five essential elements for human needs: milk, ghee, butter, buttermilk, and cheese.
151. Mona Shresta, interview by author via Messenger, April 15, 2022.
152. Mona Shresta, interview by author via Messenger.

- Discuss the implications and significance of these truths to our lives.
- Seek the Holy Spirit's guidance to discover appropriate application.

40:1–41:34 Yahweh's Second Speech

40:1–24 The Ode to Behemoth

Through a series of rhetorical questions, Yahweh had revealed his divine wisdom and his sovereign control in the administration of his creation (38–39). Here in chapter 40, he indirectly revealed to Job yet another facet of himself: his sovereign power and justice. The questions that will be addressed in relation to this chapter include the following: What kind of animal was the "Behemoth"? Will the theory of evolution suffice to answer the questions regarding the origin of life and the purpose of human existence?

40:1–5 Job's response

A second time, Yahweh challenged Job to a confrontation, using a rhetorical question to remind him that one who "contends" with the Almighty is in no position to "correct" him (40:1). He invited Job, who had accused him, to now "answer" in defense (40:2). God asked Job directly, "Will the one who contends with the Almighty correct him?" Clearly, God took Job's contention seriously. Job's response was predictable: "I am unworthy – how can I reply to you?" Since there was really nothing that Job could say in his own defense, he covered his mouth (40:3–5). Humbled and overwhelmed, Job admitted that he was in the presence of Almighty God and that his numerous words had missed their mark. Although humbled, Job had not yet come to a place of repenting of his accusations against God concerning his justice, silence, and goodness.

40:6–14 Yahweh challenged Job to listen

As in his first speech, Yahweh answered Job out of the storm, saying, "Brace yourself like a man; I will question you, and you shall answer me" (40:7; see also 38:3).

Yahweh has the power to destroy the proud (40:8–14). Responding to Job's accusations of injustice and mismanagement of the universe, God basically challenged Job to manage it better, asking if Job had not merely the wisdom but also the power and authority to ensure that true justice was enforced.

Yahweh pointed out that no one could "discredit" or annul[153] God's justice and then claim to be upright (40:8). Presented as a rhetorical question, this next statement is emphatic. In the first place, in order for Job to claim equality in power[154] with God, he should have been able to speak with a voice that thunders like God's (40:9). Moreover, Yahweh commanded Job to "clothe himself with glorious splendor" (40:10, my translation).[155] The synonymous parallelism and a hendiadys emphasize the seriousness of the challenge to Job. God also told Job that he would have to release his burning anger and make sure that he humbled all the proud (40:11b), subdued the proud and the wicked (40:12), and buried the proud-wicked in the dust (40:13). When Job had accomplished such feats – rooting out, punishing, or destroying the wicked – then Yahweh would certainly applaud him and acknowledge that Job could indeed deliver himself by his own strength (40:14).

Verses 8–14 contrast the power of God with the power of humankind. God affirmed his justice – without defending or explaining it – and showed that he is and always will be just and fair to his creatures. God alone – not Job, not the three friends, and certainly not *Satan* – administers and regulates justice. "The point of this speech is that anyone who is demanding an answer from God must become as powerful as God in order to justify that demand. Yahweh's ironic questions remind Job of his place as a created being in the universe."[156]

40:15–24 "Ode to Behemoth"

In this section – which can be titled "Ode to Behemoth" – God's own wisdom poetry stresses his power in opposition to that of human beings or *Satan* (40:15–24). Yahweh cited Behemoth as raw evidence of his power and questioned if Job had any control over this animal. "Behemoth" is the feminine plural form of the Hebrew term *behema* (beast). The plural ending can be taken to represent (a) a collective term for all animals on the surface of the earth; (b) majestic attributes, intensity, and magnitude, which could then refer to

---

153. The Hebrew term *parar*, translated above as "annul," ordinarily means "to break" or "frustrate" and it occurs three other times within the book and with the same nuance (5:12; 15:4; 16:12).
154. Literally, "right arm."
155. The NIV has "glory and splendor."
156. Rao, "Job," 610.

the largest animal that was created; or (c) an abstract idea such as life so that "Behemoth" stands simply as a title.[157]

Scholars do not agree on whether this animal should be taken literally or metaphorically.[158] When understood metaphorically, Behemoth refers to a mythical beast, "a primordial beast that cannot be defeated."[159] Rowley and Alter, among others, take Behemoth to mean a mythological creature and, therefore, not a real animal.[160] Walton also recognizes that it is not uncommon to see Behemoth as a throwback from ancient mythology, evincing connections to the world of nature and myth.[161] He says, "In the end, however, it is not the roots of the ideas or the associations they may evoke that are most important; it is their literary use in Job."[162] So, from a literary standpoint, Behemoth is compared with Job "as an illustration for Job to emulate."[163] In listing the characteristics of Behemoth and noting its submissive disposition to Yahweh,[164] the message for Job was that instead of questioning God's justice, he should have exhibited the same traits and submissive response to Yahweh.

Taken literally, suggestions about the identity of Behemoth range from an elephant, a hippopotamus, an ox, a river horse, and even a demonic being. Among these, the hippopotamus seems to be the most popular suggestion. Archer explains that, in those times, there may have been a gigantic variety of hippopotamus that outclassed the elephant.[165] If we take the term Behemoth to represent size, the elephant is a likelier candidate than the hippopotamus. However, the tails of both elephant and hippopotamus are too short to fit the description of Behemoth's tail. Instead, the description of the animal, including its tail and bones, seems to match that of a mature sauropod dinosaur, a suggestion toward which this author gravitates. Sarfati identifies this sauropod

---

157. See note on 45:15, *NET* Bible.
158. See Vicchio, *Book of Job*, 274–79. He traces how Behemoth has been viewed from the earliest reference to it in the *Apocalypse of Enoch* to select proponents of different views in the 21st century.
159. Ariela Pelaia, "The Behemoth in Jewish Mythology" *Learn Religions*, 26 August 2020
160. See Rowley, *Book of Job*, 255. Alter thinks Behemoth "represents a mythological heightening of the actual beast," Writings, 572.
161. Walton, *Job*, 407. Walton sees both Behemoth and Leviathan as throwbacks from ancient mythology.
162. Walton, *Job*, 407–8.
163. Walton, *Job*, 408.
164. Walton, *Job*, 408.
165. Gleason L. Archer, Jr. *The Book of Job: God's Answer to the Problem of Undeserved Suffering* (Grand Rapids: Baker Books, 1982), 107.

with "the 25-m-long 60-tonne Dreadnoughtus schrani with a heavily muscled 10-m-long tail."[166]

This section describes Behemoth's diet (40:15), strength (40:16–18), habitat (40:19–23), and fierceness (40:24).

> Yahweh created Behemoth, which eats grass like an ox (40:15).
> Its strength is found in his loins and in the powerful muscles of its belly (40:16).
> It bends its tail stiffly like a cedar (40:17).
> Its bones are like tubes of bronze, its limbs are like iron bars (40:18).
> It "ranks first among the works of God," and which God can approach with his sword (40:19).
> Its source of food is the mountains, where beasts of the field frolic (40:20).
> It lies down under lotuses and reeds, surrounded by willow trees (40:21–22).
> It is not alarmed even by the flooding of the River Jordan (40:23).
> No one can capture it by piercing its nose (40:24).

By bringing Behemoth into the discussion, God demonstrated that if Job could not capture or control Behemoth – which was merely a fellow creature – then he was certainly no match for God, whose power was demonstrated in his control over Behemoth. Job could not, on his own, carry out justice to destroy the proud. In the end, God remained victor and, in the process, revealed more about his divine wisdom, justice, and power.

Face-to-face with Yahweh, Job realized that Yahweh is sovereign overall. This was demonstrated in his power to destroy the proud and wicked as well as control Behemoth, which only he could destroy (40:19) and capture (40:24). Yahweh who is all-wise is the Creator of Behemoth and Job. Indeed, Job had to fully understand that God's ways are higher than his ways and that God's thoughts are far beyond his own.

---

166. Jonathan D. Sarfati, *The Genesis Account: A Theological, historical, and scientific commentary on Genesis 1–11*, 4th ed (Powder Springs: Creation Book Publishers, 2015, 2021), 241.

THE ORIGIN OF LIFE AND THE PURPOSE OF OUR EXISTENCE

Those living in Asia have not escaped the influence of Charles Darwin and his work on *The Origin of Species*. As a student of biology, I was introduced to the theory of evolution in my senior year. The theory's main tenet is that humankind evolved over a period of millions of years by a gradual natural process – from nonliving molecular forms to simple organisms, then to complex organisms, and, finally, becoming human beings. Richards and Ruse claim that after the *Origin* had been "published the fact of evolution became quickly accepted, although of course there were those who were never convinced."[1] They note that while those like Louis Agassiz – the bishop of Oxford – and Charles Hodge remained unconvinced, they were the exception and, generally, the scientific world came on board very quickly.[2]

Kutschera and Niklas also outline the basic history of the theory from the time of Darwin and claim that the evolutionary theory "is a documented fact."[3] They argue that "although many major questions in evolutionary biology remain unanswered, no credible scientist denies evolution as 'a fact.'"[4] They hasten to add, however, that "many scientists continue to explore and debate precisely how the mechanisms of evolution work."[5]

In relation to both micro- and macroevolution, several questions have not been answered satisfactorily by the theory of evolution: (a) Where did the nonliving matter that later evolved to a simple living organism come from?; (b) Where are the transitory forms *en masse* – like half-monkey and half-human – both among the living and in the fossil records?; (c) How can order and intelligent design in the universe be explained?; and (d) Assuming that the theory successfully addresses the origin of life, what is the purpose of life? Where can we find a meaningful and cohesive explanation of pain and suffering?

The Bible and the living God offer answers to these questions. When we consider life as a whole, "belief in the 'blind chance' position, it turns out, requires *considerable* faith. Such believers frequently put themselves in the difficult position of making claims of meaning in life without being able to give tangible reasons for it."[6] Johnson summarizes the implications of a staunch adherence to the tenets of naturalistic or biological evolution:

> The story of salvation by the cross makes no sense against the background of evolutionary naturalism. The evolutionary theory is a story of humanity's climb from animal beginnings to rationality, not a story of a fall from perfection. It is a story about recognizing gods as illusions, not a story about recognizing God as the ultimate reality we are always trying to escape. It is a story about learning to

rely entirely on human intelligence, not a story of the helplessness of that intelligence in the face of the inescapable fact of sin.[7]

Consider the truth that there is a living God, who made the heavens and the earth, including humankind in their full-grown status (Gen 1:27–28). Job 40:15a states, "Look at the Behemoth, which I created along with you" (my translation). Whatever that Behemoth was – and scholars have proposed various options like dinosaurs or sea creatures – it was created at the same time as the rest of creation (Genesis 1–2).

Regardless of the identity of Behemoth, it was made in the same manner (not necessarily of content) as Job – full-grown and independent beings, both created by God.

---

1. Robert J. Richards and Michael Ruse, "Envoi" in *Debating Darwin* (Chicago: University of Chicago Press, 2016), http://www.perlego.com/book/2448579/debating-darwin-pdf.
2. Richards and Ruse, "Envoi."
3. Ulrich Kutschera and Karl J. Niklas, "The Modern Theory of Biological Evolution: An Expanded Synthesis," *Naturwissenschaften 91* (2004): 256.
4. Kutschera and Niklas, "Modern Theory of Biological Evolution," 256.
5. Kutschera and Niklas, 256.
6. Fred Heeren, *Show Me God: What the Message from Space Is Telling Us About God*, Wonders that Witness (Wheeling: Day Star Publications, 1995), 264.
7. Phillip E. Johnson, *Defeating Darwinism by Opening Minds* (Downers Grove: InterVarsity Press, 1997), 111.

41:1–34 The Ode to Leviathan

In this chapter, Yahweh introduced another strange animal and described it at length using rhetorical questions. At times, he paused in his description to challenge Job more directly and drive home his message. This second poem, which can be called an "Ode to Leviathan," raises similar questions to those raised by the "Ode to Behemoth." To what does "Leviathan" refer? Is this a literal or metaphorical animal? What is the significance of the detailed description given by God to Job?

41:1–11 Leviathan's ability to avoid capture

Among the many suggestions about the identity of Leviathan – whale, dragon, creation monster, sea serpent, crocodile, and hippopotamus – a creation monster (mythological) and a crocodile (literal-natural) seem the most popular.[167] Hartley acknowledges that the "author skillfully weaves into the portrait of an earthly serpentine animal the features of a mythical dragon."[168] From a literary standpoint, Walton suggests that in the first eight verses, "Leviathan is to be compared with Yahweh."[169] These verses "discuss what *Job* can't do to Leviathan, and they are also things that Job must learn he cannot do to Yahweh."[170]

What can be known about "Leviathan" from the text? What kind of animal was it? Leviathan is described in this way:

- It could not be pulled in with a fishhook; nor could its tongue be tied with a rope (41:1).[171]
- No cord could be put through its nose; nor could a hook pierce its jaw (41:2).
- It would not beg for mercy or speak with gentle words (41:3).
- It would not agree to be a slave (41:4).
- It could not be made a pet like a bird (41:5).
- Merchants would not buy it to divide it among themselves (41:6).
- Its hide could not be pierced with harpoons; its head could not be pierced with fishing spears (41:7).

"Leviathan" was strong and invincible and could not be wounded, captured, tamed, or killed. If Job were to lay a hand on Leviathan, the resulting struggle would ensure that he would never do so again (41:8). Yahweh warned that any hopes of subduing Leviathan would be futile because the mere sight of this creature would be overwhelming (41:9).

Yahweh asked Job a rhetorical question: If no one was fierce enough to rouse Leviathan, who could possibly stand against Yahweh (41:10)? No one had any claim against Yahweh because, as he declared, "Everything under heaven belongs to me" (41:11)! The purpose in placing verses 10–11 in the middle of Leviathan's description was to show Job that someone who could not even face Leviathan dared not confront Yahweh, who had full control over

---

167. Vicchio traces and charts the different views on Leviathan during the 19th and later 20th century, noting those who take it naturally, mythologically, or a mix of both, *Book of Job*, 290–91.
168. Hartley, *Book of Job*, 530.
169. Walton, *Job*, 408.
170. Walton, *Job*, 408.
171. In the MT, Job 41:1 is 40:25.

Leviathan, which, like everything else – including Job – belonged to Yahweh! This reminder to Job, who had intended to confront Yahweh, was meant to put Job in his place and urge him to rethink his position about confronting God.

41:12–25 Leviathan's anatomy

In this section, Yahweh described Leviathan's awesome anatomy (41:12–25), including "its limbs, its strength and its graceful form" (41:12). In the descriptions below, the parts of Leviathan's body that are specifically identified in the text are shown in italics:

- No one can strip off its *outer coat* or penetrate its *coat of armor* (41:13).
- No one can open the doors of its *mouth*,[172] ringed about with fearsome *teeth* (41:14).
- Its *back* has rows of shields tightly sealed together (41:15).
- Each [shield] is so close to the next that no air can pass between (41:16).
- They are joined fast to one another; they cling together and cannot be separated (41:17).
- Its snorting throws out flashes of light; its *eyes* are like the rays of dawn (41:18).
- Flames stream from its *mouth*; sparks of fire shoot out (41:19).
- Smoke pours from its *nostrils* as from a boiling pot over burning reeds (41:20).
- Its breath sets coals ablaze, and flames dart from its *mouth* (41:21).
- Strength resides in its *neck* (41:22).
- The folds of its *flesh* are tightly joined; they are firm and immovable (41:23).
- Its *chest* is hard as rock, hard as a lower millstone (41:24).

Leviathan could easily pass for a dragon, particularly given the references to its "snorting [that] throws out flashes of light," its eyes like bright "rays of dawn," the "flames [that] stream from its mouth," and "its breath [that] sets coals ablaze" (41:18–21). Alter explains that the "poet clearly moves from the Egyptian crocodile to a mythological fire-breathing dragon.[173] Alden, in

---

172. Literally, "doors of his face."
173. Alter, *Writings*, 575. Verse 18 above is verse 10 for Alter.

referring to the smoke that "pours from its nostrils as from a boiling pot" (41:20), comments, "This sounds like the description of that dragon that is found in many ancient tales."[174]

On the other hand, these features can also be viewed as characteristics observed in the crocodile. For instance, in the "snorting" (or "sneezing"), the "noun appears to indicate the vapor or spray of moisture that emits from Leviathan's nostril."[175] The eyes that are "like the rays of dawn" is, "perhaps, a reference to the reddish hue of the eyes of the crocodile."[176] As to the "flames [that] stream from its mouth," Rowley explains that when "the crocodile issues from the water, it expels its pent-up breath together with water in a hot stream from its mouth, and this looks like a stream of fire in the sunshine."[177] When we consider the animal's anatomy and the context of its own habitat, a natural crocodile closely fits the description, especially in regard to its scaly covering (41:13, 15–17) and teeth (41:14). This author supports the view that Leviathan could very well refer to a crocodile.

Verse 25 describes the kind of fear that this animal arouses in people. When the crocodile rises up,[178] the mighty are petrified. When it crashes back down into the water, these people "retreat" in fear. The parallelism here shows that no human being can really face up to this animal.

41:26–34 Leviathan's invincibility

Any attempts to capture Leviathan – with weapons such as swords, arrows, or spears – were futile (41:26–29). These weapons would not be able to penetrate its body, which was covered with hard scales that could deflect or shred any weapon. Its underside was protected by "jagged potsherds, leaving a trail in the mud like a threshing sledge" (41:30).[179]

Three times in this chapter, the reader is made to pause and feel the impact of what is being said about Leviathan (41:10–11, 25, 33–34). Each time, there is an expression of awe at the nature and power of this animal, which, together with the hyperbole in verse 18 and the complex parallelisms in verses 26–30, all combine to drive home the point that Leviathan was fearless and

---

174. Alden, *Job*, 404.
175. Vicchio, *Book of Job*, 284. See also Rowley, *Book of Job*, 262.
176. Vicchio, *Book of Job*, 284.
177. Rowley, *Book of Job*, 262.
178. Literally, "his rising."
179. There are two figures of speech here. First is a metaphor, where the underside is directly described jagged potsherds. The second is a simile where he trails that Leviathan leaves like the trails left by a threshing sledge.

invincible, and therefore to be feared (41:34). Other majestic animals[180] were petrified before it for it was king over them all. So, both in the animal world and among human beings, Leviathan remained invincible. This message is summed up in the last two verses: "Nothing on earth is its equal – a creature without fear. It looks down on all that are haughty; it is king over all that are proud" (41:33–34).

The reader may wonder about the purpose of such a long and detailed description of this animal. If Leviathan were a sea monster, would Job – who lived in the Arabian Desert – have even had a chance to see such a creature? If, on the other hand, Leviathan were a crocodile, Job might have seen one in his lifetime.

The detailed description might have been given so that Job would think twice before lodging another complaint against God, accusing him of being unjust or tolerant of evil. Yahweh had already warned Job about the dangers of laying a hand on Leviathan (41:8). Even less should Job dare to lift his hand against God or file a case against him! There were so many things that Job did not know about Leviathan, but which God did know. If Job could not control Leviathan, how much less could he control its Creator? Moreover, how could he "tell Yahweh what he must do and how he must treat the innocent and the guilty? Yahweh is sovereign over all of creation, and so he has the freedom to do what is right and best, even if we cannot understand his purpose."[181]

This chapter informs us that only Yahweh could catch and tame Leviathan (41:1–10) because he alone is sovereign and in control over all his creation – for everything under heaven belongs to God (41:11). He alone knows everything about Leviathan – its anatomy (41:12–25) and its invincibility (41:25–30) – whereas Job was not only ignorant about all these things but also incapable of capturing and taming this creature, and afraid even of approaching it. "Job is not able to establish justice because he is not able to control evil or subdue the wicked. Divine justice includes the power to rule and the authority to control the well-being of his subjects. The power of evil is under the sovereign rule of God and is beyond Job's ability to control."[182]

Yahweh wanted to show that just as Job knew nothing of the capabilities of Leviathan, so he knew hardly anything about God's capabilities. Indirectly,

---

180. Literally, "sons of pride."
181. Rao, "Job," 611.
182. Belcher, *Finding Favour*, 125.

God was challenging Job to reconsider his intention to confront Yahweh and to drop the idea of a lawsuit.

Pause and consider these questions: When was the last time you encountered a difficulty or a trial in life? How did you respond? What were the questions that you asked? Did your questions lead you to invite God into the situation? Are you going through what you see as "undeserved suffering" at present? At this moment, how is God leading you to respond to this situation?

Earlier, Elihu had perceived some undercurrents of pride in Job, both in the content and tone of his speeches – his accusations against God (27:2, 20–23), as well as his actions (27:35–37).

A classic example of human hubris – pride – is recorded in Genesis 11. The people of Shinar (or Babel or Babylonia) wanted to make a name for themselves. To avoid being scattered, these people decided to build a city with a ziggurat that reached to the heavens. While this wish is expressed as a hyperbole, it was a plan in direct violation of God's earlier mandate to spread out and populate the earth (Gen 1:26–28; 9:7–11). God intervened in this situation before humankind could self-destruct. He showed them their folly and ensured that his purposes would be accomplished. When God confused the people's languages, their building project came to a standstill, and Yahweh scattered the people to the different corners of the earth (Gen 11:8–9).

Below are some selected maxims and proverbs on the subject of pride and arrogance in the Asian context:

> "Pride attaches undue importance to the superiority of one's status in the eyes of others. And shame is fear of humiliation at one's inferior status in the estimation of others. When one sets his heart on being highly esteemed, and achieves such rating, then he is automatically involved in fear of losing his status."[183] – *Lao Tzu, Founder of Taoism*

> "Even monkeys fall from trees." – A Japanese proverb, which "suggests that even the most skilled, can make a mistake in something they should be a master of."[184]

> "Pride is concerned with who is right. Humility is concerned with what is right.[185] – *Pakistani Proverb*

---

183. See http://www.thinkexist.com/quotation/pride.
184. See http://www.orientaloutpost.com.
185. See http://www.minimalistquotes.com.

Job

"By pride one causes virtue to decline."[186] – *Tibetan Proverb*

"Arrogance is the capital-stock of misfortune.[187] – *Persian Proverb*

These two proverbs in the Bible also talk about pride:

> "Do you see a person wise in their own eyes? There is more hope for a fool than for them" (Prov 26:12).

> "Let someone else praise you, and not your own mouth; an outsider, and not your own lips" (Prov 27:2).

Clearly, both biblical and non-biblical sources warn against self-conceited pride. Ultimately, pride does not bring good but only shame and destruction. So, time and again we must be reminded that pride is a dangerous and destructive attitude.[188]

Job was on the verge of rebelling against God and moving toward self-destruction. Yahweh intervened with the reminder that he was the one who had created the universe and continues to sustain it. Yahweh asked Job if he also intended to "discredit" or nullify God's justice (40:8). Through his presentation about two of his creatures – namely, Behemoth and Leviathan – Yahweh pointed out that if Job could not capture and domesticate these animals, he could hardly challenge Yahweh to a showdown. Job realized the truth of God's words and, as the next chapter will show, was ready to recant before Yahweh.

The topic of Behemoth and Leviathan seems to have become a never-ending discussion among scholars. Zuck argues that if both animals were symbols of chaotic evil and human beings could not single-handedly subdue them, then neither "can man conquer evil in the world which they symbolize. Only God can do that. Therefore, Job's defiant impugning of God's ways in the moral universe – as if God were incompetent or even evil – was totally absurd and uncalled for."[189] Stone explains that due to the increase in our knowledge about ANE symbols and myths, "most commentators now conclude that Behemoth and Leviathan, though perhaps modeled in part on such real animals, are in fact mythological beasts 'liminal creatures' that 'represent the frightening and alien other, bearing the terror of the chaotic in their very being.'"[190]

---

186. See http://www.proverbicals.com.
187. See http://www.proverbicals.com.
188. Earlier, we had a brief discussion on pride in Job 20 of this work.
189. Zuck, "Job," 772–73.
190. Ken Stone, "Israel's Wild Neighbors in the Zoological Gaze" in *Reading the Hebrew Bible with Animal Studies* (Redwood City: Stanford University Press, 2017), https://www.perlego.com/book/745970/reading-the-hebrew-bible-with-animal-studies-pdf.

While most scholars take Behemoth and Leviathan as either literal-natural or mythological animals, Belcher takes the middle ground and posits that perhaps the "best conclusion is that Behemoth is an animal of the natural world and Leviathan is a supernatural creature."[191] He adds that Leviathan is "engaged in physical violence in the natural world. Job has questioned the justice of God. When God confronts Job with Leviathan, he confronts him with the impossibility of subduing evil, wickedness, or even *Satan* himself. Job is not able to establish justice because he is not able to control evil or subdue the wicked. Divine justice includes the power to rule and the authority to control the well-being of his subjects."[192]

Yahweh's presentation of Behemoth and Leviathan must have been overwhelming for Job. It was now his turn to respond. The questions to be answered in this section include the following: What was the evidence of Job's vindication? What was the implication of the offering that God had required of Eliphaz, Bildad, Zophar? Why did God not address Elihu?

JOB 42:1-6 JOB'S RECANTATION

Acknowledging his limitations, Job affirmed the omnipotence of God, who is capable of doing anything and whose plans and purposes cannot be thwarted (42:1-2). Job agreed with Yahweh's evaluation of him as one who had obscured God's plans "with words without knowledge" (38:2). He admitted that he had spoken about marvelously awesome things[193] that he had no knowledge about (42:3) – a reference to the power and wisdom of Yahweh in ruling his inanimate and animate world on both the micro- and macro-levels. Job obviously did not share these attributes for "God has ordered the cosmos by his wisdom . . . Wisdom is at the heart of order."[194]

Job recounted the process that Yahweh had adopted to confront him. Yahweh had commanded Job to listen while he spoke and questioned Job (42:4) and, in verbalizing his response, Job claimed that he had paid close attention to what Yahweh had said and confirmed that he had now seen Yahweh (42:5). While Job did not actually see God, he "has been led to see the multifarious character of God's vast creation, its unfathomable fusion of beauty and

---

191. Belcher, *Finding Favour*, 124. Hartley also takes a mix of the two views, acknowledging an earthly serpentine animal and a mythological dragon, *Book of Job*, 530.
192. Belcher, *Finding Favour*, 125.
193. The verb means "to do something wonderful," "perform something unusual, a miracle," "to display marvelous power." See *HALOT*, s.v. "pele."
194. Walton, *Job*, 411.

cruelty, and through this he has come to understand the incommensurability between his human notions of right and wrong and the structure of reality."[195]

This is "the most crucial point of the book, the difference between what Job has merely heard and experienced about Yahweh compared with what Yahweh revealed about himself."[196] And, in this encounter, "Job discovered the reality of ultimate meaning as reflected in the God speeches by being exposed to a world beyond his comprehension."[197]

Vicchio lists the different ways in which Job 42:6 has been translated in the nineteenth and twentieth centuries. The most common among these include the following: "'I retract and repent on dust and ashes,' 'I repudiate my words, and repent in dust and ashes' or 'I despise myself and repent in dust in ashes.'"[198] The traditional view – which is the general consensus – is that Job repudiated his words and repented. However, another view proposes that Job was not repentant but was rejecting Yahweh in 42:5–6.[199] The translation of Job 42:6 by Curtis reflects this sentiment: "Therefore, I feel loathing contempt and revulsion [toward you, O God]; and I am sorry for frail man."[200] Curtis explains that "Job in his final words to Yahweh has rejected the god who responds to the anguished plea of his most devoted worshiper with contemptuous and arrogant boasting. . . . There is not the slightest suggestion that he recants or in remorse grovels with the divine."[201] Shultz reasons, "While some of Curtis's linguistic arguments in 42:6 are compelling, his conclusion requires him to deny the unity of the book."[202]

The Hebrew verbs *ma'as*[203] and *nakham* are key to understanding the meaning of Job's final words. Since the word *ma'as* does not have any object, the NIV supplies the word "myself." We want to know what it was that Job rejected. It was not the trumped-up sins that his friends had accused him of that Job rejected. Davy explains that Job recognized his place before Yahweh and his own limited capacity to make judgments concerning the administration of

---

195. Alter, *Writings*, 577.
196. Rao, "Job," 611.
197. Lewis, *Victor Frankl*, 117.
198. Vicchio, *Book of Job*, 294.
199. Vicchio notes some scholars who suggest that Job was not repenting in 42:5–6: Carl Jung, D. A. Robertson, K. Fullerton, *Book of Job*, 295.
200. John Briggs Curtis, "On Job's Response to Yahweh," *JBL* 98, no. 4(1979): 505.
201. Curtis, "On Job's Response," 505.
202. Carl Shultz, "The Cohesive Issue of Mišpat in Job," in *Go to the Land I will Show You: Studies in Honor of Dwight W. Young*, eds. Joseph Coleson and Victor Matthews (Winona Lake: Eisenbrauns, 1996), 174.
203. The Hebrew word *ma'as* can also mean "reject," "refuse." See *HALOT*, s.v. "ma'as."

Yahweh's governance of the world.[204] It seems likely that Job was also referring to his harsh words and accusations of injustice against Yahweh, his misunderstanding God's silence, and his misconceptions about him.

What did Job retract? The word *nakham* usually means "to regret," "be sorry," "comfort,"[205] "a change of mind," or "repent."[206] This verb can have "a forensic usage in prophetic lawsuit literature in the Bible as 'retract,' a translation which warrants consideration in 42:6."[207] Indeed, "retract" is fitting for *nakham* in this instance since, as early as chapter 7, Job planned to lodge a legal complaint against God. Now he *retracted* and chose not to pursue the case any longer. So then, Job 42:6 can be translated as "I reject my words and retract in dust and ashes" (my translation). By chapter 16, Job had assembled most of the players in a courtroom. His testimony and countercharges in chapter 31 completed all that was required for a court hearing. He was ready with his case, and he was demanding justice and vindication.

Job hoped to meet God face-to-face (19:26–27). But when the moment came, things did not happen as Job had expected. Job had wanted a chance to personally air his complaints to Yahweh. Even after Yahweh's first speech, Job still wanted to pursue his case. It was Yahweh's second speech about Behemoth and Leviathan that changed Job's mind and put an end to his clamor for justice. Job had learned by then that Yahweh sustains his universe by wisdom and care and not, primarily, by retributive justice or through compensation theology as he and his friends had believed. Job also realized that his case against Yahweh had no merit. He did not have all the facts regarding Yahweh's justice and transcendent wisdom in managing his universe. Upon realizing this, Job had no recourse but to retract his charges and dismiss the case.

While your guess is as good as mine as to how Job might have felt after his enlightenment, imagine holding on to a retribution principle and living by it for 60 or 70 years, only to discover that it is flawed. "In dismantling the retribution principle as the only way of understanding how the world works Yahweh provides a corrective to Job, and to humanity, that we cannot reduce God's operation of the universe to a simplistic or mechanical application of action and consequence. As such the book of Job offers a corrective to faulty

---

204. Davy, "A Missional Encounter with Cultures in Job."
205. See *HALOT*, s.v. "nakham."
206. See Mike Butterworth, "nacham," *NIDOTTE* 3:82.
207. Sylvia Huberman Scholnick, "The Meaning of Mišpat (Justice) in the Book of Job," in *Sitting with Job: Selected Studies on the Book of Job*, ed. Roy B. Zuck (Eugene: Wipf & Stock, 2003), 357.

religious thinking and practice that assumes that suffering must necessarily imply sin."[208]

They say, "Better late than never." Perhaps we need to pause and ask these questions of ourselves: What are the principles that I currently live by? Which of these principles are true and consistent with the teachings of Jesus Christ? Which ones, even though they may sound biblical, are flawed? Do I have any misconceptions of God that I need to acknowledge and correct?

A RECAP OF YAHWEH'S MONOLOGUES

Verse 6 of chapter 42 was Job's final response to Yahweh's second speech that ended in 41:34. What did the Yahweh speeches accomplish for both Yahweh and Job? From Yahweh's point of view, he used these speeches to expose Job's misconceptions about God, his justice, and his management of the universe. Yahweh also affirmed his desire to restore fellowship with Job – and this would happen when Job acknowledged his sinful accusations and withdrew his case against Yahweh. As for Job, Yahweh's speeches revealed God to Job – who he is and his awesome deeds. He operates and manages his world by wisdom. Job came to the point where he had to admit that God himself was the standard of justice. God uses his power and administers his justice according to his own moral perfection. Thus, whatever he does is fair, just, and good even if we do not understand it.

In the light of God's desire for restored fellowship with Job, reflect on these questions: If you are a believer in the living God, how would you assess your present walk, fellowship, and relationship with Jesus Christ? If you do not have a personal relationship with God, will you pause now and consider his offer (see Matt 11:28; John 3:16; 14:6; Acts 16:31; Eph 2:8–9)?

---

208. Davy, "A Missional Encounter with Cultures in Job," in *Book of Job and Mission of God*.

JOB 42:7–17

THE EPILOGUE

This section, like the prologue, is in narrative form, with characters, a setting, and a plot. The characters include Yahweh, Job, the three friends, as well as Job's family members, relatives, and friends. *Satan* and the angels – who were present in the prologue – are absent here, and Elihu, who served as Job's advocate, is also not mentioned.[1] From a literary standpoint, the setting is the earth, not heaven, so *Satan* and the angels need not be there. The focus is now on Job and his three friends.

The setting had changed – from a dunghill outside the city to Job's own property. Job's fellowship with Yahweh and his family, as well as his wealth and social standing, were restored. Although there is no mention of Job's health condition, it seems reasonable to assume that he was healed from his disease – even though some scars might have remained.

The plot involves several scenes: (a) Yahweh rebuked the three friends, (b) he instructed them to bring to Job the animals and sacrifice a burnt offering for themselves, (c) Job prayed for his friends, (d) Yahweh showed favor to Job and accepted his intercession on behalf of his friends, and (e) everything that Job lost was not only restored but doubled.

42:7–9 JOB'S VINDICATION
42:7 The Rebuke of the Counselors

Yahweh accused Eliphaz and his two friends of failing to speak the truth about him, unlike his servant Job had done (42:7). The three "repeatedly proffered lies – about the divine system of justice – in order to preserve their pat notion of reward and punishment. They were, in effect, corrupted witnesses on God's behalf."[2] Job, however, maintained his integrity throughout the debates.

Eliphaz, Bildad, and Zophar had come to comfort and encourage Job, and they meant well. They thought that they were doing the right thing. Despite their flawed theology and poor counsel – which Job rejected – they did three things for Job: (a) they helped Job to process what had happened to him so that

---
1. Elihu completed his role so he need not be included in the epilogue.
2. Alter, *Writings*, 578.

Job was able to express his thoughts and feelings; (b) they kept Job company the whole time that he was at the dunghill; and (c) it can be inferred that by their presence, would-be marauders and wild animals stayed away from Job.

Yahweh's repeated reference to Job as "my servant Job" (42:7–8) – almost a term of endearment – was God's way of affirming Job in the presence of his friends. God had used this same term in his conversation with *Satan* (compare 1:8; 2:3). Yahweh's affirmation was all that Job needed. He was vindicated, and he felt affirmed.

42:8 The Sacrifice of the Counselors

Yahweh commanded Eliphaz and his two friends to take seven bulls and seven rams and bring these to Job. The friends would offer a burn offering for themselves and Job would intercede for them. Yahweh promised to show favor and not deal with them as they deserved for misrepresenting Yahweh by failing to speak the truth about him (42:8). That Yahweh asked Job to mediate for his friends signifies the restoration of fellowship between Job and Yahweh, as well as the vindication of Job.

42:9 The Obedience of the Counselors

Eliphaz, Bildad, and Zophar did as Yahweh had instructed, and as promised, Yahweh showed them favor on account of Job's intercession (42:9). The situation was now reversed: Job's accusers had become the accused, while Job, whom they had accused, now mediated for them. This time together would have given Job and his three friends ample time to talk and to forgive each other. Their relationship with Yahweh, as well as with each other, was restored.

Elihu was not included in Yahweh's rebuke because, despite being younger than the rest, his evaluation of Job's situation had been more balanced than that of the friends. Elihu had considered the situation from both God's and Job's perspectives. He had not joined in the debate to condemn Job, as the others had done, but to help Job rightly assess the situation and see things from God's perspective. He had also corrected Job's faulty theology and prepared him well for his long-awaited confrontation with Yahweh.

42:10–17 Job's Possessions

After Job prayed for his friends, Yahweh restored his family and wealth – the fortunes Job had lost. Moreover, Yahweh doubled Job's former possessions (42:10)! It can be assumed that Job's fellowship with Yahweh was restored immediately after his recantation (42:6). It was only after Job offered the sacrifice for his friends – which would have involved worshiping God – that God restored what Job had earlier lost. Therefore, it cannot be said of Job that he worshiped God only because Yahweh had blessed and protected him. Indeed, it is possible for true believers in Yahweh to worship and serve him even when they are not blessed materially.

Then Job's relatives and those who had known him before the calamities came to Job's house for a celebratory feast. They comforted Job, and they even brought him gifts of money and gold rings (42:11). This celebration accomplished two things: the restoration of Job's friendships and the restoration of Job to the community as a whole. In the honor-shame culture of Job's time, this was important because it signified that Job had regained his social standing. Earlier, when he had lost everything, even young people of no consequence had disrespected him.

The gifts mentioned represent the many presents that Job must have received. In the ANE, it was customary to bring presents when visiting dignitaries, especially in times of calamity. For instance, after King Hezekiah's encounter with Sennacherib, king of Assyria, the people brought gifts to King Hezekiah, thus increasing his reputation (2 Chr 32:23). The gifts signified the acceptance of Job back into the community and his former sphere of influence.

Verses 11– 12 find connection with the NT, where James refers to Job's perseverance and restoration (Jas 5:11). Reminding his readers that the Lord is compassionate and merciful, James acknowledges that Job endured much suffering but also experienced a positive outcome in Yahweh's dealings with him. Yahweh "blessed the latter part of Job's life more than the former part" (42:12). The chart below shows the difference between Job's possessions in earlier and later times.

Job's Possessions and Children		
Job's Possessions	**Before the Calamities**	**After the Calamities**
Sheep	7,000	14,000
Camels	3,000	6,000
Oxen	500 pairs	1,000 pairs
Donkeys	500	1,000
Job's children	7 unnamed sons and 3 daughters – all feasting in the house of the eldest brother	7 unnamed sons and 3 daughters – who are named and described as the most beautiful women in the land

Job ended up with twice as much as he had lost. He had twenty children (10 with God, 10 at home). He and his wife were almost certainly reunited. Friends and relatives visited him, even bringing him gifts. God blessed him a second time with seven sons and three beautiful daughters: Jemimah (meaning "dove"), Keziah (meaning "cinnamon"), and Keren-Happuch (meaning "horn of eye paint"). Alter explains that these names "have no currency elsewhere in the Bible. The writer may have wanted to intimate that after all Job's suffering, which included hideous disfigurement as well as violent loss, a principle of grace and beauty enters his life in the restoration of his fortunes."[3] He adds that "the three daughters have names associated with feminine delicacy and the arts of attraction, and they are said to be the most beautiful women in the land."[4] Each of Job's daughters received an inheritance from their father, just as their brothers did (42:15). Giving an inheritance to his daughters was a special act on Job's part – centuries later, under Mosaic legislation, this was the exception rather than the rule (Num 27:8). Job's decision to grant both sons and daughters the right to inherit could be viewed as a special contribution of wisdom theology in relation to the equal rights of men and women, and it is a good model to follow.[5] Among the *Ibaloy* tribe – mentioned several times in this commentary – the following customary law is still in place: "When a person who has children dies, the oldest boy or girl sometimes gets more of the inheritance. The children, male and female, get the same (value) of rice fields. The boys get more animals, and the girls get more money. The adopted children get a part of the property, but not the same (amount) as the children of the dead man."[6]

This chapter, and the book of Job, ends with the comment that Job lived an additional 140 years. "Job was supposedly 60 or 70 years of age"[7] before the calamities came. If we take the 70 years for his age then, this means that he lived a total of 210 (70 + 140) years. That is twice as long as his life before the calamities. Job was able to see his grandchildren up to the fourth

---

3. Alter, *Writings*, 579.
4. Alter, *Writings*, 579.
5. A passage in Proverbs, a wisdom book, talks about a good father leaving an inheritance to his *grandchildren* (Prov 13:22). In the Hebrew text, the noun *children* (*banim*) is parsed as masculine-plural, hence these would be referring to male grandchildren, which do not necessarily include the granddaughters.
6. Moss, *Nabaloi Law and Ritual*, 251. This practice, though modified in some ways, is still observed today in this culture and attested to by this author.
7. Zuck, *Job*, 188.

generation (42:16), and he died "an old man and full of years" (42:17) – which had been his desire before the calamities came.

God showed generosity and forbearance by restoring Job's fortunes (42:10) and blessing him even more than before (42:12). Job acknowledged God's sovereignty and admitted that Yahweh could do all things and that none of his purposes could be thwarted (42:2). This recalls King Nebuchadnezzar's acknowledgment that God "does as he pleases" and no one can question him for doing so (Dan 4:35). God is sovereign over heaven and earth, over empires and people.

In this chapter, Yahweh commended Job because even in the face of doubt and pressure from a false theology, Job maintained a personal relationship with God and brought his doubts directly to Yahweh. So, *Satan's* hypothesis was proven false, and Job did not curse God as *Satan* had hoped and falsely predicted (compare 1:9–11; 2:4–5).

Yahweh did not tell Job to repent so that his pain would be explained, so that he would be vindicated, or so that his prosperity would be restored. Instead, God met with Job face-to-face. The first thing that Job discovered through this encounter was that he had been greatly mistaken in the reason for his quest. As this courageous rebel stood in Yahweh's presence, his consuming passion for vindication suddenly seemed ludicrous. Job's complete silence at this juncture showed that he had learned his lesson. He had been in error in assuming that the universe operated according to principles that humans could rationally understand. Once that putative principle of order collapsed in the face of divine sovereignty, Job's need for personal vindication vanished as well. Job's personal experience had taught him that he had also clung tenaciously to an assumption of order. He finally gave up this claim, which had hardly brought solace in his case.[8]

It had been Job's lifetime dream to die contently after having reached a happy old age (29:18–20). Job's friends had argued that dying young characterized the life of a wicked person (20:11) and that since, in their assessment, Job had sinned, his life would be cut short. But length of life is not always proportionate to one's righteousness. Sometimes, a righteous person lives a shorter life than an unrighteous person. What matters, however, is that the righteous live acknowledging God's goodness and justice, regardless of whether good or bad come their way.

---

8. James L. Crenshaw, *Old Testament Wisdom: An Introduction* (London: SCM, 1982), 124–25.

When sufferings come, we can easily become unthankful and forget God's goodness. When that happens, remember how blessed you are . . .

- Count your blessings in life.
- Ask God to give you a thankful heart for everything that happens in your life.
- Pray that God will give you the assurance to believe with all your heart that everything God does is right and good.
- Repent of all the times you have questioned God or found fault with his treatment of you. Pray that God would humble you and help you to recognize that such complaints may lead to sin.
- Be satisfied with the holy will of God, and do not complain or worry. Pray for courage and contentment.

CONCLUSION

Unknown to Job, he was the subject of *Satan's* attacks. These attacks set off a series of events that brought unparalleled calamities on Job. Even his friends, who had supposedly visited him to comfort him, became a source of discouragement. Drawing on a principle from traditional wisdom, they concluded and communicated to Job that he must have sinned to merit such calamities. Realizing that he did not stand a chance before his friends, Job decided to present his case before the Almighty. Being conscious that he had not sinned as suggested by his friends, Job felt unjustly treated by God and all the more so by God's seeming silence. To plead his innocence, Job formulated a case against God. During the long debates about questions of sin and justice, the accusations of his friends prodded Job to prepare his own defense, assemble the players in the courtroom, fulfill all other requirements for a lawsuit, and, finally, make one last attempt to vindicate himself by his testimony and countercharges. When everything was ready for the court hearing, Elihu offered himself as Job's defense attorney. Even though Job had neither invited Elihu nor indicated acceptance of Elihu's offer, the latter had assumed this responsibility. In the process, Elihu corrected Job's flawed theology, while affirming that God – even though he does not need to do so – does respond to his people. God is just, wise, and all-powerful. To a great extent, Elihu prepared Job for the confrontation with God.

Yahweh appeared in his own time and in his own style. He did not directly answer the questions that Job had wanted answered: "Why me?" and "What have I done to deserve such pain and suffering?" Instead, through a series of rhetorical questions, Yahweh gave an informative presentation to Job about his creation – the universe and everything in it – to demonstrate his ability to control, maintain, and sustain everything by his mighty power and transcendent wisdom (38:1–41:34).

How did Job respond to Yahweh's self-revelations? Job said: "I am unworthy . . . I put my hand over my mouth and am silent . . . My eyes have now seen you; therefore, I reject my words and retract" (40:4–5; 42:5–6, my translation). God's display of his sovereignty in his creation had silenced Job and prompted him to respond in humility, awe, and reverential fear. Job then dropped his charges and did not pursue his case against the Almighty.

Satan, who instigated the attacks on Job (1–2), was silenced by Job's response (42:1–6), which proved that Yahweh's confidence in Job had not been unfounded (1:8; 2:3). God needs no vindication, but the book of Job shows that undeserved suffering – accepted and borne by a believer in the living God – does, in a sense, vindicate God's gracious plan for his saints. "True wisdom, like God, defies human reason"[1] and the wrong concepts of traditional wisdom but, when properly applied by God's people during undeserved suffering, becomes a living demonstration of God's grace and a believer's faith.

The failure of traditional wisdom to answer Job's complaints reveals that the unbelieving world operates by flawed principles and that it is only through a personal relationship with God that fallen humanity can find meaning and purpose in an unjust world. *Satan*, Eliphaz, Bildad, Zophar, and even, to some extent, Job wrongly assumed that punishment of the wicked and reward of the righteous in this life was a fixed doctrine. This, however, limits God's freedom. In compensation theology, for example, rain was often seen as a reward, while withholding rain was viewed as punishment. Yet, rain falls because of God's grace to both the righteous and the wicked (Matt 5:45).

God wanted to show that neither human beings' piety nor their sin affected how God administered his plan. Both then and now, God carries out his plan by grace. As Tsevat writes, "Job behaved piously throughout, but his behavior had, in the narrated time of 1:13–31:40, no consequences compatible with the accepted idea of reward and punishment."[2] His hope had been in the positive results of a false doctrine, while his friends had extolled the negative aspects of that same doctrine. Elihu (32–37) and God (38–41) both stated that these misplaced hopes of payback or compensation for goodness have no place in the divine economy. In his final responses (40:3–5; 42:1–6), "Job acknowledges this fact and is now prepared for a pious and moral life uncluttered by false hopes and unfounded claims."[3]

This is not to say the book of Job teaches that a person has no obligation to live a moral and righteous life, and to remain committed to truth and justice in the face of sin and evil. What it does show is that believers have an obligation to examine their motivation in coming to and serving God, especially during times of trial and suffering. Furthermore, the book of Job does not support the mistaken idea that all suffering is for disciplinary purposes or that

---

1. Crenshaw, *Old Testament Wisdom*, 123.
2. Zhitlowsky, "Job and Faust," 104.
3. Tsevat, "Meaning of the Book of Job," 73–106.

suffering always results from sin and evil. God does discipline, teach, guide, and direct through suffering, but he cannot be manipulated by a system of blessing and cursing that has been devised by human beings – a system that is negatively called the theology of retribution or recompense or positively labeled the theology of prosperity. God is not obligated to humanity under any conditions. Once this is understood, believers are free to examine their suffering on the basis of God's grace. Andersen comments, "That the Lord himself has embraced and absorbed the undeserved consequences of all evil is the final answer to Job and to all of humanity. As an innocent sufferer, Job is the companion of God."[4]

Job was righteous because he had a grace relationship with Yahweh. That being the case, why did God put Job through all this suffering? Lawson says that it was primarily

> to reveal Himself to Job. . . . Through this interrogation, God had taught Job that he alone created everything – the heavens and the earth, and all that is in them – and he alone controls all that he created. He alone has the right to do with his own as he pleases. He is under no obligation to explain his actions to his creation. He alone is sovereign and not accountable to anyone.[5]

The question "Why do the righteous suffer?" cannot, therefore, be explained by just one answer. The many reasons given in Scripture for personal suffering must all be examined in the light of God's grace and the experience of the sufferer. Three sets of reasons have been suggested: The first set have as their source the book of Job; the second, other texts in the Bible; and the source of the third set of reasons is what other people think in light of their study of the Bible and their own experiences in life.

REASONS FOR SUFFERING – FROM THE BOOK OF JOB

1. There is an invisible spiritual war that is being waged beyond the realm of what human beings can see (1–2).

2. God is glorified and honored – in the invisible court proceedings in heaven – by the testimony of the believer (1:1–2:10).

3. Every person will go through suffering of some form (5:7).

---

4. Andersen, *Job*, 73.
5. Lawson, *When All Hell Breaks Loose*, 240.

4. Suffering is sometimes the result of sin.

5. God sometimes allows suffering in order to turn a person from pride and destruction (33:17–18).

6. God may use suffering to instruct, correct, or restore (33:19–30).

7. Pain can be God's ordained platform to reveal himself – who he is, what he has done, and what he continues to do (38:1–41:34).

8. Pain and suffering may lead believers to a deeper knowledge and experience of God (42:5–6).

REASONS FOR SUFFERING – FROM OTHER BIBLICAL TEXTS

1. Pain and suffering often reveal what is in our hearts (Deut 8:2–4).

2. God sometimes uses suffering for his own purposes and for his own glory (John 9:3).

3. Both personal sins (Rom 2:9, 3:9–20) and corporate sins (Isa 1:1–9) lead to pain and suffering.

4. Suffering is universal, and it comes to every person (Rom 8:22–23).

5. Suffering can serve as an antidote to arrogance (2 Cor 12:7–10).

6. Pain may be used to correct and discipline (Heb 12:5–11).

7. Suffering can be a platform to exercise faith (1 Pet 5:10).

REASONS FOR SUFFERING – FROM VARIOUS SCHOLARS

1. Suffering demonstrates that God is absolutely sovereign and can do with his creatures whatever he pleases.[6] The believer's appropriate response to God's sovereign grace is faith and submissive trust.[7]

2. There is a sense in which believers suffer by being a part of God's family.[8]

3. Suffering makes believers acutely aware of the power of evil, strips them of all their worldly securities, allows them to see Christ in his glory, and enables them to bear the fruit of the Spirit.[9]

---

6. Gregory Wayne Parsons, *A Biblical Theology of Job 38:1–42:6* (PhD diss., Dallas Theological Seminary, 1980), 151.
7. Parsons, *A Biblical Theology of Job*, 151.
8. Washington Oestreich, "The Suffering of Believers under Grace" (Th.M. thesis, Dallas Theological Seminary, 1944), 66–71.
9. Mark R. Littleton, *When God Seems Far Away* (Wheaton: Harold Shaw, 1987), 116.

Conclusion

4. Suffering is a testimony to others of a believer's love and faithfulness to God.[10]

5. Suffering is a tempering process.[11]

6. Suffering is used to test and to teach.[12] The focus in this book is on what Job learned from suffering, not suffering itself. Therefore, suffering teaches believers to look to future glory, to be obedient, to learn patience, to be sympathetic to others who suffer, to live a life of faith, to understand God's gracious purposes, to abide in Christ, to pray, to be sensitive to sin, to love God, to love the Scriptures, and to learn contentment.

7. Suffering is often given for disciplinary purposes.[13] "Job did not receive explanations regarding his problems, but he did come to a much deeper sense of the majesty and loving care of God."[14] "Knowing the answer to the question 'Who?' Job no longer needed to ask the question 'Why?'"[15] Some hold that a "no" answer is given to the problem of undeserved suffering. God is so great that if an answer were given, one could not understand it.[16]

8. "In suffering, God is saving us, delivering us into a relationship with himself where he is actually, God and Lord."[17]

Those who suffer can relate to Job's struggle and ultimate triumph. And the suffering of Job teaches the following important truths:

1. God's wisdom is above human wisdom.

2. God must not be limited to preconceived notions of retribution or recompense theology.

3. God's blessings are based solely on grace, not on some traditional, legalistic formula.

4. God does allow suffering and pain, and even death, when these things best serve his purposes.

---

10. Littleton, *When God Seems Far Away*, 54.
11. Littleton, *When God Seems Far Away*, 42.
12. Wilkinson and Boa, *Talk Thru the Old Testament*, 1:145.
13. Bode, *Book of Job*, 210–17.
14. Zuck, "Job," 776.
15. David L. McKenna, *Job*, Communicator's Commentary (Waco: Word, 1986), 315.
16. David M. Howard, *How Come, God? Reflections from Job about God and Puzzled Man* (Philadelphia: Holman, 972), 114.
17. Eric Ortlund, "Pastoral Penses: Five Truths for Sufferers from the Book of Job," *Them* 40, no. 2 (2015): 256.

5. Because God's people are intimately related to him, suffering is often specifically designed to glorify God in the unseen war with Satan.

6. Even though people may misunderstand the ways of God and the "whys" of life, having a personal relationship with God is the only way a person can truly know and understand justice.

7. A flawed retribution concept impinges on a person's view of God's ways and confines God to human standards of interpretation.

8. Satan is behind this false retribution concept and delights in using it to afflict the upright.

9. Accepting false tenets about suffering can cause a person to blame and challenge God.

10. Prosperity theology has no place in God's plan of grace.

11. Sin is not always the reason for suffering.

12. Suffering can have a preventive purpose.

13. Suffering can be faced with faith and trust in a loving God even when there is no immediate, satisfying, or logical reason to do so.

14. Life is more than a series of absurdities and unexplainable pain that must simply be endured. Instead, life for believers is linked with God's unseen purpose.

15. People do not always know all the facts; nor is such knowledge necessary to live a life of faith.

16. The greatest of saints do struggle with the problem of undeserved suffering and will continue to do so.

Suffering is a universal experience and a fact of life. It was true in the ANE, and it is true in Asia, in our lives today. While we will never have all the answers and reasons for the suffering that might come our way, our attitude and response to suffering – along with the extent to which we allow God to undertake for us – will determine whether or not we will be able to overcome these challenges. For Job, the ultimate answer for his pain was that he "saw God" and had a meaningful encounter with Yahweh that was based on grace, rather than on restored prosperity. By the time Yahweh had concluded his speeches, Job's focus was on God, not on his suffering or his material blessings (Ps 77:1–2, 10–12). Job, like all believers, experienced God's comfort *through* his suffering, and this deepened his faith and trust in God.

Conclusion

Suffering encourages believers to offer thanks in all circumstances (1 Thess 5:18) and to realize that God's purposes and plans are not hindered – and may even be furthered – by suffering (Jer 29:11). It is equally true that believers are commanded to welcome multiple trials as friends and embrace these as opportunities to display God's work in their lives (Jas 1:2–4). Although Job ended his days with twice as much as he had possessed at the beginning, he realized that these too, were the blessings of a loving and all-wise God.

As we bring this conversation about Job to a close, let us briefly consider three key questions: Is it possible to worship God solely for who he is without the motivation of his rewards? In what ways is the retribution concept – which believers knowingly or unknowingly embrace – flawed? Can a person find meaning and purpose in pain and suffering?

Concerning the First Question about Worshiping God

Satan's presupposition had been that Job only worshiped God because God had provided everything that Job needed, protected him, and blessed his life. He predicted that once God withheld his presence and blessings, Job would certainly curse God (1:11). When Job lost his properties and children, he continued to worship God and did not accuse him of any wrongdoing (1:20–22). When Job lost his health and social standing, his wife suggested that he curse God, but Job's response was total commitment to God – with a readiness to accept both the good and the bad from God – and he did not sin (2:10). It was only when he reached rock bottom that Job cursed the day he was born, but even then, he did not curse God (3:1–26). Throughout the debates, Job was brutally honest with God. He questioned what he perceived as injustice and God's silence. Although Eliphaz accused Job of committing blasphemy against God, Job did not curse or denounce God. In his second response to Yahweh (42:1–6), Job used strong words to express his change of heart. He repudiated his earlier words against God and his misconceptions about God. He retracted his earlier charges and did not pursue his case against Yahweh. Job remained faithful to God not just when he was tremendously blessed but even in the darkest days of his life, when he had nothing left but his wife and his life.

Pause and ask yourself: Will I be able to respond as Job did in the face of suffering? Will I be able to maintain a confident trust in God, who remains sovereign over local and worldwide events? When yet another calamity seems to be looming on the horizon, will I pray as Habakkuk prayed?

> Though the fig tree does not bud
>   and there are no grapes on the vines,
> though the olive crop fails
>   and the fields produce no food,
> though there are no sheep in the pen
>   and no cattle in the stalls,
> yet I will rejoice in the LORD,
>   I will be joyful in God my Savior.
> The Sovereign LORD is my strength;
>   he makes my feet like the feet of a deer,
>   he enables me to tread on the heights (Hab 3:17–19).

Concerning the Second Question about the Retribution Concept

As discussed earlier – in the section dealing with Job 4 – the three friends espoused a flawed retribution concept and applied this to Job's situation. They treated the condition of the maxim as the premise statement and the result statement as the cause statement: "Because you are suffering, you must have sinned." Their view did not accommodate the reality that "the righteous do suffer, and the wicked do prosper in life."[18] This distorted retribution concept was not life-giving for Job. As a result, he rejected the counsel of his friends. As discussed in this commentary, people may experience pain and suffering for many reasons other than sin. For Job, suffering was a preventive measure and one that led him into a deeper experience of God.

Concerning the Third Question about Finding Meaning in Pain and Suffering

By chapter 3, Job had hit rock bottom. He wished that he had never been born so that he would not have to go through the calamities he was experiencing. He had reached an "existential vacuum," a meaningless and purposeless existence.[19] He admitted that life was hard and without hope (7:1–6). Faced with the choice to either hope in God or hope in death, Job chose the former even though he feared that God would slay him (13:14–16).

When Job felt that he no longer had hope in this world (19:9–11), what kept him going? There were three things that initially pulled Job out of his pit

---

18. Refer to pages 48-50 ("Retribution Concept: When Does It Become Flawed?")
19. Lewis, *Victor Frankl*, 23.

of despondency and given him something to live for: the pursuit of a court hearing, vindication, and seeing his *go'el* (redeemer) face-to-face (19:23–27). While these things helped to slowly bring back some semblance of meaning to Job's life, ultimately, it was his personal encounter and experience with Yahweh that gave real meaning[20] and the right perspective on his pain and suffering. Blaise Pascal was right when he said that "there is a God-shaped vacuum in the heart of each man which cannot be satisfied by any created thing but only by God the Creator, made known through Jesus Christ."[21]

MY CONCLUDING PRAYER

May Yahweh, the living God, the God of Job, so grip our hearts that we will fully trust him whether in *plenty* or in *want*, whether in the *brightest* or *darkest* times of our lives, and whether we experience *joy* or *pain*. And when unexplainable circumstances and undeserved suffering come our way, may our Lord enable us to embrace these as friends (Jas 1:2–3).

When pain and suffering visit, may we make it our goal to pursue God's plan and purpose for our lives. May the Holy Spirit empower and guide us to live according to God's will and what delights him. May we become all that God has purposed us to be and, by his grace, may we accomplish all that he has ordained for us to do in our lifetime.

As God's servant-stewards, may we be faithful to our calling, to the *missio Dei*, and even when it is hard, may we plod on in whatever field he has placed us.

And when our trials and difficulties seem overwhelming, may God gently lead us to himself and to a meaningful experience of him as our loving heavenly Father, and our incomparable Savior, Jesus Christ.

To Yahweh, the living God, belongs all the glory!

---

20. Logotherapy would call this the ultimate meaning. It is beyond the person and is supernatural. See Lewis, *Victor Frankl*, 104.
21. Blaise Pascal, "Section 7: Morality and Doctrine" in *Pascal's Pensées* (New York: Dutton, 1958); The Project Gutenberg e-book of Pascal's Pensées, http://www.pgdp.net.

SELECTED BIBLIOGRAPHY

Alden, Robert L. *Job*. NAC 11. Nashville: Broadman & Holman, 1993.

Al-Fayumi, Saadiah Ben Joseph. *The Book of Theodicy: Translation and Commentary on the Book of Job*. Translated by Lenn Evan Goodman. YJS 25. New Haven: Yale University Press, 1988.

Alter, Robert. *The Writings*. Vol. 3 of The Hebrew Bible: A Translation with Commentary. New York: Norton, 2010.

Andersen, Francis I. *Job: An Introduction and Commentary*. TOTC 14. Downers Grove InterVarsity Press, 1976.

Anderson, Neil T. *Victory Over the Darkness*. Ventura: Regal Books, 1990.

Archer, Gleason L., Jr. *A Survey of the Old Testament: Introduction*. 3rd ed. Chicago: Moody Press, 1994.

———. *The Book of Job: God's Answer to the Problem of Undeserved Suffering*. Grand Rapids: Baker Books, 1982.

Avruch, Kevin. Review of *An Asian Perspective on Mediation*, edited by Joel Lee and Teh Hwee. *Peace & Conflict Review* 4, Issue 1:2.

Bakon, Shimon. "The Enigma of Elihu." *Dor le Dor* 12 (1984): 217–28.

Barkai, John. "A Cross-Cultural Mediator To Do? A Low-Context Solution for A High-Context Problem." *Cardozo Journal of Conflict Resolution* 10 (2008): 43–89.

Barnes, Albert. *The Book of Job*. Grand Rapids: Baker Books; repr. 1996.

Baucas, Biano. *Traditional Beliefs and Cultural Practices in Benguet*. La Trinidad: New Baguio Offset Press, 2003.

Beeby, H. D. "Elihu – Job's Mediator?" *South East Asia Journal of Theology* 7 (1969): 33–54.

Belcher, Richard P., Jr., *Finding Favour in the Sight of God: A Theology of Wisdom Literature*. NSBT. London: Apollos, 2018.

Bode, William. *The Book of Job and the Solution of the Problem of Suffering it Offers*. Grand Rapids: Eerdmans–Sevensma, 1914.

Brinkman, J. A. *A Political History of Post-Kassite Babylonia 1158–722 B.C.* Rome: Pontifical Biblical Institute, 1968.

Bromily, Geoffrey W., ed. *International Standard Bible Encyclopedia*. 4 vols. Rev. ed. Grand Rapids: Eerdmans, 1979–1994.

Brown, Francis, S. R. Driver, and Charles A. Briggs. *A Hebrew and English Lexicon of the Old Testament*. Oxford: Clarendon, 1907.

Budde, Karl, *Das Buch Hiob*. HAT. Göttingen: Vandenhoeck & Ruprecht, 1896.

Bullinger, E. W. *The Book of Job*. Grand Rapids: Kregel, 1990.

———. *Figures of Speech Used in the Bible*. Grand Rapids: Baker Book House, 21st printing, 1997.

Clines, David J. A. *Job 1–20*. WBC 17. Dallas: Word, 1989.

Cornill, Carl. *Introduction to the Canonical Books of the Old Testament*. Translated by G. H. Box. Theological Translation Library 23. New York: Putnam's Sons, 1907.

Crumbaugh, James C. and Leonard T. Maholick. "An Experimental Study in Existentialism: The Psychometric Approach to Frankl's Concept of Noogenic Neurosis," *Journal of Clinical Psychology* 20, no. 2 (1964): 200–7.

Cuncic, Arlin. "What is Logotheraphy?" *Verywell Mind*, 8 July 2022. https://www.verywellmind.com/ an-overview-of-victor-frankl-s-logotherapy-4159308.

Curtis, John Briggs. "On Job's Response to Yahweh," *JBL* 98, no. 4 (1979): 497–511.

———. "Word Play in the Speeches of Elihu (Job 32–37)." *Proceedings* 12 (1992): 23–30.

Davy, Tim J. *The Book of Job and the Mission of God*. Eugene: Wipf & Stock, 2020. https://www.perlego.com/book/1990350/the-book-of-job-and-the-mission-of-god-pdf.

Dell, Katharine J. *Eerdmans Commentary on the Bible: Job*. Grand Rapids: Eerdmans, 2019. http://www.perlego.com/book/2985430/eerdmans-commentary-on-the-bible-job-pdf.

———. Job: An Introduction and Study Guide: Where Shall Wisdom Be Found? T&T Clark Study Guides to the Old Testament. London: T&T Clark, 2017.

Dhorme, Edouard. *A Commentary on the Book of Job*. Nashville: Nelson, 1984.

Diamond, David. "One Nation, Overseas." *Wired*, 1 June 2002. https://www.wired.com/2002/06/philippines/.

Diewert, David Allen. "The Composition of the Elihu Speeches: A Poetic and Structural Analysis." PhD diss., University of Toronto, 1991.

Driver, Samuel Rolles and George Buchanan Gray. *A Critical and Exegetical Commentary on the Book of Job*. ICC. Edinburgh: T&T Clark, 1921.

Dyer, Charles and Gene H. Merrill. *The Old Testament Explorer: Discovering the Essence, Background, and Meaning of Every Book in the Old Testament*. Nashville: Word, 2001.

Ellison, H. L. *From Tragedy to Triumph: Studies in the Book of Job*. Grand Rapids: Zondervan, 1958.

Estes, Daniel J. *Job*. TTC. Grand Rapids: Baker Books, 2013.

Freehof, Solomon B. *Book of Job: A Commentary*. Jewish Commentary for Bible Readers. New York: Union of American Hebrew Congregations, 1958.

Gesenius, Wilhem. *Gesenius' Hebrew-Chaldee Lexicon to the Old Testament*. Translated by Samuel Prideaux Tregelles. Grand Rapids: Baker Books, 1979.

Selected Bibliography

Gnuse, Robert Karl. *Dreams and Dream Reports in the Writings of Josephus: A Tradition-Historical Analysis*. Leiden: Brill, 1996.
Gordis, Robert. *The Book of God and Man: A Study of Job*. Chicago: University of Chicago Press, 1965.
———. *Poets, Prophets, and Sages*. Bloomington: Indiana University Press, 1971.
Gray, John. "The Masoretic Text of the Book of Job, the Targum and the Septuagint Version in the Light of the Qumran Targum (11QtargJob)." *ZAW* (1974): 331–50.
Habel, Norman. "The Role of Elihu in the Design of the Book of Job." In *In the Shelter of Elyon: Essays on Ancient Palestinian Life and Literature in Honor of G. W. Ahlström*, edited by W. Boyd Barrick and John Spencer, 81–98. JSOTSup 31. Sheffield, JSOT Press, 1984.
Habtu, Tewoldemedhin "Job." In *Africa Bible Commentary*, edited by Tokunboh Adeyemo, 571–604. Grand Rapids: Zondervan, 2006.
Hallo, William W., ed. Canonical Compositions from the Biblical World. Vol. 1 of The Context of Scripture. Leiden: Brill, 1997.
Harmon, Jana. "C. S. Lewis on the Problem of Pain." C. S. Lewis Institute, Fall 2012. https://www.cslewisinstitute.org.
Harris, Laird R., Gleason L. Archer Jr., and Bruce K. Waltke. *Theological Word Book of the Old Testament*. 2 vols. Chicago: Moody Press, 1980.
Harrison, R. K. *An Introduction to the Old Testament*. Grand Rapids: Eerdmans, 1969.
Hartley, John E. *The Book of Job*. NICOT. Grand Rapids: Eerdmans, 1988.
Heeren, Fred. *Show Me God: What the Message from Space Is Telling Us About God*. Wonders that Witness 1. Wheeling: Day Star Publications, 1995.
Hess, Richard S. "Chaldea." In *ABD*, ed. David Noel Freedman, 1:886–87. New Haven: Yale University Press, 1992.
Hulme, William. "Pastoral Counseling in the Book of Job." *Concordia Journal* 15 (1989): 121–38.
Johns, David Arvid. "The Literary and Theological Function of the Elihu Speeches in the Book of Job." Ph.D. diss., Saint Louis University, 1983.
Johnson, Philip E. *Defeating Darwinism by Opening Minds*. Downers Grove: InterVarsity Press, 1997.
Johnston, Philip S. *Shades of Sheol: Death and Afterlife in the Old Testament*. Downers Grove: InterVarsity Press, 2002.
Josephus. Translated by Henry St. J. Thackeray et al. 10 vols. LCL. Cambridge: Harvard University Press, 1926–1965.
Kaiser, Walter C., Jr. *The Majesty of God in the Midst of Innocent Suffering: The Message of Job*. Fearn: Christian Focus Publications, 2019.

Kent, Charles Foster. *The Growth and Contents of the Old Testament*. London: Scribner's Sons, 1926.

Koda, Masahide, et al., "Reasons for Suicide During the COVID 19 Pandemic in Japan." JAMA Network Open. 31 January 2022.

Koehler, Ludwig, Walter Baumgartner, and Johann J. Stamm. The Hebrew and Aramaic Lexicon of the Old Testament. Translated and edited under the supervision of Mervyn E. J. Richardson. 2 vols. Leiden: Brill, 1994–1999.

Komp, Diane M. *Why Me? A Doctor Looks at the Book of Job*. Downers Grove: InterVarsity Press, 2001.

Kübler-Ross, Elizabeth. *On Death and Dying: What the Dying Have to Teach Doctors, Nurses, Clergy & their Own Families*. New York: Scribner, 1969.

Kutschera, Ulrich and Karl J. Niklas. "The Modern Theory of Biological Evolution: An Expanded Synthesis." *Naturwissenschaften 91 (2004): 255–76*.

Lewis, Marshall H. *Viktor Frankl and the Book of Job: A Search for Meaning*. Eugene: Wipf & Stock,, 2019. https://www.com/book/1483066/viktor-frankl-pdf.

Levinger, Jacob S. "Maimonides' Exegesis of the Book of Job." In *Creative Biblical Exegesis: Christian and Jewish Hermeneutics through the Centuries*, edited by Benjamin Uffenheimer and Henning G. Reventlow, 81–88. JSOTSup 59. Sheffield: JSOT Press, 1988.

Longman, Tremper, III. *Job*. Baker Commentary of the Old Testament Wisdom and Psalms. Grand Rapids: Baker Academic, 2012. https://www.perlego.com/book/2050908/job-baker-commentary-on-the-old-testament- wisdom-and-psalm.pdf.

Maimonides, Moises. *Guide to the Perplexed*. Translated by M. Friedlander. New York: Dover, n.d.

Malanes, Maurice. *Power from the Mountains: Indigenous Knowledge Systems and Practices in Ancestral Domain Management*. Geneva: International Labor Union, 2002.

McCabe, Robert V., Jr. "The Significance of the Elihu Speeches in the Context of the Book of Job." Th.D. diss., Grace Theological Seminary, 1985.

McKim, Donald K. *The Westminster Dictionary of Theological Terms*. 2nd ed. Louisville: Westminster John Knox, 2014. https://www.perlego.com/book/2100943/the-westminster-dictionary-of-theological-terms-second-edition-revised-and-expanded-pdf.

Mendenhall, George. "Covenant Forms in Israelite Tradition." *Biblical Archaeologist Reader* 3 (1970): 25–53.

Mixter, R. L. "Hand." In *Zondervan Pictorial Encyclopedia of the Bible*, edited by Merrill C. Tenney, 2:34–35. Grand Rapids: Zondervan, 1975.

O'Connor, Daniel J. "The Hybris of Job." *ITQ* 55 (1989): 125–41.

Selected Bibliography

Ortlund, Eric. "Pastoral Penses: Five Truths for Sufferers from the Book of Job" *Them* 40, no. 2 (2015) 253–62.

Pascal, Blaise. *Pascal's Pensées*. New York: Dutton, 1958. http://www.pgdp.net.

Pelaia, Ariela. "The Behemoth in Jewish Mythology." *Learn Religions*. 10 May 2018 learnreligions.com/what-is-the-behemoth-2076679.

Pope, Marvin H. *Job*. AB 15. Garden City: Doubleday, 1973.

Rao, Naveen. "Job." In *South Asia Bible Commentary*, edited by Brian Wintle, 579–612. Grand Rapids: Zondervan, 2015.

Rasmussen, Carl G. *NIV Atlas of the Bible*. Grand Rapids: Zondervan, 1989.

Reyburn, William David. *A Handbook on the Book of Job*. New York: United Bible Societies, 1992.

Richards, Robert J., and Michael Ruse, *Debating Darwin*. Chicago: The University of Chicago Press, 2016. http://www.perlego.com/book/2448579/debating-darwin-pdf.

Rowley, H. H. *The Book of Job*. NCBC. Grand Rapids: Eerdmans, 1992.

———. "The Book of Job and Its Meaning." *Bulletin of the John Rylands Library* 41 (1958): 167–207.

Sarfati, Jonathan D. *The Genesis Account: A Theological, Historical, and Scientific Commentary on Genesis 1–11*, 4th ed. Powder Springs: Creation Book Publishers, 2015, 2021.

Sarna, Nahum H. "Epic Substratum in the Prose of Job" *Journal of Biblical Literature* 76 (March 1957): 13-25.

Schaper, Robert N. *Why Me, God?* Glendale. CA: G/L Publications, 1974.

Scholnick, Sylvia Huberman. "The Meaning of Mišpat (Justice) in the Book of Job." In *Sitting with Job: Selected Studied on the Book of Job*, edited by Roy B. Zuck, 349–358. Eugene: Wipf & Stock, 2003.

Schreiner, Susan E. *Where Shall Wisdom Be Found? Calvin's Exegesis of Job from Medieval and Modern Perspectives*. Chicago: University of Chicago Press, 1994.

Seow, C. L. *Job 1–21: Interpretation and Commentary*. Illuminations. Grand Rapids: Eerdmans, 2013.

———. "Orthography, Textual Criticism, and the Poetry of Job." *JBL* 130, no. 1 (2011): 63–85.

Shultz, Carl. "The Cohesive Issue of Mišpat in Job." In *Go to the Land I Will Show You: Studies in Honor of Dwight W. Young*, edited by Joseph Coleson and Victor Matthews, 159–76. Winona Lake: Eisenbrauns, 1996.

Smick, Elmer. "Introduction" in *Job*, EBC, ed. Tremper Longman III and David E. Garland. Grand Rapids: Zondervan, 2017), http://www.perlego.com/book/560269/job-pdf.

Soulen, Richard N. *Handbook of Biblical Criticism*, 2nd ed. Altanta: John Knox, 1981.

Stern, David H. *Jewish New Testament Commentary*. Clarksville: Jewish New Testament Publication, 1992.

Stickel, Johann Gustave. *Das Buch Hiob rhythmisch gegliedert und übersetzt mit exegetischen und kritischen Bemerkungen*. Leipzig: Weidmannsche Buchhandlung, 1842.

Stone, Ken. *Reading the Hebrew Bible with Animal Studies*. Redwood City: Stanford University Press, 2017. https://www.perlego.com/book/745970/reading-the-hebrew-bible-with-animal-studies-pdf.

Teng, Sharon. "Sago Lane: 'Street of the Dead.'" *BiblioAsia* 8 (2013): 34–39. http://biblioasia.nlb.gov.sg/files/pdf/vol-8/issue-4/v8-issue4_SagoLane.pdf/.

Tsevat, Matitiahu. "The Meaning of the Book of Job." *HUCA* 37 (1966): 195.

Umbreit, Friedrich Carl. *Das Buch Hiob: Üebersetzung und Auslegung*. Heidelberg: Mohr, 1832.

Uytanlet, Samson L., and Kiem-Kiok Kwa, *Matthew: A Pastoral and Contextual Commentary*. ABCS. Carlisle: Langham Global Library, 2017.

VanGemeren, Willem A., ed. *New International Dictionary of Old Testament Theology and Exegesis*. 5 vols. Grand Rapids: Zondervan, 1997. Vicchio, Stephen J. *The Book of Job: A History of Interpretation and Commentary*. Eugene: Wipf & Stock, 2020.

Waltke, Bruce K., and M. O'Connor. *An Introduction to Biblical Hebrew Syntax*. Winona Lake: Eisenbrauns, 1990. Walton, John H. *Job*. NIVAC. Grand Rapids: Zondervan, 2012.

Wiersbe, Warren. *Be Patient (Job): Waiting on God in Difficult Times*. Wheaton: Victor Books, 1991.

Williams, Ronald J. *Hebrew Syntax: An Outline*. Toronto: University of Toronto Press, 1967.

Wilson, Lindsay. *Job*. Two Horizons Old Testament Commentary. Grand Rapids: Eerdmans, 2015. https://www.perlego.com/book/2015636/job-pdf.

Young, Edward J. *An Introduction to the Old Testament*. Grand Rapids: Eerdmans, 1964.

Zuck, Roy B. *Job*. Everyman's Bible Commentary. Chicago: Moody Press, 1978.

———. "Job." In *The Bible Knowledge Commentary*, edited by John F. Walvoord and Roy B. Zuck, 1:715–77. Wheaton: Victor Books, 1985.

———. "A Theology of Wisdom Books and the Song of Songs." In *A Biblical Theology of the Old Testament*, edited by Roy B. Zuck, 207–55. Chicago: Moody Press, 1991.

Asia Theological Association
54 Scout Madriñan St. Quezon City 1103, Philippines
Email: ataasia@gmail.com Telefax: (632) 410 0312

OUR MISSION

The Asia Theological Association (ATA) is a body of theological institutions, committed to evangelical faith and scholarship, networking together to serve the Church in equipping the people of God for the mission of the Lord Jesus Christ.

OUR COMMITMENT

The ATA is committed to serving its members in the development of evangelical, biblical theology by strengthening interaction, enhancing scholarship, promoting academic excellence, fostering spiritual and ministerial formation and mobilizing resources to fulfill God's global mission within diverse Asian cultures.

OUR TASK

Affirming our mission and commitment, ATA seeks to:

- **Strengthen** interaction through inter-institutional fellowship and programs, regional and continental activities, faculty and student exchange programs.
- **Enhance** scholarship through consultations, workshops, seminars, publications, and research fellowships.
- **Promote** academic excellence through accreditation standards, faculty and curriculum development.
- **Foster** spiritual and ministerial formation by providing mentor models, encouraging the development of ministerial skills and a Christian ethos.
- **Mobilize** resources through library development, information technology and infra-structural development.

To learn more about ATA, visit www.ataasia.com or facebook.com/AsiaTheologicalAssociation

Langham Literature, along with its publishing work, is a ministry of Langham Partnership.

Langham Partnership is a global fellowship working in pursuit of the vision God entrusted to its founder John Stott –

> *to facilitate the growth of the church in maturity and Christ-likeness through raising the standards of biblical preaching and teaching.*

Our vision is to see churches in the Majority World equipped for mission and growing to maturity in Christ through the ministry of pastors and leaders who believe, teach and live by the word of God.

Our mission is to strengthen the ministry of the word of God through:
- nurturing national movements for biblical preaching
- fostering the creation and distribution of evangelical literature
- enhancing evangelical theological education

especially in countries where churches are under-resourced.

Our ministry

Langham Preaching partners with national leaders to nurture indigenous biblical preaching movements for pastors and lay preachers all around the world. With the support of a team of trainers from many countries, a multi-level programme of seminars provides practical training, and is followed by a programme for training local facilitators. Local preachers' groups and national and regional networks ensure continuity and ongoing development, seeking to build vigorous movements committed to Bible exposition.

Langham Literature provides Majority World preachers, scholars and seminary libraries with evangelical books and electronic resources through publishing and distribution, grants and discounts. The programme also fosters the creation of indigenous evangelical books in many languages, through writer's grants, strengthening local evangelical publishing houses, and investment in major regional literature projects, such as one volume Bible commentaries like the *Africa Bible Commentary* and the *South Asia Bible Commentary*.

Langham Scholars provides financial support for evangelical doctoral students from the Majority World so that, when they return home, they may train pastors and other Christian leaders with sound, biblical and theological teaching. This programme equips those who equip others. Langham Scholars also works in partnership with Majority World seminaries in strengthening evangelical theological education. A growing number of Langham Scholars study in high quality doctoral programmes in the Majority World itself. As well as teaching the next generation of pastors, graduated Langham Scholars exercise significant influence through their writing and leadership.

To learn more about Langham Partnership and the work we do visit **langham.org**

www.ingramcontent.com/pod-product-compliance
Lightning Source LLC
Chambersburg PA
CBHW071958220426
43662CB00009B/1181